The Place-name Kingston and Royal Power in Middle Anglo-Saxon England

Patterns, possibilities and purpose

Jill Bourne

BAR British Series 630

2017

Published in 2017 by
BAR Publishing, Oxford

BAR British Series 630

The Place-name Kingston and Royal Power in Middle Anglo-Saxon England

ISBN 978 1 4073 1568 3

BAR titles are available from:

BAR Publishing
122 Banbury Rd, Oxford, OX2 7BP, UK
EMAIL   info@barpublishing.com
PHONE +44 (0)1865 310431
FAX   +44 (0)1865 316916
www.barpublishing.com

Dedicated to the memory of Margaret Gelling

Contents

Cover Image Details...viii

Abbreviations ix

Acknowledgements xi

Abstract..xii

PART I

Chapter 1. Background and Assumptions 3

Building the corpus 3

Analysing the corpus...4

Status of names in Kingston..4

Identifying Roman roads 4

Mapping the Kingstons 5

The structure of this work 6

Chapter 2. The Place-name Kingston 7

The name...7

Previous work on the place-name Kingston...8

Statistical analysis 9

Kings and kingship: early Anglo-Saxon kingdoms, royal power and its workings......................10

The Continental homelands and early Anglo-Saxon kingship..11

The earliest petty-kingdoms 12

The Tribal Hidage and the earliest English kingdoms 13

Chapter 3. Patterns and Possibilities: Distribution and Communications...............................15

The Kingston Material 15

The tables 15

The Kingston Material Group by Group...19

Group 1 Counties which comprised the core of ancient Wessex prior to 726 19

Domesday Book royal connections and ecclesiastical status 22

Wiltshire: Domesday Book, royal connections and ecclesiastical status 26

Somerset: royal connections, ecclesiastical status, and Domesday Book 27

Counties closely associated with early Wessex: Berkshire; Oxfordshire; Surrey 28

Berkshire: charters, Domesday Book, royal Connections and ecclesiastical status 29

Counties over which Wessex had established lordship prior to 726: Sussex; Kent 31

Sussex: Domesday Book, royal connections and ecclesiastical status...................................32

Kent: Domesday Book, royal connections and ecclesiastical status 33

Group 2: Counties of the Severn Valley, Welsh Borders, and the West Midlands 33

Domesday Book, royal connections and ecclesiastical status 35

Welsh border counties 36

Group 3: Counties lying between Watling Street and the Mersey/Humber Line plus East Anglia............39

Cambridgeshire, Huntingdonshire, and Suffolk 40

Group 4 Counties North of the Humber/Mersey Line 42

Chapter 4. Interpreting the Patterns...45

Kingstons: the royal connection...45

Were the Kingstons *villæ regales*? 46

Kingstons and the *Firma Unius Noctis* 49

Kingstons sited in an apparent direct relationship *villæ regales* named as such in the record 50

Kingstons and small, early 'kingdoms'..52

The *Stoppingas* 52

Kingestune (Wistow) HNT 52

The Isle of Wight: The kingdom of the *Wihtgara* 53

(Market) Bosworth/Congerstone Leicestershire 54

Conistone (Kettlewell) and Coniston (Cold) YOW 54
Kingston Kent: the Bourne people...55
Kingstons: the road connection...55
Anglo-Saxon settlement and the Roman road system...55
The 'road/string' distribution pattern 56
Kingstons and Roman small towns..57
Radmanni, radchenistri and carting obligations in Domesday England...................................58
Expanded Wessex: origins and chronology of the kingdom of Wessex and its kings 59
Documentary references for Wessex...59
The major events of the reign of Ine of Wessex 688–726...61
    The law codes of Ine and the governance of the kingdom...62
    The foundation of *Hamwīc*..63
Kingstons Sited in the Severn Valley and the West Midlands 64
    The *Hwicce* and the *Magonsæte*..64
        The *Hwicce*...64
        The *Magonsæte* 65
        Cambridgeshire and Huntingtonshire...65
The evidence so far?...67

Chapter 5. Kingston upon Thames...69
Kingston Hill and Coombe Hill 70
Anglo-Saxon Kingston upon Thames 70
A note on the 'lost' *villa regalis* of *Frǣricburna* 71
    The *villa regalis* of *Frēoricburna/Frǣricburna* and the Hogsmill/Lurtebourne valley.........71
    The site of the royal residence of *Frǣricburna*...72

Chapter 6. What Was a Kingston? 75
What Kingstons were *not*..75
What Kingstons *might* have been...75
Were the 'original' Kingstons and the 'road/string' Kingstons kin? 76
When were the Kingstons founded, what was the process, and by whose order? 76
Villæ regales and Kingstons...77
When were the Kingstons founded? 80
In Summary...80
And finally, was there an architect? 80

PART II

The Data...83
Berkshire 1 85
Berkshire 2 85
Berkshire 3 87
Berkshire 4 87
Cambridgeshire 1 89
Cambridgeshire 2 89
Devon 1 91
Devon 2 91
Devon 3 93
Devon 4 93
Devon 5 95
Dorset 1 95
Dorset 2 97
Dorset 3 97
Dorset 4 99
Dorset 5 99
Dorset 6 101
Dorset 7 101
Gloucestershire 1..103
Gloucestershire 2..103
Gloucestershire 3..105

Gloucestershire 4...105
Gloucestershire 5...107
Gloucestershire 6...107
Gloucestershire 7...109
Hampshire 1...109
Hampshire 2...111
Hampshire 3...111
Herefordshire 1..113
Herefordshire 2..113
Herefordshire 3..115
Herefordshire 4..115
Huntingdonshire 1...117
Huntingdonshire 2...117
Kent 1...119
Kent 2...119
Lancashire 1...121
Leicestershire 1..121
Northumberland 1..123
Nottinghamshire 1...123
Oxfordshire 1...125
Shropshire 1...125
Somerset 1..127
Somerset 2..127
Somerset 3..129
Somerset 4..129
Somerset 6..131
Staffordshire 1...131
Suffolk 1...133
Suffolk 2...133
Suffolk 3...135
Surrey 1..135
Surrey 2..137
Surrey 3..137
Sussex 1..139
Sussex 2..139
Sussex 3..141
Sussex 4..141
Warwickshire 1..143
Warwickshire 2..143
Warwickshire 3..145
Warwickshire 4..145
Wiltshire 1..147
Wiltshire 2..147
Wiltshire 3..149
Wiltshire 4..149
Worcestershire 1..151
Yorkshire East Riding 1..151
Yorkshire West Riding 1...153
Yorkshire West Riding 2...153

Bibliography..**155**
Index..**165**

Cover Image Details

The front cover image shows the first page of the manuscript, known as the *Textus Roffensis*, of the early seventh-century law code of King Aethelberht of Kent, compiled at Rochester, Kent in the 1120s. The reference to *cyningestune* as a specific place is at the end of line eleven and the beginning of line twelve.

Translation:

ÆTHELBERHT

These are the decrees which King Æthelberht established in the life-time of Augustine

1. *Godes feoh and ciricean XXII gylde. Biscopes feoh XI gylde. Preostes feoh IX gylde. Diacones feoh VI gylde. Cleroces feoh III glyde. CiricfriÞ II gylde. MæthlfriÞ II gylde.*

[Theft of] God's property and the Church's shall be compensated twelve fold; a bishop's property eleven fold; a priest's property nine fold; a deacon's property six fold; a clerk's property three fold. Breach of the peace shall be compensated doubly when it affects a church or a meeting place.

2. *Gif cyning his leode to him gehateÞ, and heom mon Þær yfel gedo; II bote and cyninge L scillinga.*

If the king calls his lieges to him, and anyone molests them there, he shall pay double compensation, and 50 shillings to the king.

3. *Gif cyning aet mannes ham drinicaeÞ, 7 ðær man lyswæs hwæt gedo, twibote gebete.*

If the king is feasting at anyone's house, and any sort of offence is committed there, two fold compensation shall be paid.

4. *Gif frigman cyning stele, IX gylde forgylde.*

If a freeman robs the king, he shall pay back a nine fold amount paid.

5. *Gif in **cyninges tun** man manan ofslea, L soill gebete.*

If one man slays another on the king's premises, he shall pay 50 shillings compensation

6. Gif man frigne mannan ofsleahÞ, *cyning L soill to drihtin-beage*

If a man slays a free man he shall pay 50 shillings to the king for infraction of his seignorial rights.

7. *Gif cyninges ambihtsmið oÞÞe laadrinemannan ofslehð, meduman leodgelde forgeld.*

If [he] slays a smith in the king's service, or a messenger belonging to the king, he shall pay an ordinary wergeld.

8. *Cyninges mundbyrd L scillinga,*

The king's mundbyrd shall be 50 shillings.

9. *Gif frigman frem stelÞ, III gebete, 7 cyning age Þ wite 7 ealle Þa æhtan.*

If a freemen robs a freeman, he shall pay a threefold compensation, and the king shall take the fine, or all [the man's] goods.

10. *Gif mann witð cyninges mægdenman geligeÞ, L scillinga gebete.*

If a man lies with a maiden belonging to the king, he shall pay 50 shillings compensation.

11. *Gif hio grindende Þeowa sio, xxv scillinga gebete. Sio Þridde xxii scillingas.*

If she is a grinding slave, he shall pay 25 shillings compensation. [If she is of the} third [class], [he shall pay] 12 shillings compensation.

Abbreviations

ASC   Anglo-Saxon Chronicle

CDEPN V. Watts, *Cambridge Dictionary of English Place-Names* (CUP) 2004

DB   Domesday Book. (Chichester, Phillimore, 1975-92)

DEPN   E. Ekwall, *Concise Oxford Dictionary of English Place-Names*, 4th edition, (Oxford, 1960)

EPNS   English Place-Name Society

HE   Bede, *Historia Ecclesiastica Gentis Anglorum*, ed. B. Colgrave and R .A. B. Mynors (Oxford, 1969)

HER   Historic Environment Record (formerly SMR)

JEPNS *Journal of the English Place-Name Society*

M   Roman road identification number as allocated by I. D. Margary

OD   Old Danish

OE   Old English

ON   Old Norse

OS   Ordnance Survey Maps

S   Charters as numbered in The Electronic Sawyer. www.esawyer.org.uk

TRE   *Tempore* (in the time of) *Regis Eduardi*

TRW   *Tempore* (in the time of) *Regis Willelmi*

VCH   Victoria Histories of the Counties of England

COUNTIES OF ENGLAND

The county areas are those which obtained before 1974. The abbreviations are those used by M. Gelling and A. Cole in *The Landscape of Place-Names* (Stamford: Tyas, 2000). The counties are listed alphabetically by the full county name, not by the abbreviated form. Only the counties that are reference in the text are listed here.

BRK   Berkshire

CAM   Cambridgeshire

DEV   Devon

DOR   Dorset

GLO   Gloucestershire

HMP   Hampshire

HNT   Huntingdonshire

HRE   Herefordshire

IOW   Isle of Wight

KNT   Kent

LEI   Leicestershire

LNC   Lancashire

NTT   Nottinghamshire

OXF   Oxfordshire

SFK   Suffolk

SHR   Shropshire

SOM   Somerset

SSX   Sussex

STF   Staffordshire

SUR   Surrey

WAR   Warwickshire

WLT   Wiltshire

WOR   Worcestershire

YOE   Yorkshire East Riding

YOW   Yorkshire West Riding

Acknowledgements

I have been fortunate in my research to have had the inspiration, guidance, encouragement, and, most importantly, friendship, of those mentioned below. I am indebted to them all. Without them the results of this research project would have been so much the lesser.

Emeritus Professor Charles Phythian-Adams was the inspiration for this study. It was he who suggested the idea. The late Dr Margaret Gelling, my mentor and friend for more than a quarter of a century, encouraged and supported me. Associate Professor Jayne Carroll, Director of the Institute of Name Studies (INS) at the University of Nottingham, saved me from drowning. Cheerful, optimistic, and firm! –she alone knows the debt I owe her. Dr David Parsons, formerly of the University of Nottingham and now of the University of Wales, shared his comprehensive knowledge of the Anglo-Saxon world and its words. When I was despairing of finding a cartographer who understood what I wanted, David saved the day. He stepped in, wearing his cartographer's hat, to create most of the beautiful maps that enhance this volume. Dr Stuart Brookes, of the Institute of Archaeology, UCL, created the Base Map, and the Tribal Hidage map which support the core of this study, and was extraordinarily generous with his time and ideas. It was he who made it possible for me to access the Landscapes of Governance GIS data. I have had long and rewarding discussions with Professor John Blair, of The Queen's College, Oxford, also Dr John Baker of the INS, Jeremy Harte, Director of Ewell Museum, David Bate of the British Geological Survey, and Alan Morton, Senior Planning Archaeologist for Southampton. All were unstinting in sharing their expertise and time, and all went out of their way to help. Dr Patrick Clay was my archaeological adviser and critic; Beth Bourn-Williams pre-proofed the whole manuscript, a demanding job, which she executed with great skill; Dr Peter Walker, professional editor and Reviews Editor of the *Transactions of the Leicestershire Archaeological and Historical Society* (of which I am the Hon. Editor), patiently copy-edited the final manuscript. I want to express a particular debt of gratitude to Barry Kendall, friend and colleague, for his support in so many ways, too numerous and varied to list. He knows how important his contribution has been.

The extracts from the first edition OS 1" maps are provided through www.VisionofBritain.org.uk and are the copyright of the Great Britain Historical GIS project, the University of Portsmouth, and the British Library. Details from first and second editions of OS 6" maps are obtained through the Digimap data download service. © Crown Copyright and Database Right 2016. Ordnance Survey (Digimap Licence)

Abstract

This work presents the corpus of all 70 surviving Kingston names and investigates each one within its historical and landscape context, in an attempt to answer the question: 'What was a Kingston?'

All previous published work on this recurrent place-name, both scholarship with an etymological focus and contextual scholarship which examines the names within their wider contexts, has been addressed. The connections between Kingstons and the *cyninges-tūns* and *villæ regales* of the documentary sources are explored. The concept and development of early kingship and its possible origins are presented and considered along with the laws of the earliest kings, the petty kingdoms, and emergence of the larger kingdoms for which the term Heptarchy was coined (but not used at the time); seeking to understand what the name Kingston might have represented 'on the ground'.

Particular attention is paid to Ancient Wessex, where more than half of the corpus of Kingston names are found, and to the early Anglo-Saxon kingdoms of the *Hwicce* and *Magonsæte*, where a further quarter lie. The fundamental questions of this study are addressed in the light of what is known regarding Anglo-Saxon royal power and its workings between the years 600 to 850.

The core of the work is the hypothesis that names of the type *cyninges tūn* or *cyning tūn* derive not from independent coinages meaning 'manor/farm/enclosure of a king' in some general sense, nor in direct relation to the phrase *cyninges tūn*, as it is sometimes assumed in the literature, as an equivalent to *villa regia*. These names are the compound appellative *cyninges-tun*, used for a place on a royal estate where some aspect of royal authority was implemented. Or, they were sited, in the main, on major long-distance Roman, and other known ancient roads, to enforce some aspect of Anglo-Saxon royal power. The idea that a place with the name Kingston was the centre of royal power is wrong. It was at the king's hall, the central place on a royal estate, where the king would have met with his council, the Witan, and from where decisions were agreed and the kingdom ruled.

PART I

Figure 1: Distribution map of the place-name Kingston in relation to major Roman roads and attested long distance medieval roads.

Chapter 1

Background and Assumptions

The aim of this study is to seek answers to the question: what was a Kingston and what was its purpose within an elite estate and the administration of a region or kingdom in Anglo-Saxon England?

The starting point begins from the same premise as that of Cullen, Jones and Parsons in their study of the place-name element *þorp*. In the preface to *Thorps in a Changing Landscape*, the authors observe that it would be wonderful to claim that when they embarked on their research into the place-name element *þorp*, they knew that it would result in a total re-evaluation, not only of the settlements themselves, but also of some of the fundamental processes that created the English rural landscape. This, however, was far from the truth. Yet, when they looked back on the results of their research, it seemed blindingly obvious that a group of places that shared a core name must, rather like a family, have something in common that binds them together, and that if the evidence from a variety of perspectives was interrogated, insights into their origins and development should follow. The idea is so simple, it is extraordinary that a full-length study using a similar approach had not been undertaken before.[1]

Of potentially equal significance are the wholly unexpected findings that have emerged from a similar analysis of the place-name Kingston and its significance in the political landscape of early-mid Anglo-Saxon England; findings that would not have become apparent without a detailed interrogation of the surviving evidence drawn from all available sources. A place with the common name Kingston must in origin have been at some fundamental level, as with the *þorp* names, the same type of place, founded with a common purpose.

Building the corpus

Seventy Kingston place-names (and its variant forms) were identified, and their etymologies confirmed by reference to the county volumes of the English Place-Name Society.[2] To be included in the corpus a name must have entered the written record prior to 1600, and be unquestionably a Kingston. The heart of this study is that names of the type *cyninges+tūn* or *cyning+tūn* do not derive from independent coinages meaning 'manor/farm/enclosure of a king' in some general sense, or in direct relation to the phrase *cyninges tūn* as it is sometimes used in the literature as an equivalent to *villa regia/villa regalis*. The names fall

into two main groups which, although distinct, are, in some essential respect the same, because the core of their function was toward the same overall purpose. All the Kingstons are examples of the compound appellative *cyninges-tūn*, used for places commonly sited on major long-distance Roman or known ancient routeways, where some aspect of Anglo-Saxon royal power was carried out, or for places sited in close association to the central places on important Anglo-Saxon royal estates - *villæ regales*.

In Old English place-names the element 'king' is only ever used as a specific. It derives from OE *cyning*, *cyng*, 'king', with or without the genitive singular ending *es*, or names related to the OE *cyne*, 'kingly, royal', *cyne + tūn* which produce names such as Kineton. It can be difficult, sometimes impossible, to distinguish between *cyning-* and *kyne-* names. In some cases, Old Norse *konungr* or Old Danish *kunung* also appear to underlie the name-forms. *Cyning* has a wide range of possible variations in the OE spelling system in which the initial *c* can alternate with *k*, *y* with *i*, and *ng* with *ncg* or *ngc*. Scragg, in his analysis of this element as it appears in its variant forms in all manuscripts and documents datable within the period 980–1100 (excluding inscriptions and the occurrence of the word king in place-names), concludes that there is really no strongly discernible pattern of use, and that most variations have to be put down to differences over time, space and 'one-thousand-year-old slips of the pen'.[3] In other words, no weight should be placed on the variations in spelling. Of the 70 Kingstons in the corpus, 53 (77 per cent) are in origin *cyninges-tūn*, 17 (23 per cent) are the variants *kyne-, kine-, kin-tūn*.

The names were gathered from individual county volumes published by the English Place-Name Society; (Smith 1956; Ekwall 1960; Watts 2004,). All the relevant Victoria County Histories, nineteenth and early twentieth-century trade directories, gazetteers and topographical dictionaries were checked.[4] Maps are a useful source for harvesting names and although the Index to the Ordnance Survey produced no new examples of the name, close scrutiny of the maps themselves (the one-inch to the mile, Series 6),[5] and the first and second editions of the six-inch to one-mile maps,[6] was more rewarding, particularly in the identification of long-distance Roman roads. This was

---

[1]   Cullen *et al.* 2011: p. xvii.
[2]   These are listed under author in the Bibliography.

[3]   Scragg 2008: pp. 117–22.
[4]   Directories, gazetteers, and topographical dictionaries are listed in the Bibliography. Access to these sources, even in academic libraries, is patchy. They are rare, expensive and highly collectible.
[5]   OS Series 6, one-inch to the mile map is the most easily available map with the fewest modern features.
[6]   These were accessed on line at british-history.ac.uk

of particular importance as the mapped Kingston sites revealed a previously unspotted close association with long-distance major Roman roads and known ancient track-ways.

More than 70 per cent were found to lie on or within one mile of these roads, and a further 15 per cent on roads which are known to have been used, and probably adapted by the Romans - a total of 85 per cent of all the Kingstons. Sources which might prove rewarding in the hunting down of Kingston names not recorded elsewhere are the pre-twentieth-century county, parish, tithe, and parliamentary enclosure maps. These are generally reliable, but their survival is patchy and for many places may never have existed. The collections of the Record Office for Leicester and Leicestershire turned out to be fruitful in the form of a recently discovered private estate map of the parish of Gumley. This yielded the lost names *kingshaeme* and *kingslea*, names of significance in the light of Gumley's being a *villa regia*. Two charters record the appearance at Gumley of two Mercian kings −Æthelbald in 749 and Offa *c.* 772 (for 775, 777).[7] Without the chance survival of these charters, in archives outside Mercia, nothing remains today that even hints at the august past of this tiny village.

Analysing the corpus

The material gathered for the Kingston corpus has been analysed from the perspective of geographical location, early history, royal connections, ecclesiastical status, appearance in charters, and DB. All the data are contained in Part II. The names are listed alphabetically by county, and within the county in order of first appearance in the record. There is an individual map for each place, on which is marked the site of the Kingston, and any associated Roman or other ancient road. The first editions of one-inch to one-mile OS maps have been used for this purpose. Dates, in the main, are from the first quarter of the nineteenth century.

Status of names in Kingston

The analysis and synthesis of the collected data regarding the Kingstons revealed distribution patterns which, whilst not quite as startling as the association with Roman roads (below), are, nevertheless, highly significant. Contrary to the commonly held assumption that Kingstons were important places, in fact the opposite was the case. None were assembly sites or *burhs*, they were not liable for the *firma unius noctis*, or the *trinodius necessitas*.[8] In origin they were ecclesiastically dependent, although some did develop into independent parishes later, and less than a third were listed independently in DB. Carole Hough is of the opinion that the late arrival in the record of two-thirds of the names will give added weight to the commonly held

view that Kingstons belonged to a relatively late stage of place-name formation.[9]

Identifying Roman roads

The siting of at least 85 per cent of the Kingstons on major Roman roads, or on long distance ancient routeways was wholly unexpected. Even more surprising is the distribution pattern of more than half of the corpus being sited at regular distances apart of roughly nine to ten miles apart in 'strings'. This 'road/string' pattern is most pronounced in ancient Wessex, particularly across central Dorset, the lower Fosse Way, east Devon and the Severn Valley. Hints of this road/strings distribution can also be seen elsewhere. These patterns suggested that the positioning of these Kingstons might not have been random, and when statistical analysis was applied to the sites, the results revealed a significant positive correlation between the Kingstons and Roman roads. This apparently deliberate siting of so many Kingstons on these roads suggests that when the Kingstons were founded the roads must have been significant features in the landscape, and serviceable in some way.

The standard work of reference in the identification of Roman roads is that of the landscape archaeologist Ivan Margary.[10] Margary used a combination of maps, antiquarian records, place-names and extensive fieldwork to plot the Roman road system. His work is regarded as generally reliable, but incomplete. Almost no systematic work on Roman roads has been undertaken since he published his work in 1957. Some additional Roman roads have been mapped by Heritage England, but the record is patchy as their records depend on local Heritage Environment Record officers forwarding on information gained locally, leading to some counties being well represented, others less so, some not at all.[11] The OS map of Roman Britain is updated only infrequently, so presents a partial picture only.[12] In addition to Margary and the Heritage England mapped roads, it has been possible to identify a few roads for which there is enough archaeological, documentary or topographical evidence to confirm their existence, and use, during Roman times. Close scrutiny of the earliest editions of the six-inch OS maps, containing as they do many features that have been omitted from later editions and which are not included on smaller scale maps, uncovered new information that was critical in three or four instances where several short stretches of not previously noted known Roman roads were able to be confirmed. Papers published in county journals of record often contain information not noted elsewhere; they are easily overlooked unless the researcher stumbles upon references in another publication. Kinton, in the parish of Great Ness, Shropshire, is a case in point. It did not appear to be sited close to any significant routeway until a reference in a footnote to the identification by Philip White of a unknown and unsuspected Roman road that ran

---

[7] S 91, S 109, S 114.
[8] See the Glossary for a full definition of this recurring term.

[9] Hough 1997: pp. 55–7.
[10] Margary vol. 1, 1955; vol. 2, 1957.
[11] See Part II of this work.
[12] Ordnance Survey Map of Roman Britain, 5th edn, 2001.

between Wroxeter and Whittington, broke the silence. This is the road on which Kinton lies.[13] Other indicators of roads can sometimes show up as traces of *aggers*, crop marks and parish boundaries which shadow earlier features. Even a row of trees can sometimes suggest an ancient line, as can be seen in the tree-lined drive of Kingston (Lacy) House in Dorset, where it follows the line of the Roman road from Badbury Rings to the coast at Hamworthy.[14] A line of Roman villas, sited close to the Roman road that crossed Sussex between Brighton and Chichester, enabled several gaps in its line to be completed.[15] More of this road has been confirmed recently close to Chichester, as a result of road works. Surviving milestones can also indicate roads. At the height of the developed road system there will have been thousands lining the routes. Unfortunately they are easily moved and only 17 have been identified positively as being still *in situ*. One of these lies just outside the east gate into Dorchester in the parish of Stinsford where Kingston (Maurward/Stinsford) is sited.[16] Aerial photography, LiDAR, and geophysical surveys have made an important contribution to the detection of previously unknown lines of roads, as has the identification by Anne Cole of some place-name types as route-indicators.[17] Elements such as *cæster*, *burrens*, *draycott/ton*, *wīchām* and *toot,* are some of the most commonly recurring names which suggest the existence of a road that was a significant, recognisable and probably functioning feature in the landscape when the names were coined. Cole suggests that the only place-name element that seems to be used specifically to indicate that a road is Roman is *stræt*. The function of the Kingstons sited on major Roman roads does not appear to have been as 'route-indicators'.

A further example of how the careful piecing together of small scraps of evidence can reveal the existence of a possible road is the identification by Michael Costen of a previously unrecognised Roman road in Somerset. Costen proposes a road which ran south from Combwich, a settlement with good Roman antecedents, from a point at the crossing near the mouth of the River Parrett. Nether and Over Stowey, which lie close to the northern side of the Quantocks, have early name-forms that suggest they were naming the *stan-weg* 'the stone way/path'.[18] Both the Stoweys had Norman castles, with the Nether Stowey castle overlooking the road where it runs up on to the Quantocks, an indication that it must have been still well-used in the twelfth century. On the other side of the hills, close to Bishop's Lydeard, an *ealdan stræt*,[19] 'old street/road/pathway',* occurs in the boundary clause of a charter of Æthelwulf, king of Wessex in 854.[20] The clause, which is not contemporary with this charter, is twelfth century.[21]

The road then carries on across the Brendon Hills towards Exmoor; this road might be indicated by the name 'Old Stowey' in DB.[22] A little further west, just south of Wheddon Cross the road above Old Stowey, known here as harepath, a corruption of *herepað*, 'army path', appears to be heading towards the north Somerset and Devon coast.[23]

Many miles of the Roman road system must still be awaiting discovery. Christopher Taylor is of the opinion that there might be at least 500 miles of Roman roads which have not been identified.[24] It is possible that the Kingstons for which it has not been possible to establish a connection with a Roman road or ancient routeway could well be standing on one of these unrecovered roads.

An instance of how one of these lost roads came to light is the discovery in 1973 at Slaithwaite YOW of an unsuspected section of the west-east road across the Pennines which linked the Roman legionary fortresses of Chester and York.[25] Forty years earlier, Margary had proposed that the line of this road, which would have run between March Hill and Outlane, broadly followed the line of the A640 (M712). Thirty years after Margary published his research a local farmer was taking down a ridge that crossed one of his fields when he came across, at only 25cm below the surface, a perfectly preserved metalled Roman road, the true line of the trans-Pennine road more than a mile from the A640. Margary had not looked here, so 'obvious' was the route he defined. His mistake, however, was understandable as the road had made a puzzling right-angled bend.[26] The lesson to be learned here is that seemingly secure evidence from an impeccable source can be wrong, and a lack of evidence does not mean that there is none.

Mapping the Kingstons

Given the nature of the evidence, it is difficult to be sure of the exact site of any of the Kingstons (or any other place) on the *apparent* present-day line of almost any Roman road. The position of a name on a printed map is more often than not the best attempt of the cartographer to fit it in the space available. Settlements change in form over time, sometimes shifting significant distances. The lines of parish boundaries are more reliable, but they too will have been subject to changes over time, and although proto-parishes could well have been emerging, the boundaries would have been fluid. For the purposes of this study the measurement is from the Roman road to the church, or in the absence of a church, the distance is from the road to the boundary of the parish in which the Kingston lies.[27]

---

[13] Lafflin 2001: pp. 1–11.

[14] M 4d.

[15] M 153.

[16] Milestone Society: www.milestonesociety.co.uk.

[17] Cole 2011.

[18] Costen

[19] *Stræt* is the OE term for a paved road. The only paved/metalled roads would have been Roman at this time.

[20] S 311.

[21] BL Add ms. 15350 fol 27, v.28. Costen, *personal correspondence.*

[22] DBSom (25, 21); SS 955 385.

[23] Costen 2011: Fig. 1.2, p, 14 and personal communication.

[24] Taylor 1979: p. 50.

[25] SE 07 15.

[26] Lunn, Crosland, Spence, Clay 2008.

[27] Gelling, 1977: pp. 8-26. This is the method adopted by Margaret Gelling in her study of the compound place-name *wīchām*.

The Base Map on which the Kingstons have been plotted has been created digitally. It comprises all the long-distance Roman roads described by Margary.[28] Unless they are strictly relevant, many of the more minor Roman roads have been omitted. Three ancient long-distance routeways have been included, also a few relevant roads from the Heritage England database and from other literature published post-Margary. The latter are referenced in the text and the Bibliography. All long-distance routes, often with local names such as 'salt-way', *herepath*, 'causeway', 'port-way', 'hard way', have been investigated.

The structure of this work

Firstly, this study examines all earlier research, and assumptions, related to the meaning and significance of the habitative place-name Kingston. The name is then investigated in relation to the origin and development of the idea and substance of kings, kingship, and the exercise of royal power, its workings, royal communications, early Anglo-Saxon kingdoms, and the earliest English laws. The relationship between names in Kingston and instances of the phrase *cyninges-tūn* in the documentary records is explored.

The distribution patterns of the 70 examples are analysed in Chapter 3 in the broad context of their geographical location, early history, royal connections, ecclesiastical status, listing (or not) in Domesday Book; and other relevant documentary and archaeological evidence. In Chapter 4 they are explored further in relation to long-distance Roman roads, other major ancient routeways, and the wider landscape. The distributional patterns associated with these roads is also addressed in this chapter, along with the possible reasons for the greater majority of them being sited along these roads in a seemingly planned fashion, and what this suggests about their origins, purpose and function. The name clearly indicates royal ownership of some kind, but the deliberate distribution patterns suggest that the name signifies more than a simple statement of ownership. If the Kingstons were created to serve a specific royal purpose, what might that purpose have been? Their being sited on the main Roman highways suggests that their function must have been related to royal control and communications in some way. The probable condition of the Roman roads at the time of the foundation of the Kingstons was also explored. The broad consensus now is that in the early/mid-Anglo-Saxon period, most of the major Roman roads, and even some minor ones, would not only have still been recognisable earthworks in the landscape, and they would almost certainly have been serviceable enough to provide the basis of a coherent, usable road network. David Pelteret is of the opinion that the absence of discussion regarding the roads in many textbooks is not a reflection of the paucity of the material, but more likely is a failure to look for topographical explanations for significant political, social and cultural developments in Anglo-Saxon history.[29]

There is also a pronounced distributional bias towards the counties which comprised the heart of ancient Wessex, with Hampshire, Dorset, Wiltshire, Somerset and Devon. When the counties which had close associations with ancient Wessex – Berkshire, Surrey and West Oxfordshire – and those over which Wessex had established lordship prior to 726 – Sussex and Kent – are added, they comprise more than 77 per cent of the whole corpus. Eighteen Kingstons, almost a quarter of the total, are found in the lower Severn Valley and the West Midlands, in the main within the Anglo-Saxon kingdoms of the *Hwicce* and *Magonsæte*. Together these groups account for 80 per cent of the total. These patterns are discussed in Chapter 3.

Kingston upon Thames in Surrey is the only Kingston in the corpus which stands out as being, in some essential respect, different from all the others. Peter Sawyer, in his study of *villae regales* 'royal estates' in Anglo-Saxon England, has devised a list of criteria by which these *villae regales* can be identified. Kingston upon Thames *appears* to meet many of these criteria: none of the remaining 69 meets any.[30] Something is not quite right here and several scholars have noted that there is a puzzle at the heart of this place. These contradictions are addressed fully in Chapter 5, where it is suggested tentatively that the answer may lie, at least in part, with Kingston on Thames being confused with the, as yet, unidentified Surrey *villa regia* of *Freoricburna*.

The paucity of evidence for the early/mid-Anglo-Saxon period means that our understanding of the name can be only partial at best. Regardless of this, sufficient evidence, both circumstantial and explicit, has been uncovered to suggest a probable foundation date, and to propose something of the circumstances that might have applied at that time.

---

[28] Margary, 2 vols, 1995, 1997.
[29] Pelteret 1999: p. 395.
[30] Sawyer 1983: pp 273–99.

Chapter 2

The Place-name Kingston

James Campbell's essay, *Bede's Words for Places*, concludes:

> In exploring the in some ways oddly orderly world of early England, the identification of places with special functions is of particular importance. The study of vocabulary has at least this to contribute to the much-to-be-hoped-for historical gazetteer of early England. It permits the formulation of questions that go with the grain of sources. 'What and where were the metropolises civitates, urbes, villae/vici regales and portus?' are not questions which hold forth the hope of complete and unambiguous answersbut they are in large measure answerable.[1]

The name

Richard Jones, in his introduction to the published seminar series *Sense of Place in Anglo-Saxon England*, observes that place-names which derive from natural features have been shown to be extremely precise, and that there is every reason to suppose that names which derive from habitations and structures are equally precise. However, the major barrier to the drawing of definitive conclusions is that the features and circumstances to which a name alludes have long disappeared or been obscured. This makes it difficult, sometimes impossible, for definitive conclusions to be drawn about what *exactly* these habitative names denoted.

The place-name Kingston is such a name, superficially obvious but on closer examination opaque. Place-name scholars are generally in agreement that *-tūn* names such as Kingston (*cyning* 'king'), Chilton (*cild* 'child'), Bish(op)ton (*biscop* 'bishop'), Knighton (*cniht* 'youth, retainer/servant, (later) knight') and Preston (*prēost* 'priest') are reasonably easily understood both in their etymologies and their significance, and that because they refer to social and administrative roles which belong to a relatively late stage of social organisation in Anglo-Saxon England, they therefore must be of relatively late coinage.[2] Recent work has questioned this assumption in relation to these Kingston names, suggesting they could date from a much earlier time.[3]

It has already been noted that 73 per cent of the corpus of names in Kingston are in the form *cyning(e)s-tūn*, and 27 per cent are derived from *kyne* or uninflected *cyning*. The use of *tūn* as a place-name-forming element seems to have become increasingly widespread after the mid-eighth century, although there is evidence of its use throughout the Anglo-Saxon period. This element is still not fully understood despite its being the most common generic in English place-names. The generally accepted interpretations are considered to be 'enclosure', 'village', 'farmstead', 'estate', 'manor', 'township', although the precise meaning in individual cases can be hard to determine. Barrie Cox, in his examination of names which occur in the earliest sources (to AD 731), found only six place-names with the element *tūn*, all of which seem to carry the meaning of 'enclosure' or 'farmstead'.[4] When Campbell added to Cox's list the names ending in the element *tūn* recorded in the *Anglo-Saxon Chronicle* between 731 and 800, Bensington, Taunton, Somerton, *Meretun* and *Seletun* come into view.[5] Notably these places differ significantly from the other *tūn*s in the list. Campbell does not quibble with Cox that the term *tūn* in the pre-731 list meant a farmstead or enclosure of some sort, his judgement is that three of the names in the list, Bensington, Taunton, and Somerton, were *not* small farming settlements but were almost certainly *villæ regales*. *Meretun* and *Seletun* have yet to be identified. This early use of *tūn* is confirmed by the entry in the *ASC* for AD 571. Here the plural *tūnas* is used as a generic term for Aylesbury, Bensington, Eynsham, and Limbury, four places that were captured by Cuthwulf from the Britons. Clearly the term was used for places of consequence.

As the data for this study came together it became clear that the generally accepted understanding of what Kingstons were was mistaken. Not only were they not *tūn*s in the sense of farming settlements, but neither were they *villæ regales*; in fact, it became clear that in origin they might not have been settlements at all but were points in the landscape where some aspect of the exercise of royal power took place. If that had been the case and they became redundant, many of their names might also have fallen out of use. Of the 70 survivors the majority are minor, dependent places, some strikingly so. Two are farm names; three are the names of small estates and houses of minor gentry, one survives as the name of a hospital, another as the name of a small railway station, two are recorded as names in the charter bounds of neighbouring places, one is a street name, another a small council-house estate, one is the name of a barn now used for motor bike repairs, and, humblest of all, one is an amusement arcade.

---

[1] Campbell 1986: p. 116; Cameron 1996: pp. 123–4.
[2] Gelling 1997: p. 125.
[3] Hough 1997: pp. 55–57.
[4] Cox 1975/1976: p. 51.
[5] Campbell 1986: pp. 49–50.

It is probable that we have most of the recoverable Kingston names although no doubt a few could be still be lying fugitive, retrievable perhaps in the 25-inch to the mile first edition OS maps, tithe and estate maps, and documents still in private hands. Survival is a significant factor which must be borne in mind when assessing a recurrent place-name and its distribution: is their survival random or was there a regional variation in the coining of the name that accounts for the bias observed in their distribution?

Previous work on the place-name Kingston

It has been noted already that the generally held opinion of most place-name scholars regarding the name Kingston is that expressed by Margaret Gelling in her introduction to *Signposts to the Past*:

> Some categories of habitative names must be of relatively late coinage because they refer to social and administrative arrangements which cannot go back to the first coming of the English. Kingston 'royal manor', Bishton 'episcopal manor', Knighton 'estate of the young retainers', Preston 'estate of the priests', Chilton 'estate of the young noblemen', refer to manorial arrangements which belong to a relatively late stage of social organisation, not to the conditions of the migration period [...] and may be supposed to have replaced earlier names in the English language. [6]

Kenneth Cameron concurs, stating 'what evidence is available to date suggests that Kingstons belong to a later rather than an earlier period in Anglo-Saxon England'.[7] Of the examples of which he was then aware, he observed that fewer than 29 were derived from *cyning* or *cyne,* or had known royal associations during their recorded history. He did acknowledge, however, that clearly they all must have been royal manors or estates when the names were coined, although there were still unanswered questions about the name, and that more work remained to be done before its definition, meaning, and significance could be understood more precisely.[8]

In general, place-name scholars are in agreement with Gelling and Cameron that the name is relatively late. Carole Hough accepts that although this may be true for the other names in the group, such as Preston and Chilton, it may not be for the name Kingston. She questions the commonly held view that the name Kingston is late, pointing out that the term *cyninges tūn* was in use at the very latest by the early seventh century, and possibly earlier. Hough notes that some re-thinking is required and that the testimony of the early laws makes it 'wholly unnecessary to attribute place-names reflecting sophisticated social arrangements to the later period'.[9] In her opinion, despite the lateness of the extant sources, at least some of the Kingston names

must reflect conditions considerably earlier than their recorded history. Hough does not regard it as conclusive, and that because the Kingston names in the main are recorded in relatively late sources, they are necessarily of late foundation.

The term *cyninges tūn* occurs in the late sixth/early-seventh century laws of King Æthelberht of Kent, the earliest extant document written in the English language. Chapter five of the laws reads: *Gif in cyninges tune man mannan ofslea, L scill' gebete* 'if anyone kills a man in a *cyninges tūn* he shall atone with 50 shillings' (that is, in addition to the usual wergild payment. There is every reason to assume that the function of a place described as a *cyninges tūn* would have been understood.[10] The term appears again in the late ninth century in Ch.1§2 of the laws of King Alfred. This law states that 'one who breaks an oath will be imprisoned *on cyninges-tūn* for 40 days and undergo there whatever penance the bishop prescribes for him.[11] The existence of these laws is evidence enough that both the term and its physical manifestation would have been understood by most contemporaries. Hough concludes that the term *cyninges tūn* refers not to manorial arrangements but to a legal structure, relating to an area of jurisdiction within which crimes attracted a special penalty, and which was already in place by the early seventh century. She notes that *cyning* had a range of meanings in Old English: a tribal leader or petty ruler among others, which are not reflected in Modern English, and would not have been used for the king of all England until much later in the Anglo-Saxon period. She suggests that perhaps it this later use of the term which has dictated the common assumption that Kingston place-names belong to this later time.

More recently, Duncan Probert, in his distributional study of the place-name Kingston, set out to establish what the name actually signified to contemporaries.[12] His study identified 61 Kingston names which he examined in their historical, administrative and tenurial contexts. He too questioned the received opinion that the name cannot be assigned to an early phase of Anglo-Saxon settlement, concluding, like Hough, that the *cyninges tūna*s of the laws of Æthelberht and Alfred had a legal function, and that by the early seventh century at the latest they must have had a physical existence recognised by contemporaries. Probert notes that the evidence does not allow us to say whether a place with this function existed at an even earlier date, or in areas outside Kent and Wessex. He does, however, cite a reference to the imprisonment of Bishop Wilfred in an *urbs regis* (possibly Durham) in the late seventh century, and a further Mercian example of imprisonment at a *villa regalis* the early eighth century.[13] He also points to a detail

---

[6] Gelling 1997: p. 125.
[7] Cameron 1996: p. 134.
[8] Cameron 1996: pp. 133–4.
[9] Hough 1997: p. 5.

[10] Hough 1997: p. 5.
[11] The precise date of the promulgation of the laws is unknown. Attenborough considers Liebermann's judgement (III, p. 34) that a date of *c.* 892–3 is too late, suggesting instead, that as Alfred describes himself as *Westseaxna cyning* an earlier date is more likely, as later in his reign Alfred adopted the Latin term *Angul-saxonum rex* or *Anglorum Saxonum rex*. Attenborough 1922: p. 35.
[12] Probert 2008: pp. 7–19.
[13] S 180.

in an early ninth-century charter of Offa of Mercia, in which the royal *feorm* from Westbury-on-Trym is to be taken *ad regalem vicum*, 'to the royal estate', the key point here being that the term was used as a conceptual label without the need to specify the name of the whole royal estate. He suggests that in early ninth-century Mercia, as in seventh-century Kent and late ninth-century Wessex, the term *cyninges tūn*, or its Latin equivalents, could have had a meaning that described the function, or functions, of certain places within contemporary patterns of landscape organisation, and that these names originated as artificial administrative labels. His view is that, although a *cyninges-tūn* may have had a particular role within a royal estate structure, it was not a central one; neither need it have had only one function. He goes on to suggest that not all of the Kingston names were necessarily the same type of place.

When Probert addresses what he calls the 'problem' of Kingston upon Thames, he considers, on the evidence of the three sound Canterbury charters issued from there, plus a somewhat dubious Winchester charter, that it is clear that there was a place already known as *Cyningestūn* when a royal assembly was held there in 848 (see Chapter 5 for a full discussion of this). The problem, as Probert recognises, is the uniqueness of Kingston upon Thames; none of the other Kingstons display any of its impressive array of royal and administrative characteristics, and yet it has become the yardstick by which the others are measured. He warns that we must beware of making assumptions about the meanings of terms such as *cyning(es) tūn* and *villa regalis* and they should not be used as convenient labels for our ideas and models, confusing modern usages with the meanings that these terms had originally. His opinion is that most of the Kingston names arose as a consequence of some not yet properly-defined function or functions that applied at the time of their coining. Furthermore, he says that the answer to the question 'what was a Kingston?' will only be found by investigating each name in its immediate historical, administrative, and tenurial context, along with regard to the wider patterns of local landscape organisation within which it existed. He does not suggest what these proposed functions may have been, other than to concur with Hough that one function at least must have been concerned with the delivery of justice. He notes that a distribution map shows the Kingstons to be essentially a Wessex phenomenon and that Kingston upon Thames is the only example of the name to feature in the known royal *villæ regales* listed by Sawyer.[14] Surprisingly, he does not appear to have noticed the association between the Kingstons and Roman roads.

Statistical analysis

Rigorous, sophisticated, and independent analysis was applied to the data relating to the apparent association between the Kingstons and Roman and other long-distance roads.

Keith Briggs applied statistical analysis to the distribution of the name in relation to Roman roads, using the Kolmogorov-Smirnov test, which demonstrated that there is a statistically significant bias towards Roman roads with Kingstons that lie at distances one and a half miles or less from the road.[15] Briggs records his results but has not commented on them. When Anne Cole applied the chi-squared test to the same data a similar result was obtained, producing a range of values of between one, and one and three quarters, which indicates that they should be considered to correlate with the roads.[16] A third, and somewhat wider-ranging statistical test, was undertaken by Giacomo Zanella, a statistician in the University of Warwick.[17] The data set, which was compiled by John Blair and Ann Cole, comprised 20 different place-name types, and a total of 1,316 Anglo-Saxon settlements known to have been in existence between 750-850. The hypothesis was that the settlements were organised into administrative clusters, which tended to be composed of a variety of complementary place-names in each cluster. Kingston was one of these names. The analysis relating to the Kingstons proved that their siting was purposeful and unquestionably not random. The results have been described by John Blair as spectacular.

Stephen Bassett, in his research into the mother church, and extensive parochia, of St Peter's, Wootton Wawen WAR, discusses the role that Kington (Grange), one of many component parts of the estate, might have played within the estate. Bassett asks how reliably can we discover the extent of large mother-church parishes, date their origins, and grasp the historical significance of their individual shapes and sizes. He aims to understand the processes, and chart the stages, of the 'slow fission' of most of the mother-church parishes, a trend which by 1200 had set in motion the creation of the parochial geography of recent centuries.[18] Wootton Wawen is undoubtedly a minster of early foundation which today covers 3,187 hectares; this is the residual area of the original *c*.7,000 hectares the church served in the late Anglo-Saxon period. Claverdon, once an ecclesiastical daughter of the *parochia* of Wootton, had by 1200 become the most important secular centre in the area. It was by then a (lesser) mother-church with six dependent chapelries of its own, one of which was Kington. Bassett thinks Kington was 'an Anglo-Saxon royal farm – the king's *tūn* to which the population of the area were required to take the *feorm*'.[19] He suggests that Kington may have been so named because this is where the royal residence was sited, or alternatively it was not known as the 'king's *tūn*' until it was the last piece of royal land in the area that, for reasons that are now obscure, remained in the king's hands. The latter 'last toe-hold' theory is plausible, but unlikely, a suggestion but no more than that. If that was the case, similar conditions would have applied across the country

---

[14] Probert 2008: pp. 7–19.

[15] Briggs 2009: pp. 43–57.
[16] Cole 2011.
[17] Zanella 2014.
[18] Bassett 2007: p. 115, fn. 1.
[19] Kingstons are discussed in relation to the *firma unius noctis*, in Chapter 4.

with the processes of fission breaking up up royal estates, resulting in numerous vestigial fragments of land being retained for reasons unknown, and probably unknowable, and becoming known as Kingston.

Kington Grange (Claverdon) is one of only two Kingstons out of the ten sited within the kingdom and diocese of the *Hwicce*, for which it has not been possible to make a secure connection to a known long-distance Roman road. The other is Kington WOR. There is, however, a road one mile to the west of Kington, which clearly follows an ancient line, running north south through Wootton Wawen in the general direction of Stratford upon Avon. The line of this road, which originates at Metchley Park, Edgbaston, is known for much of its length as Monkspath Street, and is understood to be following a Roman line for the first few miles of its length, after which the line is lost.[20]

When the boundaries of St Peter's *parochia* are superimposed on a map of the local drainage pattern, it is immediately clear that the district which the church served initially comprised the middle section of the drainage basin of the River Alne, and that the undivided territory is reminiscent of the riverine estates that have been identified elsewhere in lowland Britain.[21] This area corresponds broadly to the 20 hides of land granted in 716 (x 37) by Æthelbald, King of Mercia and the South Angles, to Æthelric, *in regione ... Stoppingas*. Bassett notes that the name *Stoppingas* must reflect the natural topography of the district which is a *stoppa*, a 'bucket-shaped hollow', confirming that the formal territory of Wootton Wawen's church was not an aggregation of separate manors for ecclesiastical purposes, but was a primary unit of Anglo-Saxon settlement and land use.[22] The location of Kington in an attested early Anglo-Saxon small kingdom adds support to the proposition that the name might be of early origin. The close association of a Kingston with the central place in what might also have been an early small kingdom, might also have been the case with several other Kingstons (this is discussed fully in Chapter 3).

Kings and kingship: early Anglo-Saxon kingdoms, royal power and its workings

Little is known with any degree of certainty about the state of Britain after the collapse of the central authority of Rome in the early years of the fifth century. Campbell described the years between 400 and 600 as the 'lost centuries', and 'dangerous territory'.[23] Notwithstanding these constraints, there is no choice but to enter this territory as these are the centuries during which kingship was developing, the early kingdoms forming in conditions and circumstances that led to the creation of places for which the name Kingston was coined. Any study of a place-name containing the element

cyning must wrestle with the concept of what it might have signified at various stages in the Anglo-Saxon period.

It is unclear as to how the Anglo-Saxon raiders and settlers were able to create their own kingdoms, how they evolved, who these early kings were, what was actually meant by the term *cyning* and the institution of kingship, or how royal power was transmitted. Were any structures inherited from pre-Anglo-Saxon times, or were they newly created? The reliable written evidence called for to answer these questions is simply lacking. Early continental European medieval kings were able to increase and cement their power by drawing on surviving Roman institutions and monopolistic rights, but in Britain there seems to have been no such transmission of Roman authority. Political control passed to the Anglo-Saxon incomers, with their own gods, language, and social organisation being the dominant cultural values. Much has been written about this subject, views that are summarised by Bassett in his introduction to *The Origins of the Anglo-Saxon Kingdoms*.[24] Basset proposes two 'ideal' types of kingdom formation (which he acknowledges are not the only possible types). The first ideal type is the coalescence of neighbouring areas of settlement, accompanied by the translation of the leaders of dominant tribes into kings, a process he sees as taking place during the years of the migratory period at different rates of speed in different areas. His second ideal type is the take-over by the incoming Anglo-Saxons of existing territorial units in the early post-Roman period. Both of these broad types could, and probably did, apply to early Anglo-Saxon England, with some areas being newly settled and brought into agricultural production, whilst others continued to be worked by Britons who had been taken over by the newcomers by force or agreement. These 'ideal' types are not proposed as either/or, and there will have been many variants. In either situation hierarchies would have developed, or already existed, within the various groups of newcomers, out of which kingship evolved. These groups could have been of extended family kin, who may have arrived with their leaders and carried on, at least initially, a variant of life on the continent. They almost certainly have been groups such as that led by Penda of Mercia, whom Stenton suggests was 'a landless noble of the Mercian royal house fighting for his own hand'.[25] No details of these early kings are known, but when they come into view, both archaeologically and documentarily, in the first half of the seventh century at Sutton Hoo, Taplow, Prittlewell, and, more recently, the gold hoard at Hammerwich, Staffordshire, our breath is taken away by their splendour. Nevertheless, despite the fabulous material evidence of their power, we still do not know for certain who was buried in these graves, or who buried the hoard, or why. Informed suggestions can and have been made but certainty is not possible.

The concept of kingship could have been imported by Germanic immigrants in the fifth and sixth centuries, creating

[20] Leather 1994: p.103.
[21] Bassett 2007: pp. 140–42, fn. 68.
[22] Bassett 2007: p. 142, fn. 72.
[23] Campbell 1982: p. 20.
[24] Bassett 1989: pp. 3–27.
[25] Stenton 1971: p. 45.

something similar in Britain to that which had existed in their homelands. Alternatively, a peculiarly Anglo-Saxon idea of kingship may have developed in those early years of settlement. Another possibility is that, irrespective of the type of kingship that might have existed in the Germanic homelands, initially, the newcomers might not have been able to choose their own systems of government. If this was the case, what might these very early systems have been, by what means were they replaced, and what kind of people became their first rulers?[26] There is no direct evidence to answer these questions, although progress is being made by the careful following-up of every lead and clue, and by historians, archaeologists, place-name, and literary scholars beginning to talk to each other.[27]

David Dumville is of the opinion that the origins of the kingdoms that emerge from the earliest documentary sources do not to go back to the earliest years of the Anglo-Saxon age, but are more likely to be of sixth rather than the fifth century date.[28] Although the information is still patchy and often unreliable, by the end of the seventh century we are firmly in historic times, and by looking back from seventh and eighth-century sources it is possible to understand something of the earlier years, although the earliest times may never be understood satisfactorily.

The *Anglo-Saxon Chronicle*, Bede's *Ecclesiastical History of the English People*, and charter evidence, are the most extensive, important, and richest sources for this period. However, it is essential to keep in mind that although they record the events of earlier times they will have used the terminology of their own time to do so, with the attendant possibility that some subtleties of meaning might have been lost.[29] The events described in these written sources might have been manipulated, deliberately falsified perhaps, even by the kings themselves, to achieve a variety of ends. The scribes might also have tended, albeit unconsciously, to idealise (or vilify) the lives of the kings and their deeds to fit the demands of changed circumstances. The implications of this for this study, which has at its core the concepts, 'king', 'kingship', and 'kingdom', are considerable.

The *Anglo-Saxon Chronicle* contains only two entries relating to the very early English kingdoms – the accession of Ida in Bernicia in 547 and Ælle in Deira in 560, whereas Bede records much more concerning the early kings and their kingdom; his *Ecclesiastical History* of the English people is dedicated to a king. His account although fulsome was written two hundred years or more after the arrival of the first Anglo-Saxons, and more than 100 years after the close of the sixth century, by which time many of the Anglo-Saxon kingdoms had come in to being already. Bede's

account of these times is based largely on the writings of Gildas, the sole contemporary British written source for the period.[30] Gildas described the events of his own times and of the previous century, referring mainly to south-western England and Wales. His account is predominantly a moral diatribe against the rulers of his day, in which he condemns the sinfulness of contemporary religious and secular people who had provoked the wrath of God.[31] However, unreliable as it is, the testament of Gildas is crucial as it does at least offer some sort of framework for a discussion of the times.[32]

Bede's own, sometimes prejudiced, opinions will also have influenced his selection of material and the perspective he brought to it. He is not always consistent, neither does he consider a kingdom to be worth mentioning, except in passing, unless or until it had its own bishop. His terminology is inconsistent, for example, his use of the terms *provinciæ* and *regiones* for areas which were manifestly of widely differing importance and size. Campbell thinks Bede's often messy and ambiguous terminology is probably a reflection of the unstable world of which he is writing.[33] However, none of these caveats should lead us to a wholesale rejection of his testimony. Cameron draws our attention to the accuracy of some of Bede's information regarding, for example, the desertion of the areas from which some of the immigrants came. Recent archaeological research confirms that in the fifth century extensive areas of the homelands were badly affected by rising sea-levels, leading to the wholesale abandonment of settlements.[34] A few twelfth and thirteenth century annals survive, but they cast little light on the period and are generally regarded as unreliable, particularly in respect of the dates they give.[35]

The Continental homelands and early Anglo-Saxon kingship

It is to the homelands of the various regions of northern continental Europe from which the various groups came that we need to look for the roots of the customs and practices that evolved in Britain. The various tribal groups, although broadly similar, would have had many dissimilarities in their traditions of leadership. Germanic kingship was known to Tacitus, who writes in *Germania* of the practices of some of the tribes known to him. He notes that they chose their kings for their noble birth, but their commanders for their valour. He refers to the 'king' or the 'chieftain', but it is not clear if these were alternative terms for the same role or two distinct offices.[36] He lists those Germanic peoples who were ruled by kings and seems to suggest that some, but not necessarily all, of the Germanic

---

[26] Bassett 1989: p. 3.
[27] Bassett 1989: pp. 3–5.
[28] Dumville 1977a: pp. 90–3.
[29] Bede's *Ecclesiastical History of the English People* was completed in 731; The Anglo-Saxon Chronicle began to be compiled towards the end of the ninth century; the corpus of extant charters numbers over 1,000 texts, which range from the last quarter of the seventh century onwards.

[30] Gildas was a British monk of mid-sixth century whom Bede made famous by using his material, probably because there was no other evidence available to him writing 200 years later.
[31] *De Exidio Brittanae*, Lapidge 1999: p. 204.
[32] Yorke 2006: pp. 15-16.
[33] Campbell 1986: p. 86.
[34] Campbell 1982: p. 30.
[35] These are listed and discussed by Campbell 1982: p. 26.
[36] Tacitus, *Germania*: ch. 7; Mattingly and Handford 1970: p. 22.

tribes were governed by kings. The continental Saxons were one such group. The tribes with kings chose them according to their degree of nobility, that is, how close they were in blood ties to a previous king or his family. The king was customarily a war-leader with proven prowess in battle, although, as noted above, this was not invariably so. Above all, the king had to be of 'the blood royal'. This, significantly is how he described King Ine of Wessex, more of which later.[37]

Green considers the various terms that were used for a leader, principally the three vernacular terms for 'king': the Gothic *þiudans*; Old High German *truhtin*; and Old High German *kuning*.[38] The term *þiudans* derives from *þiuda*, 'people' – a ruler over a people, *truhtin* could refer to a war-leader who may also have been a king but not necessarily so, and *kuning* 'king', the warrior leader of the kin. For this study this is the most significant of these terms.

In all well-attested Germanic languages, with the exception of Gothic, cognates of *kuning/cyning* survive as the term for 'king', despite it being linguistically the most difficult to explain of all the various terms related to leadership.[39] In origin it appears to have been applied to small-scale kingship –'petty kings', to distinguish them from *þiudans*. A runic inscription from Rök in Östergötland refers to 20 kings banded together for war-like ventures. These would almost certainly have been petty kings, and the five Wessex kings killed in one battle in 626 would almost certainly have been of a similar status.[40] In that year seven kings in total are recorded as being killed in Wessex; the additional two were Cynegils and Cwitchelm, who fought, and lost, against Penda of Mercia at Cirencester.[41]

To turn to Bede for an answer to the question 'what is a *rex*?' is not to find a simple answer. He uses the term *rex* for rulers of widely differing levels of power, from the *reges* of Northumbria, Wessex and Mercia to the *rex* of [the isle of] Wight.[42] His use of *principes* is equally unclear as does not always use the term as a synonym for *reges*, as his *principes* sometimes includes *reges*.[43] This inconsistency means that we cannot look to Bede to provide a clear cut answer to what the term *cyning* meant. His terminology for kingdoms and peoples is equally inconsistent. Campbell in his analysis of the terms Bede used for leaders and peoples concluded that Bede's inconsistency probably reflected the

unstable nature of the kings and their kingdoms at the time he was writing.[44]

Having established that there is no direct evidence that allows us to say what the word *cyning* meant in England before the seventh century, it is, nevertheless, safe to say that the term and the concept of kingship would have been understood and broadly available for use by the leaders of the war-bands who arrived in Britain, some of whom could well have been petty kings in their own lands. Did they bring the concept of kingship and kingdom with them? We simply do not know. All that can be said with certainty is that by the time of the earliest records, *cyning* is the word used to describe their leaders.

In origin, *cyning* seems to have carried family or dynastic undertones, signifying members of a specially selected kindred divinely called to rule over a people. All of the (much later recorded) kingly genealogies and foundation myths claim descent, usually althought not exclusively, from pagan gods. Descent from a god raised a king above his followers and imbued him with sacred authority. Kingship was sought for power and property, which in turn were used for the benefit of self, family, and companions. War booty, gained by pillage and by the exaction of tribute, was vital if the king was to retain his war-band, the basis of his power, men who fought to the death if necessary, who were then rewarded with gifts from the king –the 'ring-giver'. To survive the king had to keep giving, and to keep on giving he had to keep on fighting and giving. A 'ring-stingy' king did not last long.

The earliest petty-kingdoms

Studies of the northern Germanic tribes show that many of these war-bands and their kings were of relatively new origin, in all probability no earlier than the third or fourth centuries, reflecting the political geography of northern *Germania* at this time, which was also relatively recent. This shift would have opened up the opportunity for war-bands to spring up around successful local leaders, many of whom might well have been some of the earliest settlers in England. They would have brought with them their established social and cultural structures, but with old constraints weakened new patterns of social and political expression would have been easy to establish when there was no over-arching political power structure to prevent it. Germanic settlement in Britain began before the end of the fourth century and continued into the sixth century at least, a century and a half of almost certain anarchy, a long time for what must have been largely a free-for-all. There would have been regional variations, and the incomers were not of the same type. Excavated settlements and cemeteries reveal not only warriors buried with their weapons, but also lesser folk, driven from the crowded North Sea regions. There is an abundance of legend, but no documentary record of the rulers of the British kingdoms encountered by the Anglo-Saxons when they arrived, or what opposition the

---

[37] *HE* vol. 7, 276.

[38] Green 1998: pp. 121–40.

[39] The ninth-century Rök runestone features (Ög 136; www.nordiska. uu.se/forskna/samnord.htm), the longest known runic inscription in stone. It refers to 20 *kunungar* 'kings', four groups of five brothers and their fathers, who were also four brothers.

[40] *ASC* 626 'And then he (Edwin) went into Wessex with an army and felled 5 kings there'.

[41] *ASC* 628.

[42] Campbell 1979: p. 1.

[43] Peada, son of Penda, is one such case. Campbell 1979: p. 3 suggests that Bede was clear in regarding some potentates as indubitably *reges*. He is inconsistent about others whose status about which he felt there was some ambiguity, but nevertheless had something regal about them.

[44] Campbell 1986: p. 87.

Figure 2: Map of the possible areas of the kingdoms listed in the tribute list known as the *Tribal Hidage*, with Kingstons superimposed. Reproduced courtesy of Stuart Brookes.

incomers, numbers still essentially unknown, would have encountered. Was there a mass migration, a political and aristocratic take-over, or both? The debate continues.

Later evidence suggests that, out of what must have been a fluid and often chaotic society, a few strong British kingdoms emerged – mainly in the north and the west; fewer are known in the east and south-east. There are wide geographical variations in the archaeological record of the early Anglo-Saxon settlement and no single model provides an explanation of its diversity, although some broad observations can be made. Barbara Yorke is of the opinion that the origins of the Anglo-Saxon kingdoms were perhaps more diverse than is suggested at the point when they come into the record.[45]

The Tribal Hidage and the earliest English kingdoms

By the seventh century at least twelve kingdoms/provinces had emerged with *reges* as rulers. Within some of these kingdoms there is evidence of smaller sub-districts, almost certainly ruled by petty, tribal kings, with many other similar groups having disappeared before recorded history. The folk groups listed were assessed in hides and varied in size. Many of those listed have been hard to locate.

The Tribal Hidage is now agreed to be a tribute list of 34 kingdoms and tribal territories south of the River Humber. Its most probable date is the second half of the seventh century; it is not known why the list was compiled, or even if it is all of one date.[46] It could be a Greater Mercian document, although there is the possibility that it is a Northumbrian list of King Oswald, or his successors Oswiu or Ecgfrith. Blair argues for its being Mercian, Brooks and Higham, on the other hand, argue for a Northumbrian context.[47] The document is generally agreed to be of central importance, revealing as it does the existence of what Bassett calls a 'miscellany of peoples' – small tribal groups, many with -*ingas* names. These were the building-blocks of the kingdoms, yet without the survival of the Tribal Hidage we would never even have known of their existence – as must be the case with countless other similar groups.[48] The territory of the *Stoppingas* (above), although not listed in the Hidage, must have formed one such petty-kingdom. Its absence from the list suggests that it could well have lost its independent status before the document was drawn up. It is also possible that the putative territory of the *Hurstingas,* with a 1,200 hide assessment in the Tribal Hidage, may be represented by the later Hundred

---

[45] Yorke 1999: p. 28.

[46] Tribal Hidage (Harleian MS 3271 fol 6v.

[47] Blair 1999: pp. 456–7; Bassett 1989: p. 17; Brooks 1989b: p. 159; Higham 1995: pp. 74–113.

[48] Dumville 1989: pp. 225–30; Hart 1971: pp. 138–57; Davies and Vierk 1974: pp. 223–7, 937; Blair 1999: pp. 456–7; Yorke 1990: pp. 9–15.

of Hurstingstone HNT, in the centre of which *Kyngestune/ Wistow* lies. This kingdom, and other possible examples within whose putative boundaries a Kingston lies, are discussed in Chapter 4.

Bassett asks whether these short-lived and dimly perceived territories were of any importance. In the early sources they are referred to in exactly the same terms as the major kingdoms, that is *provinciae* and *regiones*. He is also of the opinion that they were kingdoms on the point of extinction.[49] Barbara Yorke thinks that not all of these small sub-kingdoms were necessarily self-governing units which were later incorporated into more successful neighbouring kingdoms. They could have been one kingdom subsumed as a sub-kingdom into the other, which is what seems initially to have been the case with Deira in relation to Bernicia.[50] Pauline Stafford notes that the Tribal Hidage is a timely reminder that the well-organised taking of dues and tribute is an ancient phenomenon in English history which was not new in the late seventh century, by which time the assessment units were already frozen.[51]

Within these early kingdoms there would have been a range of regnal practices. In Wessex the record shows a complex and fluid pattern of kingship: sometimes with more than one king, sometimes with a dominant king who may have reigned alone or at the same as the sub-kings. This seems to have been the case with Ine of Wessex (688-726) and his father Cenred, who was king of a component part of Wessex, probably Dorset, at the same time as Ine was king and acknowledging his father Cenred in the introduction to his law codes. It is possible that at this time Ine held an *imperium* over all sub-territories of Ancient Wessex, of which Dorset was one.[52] Chadwick is of the opinion that in Wessex, at least, it was probably the norm for the kingdom to be divided among *sub-reguli* under a 'main king' and that these would have been the ealdormen of Ine's laws.[53] Kent, in contrast, at this time seems to have had a regularised system, with the senior king in east Kent and the junior king in west Kent.[54]

By the seventh century, in both Celtic and Anglo-Saxon societies, kingship was the established, basic political institution of England, with a multiplicity of kings of differing levels. From the seventh century onwards the record reveals a society becoming gradually more stable, but still based on warfare with the king customarily being the war-leader, with a structure of emergent royal and ecclesiastical 'estates' increasingly underpinning his power. The practical governance of a kingdom would have been undertaken by officers of the king whose prime duty was to support him as war-leader.[55] The king was itinerant, this way he could exploit the produce of his lands. He could

be seen by and create awe in his subjects, as he and his considerable entourage progressed around the kingdom. The progress of the king, his family, and retainers would have demanded considerable organisational skill. Bede describes a vivid tableau of itinerant kingly power in his account of King Edwin, accompanied by his *thegns*, progressing around his *civitates*, *villæ*, and *provinciæ* with the *tufa*, the royal standard, carried before him.[56]

Having established the wider context out of which the Kingstons emerged we turn now to the data on which interpretations and theories can be built.

---

[49] Bassett 1989: p.18.
[50] Yorke 1999: p. 27.
[51] Stafford 1985: p. 94.
[52] Attenborough 1922: p. 37.
[53] Chadwick 1905: pp. 282–90.
[54] Brooks 1989a: pp. 67–74.
[55] Lloyn 1984: pp. 5–29.

---

[56] *HE* ii, 17.

Chapter 3

Patterns and Possibilities: Distribution and Communications

The Kingston Material

The data on which this chapter is based is contained in **Part II**. This chapter is, therefore, in general _lightly footnoted_. However, if information is not included in **Part II**, or if it seems particularly helpful to provide the reader with a specific reference _in situ_, it is footnoted within the text.

The 70 Kingston-names have been grouped into four geographical **Groups** determined by the distribution pattern of the names.

Group 1
- **i** Counties which comprised the core of ancient Wessex prior to 726
- **ii** Counties which had close associations with ancient Wessex prior to 726
- **iii** Counties over which Wessex had established lordship prior to 726

Group 2 Counties of the Severn Valley, Welsh Borders, and the West Midlands

Group 3 Counties lying between Watling Street and the Mersey/Humber line

Group 4 Counties lying north of the Mersey/Humber line

In **Groups 1** and **2** the material relating to the physical context of each Kingston is discussed first, followed by the documentary and archaeological evidence. In **Groups 3** and **4** where the evidence is slight the material is not sub-divided.

The tables

Table 1 lists the Kingstons alphabetically by pre-1974 counties.

Table 2 lists the names in order of their first appearance in the record.

Table 3 lists the name-forms _cyninges_ + _tun/kyne_ (and variants) by pre-1974 county. This table has been included for information even though, as discussed in chapter one, there is no discernible significance in the variant forms.

Table 4 lists Kingstons sited in relation to Roman roads or other ancient routeways.

Table 1. Kingstons listed alphabetically by pre-1974 counties

1. SP 522 025	Kennington BRK
2. SU 407 981	Kingston (Bagpuize) BRK
3. SU 326 876	Kingston (Lisle) BRK
4. SU 263 857	Kingstone (Winslow) BRK
5. TL 320 661	Conington CAM
6. TL 345 550	Kingston CAM
7. ST 252 943	Kingsd(t)on* (Colyton) DEV
8. SY 065 877	Kingston (Colaton Raleigh) DEV
9. SX 846 540	Kingston (Dittisham) DEV
10. SX 904 515	Kingston (Facy/Brixham) DEV
11. SX 635 478	Kingston (Modbury) DEV
12. SY 956 797	Kingston (Corfe) DOR
13. ST 750 098	Kingston (Haselbury Bryan) DOR
14. SY 978 013	Kingston (Lacy) DOR
15. SY 720 912	Kingston (Maurward/Stinsford) DOR
16. SY 582 913	Kingston (Russel) DOR
17. SY 862 976	Kingston (Winterborne) DOR
18. ST 763 232	Kington Magna DOR
19. SO 777 148	Kineton Green (Elmore) GLO
20. SP 097 265	Kineton (Temple Guiting) GLO
21. SO 618 019	Kingston (Aylburton) GLO
22. SO 733 038	Kingston (Slimbridge) GLO
23. _c_. ST 55 93	Kingston (Tidenham) GLO
24. ST 620 904	Kington/Kyneton (Thornbury) GLO
25. ST 538 779	Kingsweston GLO
26. SU 149 020	Kingston (Cross, Ringwood) HMP
27. SU 655 013	Kingston (Fratton/ Portsmouth) HMP
28. SZ 480 814	Kingston (I of W) HMP
29. SO 424 357	Kingstone (Thruxton) HER
30. SO 631 246	Kingstone (Weston under Penyard) HER
31. SO 291 568	Kington (Welsh Border) HER
32. SO 405 747	Kinton (Leintwardine) HER
33. TL 180 859	Conington HNT
34. TL 279 810	_Kyngestone_/Wistow HNT
35. TR 022 452	Kennington (Wye) KNT
36. TR 198 513	Kingston KNT
37. SD 302 976	Coniston LAN

38. SK 366 054	Congerstone LEI
39. NZ 225 675	Kenton (Gosforth) NTB
40. SK 591 845	Kingston (Carlton in Lindrick) NTT
41. SU 739 995	Kingston (Blount) OXF
42. SJ 372 195	Kinton (Great Ness) SHR
43. ST 547 301	Keinton (Mandeville) SOM
44. ST 401 669	Kingston (Seymour) SOM
45. ST 223 297	Kingston (St Mary, Taunton) SOM
46. ST 553 165	Kingston (Yeovil) SOM
47. ST 379 136	Kingstone (Ilminster) SOM
48. SK 060 295	Kingstone STF
49. TL 955 781	Coney Weston SFK
50. TM 191 659	Kenton SFK
51. TM 270 475	Kingston (Woodbridge) SFK
52. TQ 312 776	Kennington (Lambeth) SUR
53. SU 891 491	Kingston (Seale) SUR
54. TQ 179 693	Kingston upon Thames SUR
55. TQ 235 052	Kingston (Bucy) SSX
56. TQ 262 383	Kingston (Croft/Ifield) SSX
57. TQ 086 020	Kingston (Ferring/Angmering) SSX
58. TQ 392 082	Kingston (Lewes) SSX
59. SP 335 511	Kineton WAR
60. SP 125 815	Kineton Green (Solihull) WAR
61. SP 352 583	Kingston Farm (Chesterton) WAR
62. SP 180 642	Kington Grange (Claverdon) WAR
63. ST 813 776	West Kington WLT
64. SU 241 559	Kingston (Collingbourne) WLT
65. ST 845 370	Kingston (Deverill) WLT
66. ST 903 773	Kington (St Michael) WLT
67. SO 990 559	Kington WOR
68. TA 104 297	Kingston upon Hull YER
69. SD 902 552	Coniston (Cold) YOW
70. SD 981 675	Conistone (Kettlewell) YOW

* This name occurs interchangeably as both Kingsdon and Kingston.

Table 2. Kingstons listed by date of first documentary reference

Name	County	Date	Source
Kennington	BRK	821	S 183
Kingston upon Thames	SUR	838	S 281
Kingston (St Michael)	WLT	934	S 426
Conington	HNT	957	S 649
Kingston (Bagpuize)	BRK	959	S 673
Kingston (Tidenham)	GLO	c. 1000	S 1555
Kineton	WAR	969	S 773
Kineton Green (Solihull)	WAR	972	S 786
Kington	WOR	930	S 786
Kyngestone/Wistow	HNT	974	S 978
Conington	CAM	975	S 1487
Kingston (Woodbridge)	SFK	1042	S 1051
Coney Weston	SFK	1051	S 1080

First recorded in DB

Name	County		
Kingston	CAM		
Kingston (Corfe)	DOR		
Kington Magna	DOR		
Kingston (IOW)	HMP		
Kingstone (Thruxton)	HER		
Kingstone (Weston under Penyard)	HER		
Kington	HER		
Kennington (Wye)	KNT		
Congerstone	LEI		
Kingston (Blount)	OXF		
Kingston (Carlton in Lindrick)	NTT		
Keinton (Mandeville)	SOM		
Kingston (Seymour)	SOM		
Kingstone (Ilminster)	SOM		
Kenton	SFK		
Kennington	SUR		
Kingston (Bucy)	SSX		
Kington (Grange/ Claverdon)	WAR		
Conistone (Kettlewell)	YOW		
Coniston (Cold)	YOW		

First recorded post DB

Name	County	Date	
Kingston	KNT	1087	
Kingston (Lewes)	SSX	1087	
Kingston (St Mary, Taunton)	SOM	1155	
Coniston	LAN	1157	
Kingstone	STF	1166	
Kineton (Temple Guiting)	GLO	1185	
Kingston (Lacy)	DOR	1191	
Kingston (Winterborne)	DOR	1194	
Kingtton (Fratton/ Portsmouth)	HMP	1194	
West Kington	WLT	1195	
Kinton (Great Ness)	SHR	1203	
Kingston (Seale)	SUR	1210	
Kingston (Russel)	DOR	1212	

Kingston (Lisle)	BRK	1220		Kingstone (Wilmslow)	BRK	1252
Kingston (Aylburton)	GLO	1221		Kingston (Croft/Ifield)	SSX	1261
Kingston (Colaton Raleigh)	DEV	1227		Kingston Farm (Chesterton)	WAR	1279
Kingston (Modbury)	DEV	1242		Kingston (Cross, Ringwood)	HMP	1280
Kenton (Gosforth)	NBL	1242		Kingston (Facy/ Brixham)	DEV	1292
Kingston (Deverill)	WLT	1243		Kingston upon Hull	YER	1299
Kngston (Maurward/ Stinsford)	DOR	1247		Kingston (Collingbourne)	WLT	1306
Kingston (Slimbridge)	GLO	1248		Kingston (Ferring/ Angmering)	SSX	1312
Kington/Kyneton (Thornbury)	GLO	1248		Kingston (Dittisham)	DEV	1438
Kingsweston	GLO	1248		Kingsd(t)on (Colyton)	DEV	1539
Kingston (Leintwardine)	HER	1249		Kingston (Haselbury Bryan)	DOR	1580
Kenton Green (Elmore)	GLO	1250				

Table 3. Distribution of *cyninges* + *tun/kyne* (and other variants) by pre-1974 county
Group 1a. Counties which comprised the core of ancient Wessex before 726

	cyninges-tūn	*king (and variants) -tūn*	Combined
Dorset	6	1	7
Hampshire	3	0	3
Wiltshire	2	2	4
Somerset	4	1	5
Devon	5	0	5
Totals	**20**	**4**	**24 (34%** of all Kingstons**)**

Group 1b. Counties which had close associations with ancient Wessex before 726

	cyninges-tūn	*king (and variants) -tūn*	Combined
Berkshire	4	0	4
Surrey	3	0	3
Oxfordshire	1	0	1
Totals	**8**	**0**	**8 (11% of all Kingstons)**

Group 1c. Kingstons in counties over which Wessex had established lordship prior to 726

	cyninges-tūn	*king (and variants) -tūn*	Combined
Kent	2	0	2
Sussex	4	0	4
Totals	**6**	**0**	**6 (9% of all Kingstons)**

Group 1 comprises 54% (38) of all Kingstons.

Group 2. Kingstons sited in the lower Severn Valley and the West Midlands

	cyninges-tūn	*king (and variants) -tūn*	Combined
Gloucestershire	4	3	7
Herefordshire	3	1	4
Shropshire	0	1	1
Staffordshire	1	0	1
Warwickshire	1	3	4
Worcestershire	0	1	1
Totals	**9**	**9**	**18 (26% of all Kingstons)**

Groups 1 and 2 combined comprise 80% (56) of all Kingstons.

Group 3. Kingstons sited between Watling Street and the Mersey/Humber line

	cyninges-tūn	*king (and variants) -tūn*	Combined
Leicestershire	1	0	1
Nottinghamshire	1	0	1
Huntingdonshire	1	1	2
Cambridgeshire	1	1	2
Suffolk	2	1	3
Totals	**6**	**3**	**9 (13%** of all Kingstons**)**

Group 4. Kingstons sited in counties north of the Mersey/Humber line

	cyninges-tūn	*king (and variants) -tūn*	Combined
Lancashire	1	0	1
Yorkshire East Riding	1		1
Yorkshire West Riding	2	0	2
Northumberland	0	1	1
Totals	**4**	**1**	**5 (7%** of all Kingstons**)**

Table 4. Kingstons sited in relation to Roman roads or other ancient routeways
A. Kingstons sited either within one mile of a long-distance Roman road, or within a parish that does

SU 326 876	Kingston (Lisle) BRK	TL 180 859	Conington HNT
SU 263 857	Kingstone (Winslow) BRK	TR 198 513	Kingston KNT
SP 522 025	Kennington BRK	TR 022 452	Kennington (Wye) KNT
TL 320 661	Conington CAM	NZ 225 675	Kenton (Gosforth) NTB
TL 345 550	Kingston CAM	SU 739 995	Kingston (Blount) OXF
SY 065 877	Kingston (Colaton Raleigh) DEV	SJ 372 195	Kinton (Great Ness) SHR
ST 252 943	Kingsd(t)on (Colyton) DEV	ST 547 301	Keinton (Mandeville) SOM
ST 763 232	Kington Magna DOR	ST 401 669	Kingston (Seymour) SOM
SY 978 013	Kingston (Lacy) DOR	ST 379 136	Kingstone (Ilminster) SOM
SY 862 976	Kingston (Winterborne) DOR	ST 553 165	Kingston (Yeovil) SOM
SY 582 913	Kingston (Russel) DOR	TL 955 781	Coney Weston SFK
SY 720 912	Kingston (Maurward/Stinsford) DOR	SK 060 295	Kingstone STF
ST *c.* 55 93	Kingston (Tidenham) GLO	SU 891 491	Kingston (Seale) SUR
SO 618 019	Kingston (Aylburton) GLO	TQ 312 776	Kennington (Lambeth) SUR
SO 733 038	Kingston (Slimbridge) GLO	TQ 235 052	Kingston (Bucy) SSX
ST 620 904	Kington/Kyneton (Thornbury) GLO	TQ 086 020	Kingston (Ferring/Angmering) SSX
SP 097 265	Kineton (Temple Guiting) GLO	TQ 392 082	Kingston (Lewes) SSX
ST 538 779	Kingweston GLO	SP 335 511	Kineton WAR
SO 777 148	Kineton Green (Elmore) GLO	SP 125 815	Kineton Green (Solihull) WAR
SU 149 020	Kingston (Cross, Ringwood) HMP	SP 352 583	Kingston Farm (Chesterton) WAR
SO 405 747	Kinton (Leintwardine) HER	ST 813 776	West Kington WLT
SO 424 357	Kingstone (Thruxton) HER	ST 845 370	Kingston (Deverill) WLT
SO 631 246	Kingstone (Weston under Penyard) HER	SU 241 559	Kingston (Collingbourne) WLT
		SD 981 675	Conistone (Kettlewell) YOW
		SD 902 552	Coniston (Cold) YOW
		Total	48 = 68%

B. Kingstons sited in close association to roads which are known to have been used by the Romans or have features that suggest that they might have been

SU 407 981	Kingston (Bagpuize) BRK
SY 956 797	Kingston (Corfe) DOR
SD 302 976	Coniston LAN
TM 191 659	Kenton SFK
SP 180 642	Kington Grange (Claverdon) WAR
Total	**5 = 7%**

Groups A and B comprise 75 per cent of all Kingstons.

C. Kingstons sited on old-established long-distance roads

ST 750 098	Kingston (Hazelbury Bryan) DOR
SO 291 568	Kington (Welsh Border) HER
TL 279 810	*Kyngestone*/Wistow HNT
SK 366 054	Congerstone LEI
SK 591 845	Kingston (Carlton in Lindrick) NTT
ST 223 297	Kingston (St Mary, Taunton) SOM
TQ 262 383	Kingston (Croft, Ifield) SSX
ST 903 773	Kington (St Michael) WLT
SO 990 559	Kington WOR
Total	**9 = 13%**

D. Kingstons sited in relation to a river or the coast.

SX 904 515	Kingston (Facy/Brixham) DEV
SX 635 478	Kingston (Modbury) DEV
SX 846 540	Kingston (Dittisham) DEV
SU 655 013	Kingston (Fratton/Portsmouth) HMP
SZ 480 814	Kingston (I of W) HMP
TQ 179 693	Kingston upon Thames SUR
TM 270 475	Kingston (Woodbridge) SFK
TA 104 297	Kingston upon Hull
Total	**8 = 12%**

The most striking characteristic of almost all of the Kingstons is their close association to long-distance Roman roads or other ancient routeways. Margaret Gelling, in her study of the place-name *wīcham* and its association with Roman roads, took *close* to mean lying within one mile of the road, or within a parish that conforms to that rule.[1] These are the criteria are used here.

As noted above, all three statistical tests that were applied to the Kingston corpus produced a significant correlation between the Kingston sites, and major Roman and ancient roads: 70 per cent lie on or close to these roads, and a further 15 per cent on roads which are known to have been used, and probably adapted for use, by the Romans. Of the remaining 15 per cent, 5 per cent lie on important through-roads; two lie on rivers, the Thames and Deben, and four are close to the coast, three in Devon and one on the Isle of Wight. This is a highly significant pattern of distribution, with every Kingston, irrespective of region, sited on a major line of communication.

The Kingston Material Group by Group

Group 1   Counties which comprised the core of ancient Wessex prior to 726

There are seven Kingstons in the county of Dorset, all of which give the appearance of being sited purposefully in relation to each other at regular intervals, roughly eight to ten miles distance apart along long-distance major Roman or other ancient roads. This 'road/string' pattern can be seen at its most obvious with the Kingstons positioned along the line of the London to Exeter Roman road, as it crosses the central Dorset downs and into east Devon. This road, known in Dorset as Ackling Dyke, dates from the earliest years of the Roman occupation of southern Britain. It entered the county in the north-east from Old Sarum, ran on to Badbury Rings north of Wimborne Minster, then to Dorchester and Exeter. This road, which Taylor considers to be the best surviving length of Roman road in Britain, is still a striking earthwork in central Dorset.[2] Badbury Rings, on which the road was aligned, is an imposing Iron Age hill-fort next to which stood the Roman small town of *Vindocladia*. The road at this point was intersected by the Roman road that crossed the country from Sea Mills (*Abonæ*) (M 54) in South Gloucestershire, to Bath *Aquæ Sulis*, and on to Poole Harbour (M 4d, M 52, M 56, M 4d) on the south coast. A mile south of Wimborne Minster in the parish of Corfe Mullen, and lying just off this road to the east, is Lake Farm where the Romans established the main base for their campaign against the Durotriges. Close to this point a road struck off eastward into west Hampshire, where, nine miles on, in the parish of Ringwood, a Kingston is sited in direct relationship to the string of Kingstons that cross central Dorset.

Kingston (Lacy) stands close to the intersection at Badbury Rings. The drive of Kingston (Lacy) House follows the line of the road to Poole road. Nine miles west of Kingston (Lacy), on the London/Exeter road, Kingston (Winterborne) stands on the line of the road. A further nine miles westwards is Kingston (Maurward/Stinsford) in the parish of Stinsford, adjacent to Fordington and Dorchester. A pronounced *agger* can be seen crossing the grounds of Kingston House.

Between Kingstons Winterborne and Maurward/Stinsford, where the road crosses Puddletown Forest, a remarkable half-mile stretch of this road still stands 5m high and 26m wide. The paved central street which would have been used

---

[1]   Gelling 1997: pp. 8–26.

[2]   Taylor 1979: p.186–7.

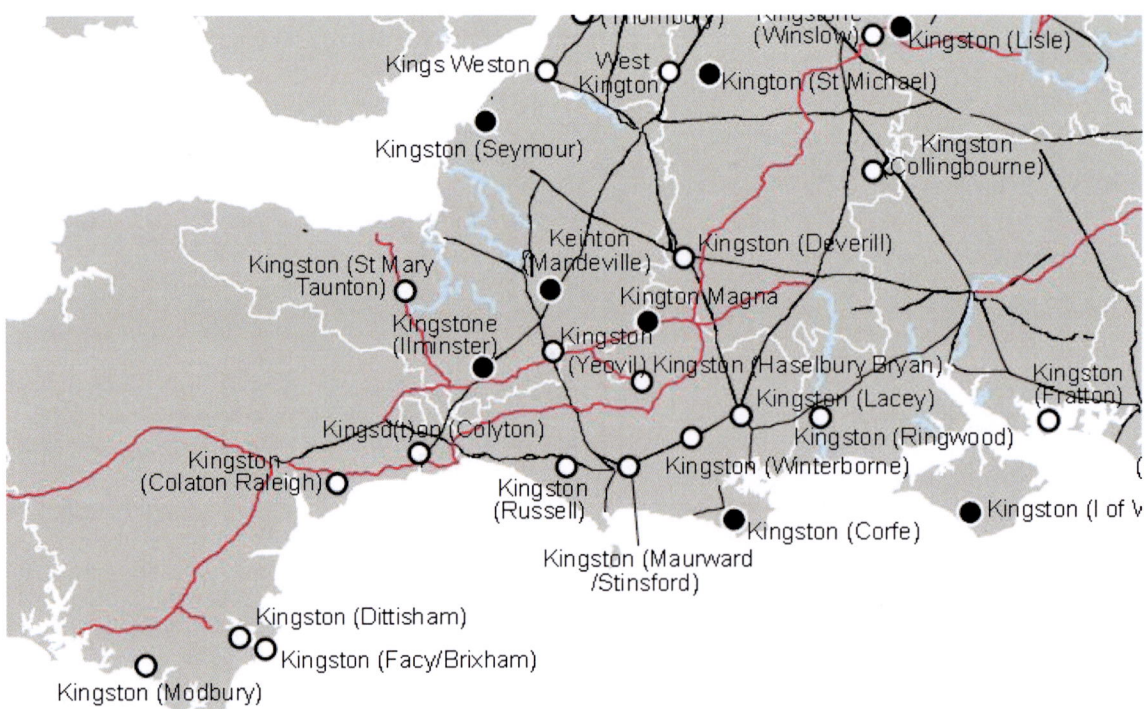

Figure 3: Devon, Somerset, Dorset, Wiltshire, Hampshire.

for rapid troop movement can still be seen, as can the wide outer droving-roads for the movement of livestock, and the drainage ditches. There is no observable, compelling topographical reason for the road to be so high and wide at this point. The English Heritage archaeologists who undertook excavations here consider it to be the most noteworthy stretch of Roman road ever found in Britain; no other known stretch of Roman road in Britain begins to approach dimensions of this scale.[3] When the incoming Anglo-Saxons arrived several hundred years after its construction it would still have been an impressive sight.

In Kingston (Maurward/Stinsford) parish the Roman road is joined by the modern road from Wimborne Minster to Dorchester. The point where these roads meet is the parish boundary of Kingston (Maurward/Stinsford) where a cylindrical stone pillar stands, generally considered to be a Roman milestone *in situ*, set deep into the southern bank of the Roman road. It is severely weathered with no surviving inscriptions.[4] Onward from this point the precise line of the Roman road as it approached and entered Dorchester is not clear (see below).

The road continues west of Dorchester where it is still visible in the landscape, although less pronounced than in the east. Nine miles from Dorchester is Kingston (Russel) the northern parish boundary of which follows the line of the Roman road. Thirty miles further west, in east Devon, in the parish of Colaton Raleigh, is another Kingston, sited in

Newton Poppleford, a daughter of Colaton Raleigh, on the Roman road. The line of the road here has been confirmed by an archaeological excavation. A further nine miles along the road is Exeter, where, given the pattern observed along this road, there is a reasonable expectation that a Kingston might be sited. However, in spite of much searching, no Kingston has as of yet been identified.

Margary identified much of the line of this road as it crossed Dorset and east Devon, but in several places he was uncertain as to its precise line.[5] Close scrutiny of the first edition of the six-inch OS map, along with the evidence of LiDAR,[6] has made it possible to fill in almost all the gaps and to establish with a greater accuracy the Kingstons that lie along it.

The position of the Kingstons, spaced out along this road at regular distances apart, would seem to indicate that we are looking at a planned system that might well have applied along the whole length of this road from east Dorset to Exeter (see below). This being so, it is possible to propose where other (now lost) Kingstons might once have stood. In east Devon, 30 miles west of Kingston (Russel), is one such case. The Kingston that stood here, recorded in 1539 for the first time as *Kingsdūn/Kingstun*, is memorialised in the name of a (now closed) rural railway station. This example also llustrates how problematic it can be sometimes to detect what the original form of a name

---

[3]   Peter Addison, Historic Environment Field Advisor, and Pete Wilson, Head of Research Policy (Roman Archaeology) at English Heritage. 'Puddletown Forest Roman Road', short report, in *Current Archaeology*, 253, April 2001.
[4]   Margary 1955, vol 1, pp. 100.

[5]   Margary 1955: vol. 1: pp. 99–105.
[6]   LiDAR - Light Detection and Ranging is a remote sensing method that uses light in the form of a pulsed laser to measure ranges (variable distances) to the earth. These light pulses generate precise three dimensional information about the shape of the earth and its surface characteristics. It is increasingly used by geographers and archaeologists.

might have been. The first edition of the six-inch to the mile OS map records the name here as Kingsdon. Thereafter, on subsequent OS maps, the forms Kingsdon (*dūn*) and Kingston (*tūn*) are used interchangeably. Occasionally the place-name elements *dūn* and *tūn* are not stable, and other evidence is needed to establish which is the more likely. In this case the complete absence of any forms prior to 1539 makes it impossible to say whether *dūn* or *tūn* was the original second element. Margaret Gelling has written extensively on what she calls 'the massive confusion of -*dūn* and -*tūn*', citing Bullington HMP, Buston NTB, Dixton GLO, Hartington DRB, and Hillerton DEV as examples of this.[7] In this instance, the non-place-name evidence for *Kingsdūn/tūn* being a Kingston is confirmed by the compelling topographical evidence of its position lying in the angle formed by two Roman roads: the London to Exeter road and the Fosse Way.

The midway point of the 20 miles of Roman road between Kingston (Russel) and Kingsd(t)on (Colyton) is where another Kingston might be expected to be found− somewhere in the area around Whitchurch Canonicorum, Bridport, Burton Bradstock or Charmouth. To date, despite an intensive study of the area both in the field and Record Office, no evidence has been uncovered. Anne Cole has drawn my attention to the possibility that if there had been a Kingston in this region it could have been lost to the sea, as has happened to so much of the coast there.

Returning to east Dorset, the line of the road has been identified continuing eastwards into Hampshire, where, three miles across the county boundary in the parish of Ringwood, another Kingston lies. This eastward running road is connected to the Devon/Dorset string system via the Roman road from Poole to Winchester, which struck east through Ferndown (now a suburb of Bournemouth) to a point just across the county boundary with Hampshire, where it turned north-east to Ringwood and eventually on to Winchester. Margary had difficulty in establishing the precise line of this road east of this point but he did identify the point on the county boundary where it left the more important road and veered towards Ringwood.[8] From this fork the road took a straight line east to the crossing point on the River Avon, known as Watton's Ford and Kingston (Ringwood).[9] Today, this road ends where it meets the modern Bournemouth to Ringwood road (A338), but it is traceable on earlier maps and with LiDAR as a straight line to Watton's Ford.

In 2003 unquestionable evidence of this road system was confirmed by the late Arthur Clarke, Archaeology Officer of the Ordnance Survey, who set out to confirm the authenticity of the line of the Roman road from Applemore Hill to Lepe.[10] Clarke was not only able to confirm the line of the road in question, but also to trace it north-

west to Shorn Hill, where it joined the Roman road from Otterbourne to Stoney Cross, Picket Hill, Hightown, and Watton's Ford. He was also able to confirm that the road continued to the vexillation fortress at Lake Farm, where it joined the Ackling Dyke road to Dorchester. Clarke not only established that this was a *bona fide* Roman road, he also identified the primary sight-lines which would have been used by the Roman surveyors who set out these roads. He is of the opinion that this was an early military road constructed as part of the operations for the capture of the Isle of Wight.

Kington Magna, Kingston (Corfe) and Kingston (Haselbury Bryan) differ from the other four Dorset Kingstons in that they do not appear to have been associated with major Roman roads. However, they are all sited on or close to long-distance ancient routeways. It is significant that whilst they do not appear to have been part of a 'string' system, they are, nevertheless, sited in direct and regular relationships to the other Dorset Kingstons, and to Kingston (Cross, Ringwood), Kingsd(t)on (Colyton), Kingston (Colaton Raleigh), and Kingston (Deverill) in south-west Wiltshire. There are hints that this system might have included the lower end of the Fosse Way in Somerset.

The southern boundary of the parish of Kington Magna, the most northern of the Dorset examples, follows the line of the Sherborne Causeway, a long-distance ancient routeway which crosses the county from Shaftesbury to Yeovil SOM, where it meets the Roman Ilchester to Dorchester road (M 47). East of Kington Magna the Sherborne Causeway, known along this section as the *Herepath*, intersects the Roman road from Badbury Rings to Old Sarum (M 4c). A further ancient road connecting Kington Magna with Kingston (Deverill) in the south west appears to be part of the 9/10-mile system.

Kingston (Haselbury Bryan) lies in central Dorset, nine miles from Kingstons Lacy, Winterborne, Maurward/ Stinsford, and Kington Magna, two miles north of an ancient routeway which crosses the county east/west from Shillington to Buckland Newton, where it intersects the present-day B3143 three miles south of Kings Stag. The positioning of a Kingston here is worth mentioning as this is the *truncum qui stat in tribis divis* 'the trunk which stands at three boundaries' and from which several roads radiate out in all directions.[11] Haselbury Bryan lies a mile east of a now minor but clearly defined ancient through-road, running south from King's Stag to join the London to Exeter Roman road just south of Puddletown.

Close to the coast of Dorset **Kingston (Corfe)** is sited on the Isle of Purbeck, on the road between Wareham and Swanage. It is possible that this Kingston also might have been part of the system described above. There is evidence of extensive Roman industrial activity in this area, with the marble quarried from here being used in London from as early as *c.* AD 70, and subsequently throughout the Roman

---

[7] Gelling and Cole 2000: p. 167-73; Margaret Gelling confirms this. Personal correspondence.
[8] Margary 1987: vol 1, pp. 87, 98.
[9] SU 104 023.
[10] Clarke 2003: pp. 35, 50.

[11] ST 724 105. First recorded in 1216, PNDo, vol. iii, p. 349.

period.[12] Putnam notes that microscopic analysis of the coarse pottery found on a typical excavation on Hadrian's Wall has identified over 50 per cent as originating from Purbeck, presumably shipped from Poole to Newcastle.[13] Poole is generally accepted to have been the harbour where the second legion *Augusta* disembarked. Nearby Hamworthy was a Roman naval station,[14] with the Legionary headquarters based at Lake Farm near Wimborne Minster. The quantity and variety of Roman activity on the Isle of Purbeck suggests that, although they have not yet been identified securely, there will have been Roman roads here. The road that runs into Dorset north east from here is the one on which Kingston (Corfe) stands and is likely to be, Roman although there is no direct evidence to support this. The nature of the topography here will have determined this line between Wareham and Swanage. From here there is a direct route to Bere Regis, next to which Kingston (Winterborne) is sited. Lavelle suggests that the connection between these two places might be related to the *firma unius noctis*.[15]

Domesday Book royal connections and ecclesiastical status

Turning to an examination of the counties Dorset, Hampshire, Wiltshire, Somerset, and Devon in relation to their respective histories, particularly any royal connection (other than the name) that can be established, the most striking characteristic is that, with the exceptions of Kington Magna and Kingston (Corfe), none were recorded in DB. All of them, even if they became parishes later, were in origin daughters of a mother church. The two that stand out as slightly dissimilar are Kingston (Corfe), which became an independent parish but in origin was a daughter of Wareham, and Kington Magna, a daughter of Gillingham. Significantly, perhaps, although it has not been possible to establish what this might be, these are the only Dorset examples that are recorded in DB.

The DB entry for Kingston (Corfe) records: 'Of the manor of Kingston the king (William) has one hide, on which he built Wareham Castle, for it he gave to St Mary's (Shaftesbury Abbey) the church of Gillingham, with its dependencies'. In 948 King Eadred had made this grant of land at Kingston to Shaftesbury Abbey, in whose hands it remained until the dissolution of the monasteries. Wareham, the most likely Anglo-Saxon royal estate of which Kingston was a component part, was a Roman settlement, a centre of British Christianity, and a Saxon minster site with several royal connections. In 802, King Beortric of Wessex was buried here, King Edward the Martyr was murdered on this estate in 978, close to the site, as a local legend tells, of the future Corfe Castle. Wareham was one of Alfred's *burh*s and DB records that it was held both TRE and TRW by the king. It was also

one of the four Dorset DB boroughs, and from time to time there was a mint here. No direct royal connection has been established for Kington Magna, although one of the three manors here was listed under the Land of the King's Thanes. The three manors all had different landholders both TRW and TRE. The most likely *villa regalis* of which Kington Magna must have been a component part is Gillingham, with which it shares a boundary on the north-west. Gillingham was also a DB borough, liable for the *firma unius noctis*, and held both TRE and TRW by the king. Three miles south-east of Gillingham is Shaftesbury, another DB royal borough whose abbey of St Mary's had been granted the church at Gillingham and all its dependencies in return for land at Kingston (Corfe). Neither of these boroughs have a Kingston within their estate lands.

Kingston (Haselbury Bryan), the third non-string Kingston in Dorset, is not listed in DB, and neither is Haselbury Bryan. Both of these places were probably subsumed under the entry for Sturminster Newton, the closest and most likely central place of which they might have been a component part.

Kingston (Lacy) is a daughter of Wimborne Minster, the central place of an estate with impeccable royal connections which at DB was held both TRW and TRE by the king, and was liable for the *firma unius noctis*. It was here that King Ine of Wessex founded *c.* 705 one of the leading West Saxon royal nunneries. This was for his sister Cuthburgh who had been the wife of Aldfrith King of Northumbria, a marriage that confirms the status of the Wessex kings at this time.

Although modest in status, Kingston (Lacy), a component member of the Wimborne royal estate, has been witness to actions of national significance. After the death of King Alfred in 899 and the accession of his son Edward the Elder, Æthelwold, cousin to Edward and son of Alfred's older brother Æthelred (who was buried at Wimborne), challenged Edward's claim to the succession. He seized the minster at Wimborne, along with the adjoining royal estate of Twynham (present-day Christchurch). The *Chronicle* for 899 records 'Edward rode with his army until he camped at Badbury'. This will have been a mustering point and one that could not be missed with its dramatic earthwork. It is here that Kingston (Lacy) lies. Was it sited here purposefully, with one of its functions being to serve the mustering point in some way? In the event there was no battle. Æthelwold escaped under darkness to join forces with the Vikings.[16] Wimborne was an important royal centre before Ine founded the minster; it lies close to a Roman villa site, and there is some evidence that it might have been a pre-Christian cult centre.

Kingston (Winterborne) is not listed in DB. In origin it was a daughter of nearby Bere Regis. Kingston lies in

[12] Jones and Mattingley 1990: pp. 217–18.
[13] Putnam 1984: pp. 77–9.
[14] Putnam 1984: pp. 14–16.
[15] Lavelle 2007: p. 35.

[16] *ASC* A, D 901.

Bere Hundred, where at DB the entry for Bere itself, along with one other unnamed place, is an entry for 'the Land of the King's Thanes', assessed at one hide with land for one plough. Thorn and Thorn consider that this might be a reference to Kingston.[17] Bere was held by the king TRE and was liable for the *firma unius noctis*.

Neither Kingston Maurward nor Stinsford, in which parish Kingston now lies, are recorded in DB. Kingston's geographical position suggests that it might have been sited in relationship to Dorchester, a Roman *civitas* capital for which there is evidence, albeit slight, that it might have continued to function as an important central place from Romano-British times through into the Anglo-Saxon period, when the record confirms it is an important royal *vill*.[18] There is an alternative possibility that Kingston (Maurward/Stinsford) might be associated with Fordington which lies immediately outside the Roman gates of Dorchester. Keene is of the opinion that the church at Fordington might well be earlier than the earliest church in Dorchester, and that the earliest Anglo-Saxon royal residence, which has heretofore been assumed to lie inside the old walled town, may in fact have been outside the Roman walls at Fordington.[19] If this was the case the royal estate centre, of which Kingston was a component part, would have been Fordington. Fordington at DB was held both TRW and TRE by the king, and was liable for the *firma unius noctis*. However, there is no doubt that Dorchester had a royal residence by the year 833 when King Egbert issued a charter from here, the first of seven.[20] The date of the first of these charters is relatively late for a centre of such importance to enter the record for the first time. Perhaps this reflects the creation of a new royal palace which replaced the (putative) earlier one suggested by Keene. An early Anglo-Saxon royal residence at Fordington would explain the confused line of the ancient roads as they approach the gates. Dorchester was the largest of the four Dorset boroughs at DB, held both TRE and TRW by the King, and liable for the *firma unius noctis*. In 1894 part of Holy Trinity, Dorchester, beyond the limits of the borough on the north-east, together with Stinsford and a part of Fordington parish, were joined together as one parish. If Keene is correct this could be a reinstatement of the previous ecclesiastical unit.

Kingston (Russell), which was not listed independently at DB, was probably subsumed under the DB entry for Long Bredy. Little Bredy was listed separately at DB under the lands of St Peter's of Cerne Abbey, where there is a thane with one hide and one plough. At DB the two Bredys were taxed separately TRE at nine hides each. It is possible that the group of royal manors which lay predominantly in the south-west of the county may have had Bere Regis and Colber added to them at DB and that an outlying portion of one of the manors of this group might have

been Kingston Russell.[21] The early tenth-century Burghal Hidage records a stronghold at *Brydie*, which might be Bredy, on the River Bride.[22] It is possible that Bridport, which may have replaced Bredy as a burghal centre in the tenth or eleventh centuries, was originally a satellite of Bredy. *Brydie* is a river name, and a settlement bearing the name could have stood at any point along its length.[23] On the boundary between Kingston (Russel) and Little Bredy there is a fortress known as the 'Old Warren', which Nicholas Brooks thinks might be the site of *Brydie*.[24] Might there have been a connection between Kingston (Russel) and this putative *burh*? Perhaps this site was regarded as an appropriate site for a *burh* because the Kingston and fortress were already in existence, with Bridport later being considered to be a better site. Brooks speculates that the broken-down state of the fortress at Little Bredy, known as the 'Old Warren', might be because it had never been completed or, if completed, it could have been slighted by the Danes. Kingston (Russel), now an independent civil parish, is a daughter of Long Bredy. There is a tantalising reference in Lewis's *Topographical Dictionary of England* to Kingston (Russel) being 'anciently in the parish of Whitchurch Canonicorum', sited nine miles to the west.[25] It has not been possible to confirm this.

The two east Devon Kingstons which lie on the London to Exeter Roman road are small dependent places, not listed in DB and both ecclesiastically daughters. Kingsd(t)on lies immediately to the east of Colyton which at DB was the chief manor in its hundred and held TRE by the king.

The distribution of Kingstons in Dorset, east Devon and west Hampshire has every appearance of being a planned system of points in the landscape sited at regular intervals of nine-ten miles apart, along the London to Exeter Roman road as it crossed central Dorset and east Devon, rather like a spine, to which Kington Magna, Kingston (Deverill), Kingston (Haselbury Bryan), Kingston (Corfe) and Kingston (Cross, Ringwood) were connected by road at almost the same distance each from the other, forming a 'spider's web' of communications. A hint of an extension of this distribution can be seen on the lower Fosse Way in Somerset (see below).

There is no evidence that the line of Kingstons observed in Dorset and west Hampshire continued eastwards from Kingston (Cross, Ringwood). If there were other Kingstons in this area, the creation of the New Forest after the Conquest will almost certainly have obliterated the evidence. It has not been possible to establish any connection between Kingston (Ringwood) and Kingston (Fratton/Portsmouth) on Portsea Island. The island is separated from the mainland by Hilson Creek, a narrow

---

[17] Thorn and Thorn 1983: see appendix under KIngstonn (Winterborne)
[18] Trevarthen 2008: pp. 6–10.
[19] Keen 1984: pp. 206, 229.
[20] S 277, S 336, S 333, S 340, S 391, S 434, S 345.

[21] Thorn and Thorn 1983: Appendix under Bere Hundred.
[22] Carroll & Parsons 2007: pp. 36–42.
[23] For discussion of this name, see Watts 2004: p. 83.
[24] Brooks 1996: p. 134; p. 148, fn. 32.
[25] Samuel Lewis 1883: vol. 2 (no pagination). It is possible that Lewis misinterpreted the significance of Kingston Russell being in the rural deanery of Whitchurch.

stretch of water which before the construction of the present road on the north bank was 400 yards wider than it is now. This road is a continuation of the Roman road that crossed Sussex, originating from a point *c.* four miles to the north of Brighton (M 43). Kingston (Ferring/Angmering) and Kingston (Bucy), two of the four Sussex Kingstons, lie on this road.

Kingston (Fratton/Portsmouth) and Kingston (Isle of Wight), both of which lie in what was originally Jutish territory, were independent of their West Saxon neighbours until Arwald, the King of Wight, was defeated and killed in 686 by Cædwalla of Wessex, who then went on to slaughter the inhabitants of the island.[26]

No association has been securely identified between the Kingstons in Jutish Hampshire and those in ancient Wessex, although it is not impossible that one might have existed. This seems to have been the case at DB where the New Forest manors of Ringwood (where there is a Kingston), Eling, Holdenhurst, Breamore, Stanswood and Twynham are recorded as holding land on the Isle of Wight. All of these manors were held TRW by the king. The TRE landholder for Ringwood was Earl Tosti. No TRE holder is given for Eling but there is some evidence that at least part of this manor may have been liable for the *firma unius noctis*. The king held Breamore and Stanswood TRE. Two landholders are listed at Twynham, one of which was the king, both TRW and TRE, whilst the other, the manor with the Isle of Wight connection, was the Canons of Holy Trinity, Twynham, who claimed that the Isle of Wight lands had always been in the hands of the church.[27] It was from the royal *vill* at Twinham that Æthelwold launched his campaign to seize the throne from Edward the Elder.

Katharina Ulmschneider suggests that there would have been a network of contacts between royal and ecclesiastical estates in the two areas. It was not long after Cædwalla's conquest of the island in 686 that the archaeological evidence from the productive site of Bowcombe/Carisbrooke shows that it was about this time that the 'market' there was established.[28] Coins minted at *Hamwīc* have been found on the site, the earliest being from the late sceatta phase, *c.* 700–10.[29]

Kingston on the Isle of Wight lies in West Medina Liberty, two miles from the coast in the south-west side of the island, five miles from Newport and five miles from Carisbrooke. It is linked by road to other settlements on the island, but does not appear to be sited in relation to the ancient track-way that runs east west along the crest of the central

chalk ridge across the centre of the island. The position of Kingston, close to the coast but not on the shoreline, is similar to Kingstons Modbury, Dittisham, and Brixham DEV (see below). None of these are, or were, ports.

Kingston (Isle of Wight) is recorded in DB as *Chingestune*, assessed as the lowest value on the island. It was held TRW by the king, and TRE was held jointly by the king and Wulfric. It was a lay manor held of Carisbrooke, a connection which, although unclear, could be significant. In all the medieval documents in which the church appears it is recorded as *capella*, but with no reference to which church it was a daughter. Hase notes that Kingston might have been a dependency of Gatcombe, which lies between it and Carisbrooke.[30] At DB Gatcombe was held TRW by the king, son of Stur, and TRE by three brothers who held it jointly from the king.[31] In 686, Cædwalla granted an estate of 600 hides on Wight to Wilfred (later saint). To date, this estate has not been identified securely; neither has it been possible to establish a connection with the royal central place and mother church of Carisbrooke/Bowcombe. There does not appear to be any connection between these lands and Kingston, for which it has not been possible to suggest a context.

Kingston (Fratton/Portsmouth) is not listed in DB, subsumed most probably into the entry for *Frodintone* (Fratton) which was held TRW by William of Warenne and TRE by *Ketel*, who 'held it from King Edward in freehold'. Although slight, this gives Kingston a royal connection, but to which royal *vill*? On the mainland, almost opposite Portsea, lies the royal *vill* of Cosham held at DB both TRW and TRE by the king. It is possible that this could have been the royal centre with which Kingston was associated. There is of course Saxon Portsmouth, which has yet to be identified but is known to have existed.[32] The *ASC* for the year 501 records: 'Here Port and his two sons, Bieda and Mægla came with two ships to Britain at the place which is called Portsmouth'.[33] Whilst the events recorded in the *ASC* are unlikely to be an exact reflection of historical reality, this entry confirms that Portsmouth must have been founded by the end of the ninth century at the latest when the 'A' text of the *ASC* was compiled. Swanton suggests that the reference may be to the Roman fortress at Porchester, for which there is evidence of Saxon occupation from the early sixth century onwards.[34] It is Portsmouth that is recorded in the Chronicle, not Porchester; however, it is Porchester that is listed in DB not Portsmouth. Porchester has been excavated extensively, whereas present-day Portsmouth has not. The answer will be found when Saxon Portsmouth

---

[26] Arwald is the only historically known King of the Isle of Wight. He may have been related to the Jutes of southern Hampshire and the South Saxons.

[27] DBHa. 1,30; 1,27; 1,37; 1,26; 17,1.

[28] This term was first used by numismatists in the 1980s when metal-detecting activity produced sometimes quite large quantities of coins and metalwork on certain sites. See Ulmschneider and Pestell 2003: pp. 1–10 for discussion of the significance of this type of site.

[29] Ulmschneider 2003: p. 81.

[30] Hase 1994: p. 65 and fn. 72.

[31] DBH (I of W 52, d).

[32] Alan Morton, Senior Planning Archaeologist, Southampton, pers. comm.

[33] *ASC* 501, A. *Her cuom Port on Bretene 7 his .ii. suna Bieda 7 Mægla mid .ii. scipum on þære stowe þe is gecueden Portesmuþa* 'Here Port and his two sons Bieda and Mægla came with 2 ship to Britain at the place which is called Portsmouth'

[34] Porchester has been identified with *Ardaonium* in the Ravenna Cosmography. Rivett and Smith 1979, p. 206; Swanton 1996: p. 15, fn. 13.

is identified and excavated. Alan Morton, Senior Planning archaeologist for Southampton for 25 years, is of the opinion that it is on Portsea Island that we must continue to look for Saxon Portsmouth.[35]

Four Kingstons are found in Wiltshire; Kingston (Deverill) in the south-west of the county, is on the border of Somerset; West Kington lies in the north-west of the county, also on the boundary with Somerset; Kington (St Michael) is sited immediately to the north of Chippenham; and Kingston (Collingbourne) is in the north-east of the county. All except Kingston (St Michael) lie on Roman roads.

The parish of Longbridge Deverill follows part of the valley of the River Deverill. It comprises six settlements on the Wiltshire Downs, where the western edge of Salisbury Plain dips into Somerset. Longbridge is the principal settlement, and its parish comprises, Crockerton, Hill, Brixton, Monkton, and Kingston.

Two Roman roads crossed at the ford at Kingston (Deverill), one from Portchester and the other from Poole. They meet at what is now the boundary between Monkton and Kingston (Deverill). A decisive battle between Alfred and the Vikings took place at Edington, after which the Viking leader agreed to be baptised and withdrew fom Wessex. Alfred's forces mustered at Court Hill one mile west of Kingston (Deverill). Court Hill is not to be confused with close by King's Court where there are three Sarsen Stones close to the church. These are reputed have been used as markers of a mustering point.

As already noted, Kingston (Deverill) lies in the south-west of the county, 10 miles north-east of Kington Magna in DOR. It lies at the intersection of two major Roman roads,[36] the Sea Mills to Poole road, on which, at Badbury Rings, Kingston (Lacy) lies; and the road that ran between Old Sarum and the Fosse Way. The road which runs south from Kingston (Deverill) to Kington Magna, via Gillingham, follows an ancient line. The siting of Kingston (Deverill), in relation to Kington Magna and the other Dorset Kingstons, suggests that it could have been part of the road/string system observed so clearly in central Dorset. The location of Kingston (Deverill) at the point where major Roman roads intersect is similar to that of Kingston (Lacy), sited 21 miles to the south-east at Badbury Rings where, at the intersection of the road by the Exeter to London road, Kingston (Lacy) stands. Kings Weston lies where the Poole to Sea Mills road ends, adjacent to the Roman port of *Portu Abone*, which was listed in the Ravenna Cosmography.[37]

West Kington lies on the county boundary with Somerset, six miles west of Chippenham and seven miles north of Bath, on the major Roman road, known for all of its length

as the Fosse Way. Nettleton, West Kington's immediate neighbour, was the site of a Roman small town where excavation has revealed a series of second-and third-century temples, located on what is known to have been a tribal boundary.[38] The temples were abandoned towards the end of the third century when the town, which produced pewter, began to develop on the same site.[39] West Kington is one of seven Kingstons in the corpus that lie immediately adjacent to Roman small towns.

The siting of West Kington and Kington (St Michael), within six miles of each other, raises the question as to whether they were the same sort of place. Did they serve the same function and what is the significance of their respective locations? West Kington lies on a major Roman road, whilst Kington (St Michael), standing adjacent to, and, as charter evidence confirms, originally dependent upon the important *villa regalis* of Chippenham, raises the question that its function might have been different. Five other Kingstons in the corpus present a similar picture.

Kington (St Michael) is the only Wiltshire Kingston that is not sited on a long-distance Roman road. It does, however, lie on an ancient through routeway which left Chippenham from the north-west to join the Fosse Way at Lordswood Farm, six miles to the north.[40] One mile from Kington (St Michael) a Roman villa has been identified on this road.[41] It is possible that this was a private road for the known villa estate, along which there might have been be other villas. To the south-east this road left the Chippenham road to join the Roman road from Silchester to Bath.[42] The Roman small town of *Verlucio*, which is named in the Antonine Itinerary, lay close to this junction.

In the east of the county, close to the boundary with Hampshire, Kingston (Collingbourne) lies between the Roman road from Old Sarum to Ermine Street[43] and the Cirencester to Winchester road.[44] The western boundary of the extensive parish of Collingbourne follows the line of the Old Sarum road, with the tip of its eastern boundary meeting the Winchester to Cirencester road at Silver Down and Scot's Poor, where the boundaries of Wiltshire, Berkshire and Hampshire meet. The road here is compelled by the topography to make a sizeable meander-like detour around Tidcombe and Fosbury Downs, on which a cluster of pre-historic monuments are sited. This configuration is akin to the meeting point at King's Stag DOR, the 'king's boundary stake', where Kingston in Haselbury Bryan, Pulham and Radlynch meet.

---

[35] Alan Morton pers. comm. I want to record my thanks to Alan Morton for his generosity in finding time to show me around the area and sharing his thoughts on early Anglo-Saxon Wessex.

[36] Margary 45b; Margary 46; Margary 52.

[37] Rivet and Smith 1979: p. 206.

[38] Jones & Mattingley 1990: p. 290.

[39] De la Bédoyère 1991: p. 114; Jones & Mattingley 1990: p. 290.

[40] ST 870 841.

[41] SU 897 797.

[42] Margary 53.

[43] Margary 44.

[44] Margary 43.

Wiltshire: Domesday Book, royal connections and ecclesiastical status

Kingston (Deverill) first appears in the record in 1243 as *Deverel Kynston* and as *Kyngestone* in 1291. Here there were four DB manors. The manor that has been identified as Kingston was held TRE by Queen Edith, a secure royal connection. Monkton Deverill was held by the church at Glastonbury and Brixton Deverill was held TRW by Queen Matilda, who gifted it to the church of St Mary of Bec. It was held TRE by Brictric.

The appearance in the record of West Kington 1195 was as *Westkinton*, presumably to distinguish it from Kington (St Michael) six miles to the west. It is not listed in DB, subsumed probably under the DB entry for Nettleton where there was one manor, held TRW by the Church of Glastonbury. No TRE holder is listed. There is a slight royal connection here by association with Glastonbury Abbey.

Kington (St Michael), in contrast, has secure royal connections. It stands adjacent to Chippenham, which is described in 853 as *villa regalis* and is listed in the will of King Alfred. It was here at midwinter after Twelfth Night 878 that the Danish army made a surprise attack and Alfred was forced to flee.[45] Domesday confirms Chippenham as the central place of an extensive royal estate held both TRW and TRE by the king. The manor, along with all its dependencies, was liable for the *firma unius noctis*. Kingston (St Michael) is recorded in two pre-DB charters. In 934 it is recorded as *Kingtone* in a charter of King Æthelstan, and in 987 as *Kyngtune* in a charter of Æthelred granting 40 hides to Glastonbury Abbey. The lands in this charter comprised both Kington (St Michael) and its neighbour Kington (Langley); these two were in origin a single land unit which had been purchased prior to 987 by Ælfswith from King Edgar. Kington (St Michael), which is listed independently as *Chintone*, was a small manor of one and a half hides held TRW from Glastonbury Abbey by Ralph Mortimer and TRE by Alwyn. In contrast, at DB Kington (Langley) was an extensive manor of 29 hides held both TRW and TRE by Glastonbury Abbey. The granting of these tenth-century charters probably led to the fission of the earlier unit. Whatever the original function of Kington (St Michael) was in relation to the royal *vill* of Chippenham, that function would almost certainly have changed when the king granted away the land.

It is interesting to note here that at almost the same time a similar state of affairs might have applied at Kineton WAR, where in 969 King Edgar granted 10 hides at *Cyngtun* to his minister Ælfwold. The bounds of the land states *Ðis synt ða lond gemæra into cyngtune of weles burnan*, 'this is the land on the boundary of *cyngtune* and *weles burnan* '.[46] By DB *Cyngtune* was back in the king's hands where it was listed with Wellesbourne, described as 'the manor (that is Wellesbourne) and the outlier' (Kineton).[47]

There are other similarities: both West Kington, sited six miles from Kington (St Michael), and Kingston Farm (Chesterton), sited six miles from Wellesbourne, lie on major Roman roads, the same distance from their respective estate centres. They also lie adjacent to Roman small towns and on ancient tribal boundaries (below). This configuration raises the question as to whether Kingstons sited immediately adjacent to the central place of a royal *villa regalis* served a different function from those (by far the greater majority) that were sited on Roman roads. The royal *villa regalis* of Taunton and its immediate neighbour Kingston (St Mary) present a similar pattern.

Kingston (Collingbourne), first recorded in 1306 as *Colingebourne Kingeston*, is a daughter of Collingbourne, as are the tithings of Aughton, Cadly, Brunton and Southton. Collingbourne featured in two ninth-century royal charters. The first, issued by King Edward from Southampton in 903, granted land at *Colengaburnan* for the founding of the New Minster at Winchester.[48] The second, also of King Edward, was issued in 921 from Wilton, granting land at '*de villa de Colingborne*'. This has been identified as that part of the estate of Collingbourne which later became known as Kingston.[49] This DB entry and the charter evidence provide Kingston with a strong royal connection. Collingbourne Ducis was held TRW by the king and by Earl Harold TRE.

The name Collingbourne may be significant. There are two possible meanings. *Coll* might have been the name of the stream, which generally is accepted as meaning the 'stream of the *Collingas*', or 'the people called after/followers of *Col(l)a*'. This is the OE male personal name *Colla* + *ingas*.[50] There really is no way of knowing which of these is correct. If it is the latter then this could be another example of a Kingston, sited centrally in an early Anglo-Saxon 'original kingdom', defined by a river valley as has been suggested to have been the case with the *Stoppingas* of Wootton Wawen WAR and 'the Bourne people' in Kent.

Four examples of the name Kingston are found in Somerset. Three are sited on Roman roads, and whilst none seem to be unambiguously part of a 'string' system there are hints with Keinton (Mandeville), whose eastern parish boundary follows the line of the Fosse Way and Kingstone (Ilminster), which lies 20 miles from along the Fosse Way that a road/string system might have existed.[51] The first edition of the six-inch to the mile OS map has not uncovered another secure Kingston, although there is a possible candidate six miles from Keinton (Mandeville). This is Kingsdon, near to Ilchester, lying in the fork of the road where the Roman road from Dorchester to Puriton branches off the Fosse Way. The place-name evidence for Kingsdon points

---

[45] *ASC* 878/9 A, E.
[46] S 773.
[47] DBWa 1, 2.
[48] S 370.
[49] S 379.
[50] Watts 2004: pp. 150–1.
[51] Margary 5 and 5b.

to *dūn* 'hill' as the second element, and the topography supports this. However, given the difficulties there can be in determining whether an element is a *dūn* or *tūn* in some early forms, the possibility that this might be a Kingston is worth noting, particularly as further south along the Fosse Way in the parish of Colyton DEV, Kingston is sited in the fork formed by two major Roman roads. This positioning of a Kingston in the angle between major Roman roads can be seen at Conington CAM, Kingston (Deverill) WLT, and Kingston (Lacy) DOR.

Kingston (Seymour) lies close to the north coast of Somerset between Clevedon and Weston-super-Mare. It is likely, although (as yet) not proven, that starting from the river bank opposite the Roman port and small town of *Abonæ* (Sea Mills) GLO, where Kingsweston is sited, a Roman road ran south shadowing the coast. If this road is projected further it would form the north-east/south-west boundary of the parish of Kingston (Seymour), where a Roman villa has been identified. The line of this road can be seen on the first edition of the six-inch to one mile OS map running north-east from Kingston through the parish of Yatton, where the site of a Roman temple has been found in the south-east corner of the parish immediately adjacent to Congresbury and the Iron Age hill fort of Cadbury. The line of the road continues on to Nailsea and Wraxall where, between these two parishes, a Roman villa lay just off the road. After this the line onwards towards the River Avon is lost. This road can be traced south-west from Kingston (Seymour) and Bourton, beyond which it has not been possible to trace the line with any certainty, although it looks as if it might have continued towards Puxton, Sandford and Winscombe, where, at the western edge of the Mendips, it would have met the Roman road coming over the Mendips from the Fosse Way, two miles north of Shepton Mallet. This road, which originated in Old Sarum, is the one on which Kingston (Deverill) is sited. After Winscombe this putative road may have run due south to Axbridge, then south-west to where it would have met the Roman road which left the Fosse Way two miles south of Keinton Mandeville. From Puriton it might have carried on to Bridgwater and Taunton. This is admittedly speculative, but a major routeway would be expected somewhere in this region.

Kingston (St Mary, Taunton) lies three miles north of Taunton on the southern edge of the Quantocks, close to several good communication routes. It has not been possible to establish a Roman or other long-distance ancient routeway here, although a small Romano-British settlement has been identified at Holloway on the south-east edge of Taunton.[52] A network of roads radiate from Taunton. The road to the north leads to Kingston (St Mary, Taunton), where at Mill Cross it runs in a north-westward direction around the foot of the Quantocks to the royal centre of Williton and the coast at Watchet. The road running north from Kingston St Mary goes to Nether Stowey, the OE *stān* 'stone' + OE *weg* 'road', where it meets the road from Bridgwater to

Williton. Could this 'stony' path have been a paved Roman road? The OE element *stræt* would be the expected term for such a road, but *weg* is possible. The road terminates at Burton in the parish of Stringston. At Lydiard St Lawrence it is joined by the road from Taunton. In the other direction the road skirts the south-eastern edge of the hills before turning north-east to join the Taunton–Bridgwater road. It then carries on to the River Parrett, where at Dunhall and Puriton it joins the Roman road which crossed the Polden Hills after leaving the Fosse Way at either Charlton Adam or Northover.

Somerset: royal connections, ecclesiastical status, and Domesday Book

The *villa regalis*, of which Keinton (Mandeville) may once have been a component part, is Somerton which lies four miles to the south-west, with Charlton Mackrell and Charlton Adam separating them. Keinton (Mandeville), listed in DB as *Chintune*, was held TRW by Mauger from the Count of Mortain, and TRE by two thanes. The DB entry for Barton St David, Keinton's neighbour on the north-west, records that one hide of Keinton Mandeville 'lay in that [Barton] manor before 1066'.[53] Barton at DB was listed under the lands of Roger of Courseulles, Alstan held it TRE. Keinton (Mandeville), Barton, the two Charltons, and Kingsdon (which is not listed in DB) are likely to have been component parts of the *villa regalis* of Somerton.

Somerton, the first entry in the Somerset DB, was held both TRE and TRW by the king, it 'never paid tax' and was liable for the *feorm*. This is the *tūn* of the *Sumortūn-sǣte* 'the people who live at, or who are dependent upon, Somerton', a hill-top site between the rivers Carey and Yeo.[54] The shire of Somerset takes its name from Somerton. The *ASC* records for the year 733 that Somerton was captured from Æthelheard, king of the West Saxons, by Æthelbald, king of the Mercians, who, on becoming king in 719, began a campaign to extend his authority beyond his own kingdom. Bede notes that by 731 he had 'subjected all the southern kingdoms up to the Humber'.[55]

The place-name evidence for Kingstone (Ilminster) is slightly ambiguous, although the balance of probabilities suggests that it is a Kingston. It was first recorded in DB as *Chingestone*, and in the Exon DB as *Chingestana*. The paucity of early forms of the name (there are only three) – *Kinestan* 1194 and 1212, and *Kingeston* in 1610 – offer little help in determining whether this is a *tūn* or a *stane* as the identification of this form is not certain. Margaret Gelling states that place-name evidence alone suggests 'stone', but she does accept that in this case, and with so few early forms, this is almost certainly a Kingston given that it appears to be part of the road/string system.

---

[52] ST 246 238.

[53] Kingweston, Keinton's neighbour to the west, is not a Kingston, neither is Kingston Pitney, west of Somerton.
[54] CDEPN 2004: p. 348.
[55] *HE* v, 23.

[56] Ilminster, its immediate neighbour, is the most likely *villa regalis* of which Kingstone was almost certainly a member. In 725, Ine, King of Wessex, granted twenty hides at Ilminster to Abbot Froda and the community at Muchelney;[57] at DB one of the manors listed here was still held by the church of Muchelney. The second manor was held TRW by Hubert of St Clair from the Count of Mortain, and TRE by Glastonbury Abbey, a religious foundation with close associations with Ine.[58] The present-day parish of Kingstone has absorbed the neighbouring hamlets of Allowenshay and Ludney; together they occupy the gap between Kingstone and the Fosse Way.

Kingston (Seymour) is recorded in DB as *Chingestone*. Two manors were listed here; both were held TRW by William de Moncells from the Bishop of Coutances. One of these manors was held TRE by four thanes 'free from all dues'. Congresbury, lying two and a half miles to the south-east, is the most likely royal estate of which Kingston (Seymour) may once have been a constituent part. Congresbury is mentioned by Asser as a derelict monastery where St Congar was buried.[59]

Kingston (St Mary) lies three miles north of Taunton, the *villa regalis* of which it was a component part. It is not listed in DB, being first recorded in 1155–8 as *Kyngestona*. Taunton is recorded in the *ASC* under the year 722 as the place 'that Ine built', and which Æthelburh, Ine's queen, 'threw down Taunton which Ine built earlier'.[60] This intriguing reference hints at trouble. We know nothing of Ine's wife other than she might have been of the same family as his successor Æthelheard, Taunton must have been restored as it later became one of Alfred's *burhs*. It featured in seven royal charters between the years 737 and 978, and in the tenth century it had a mint. At DB it was held TRW by the Bishop of Winchester; it was held TRE by Stigand, Archbishop of Canterbury. Both Kingston (St Mary) and Taunton stand at a point of easy access to good communication routes. No Roman or other known long distance ancient routeway has been identified positively here, but there can be no doubt they existed. Taunton is noted as a minor settlement on the OS map of Roman Britain. A small Romano-British settlement has been excavated in the suburb of Holway. To date this is the only evidence of any activity here in the Roman period.[61]

None of the three Kingstons that lie in south Devon has an association with any known Roman road or other ancient routeway. Their road connections are essentially local. None appears in DB; they are all minor places and ecclesiastically they are daughters.

Kingston (Facy/Brixham) is sited one mile inland, opposite Dartmouth on the east bank of the River Dart.[62] It lies next to Kingswear, which Watts notes has been named so because of the importance of its revenues from fish.[63] It is a chapelry of Brixham, recorded for the first time as *Kyngeston Facy juxta Dertemuth* in 1292. Brixham is listed in DB. Kingston may be subsumed within the entry.

Kingston (Dittisham) lies on the west bank of the River Dart, one and a half miles inland in the parish of Dittisham, of which it is a chapelry. The parish boundaries of Dittisham on the River Dart go down to the river. Kingston (Facy/Brixham) is on the opposite bank of the river. The two Kingstons are inter-visible. Kingston is first recorded in 1438 as *Kyngestone*. At DB it will almost certainly have been subsumed under Dittisham which was held by Baldwin, the sheriff.

Kingston (Modbury) lies south-west of Modbury, three and a half miles inland at the mouth of the River Erme. The parish boundaries of Modbury go down to the sea where there is a Beacon Point. Kingston, which is first recorded as *Kingeston(e)* in 1242, is a chapelry of Ermington, as is Modbury, the patronage of which alternates between the Crown and the Rector. Modbury is now an independent civil parish. At DB Ermington was the chief manor in its hundred. It was held by the king TRW, but was not royal land before DB as it had been acquired by the king in exchange for Bampton.

It has not been possible to uncover any evidence to suggest a wider context for these three south Devon Kingstons, other than they might have been beacons themselves, or associated with them. A beacon is noted on the OS map but, without a context no further progress can be made.

Counties closely associated with early Wessex: Berkshire; Oxfordshire; Surrey

The three neighbouring counties of Berkshire, Oxfordshire, and Surrey are generally considered to have emerged as counties in the seventh and eighth centuries. They are treated here as a group as they share similar early political histories

In 648, Cenwealh, King of Wessex, granted to his nephew Cuthred, 3,000 hides of land in Ashdown, west Berkshire, - the size of a small kingdom. This region, which lay between the kingdoms of Wessex and Mercia, was regularly fought over throughout the early and mid-Saxon period, becoming known as the 'debateable lands'.

There are four Kingstons in Berkshire: Kingston (Bagpuize), Kingston (Lisle), Kingstone (Winslow), and Kennington. Kingston (Bagpuize) lies on the Thames, and although not sited on a Roman road it does stand on

---

[56] Margaret Gelling: personal correspondence.
[57] S 249.
[58] DBSom. 8, 39; 19,10.
[59] Watts 2004: p. 154.
[60] *ASC* A 722.
[61] OS map of Roman Britain, 5th ed.

[62] 'Neighbouring Bury Head is said to have been a Roman fortress' Lewis vol. i (no pagination).
[63] Watts 2004: p. 348.

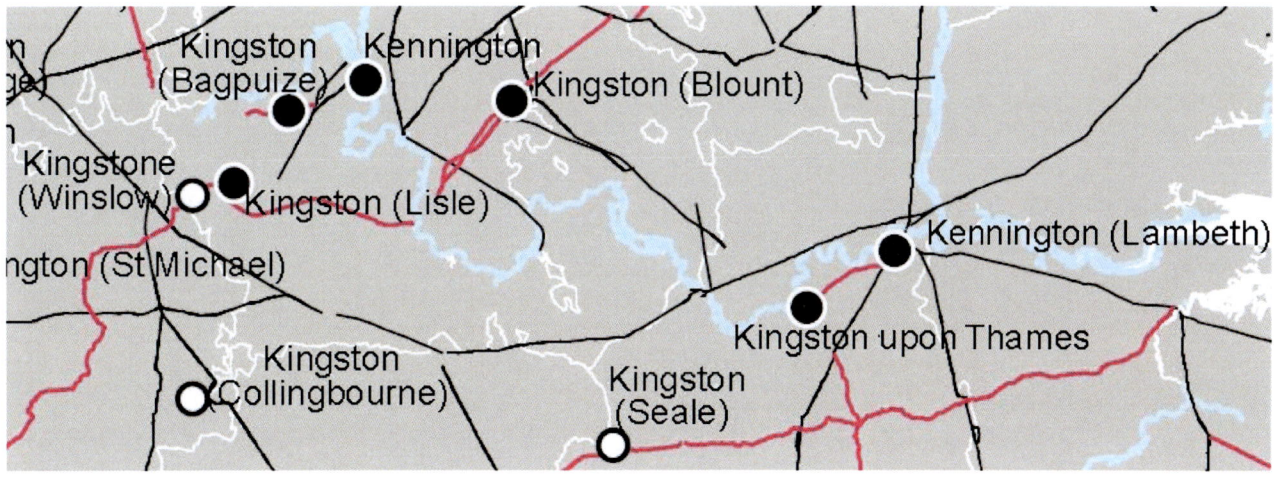

Figure 4: Kingstons in Berkshire, Oxfordshire, and Surrey.

a known long-distance routeway which crosses the north of the county, broadly following the line of the Thames. Two and a half miles west of Kingston (Bagpuize) this road forks, the upper road (A420) taking a north-westerly line via Farringdon to Shrivenham, the lower road (B4508) going directly to Shrivenham where the roads merge, continuing on to Swindon to join the Cirencester to Silchester Roman road at Stratton St Margaret, east of Swindon.[64] Two roads run eastwards from Kingston (Bagpuize) one taking a north-easterly line towards Oxford; the other running due east via Frilford to join the Roman road that ran northwards from Wantage to the river-crossing on the Thames near Hinksey, where **Kennington,** the first Kingston to enter the record, is sited on the west bank of the Thames in the angle formed by the river and the Wantage road. The road crosses the river between New Hinksey and Ifley, continuing north-east to Headington where it met the Silchester to Towcester Roman road.[65] Both Kingstone (Winslow) and Kingston (Lisle) lie on this road as it crosses central Berkshire. Along much of its length this road is shadowed by an ancient routeway known variously along its length as 'Port Way', 'Icknield Way', and 'Lower Icknield Way'. These Kingstons stand five miles apart, with their parish lands cut through by the roads. Two miles west of Kingstone (Winslow), on the boundary with Wiltshire, these roads meet the Roman road from Cirencester to Silchester (M 41b). These two Kingstons, now separated each from the other, once might have been one land unit; however, there is no evidence to support this.

Berkshire: charters, Domesday Book, royal Connections and ecclesiastical status

There are four direct references to **Kingston (Bagpuize)** in pre-Conquest royal charters and one that appears in the boundary clauses of a neighbouring land grant (Longworth). The first, in 970, is a land grant of King Edgar of seven hides to Brihtheah his 'faithful *diaconus*' at a place appellatione

dicitur *Cinges tūn,* 'free of all but the three common dues'.[66] This is the sole Kingston in the corpus to which there is a reference to the common dues. The next is a charter of 956 (for 975 x 978) of King Edward (the Martyr) of 13 hides *æt Cyngestun*;[67] The third in 965 (for 975 x 978) is also of King Edward of seven hides *aet Cyngestune*.[68] The fourth is named in a boundary clause of a charter of King Edgar of 958 (for 959). The clause refers to *ondlang Temese to þa þorn stybbe aet Cingtuninga gemære,* 'along the Thames to the thorn bush on the boundary with Kingston'.[69] These charters confirm a royal connection. Kingston (Bagpuize) is now an independent parish', originally it was a daughter of neighbouring Longworth in whose charter bounds it appears. Two manors are listed in DB although despite their earlier royal connections they were in the hands of the king TRW or TRE DB. Henry of Ferrers held one himself TRW and Stankell held it TRE. The other was held TRW by William, son of Ansculf, and TRE by Thorkell, who held it from King Edward. It is not clear which was the royal estate of which Kingston Bagpuize may once have been a component part. The most likely candidate, given the proximity of the ancient road that connects them, is Wantage, the birthplace of King Alfred.

Kennington is the first Kingston to enter the record, where in 821 it appears as *Chenigtun* in a charter issued by Coenwulf, King of Mercia to Abingdon Abbey.[70] It appears again in 956 as *Cenigtun(e)* in a charter of King Eadwig, to Brihthelm his faithful *presbyter,*[71] and in 956 as *æt Cenintune* in an agreement between Bishop Brihthelm and the Abbot of Abingdon.[72] At DB Kennington is recorded TRW as *Chenitun* and *Genetun* under the lands of Abingdon Church. 'Warin holds 4 hides of the same manor and (amongst others) the same land in *Chenitun*; Alwin one hide in *Genetun*'. TRE six Englishmen held these lands but

64   M 41a/b/c.
65   M 160b/160c.
66   S 778.
67   S 828.
68   S 829.
69   S 673.
70   S 183.
71   S 614.
72   S 1292.

'they could not withdraw from the church'. Kennington is now a parish but formerly was a daughter of Sunningwell, the *welle* 'spring' of the tribal group the *Sunningas*. This is one of the six Kingstons sited in the territories of a named early Anglo-Saxon tribal group.

Kingstone (Winslow) lies in the parish of Ashbury, close to the county boundary with Wiltshire and two miles east of the Roman road from Cirencester to Winchester. It is not listed in DB, probably subsumed under the entry for Ashbury which was held both TRW and TRE by Glastonbury Abbey. It is recorded first in 1252 as *Kyngeston Wendelsclev*. *Wend(e)l(es)cliva(m)* was the original name of the nearby escarpment. In 947, King Eadred granted 20 hides *at Aysshedoune*, the bounds of which contain a reference to *on kingesdich*. It is possible that this could be a reference to Kingstone (Winslow), which may have been a member of the royal estate of Lambourne, the neighbour to the south-east of Ashbury. At DB Lambourne was held both TRW and TRE by the King.

Kingston (Lisle), first recorded as *Kingestan* in 1220, lies six miles to the east of Kingstone (Winslow), also on the Icknield Way. It is in the parish of Sparsholt of which Fawler, a neighbour of Kingston, is also a chapelry. Kingston might have been in existence as early as 963, when its existence is implied in grant of King Edgar of 10 hides *æt Speresholte*, which is generally accepted to be Fawler.[73] The bounds of the charter refer to, *þæs cinges scypena* [...] *þæs cingestun þornas*, the 'king's cow-shed' and 'the *cingestun* thorns'. Although Kingston (Lisle) is not recorded in DB, it is almost certainly one of the three manors of Sparsholt held TRW by the king and TRE 'by three free men who held it as three manors', the other manors being Fawler and Sparsholt.[74] Only one of the manors was royal desmesne, this was probably Kingston (Lisle). It is unclear of which central place Kingston (Lisle) was once a component part. It was in Shrivenham Hundred at DB as also was Kingstone (Winslow), yet Sparsholt, of which it was a daughter, was in Wantage Hundred at DB. Lambourne, which shares the southern boundary of the parish, is another possibility, as is Wantage which also shares a boundary, and which was held by the king both TRW and TRE. The Domesday hundreds can serve as guidance only, as they do not necessarily reflect an earlier situation. The resolution of these anomalies might lie in the possibility that Lambourne and Wantage might once have been a single *villa regalis* whose territory comprised the whole area of the downs here. They were both in royal lands, they were neighbours and their boundaries were contiguous, each could have had a different administrative role, each of which might have needed a Kingston. Wantage, positioned at the junction of the Icknield Way and the Roman road coming south from Oxford, probably had the greater claim being the central place of this extensive putative territory, the importance of which is confirmed by its being the birthplace of King Alfred. The ecclesiastical

connections, however, do not support the suggestion that Kingston (Lisle) and Kingstone (Winslow) may once have been one. Kingstone (Winslow) is a daughter of Lambourne and Kingston (Lisle) a daughter of Wantage. Ecclesiastical connections are usually definitive, although, as Stephen Bassett has shown in his study of the territory of the *Stoppingas* in Warwickshire, where the *parochia* of St Peter's at Wootton Wawen originally mirrored the territory of the *Stoppingas*, it was split eventually into two units, with Claverdon, originally a daughter of Wootton, itself becoming a mother church.

The Kingstons Wilmslow and Lisle hint at the possibility that they could have been sited deliberately (although only five miles or so apart) along the Roman road, as were the Dorset 'string' Kingstons. They are also minor places, ecclesiastical daughters, late entrants into the record, and with impeccable royal connections.

A hint of the pattern seen in Berkshire has an echo in Oxfordshire where, at the foot of the Chilterns, sited on the same long-distance routeway as Kingston (Lisle) and Kingstone (Winslow), **Kingston (Blount)** is close to the boundary with Buckinghamshire. The central/eastern stretch of this road, known along much of its line as the Icknield Way, is generally accepted as having been upgraded by the Romans; ten miles to the east this routeway crossed the Roman road between Bicester/Alchester and St Albans at Aston Clinton.[75] Close by is Grim's Ditch, the substantial linear earthwork built across the west end of the Chilterns, cutting off the loop of the Thames between Wallingford and Henley. This earthwork can still be seen at nearby Princes Risborough.

Kingston (Blount), a chapelry of Aston Rowant, is first recorded in DB as *Chingestone*. Two manors are listed, neither of which had royal connections.

Kingston upon Thames is the sole example of a Kingston that appears to be a royal place of high status. It first appears in the record in 838 as, *in* [v]*illa famosa loco quæ appellatur Cyninges tūn in regione Suðregiae*, 'the famous/well-known place that is called *cyninges tūn* in the region of Surrey'. This 'famous' place has generally been accepted as reference to Kingston, upon Thames, the site of a meeting between the Archbishop of Canterbury and Ecgberht King of Wessex. At least two later Anglo-Saxon kings were crowned there, and at DB it was held both TRE and TRW by the king. It was head of its own hundred and had a minster church. The assumption that Kingston was the *cyninges tūn* of the charter is more than understandable. Despite all these characteristics suggesting that Kingston was a *villa regalis* of major significance, close scrutiny of all the evidence suggests that all may not have been quite what it seemed, and that there are several puzzling questions which need to be answered before we can be certain that Kingston upon Thames may not have been a *villa regalis*. This is explored in Chapter 4.

---

[73] S 713, Gelling 1979: p. 59.
[74] Gelling, 1979: p. 59.
[75] M 16a.

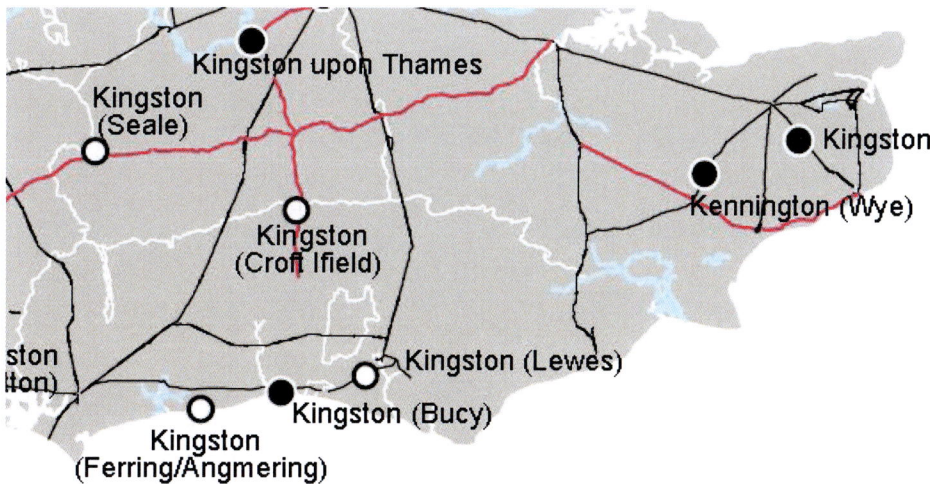

Figure 5: Kingstons in Sussex and Kent.

Kennington (Lambeth) lies in a loop of the River Thames in the parish of Lambeth, on the south bank of the river opposite Westminster. Kennington Park Road follows the line of the long-distance Roman road, known as Stane Street, which ran from London Bridge to Chichester.[76] Kennington is first recorded in DB as *Chenintune* when Theodoric, a goldsmith, 'held it himself from King Edward', an interesting and possibly significant royal connection. Kennington's royal pedigree is confirmed by the dramatic death at his royal palace here, of Harthacnut, Danish King of England between 1040 and 1042. The king is reputed to have been attending a wedding when he 'died as he stood at his drink when he fell to earth in awful convulsions [...] and he spoke no word afterwards'.[77] He was buried with his father Cnut at the Old Minster, Winchester.

Kingston (Seale) lies four miles east of Farnham on the long-distance routeway, known for much of its length as the Pilgrim's Way and which is marked as such on the first edition of the six-inch to the mile OS map. Ecclesiastically, a daughter of Farnham, Kingston (Seale) is first recorded in a rental of 1288 as *Kyngeston in Sela*. Neither Kingston nor Seale are listed in DB, the first reference to Seale is as *Sela* in a farm rental of 1210. *Sela* is an interesting place-name in this context. There are two possible meanings. It could possibly be the OE *sēale* 'at the willow(s)', although this is unlikely. The other meaning is the OE *sele*, 'a hall' or 'a building'. If this is 'hall', the structure to which the name refers will have to have been particularly remarkable for the name to be meaningful. A tenuous parallel to this can be seen in Huntingdonshire where *Kyningestune* is closely associated with Wistow, another 'dwelling place' of such renown that it needs no qualification. Watts has suggested that *wīc-stōw* may have meant 'site of the [royal] house'. There does seem to be a prima facie case for suggesting that Kingston/Seale and *Kyningestune*/Wistow may be in some way comparable.

From the end of the seventh century all of Farnham hundred was held by the Bishops of Winchester and featured in five royal charters, thus giving Kingston (Seale), by association, a royal connection.[78] It is hard to see how these three Surrey Kingstons could have been the same type of place, serving a same or similar function as each other in Anglo-Saxon royal administration. However, it will be shown later, that in origin they were the same type of place.

Counties over which Wessex had established lordship prior to 726: Sussex; Kent

Three of the four Sussex Kingstons lie in the south of the county; all are sited on Roman roads. The fourth, **Kingston (Croft/Ifield)**, is in the parish of Ifield which lies north of the angle formed by the county boundaries of Surrey, and West and East Sussex, a location that looks as if it was a deliberate choice. Although the formalisation of the boundary between East and West Sussex is relatively recent, the line is known to be ancient.[79] No long-distance Roman road has been identified here, although the road which forms the eastern boundary of the parish of Ifield follows a known ancient line. The line of the road was described in detail by Patterson in 1799.[80] It starts from Kennington in Lambeth SUR on the south bank of the Thames, opposite Westminster Bridge, which was also the starting place for the Roman road from London to Chichester. The route to Kingston (Croft/Ifield) ran south via Clapham Common, Reigate, and Crawley, and eventually to *Brighthelmstone* (Brighton). The boundary between East and West Sussex follows roughly the line of this road.

Just to the north of *Brighthelmstone* the Roman road from Kingston (Lewes) (M 153) crossed the London/south-coast road carrying on south-westwards, taking a line between the foot of the downs and the sea, towards Chichester and onwards. **Kingston (Lewes)** lies immediately adjacent to Lewes in the south-west, and nine miles north-east of

[76] M 15.
[77] ASC C, E. 1042.

[78] S 235, S 1263, S 382, S 823, S 1274.
[79] Greg Shuter, County Archaeologist for East Sussex, pers. comm.
[80] Patterson 1799: pp. 35–6.

Kingston (Bucy). This road, which has been identified archaeologically, crosses the centre of the village of Kingston. The line of this road makes complete sense if there was a Roman port at Shoreham, the closest south coast port to London. Although there is no secure archaeological or documentary evidence of this proposed port there are many circumstantial indicators of its existence.

Kingston (Bucy) and **Kingston (Ferring/Angmering)** lie on the Roman coastal road, the line of which is broadly understood, although in parts, particularly where it had to negotiate river estuaries, of which there are several, the precise line is hard to determine. Coastal erosion and the movement of shingle banks have obliterated the line in many places, with some settlements being lost to the sea completely. Both Kingston (Bucy) and Kingston (Ferring/Angmering) have been affected badly by coastal erosion.

Kingston (Bucy) lies close to the harbour east of Old and New Shoreham, bounded on the north by the downs and on the south by the River Ardur.[81] The earlier boundaries are hard to retrieve as the parish has been affected badly by significant changes in the course of the River Ardur. The shingle bank has shifted many times over the centuries and on one occasion the entrance to the harbour was blocked completely. The full extent of the land loss is unclear, but the eighteenth-century records note that it had become necessary to build a completely new road, much further inland, as the earlier road had been washed away. This is the line that we see today. Massive erosion at neighbouring Shoreham is thought to have removed a Roman harbour and port. The surrounding place-names and street patterns, suggest that this was almost certainly an Anglo-Saxon harbour. At least half of the lands of *Brighthelmstone* where it is has been suggested there was Roman settlement, have also been lost to the sea.[82]

Kingston (FerringAngmering), sited nine miles to the west, lies in the rape of Arundel. A sixteenth-century document refers to Kingston (Ferring/Angmering) as 'the Chappell of *Kyngston* which is now in the sea'.[83] This 'chappell' was a daughter of Angmering. A Roman villa has been identified close to Angmering, and a second at Rustington adjacent to East Preston, a neighbour of Kingston.

Although the two Kingstons on the coastal road and the Kingston at Lewes do not necessarily constitute a system, the nine miles' distance between them more than hints at the possibility that there might have been a connection between them, and that their positioning might not have been random.

Close examination of the first edition of the six-inch to the mile OS map from Kingston (Ferring/Angmering) to Chichester and beyond has not yielded any more examples of the name. There is a Kingsham half-mile or so south-west of Chichester on the Roman road (M 156) to Selsey Bill. Although no early forms of this name have been identified, the name has been noted because of its position, nine miles from Kingston (Angmering) and on the same road. The site of Anglo-Saxon Chichester is yet to be identified.

Sussex: Domesday Book, royal connections and ecclesiastical status

Kingston (Croft/Ifield), which first entered the record in 1261 as *Kingeston*, is now represented by the name of a farm marked on the second edition of the six-inch to the mile OS map but omitted from the first edition. It has not been possible to establish a context for this Kingston which, presumably, is a daughter of Ifield. This Kingston is a model example of the fragility of the chance survival of so many of these Kingstons.

The first appearance in the record of Kingston (Ferring/Angmering) is in 1312 as *Kingeston*. Its royal connection is via its mother settlement of Angmering, an Alfredian manor, and the surrounding neighbours, all with royal connections. Ferring, the neighbour to the west, features in a grant of 762 issued by King Osmund (of Sussex) to his *comes* '12 hides at *Ferryng* for the construction of a minster'.[84] Neighbouring West Preston, which was listed at DB as 'Nunminster', was held TRW by the Bishop of Winchester and TRE by a priest, who 'held it from King Edward'. There were two DB manors at Angmering; one was held TRE by Earl Godwin, the other by three 'freemen'.

Kingston (Bucy) lies close to the site of a large Roman villa. The Saxon settlement would most likely have been near the present church in which there is evidence of eleventh-century structures. Kingston is now a parish but originally might have been a daughter of Shoreham. In DB two manors are listed at *Chingeston*. One was a substantial manor of 20 hides, with a church, six salt-houses and three men-at-arms. It was held TRE by Azor who held it from King Harold. The second, a manor of seven hides, was held TRE by Gunhild who also held it from King Harold. A further eight and a half hides, listed under the entry for Hangleton, 'lay in the lands of Kingston'. These lands were held TRE by Azor from King Edward. Neighbouring Shoreham was also held TRE by Azor from King Edward and assessed at 12 hides. Southwick is not listed in DB, although it does appear to have been associated with Kingston with whose lands it intermingles on its western boundary. There can be no doubt about the status of Kingston (Bucy)'s royal connections. It was listed in DB and assessed at 35½ hides: this was a large Anglo-Saxon estate which in addition to Kingston included Shermanbury, Southwick and Hangleton. Brandon considers that the origin of this estate

---

[81] The name Ardur came to be used in the seventeenth century on false antiquarian grounds, which identified it with *Portus Arduri*, the Roman name for Porchester.

[82] John Mills, County Archaeologist, West Sussex, pers. comm.

[83] *Sussex Archaeological Collections* XXII, MDCCCLX, p. 97.

[84] S 48.

may be pre-Roman.[85] The post-Conquest reorganisation of the land into rapes led to the break-up of this estate unit, but the connection between Kingston and Shermanbury survived into the eighteenth century. The lordship of the manor of Kingston descended with the lordship of the rape. What this extensive Saxon estate might represent is discussed further below.

Although **Kingston (Lewes)** is not listed independently in DB, it will have been in existence as it enters the record in 1087 only one year later as *Kingestona*. The presumption is that it was subsumed under the entry for Lewes. In DB multiple land holders are listed under Lewes TRW, but TRE it was held in the main by the king. An excavation of a late sixth-early seventh-century Anglo-Saxon cemetery at Lewes produced many high-status grave goods. Kingston (Lewes) is the only example in the corpus associated securely with a place listed in the Burghal Hidage. It has been suggested that Kingston (Russel) DOR, lying adjacent to Long Bredy, might have been the site of a *burh* which was abandoned later in favour of Bridport (see above). Although this Kingston is only a small hamlet, it is now an independent parish of which nearby Iford is a part. Originally both were daughters of Lewes, next to which they stand in the same relationship to a royal centre of importance as Kingston (St Mary, Taunton) SOM and Kingston (St Michael) WLT.

Kent: Domesday Book, royal connections and ecclesiastical status

There are two examples of the name in Kent: they both lie in west Kent on major Roman roads. **Kennington (Wye)** lies between Wye and Ashford on the Roman road that ran south-west from Canterbury to the Weald. The *villa regalis* of Wye lies on this road and also on the ancient long-distance routeway, known along much of its length as 'The Pilgrims' Way', which crosses the North Downs, dropping down to the ford on the River Great Stour here.

Kingston lies 10 miles south-west of Canterbury on the Roman road to Dover. This was probably part of the riverine estate, reconstructed by Alan Everitt, of 'the Bourne people', an early Anglo-Saxon clan or tribe similar to the *Stoppingas* WAR (Bassett above and Chapter 4).[86] The famous Anglo-Saxon jewel, the Kingston brooch, was excavated from a high-status burial in a barrow on Kingston Down. Where the royal residence of the people interred in the barrow lay has not yet been identified.

Kennington (Wye) is listed in DB as *Chenintone*: TRW it was held by St Augustine's Church, 'the Abbot holding Kennington himself'. TRE it lay in the lands of Burmarsh where 'the villagers held it before 1066'. Burmarsh, which is not listed independently in DB, was also held by the Abbot. Wye is the only possible *villa regalis* to which Kennington could have been attached. Four charters testify

to its royal status. In two of these it is specifically called a royal estate – *ad villam regalem qui nominator*[87] (762) and *in villa Regis*[88] (839). At DB it was still in royal hands.[89] There were four manors, the most extensive of which had land for 52 ploughs that King William gave to Battle Abbey. There were three additional land-holders who before 1066 paid 'full jurisdiction and all the penalties from 22 Hundreds which rightly belong to the king belong to this manor'. Several of the manors, parts of whose lands 'lay in Wye', were liable for customary dues for carts, eels, yokes, escorts, and 'men (in Lympe Lathe) to guard the King at Canterbury or at Sandwich for three days if the king comes there'.[90] Leintwardine HER, next to which Kinton lies, and Kingston CAM both have similar obligations to guard and/or provide horses for the king when he visits.

Kingston is not listed in DB, although it appears in the record one year later in 1087 as *Kyningtune* in the *Domesday Monachorum* – a list of the Easter customs received by the archbishop. *Kyningtune* paid seven *denarios*, with 10 *denarios* being the highest assessment and seven the lowest.[91] It was of the lowest status, certainly not a *villa regalis*. Kingston is not an ancient parish. The church, dedicated to St Giles, is sited on the line of the Roman road. Notably the first reference to the term *Cyninges tūn* occurs in a Kentish document, the late sixth/early-seventh-century law-code of King Æthelberht of Kent.

Although the Kent and Sussex examples of Kingstons lie outside the core territory of ancient Wessex, they all present many of the most commonly recurring characteristics of a Kingston. It is possible that the two-year overlordship of Cædwalla of Wessex, followed by the 38 reign of his successor Ine of Wessex, might be connected in some way with the Kent and Sussex Kingstons, There is, however, no evidence to support this assertion.

Group 2 Counties of the Severn Valley, Welsh Borders, and the West Midlands

The present-day county of Gloucestershire is an artificial unit which was not recorded until 1016, when the various land units that made up the county were arbitrarily united. The new entity comprises the much older units of Cirencester with its seven hundreds, plus the small kingdom of Winchcombe, whose territory was essentially that of the Vale of Gloucester, along with lands west of the Severn which were annexed from Herefordshire.[92]

There are seven examples of the place-name Kingston in present-day Gloucestershire. With the exception of Kineton (Temple Guiting), they all lie on major Roman

---

[85] Brandon 1978: p. 90.
[86] Everitt 1986: pp. 79–81.

[87] S 25.
[88] S 287.
[89] D 24 1 b, c.
[90] DBKt. D 24, 6, 1.
[91] The *Domesday Monachorum* is a Domesday-related text which deals with estates of the archbishop of Canterbury, the monks of Christchurch, Canterbury, the bishop of Rochester and some other landholders in Kent.
[92] Finberg 1973: p. 21.

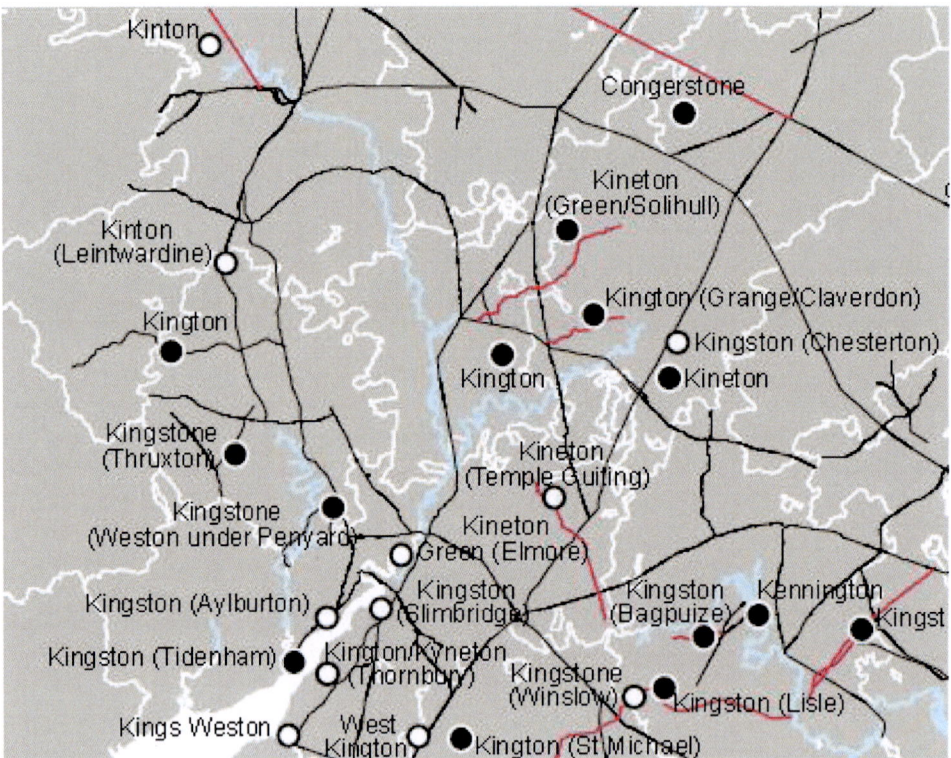

Figure 6: Gloucestershire, Herefordshire, Shropshire, Staffordshire, Worcestershire, Warwickshire.

roads that follow the lower Severn valley. The road (M 541) on the east bank of the river ran from Gloucester to the Roman port of *Abonæ* (Sea Mills) on the River Avon, and on the west bank from Gloucester to Caerleon via Chepstow (M 60a). All of these six Kingstons present characteristics that suggest they might have been part of a system similar to the one observed crossing central Dorset and the east Devon coast. These Severn valley Kingstons are considered as a group; Kineton, in the parish of Temple Guiting, is discussed separately.

The Roman road following the lower Severn valley on the east bank cuts across the parish boundaries of the Kingstons that lie along it, this suggests that the land units they define probably pre-date the road in origin. The four Kingstons all lie at regular distances apart of about nine miles.

The most northerly example is **Kineton Green (Elmore)** in the parish of Elmore, lying three miles south of Gloucester between the River Severn and the road to the Avon (M 541). The Roman and medieval landscape in this region has altered to a great extent over time. There have been many natural changes in the course of the river and land reclamation, canals, railways, and modern roads, make it hard, and in some cases impossible, to be sure of the original line of the road, although its general line is known.

Kingston (Slimbridge), in its own parish, lies on this road nine miles south of Kineton Green (Elmore). It survives as the name of a farm which lies to the west of Slimbridge church, less than a mile from the River Severn and one mile from the Roman road.

Kington/Kyneton (Thornbury) is sited nine miles south of Kingston (Slimbridge) in the parish of Thornbury. Archaeological investigation has revealed a settlement of Roman date underlying the medieval town of Thornbury. The earliest Anglo-Saxon settlement has been identified situated close to the church and castle, with an earlier high-status house lying under the castle, but not fully excavated.[93] Two forms of the name survive here, used variously over time, but there is only one place. The first edition of the six-inch to the mile OS map records a 'Kington House' and a 'Kyneton Quarry' standing side by side, a few hundred metres to the west of the church. The line of the road here is especially problematic to trace, its line having been largely destroyed by the succession of road-widenings of the A38 and the town by-pass. Thornbury lies on one of the three main salt routes that crossed Gloucestershire. Its route, described by Darby, approached Thornbury from Rockhampton to the north.

The distances seen between the first three Kingstons on the Gloucester to Sea Mills road can be seen again between Thornbury and Kingsweston, which presents a constellation of features characteristic of a Kingston. **Kingsweston** lies where the Gloucester to Sea Mills road terminates at the confluence of the River Avon and the Trym. It was here that the Roman harbour and small town of *Abonæ* lay. The remains of the Roman town can still be seen in places and a Roman villa has been excavated and preserved just to the east of this road. Although some stretches of the line road between Thornbury and Kingsweston are uncertain, the lower part of the road as it approaches Sea Mills is secure.

---

[93] Leech 1975: p. 22.

The most uncertain stretch is near Cribbs Causeway, roughly mid-way between Thornbury and Kingsweston. Here the road could have taken a line either side of Henbury Hill (M 541). Near Almondsbury a Roman road branched off west to Aust from where the *Trajectus* listed in *Iter XIV*, is thought to have crossed the Severn.[94] Access to the ferry on the west bank of the river would have been via Margary 60aa, a road that branched off the Caerwent to Gloucester road at Crick. A medieval ferry between Aust and Beachley has been known from at least the twelfth century.[95] If there was a ferry in this area in the Anglo-Saxon period, and it is generally accepted that there must have been, Aust to Bleachley route would have been the most likely.

On the west bank of the River Severn, a mile to the north of Beachley, sited on the county boundary with Monmouthshire at the confluence of the rivers Wye and Severn, is Sedbury, the *suð burh*, the most likely site of a 'lost' Kingston. Sedbury may refer to the site of a Roman camp which overlooked the River Severn at this point, positioned strategically between the banks of the rivers Severn and Wye. If the proposed site of Kingston was adjacent to Sedbury it would have been sited on the road between Caerleon and Newnham (M 60a) which crossed the Wye near Chepstow, continued on through Tidenham and terminating at Sedbury Cliffs on the Severn estuary.

Another Kingston lies nine miles north of Sedbury in the parish of Aylburton. The first edition of the six-inch OS map shows a hamlet of a few houses straggling along the line of the road, which is labelled variously 'British Road' or 'Roman Road'. The present-day main road by-passes Kingston and continues on to Lydney where the road diverged, the left fork striking north into the Forest of Dean (M 614) into Herefordshire, and the iron-working centre and Roman small town of Weston under Penyard (*Ariconium*),[96] next to which stands a Kingston. The M 60a continues to Blakely and Newnham which lie on the west bank of a great meander in the river from where a Roman ferry crossed to Arlingham on the east bank and from where a Roman road (M 543) crossed the peninsula to Whitminster where it met the Gloucester to Kingsweston road. It is a short journey, cutting off a detour of almost 30 miles up to Gloucester and back down again. It seems unlikely that there was not an Anglo-Saxon ferry here.

Domesday Book, royal connections and ecclesiastical status

The parish of Elmore lies in a wide bend in the River Severn and **Kineton Green** is barely a hamlet within the parish of which it is a daughter. The first edition of the six-inch to the mile OS map shows Kineton Green to be just

that – a small open space in the centre of the village. It is first recorded as *Kyngtone* and *Kington* in 1263. Elmore is listed in DB where there were two manors. One was listed TRW under the Land of the King's Thanes and TRE was held by Edward from the King Edward. This gives Kineton Green a respectable royal connection. The second manor was also listed under the Land of the King's Thanes, with no TRE holder given.

Kingston (Slimbridge) is not listed in DB, but is almost certainly subsumed under the entry for Slimbridge which was one of 19 outlying *berewicks* of Berkeley. It was held TRW by the King from whom Roger held two hides. No TRE information is given. Kingston is recorded first in 1154 as *Kingestona*. Its royal connection is via the king holding Slimbridge TRW at the time of Domesday.

Kington/Kyneton (Thornbury) is a tithing in the ancient parish of Thornbury. It first appears in the record as *Kington* in 1248 and as *Kyneton* in 1262. At DB it was probably subsumed under the entry for Thornbury which was held by the king TRW, but had been a manor of William's queen, Matilda, who died in 1083. Thornbury was held TRE by Brictric, a Thane of King Edward, the same Brictric who held Temple Guiting, a Gloucestershire manor in which Kyneton lies between the manors of Temple Guiting and Guiting Power (below). At Thornbury, 18 *radchenistre*, 'riding men' were listed; they held 21 ploughs.

Kingsweston is the only Gloucestershire Kingston listed independently in DB. It is first recorded in DB as *Weston(e)*; it is also one of the nineteen *berewicks* 'outliers' of Berkeley (as also is Slimbridge). Its neighbour Lawrence Weston is now a separate parish, but in origin it was one with Kingsweston. Both are chapelries of the extensive parochia of Henbury, whose other chapelries included Northwick, Redwick, Stowick, Charlton, Compton and Aust.

Kingston (Tidenham) was a tithing of the extensive parish of Tidenham. It is first recorded as *Cinges tün,* a holding of five hides in a late tenth/early-eleventh century survey of the bounds of Tidenham.[97] It is not listed independently in DB, subsumed no doubt under one of the four manors that were listed. The most important and sizeable manor listed under Tidenham in DB was assessed at 30 hides. It was held TRW by the Abbot of Bath from the king. This manor, which did not pay taxes TRE, probably represents the 30 hides granted in the charter. The other three manors, all with much lower assessments, were held TRE by Archbishop Stigand (of Canterbury). Presumably, Kingston lay within the extensive manor granted by King Eadwig.

Kingston (Aylburton), now in the parish of Aylburton, was a daughter of Lydney. It is not listed in DB, probably subsumed into the Lydney entry. At DB Lydney was held TRW by the king and TRE by Earl William, who 'made one manor from the lands of the Bishop of Hereford, the monks of Pershore, and two thanes'. Lydney, which was a

---

[94] Rivet & Smith 1979: p. 177.

[95] In the twelfth century, manorial lords of Tidenham granted passage to monks of Tintern; the manor of Tidenham had rights over this passage, and received rents from Aust and Beachley until the nineteenth century. VCH Gloucestershire vol. 10, pp. 50–62.

[96] Finberg 1977: p. 43. Described by him as 'the Birmingham of Roman Britain'.

---

[97] S 1555.

cult centre of *Mars Nodens*, the Roman god of healing, was also the site of the Roman small town of *Nemetobala*.[98] At four miles' distance, it lies just a little too far from Kingston (Aylburton) to claim an association between them. An association between Kingstons and small Roman towns has been observed in seven Kingstons in the corpus (below). Kingston (Aylburton) enters the record in 1221 as *Kinegerst* and *Kingesterne*. The predominant forms recorded between the years 1385 and 1565 are *Kingeston* and *Kyngeston*. It has been suggested that the earlier forms could be a compound of the OE *cyne* or *cyning* with *gærs-tūn*, 'a pasture enclosure'.[99] Smith, however, does not even consider this possibility,[100] neither do Margaret Gelling or David Parsons.[101]

Kineton (Temple Guiting) lies between the present-day village centres of Temple Guiting and Guiting Power. These now separate settlements lie less than one mile apart at the centre of an Anglo-Saxon royal estate that lay between the Roman Ryknield Street and a major salt-way. Ryknield Street branched off the Fosse Way at Slaughter, close to the Roman small town of Bourton on the Water, its long-distance destination being Wall, on Watling Street, in Staffordshire.[102] The eastern boundary of the parish continues down to Ryknield Street Bridge at Bourton on the Water. The western boundary of the parish follows the line of a major Salt Way from the brine springs in Droitwich, entering north Gloucestershire at Dumbleton, then taking a broadly southern direction through Toddington, Stanway, Hailes, the Guitings, Sherborne and Eastleach to Lechlade.

Kineton, a daughter of both Guitings (in origin they would have been one land unit), is first recorded in 1185 as *Kinton* and *Kintone*. It is not listed independently in DB, where it must have been subsumed under the entry for Guiting. The first reference to Guiting is in 814 in a land grant of Ceonwulf, King of Mercia, issued from Tamworth, Staffordshire, to the bishop of Worcester, of eight hides at *Sture* (unidentified), in exchange for 12 hides *bi Gythinge*.[103] It is this charter that gives Kineton its royal connection. At DB there were three manors at Guiting: two were substantial; one was much smaller. The manor that has been identified as Guiting Power was held TRE by the king with two 'riding men' listed. Temple Guiting, the second manor, was held TRE by Brictric, a powerful thane of King Edward. A further seven 'riding men' are listed here. Brictric also held Thornbury where 18 'riding men' were listed. Riding men are found in considerable numbers on estates that bordered Wales; away from these areas few are recorded. The references to entries with riding men are discussed in Chapter 4.

The distribution pattern of these lower Severn Kingstons is comparable to the Dorset/east Devon road/string pattern. Their most striking characteristic is this pattern. They all lie at 9-10 miles distance from each other in parishes whose boundaries either touch or straddle the Roman roads following the banks of the river. Kineton Green (Elmore), Kingston (Slimbridge) and Kington/Kyneton (Thornbury) all lie between the road and the river. The exception is Kingsweston which is sited in relation to the Avon and Trym, not the Severn.

Welsh border counties

All of the Kingstons in these counties lie on major Roman roads or close to Offa's Dyke. A major Roman road ran north south through Herefordshire from Whitchurch (*Mediolanum*) to Wroxeter (*Viriconium*), Leintwardine (*Bravonium*), and Kenchester (*Magnis*), at which point it turned due east to Stretton (Grandison) and then south-east to Weston under Penyard (*Ariconium*), where a branch struck off to Gloucester. The line of this road then continued on towards the River Severn where it followed the west bank to Chepstow and, eventually, to Caerleon. Kingston (Aylburton) and Kingston (Tidenham), Gloucestershire, are sited on this road.

Kinton (Leintwardine) Herefordshire lies in the north-west of the county just south of the Shropshire border, on the Roman road known as Watling Street West (M 630), which ran from Caerleon to Wroxeter. Kinton stands immediately adjacent to the Roman garrison and small town of *Bravonium*, on which Leintwardine is built. This has been identified as *Bravonio* in the Antonine Itinerary.[104]

Kinton (Leintwardine), first recorded as *Kynton* in 1249, is a chapelry of Leintwardine. The DB entries for Leintwardine, which, perhaps significantly, are included in the Shropshire folios, list two manors. One was held TRW by Earl Roger, with no TRE holder given. This is the same Earl Roger who also held Great and Little Ness in south Shropshire, where another Kinton lies. The second manor was held TRW by Ralph Mortimer and TRE by the king with 'a reeve, 2 riders, a priest and a Man at Arms'. There was an obligation attached to the smaller manor: 'When the King left the City of Shrewsbury, the Sheriff sent him 24 horses from *Lenteurde* (Leintwardine) and the King took these as far as the first manor in Staffordshire'. This is one of several Kingstons in the corpus with obligations regarding special riding duties, usually for the king (see below).

Kington (Welsh Border), south-west of Leintwardine, lies on the border with Wales. Its position, with its high and wide views westward into Radnorshire, would have given it a strategic and tactical importance. No Roman road has been identified here or nearby. It does, however, lie on an ancient routeway into Wales, and Offa's Dyke forms the parish boundary on the north and east, with Kington sited, surprisingly, on the Welsh side.

Kington (Welsh Border) seems to be a much reduced place at the time of DB, where it is recorded independently as

---

[98] Jones & Mattingley 1990: p. 280; the Ravenna Cosmology, Rivett and Smith 1979: p. 207.
[99] PNs Glo. iii, p. 266.
[100] *EPNE*, Pt 1: p. 191.
[101] Parsons, pers. comm.
[102] Guiting Power, but not Temple Gower was held TRE by the king.
[103] S 171.
[104] Rivet and Smith 1979: p. 275.

Chingtune. It was a small manor, assessed at four hides, all of which are described as 'waste'. It was in the hands of the king TRW, and TRE by Earl Harold, an indication (along with its name) of royal ownership at some point in its past. It is an ancient parish, with seven daughter settlements.

Five miles south-west of Hereford, on the line of the long-distance Roman road from Kenchester to Abergavenny (M 630), lies **Kingstone (Thruxton)**. This road branches off the Wroxeter to Caerleon and Caerwent road (M 6c). This region of Herefordshire was the territory of the small kingdom of *Ergyng* (northern Gwent), whose later name was *Archenfeld*. It is now an independent parish, but was originally a daughter of Thruxton. This independent manor was recorded first in DB as *Chingestone*, and held both TRW and TRE by the king. The tithe of the whole manor was held TRW by the Church of Cormeilles who 'pay tax and do service in Gloucestershire, but the men who live there come to pleas in this Hundred to give and receive right'. At the time of DB the boundary between Herefordshire and Gloucestershire was still fluid. Also listed is 'a wood named Treville which pays no customary dues except hunting rights. The villagers who lived there before 1066 carried the produce of the hunt to Hereford and did no other service'.

Kingstone (Weston under Penyard) lies in the south-east corner of the county close to the Gloucestershire border, in an angle formed by the Roman road that ran between Gloucester and Hereford (M 61, 611, 613), and that ran from Ross-on-Wye to Lydney and on via Chepstow to Caerleon (M 614). This road connects Kingston (Weston under Penyard) with Kingston (Aylburton) and Kingston (Tidenham), Gloucestershire; it is also one of six Kingstons which are sited either at intersections or in right angles formed by Roman roads.[105] Kingstone (Weston under Penyard) lies immediately next to the site of the Roman small town of *Ariconium*, which appears to have been the administrative centre for lead-mining in the area. This is also one of six Kingstons that adjoin Roman small towns (see below, Chapter 4).

Kingstone (Weston under Penyard) first appears in the record at DB as *Chingestone*. Two manors were listed. TRW the Church of Cormeilles held two hides here: 'They pay tax and do service in Gloucestershire, but the men who live there come to pleas in this Hundred to give and receive right'. There is no TRE information listed. This is another example of the boundary between Herefordshire and Gloucestershire still being undefined at the time of DB. The second manor is listed under Westbury in Gloucestershire, where there is a reference to eight hides in Kingstone.[106] This Kingstone has been identified securely as the one near Weston under Penyard. The confusion was caused by the documentation being filed wrongly soon after DB was compiled.

Kinton (Great Ness) Shropshire, the most northerly example in this group, lies in the south of the county, on the boundary of Herefordshire, the modern A5 road, midway between Shrewsbury and Whittington. This stretch of the A5 was not regarded as being Roman until Roger White of the University of Birmingham European Research Institute, spotted that the vexillation fortress at Rhyn Park did not seem to have any connecting routes and, knowing that there must have been at least one road to the fort, set out to find it.[107] White has now demonstrated beyond doubt that the A5, leaving Wroxeter to the north, follows a Roman line.[108] He proposes a road that left Margary 64 at Washford, where it crossed the Rea Brook,[109] then took a north-west line to meet the A5 at Margary 140.[110] Kinton (Great Ness) is sited on the west side of this road, the Roman sites at Nesscliffe on the east.[111] This, as we have seen already with Clarke's work in Hampshire (above), is a powerful example of what literally, remains to be unearthed.

Kinton is first recorded in 1203–4 as *Kinetu'*, *Kineton*. It is a chapelry of Great Ness where at DB there were two manors. The manor which today is represented by Great Ness was held by the landholder Earl Roger, along with four berewicks; TRE it was held by Earl Morcar. The second manor, Little Ness, was held by the sheriff from Earl Roger TRW; TRE it was held by Siward. It has not been possible to suggest a wider context for Kinton.

Kingstone Staffordshire is the sole example of the name in the county. It lies three miles from Uttoxeter at a fording place on the River Blythe, close to the Derbyshire border,[112] on the Roman road that originated in Colchester. This road has been confirmed archaeologically by the University of Leicester Archaeological Services team.[113] The precise siting of Kingstone, close to the fording place on the River Blythe, on the coaching route between Uttoxeter and Stafford, and on the Roman road, is testimony enough as to its importance, although it has not been possible to identify a royal connection or any significant wider context for this place. Uttoxeter, which at DB was held TRW by the king and by Earl Agar TRE, is a possibility, although the only link between them, apart from the coaching road, is that they lay in the same DB hundred, a slim association at best.[114]

Kingstone is first recorded in 1166 as *Kingeston*. Ecclesiastically, it is a daughter of its neighbour Gratwich which was listed in DB under the lands of Robert of Stafford, and held TRE by Goding, 'a free man'.

Warwickshire is home to four Kingstons: Kineton Green (Solihull), Kingston (Chesterton) and Kineton. Kington

---

[105] Other examples are Kingston (Lacy) DOR, Kingston (Deverill) WLT, Kingston (Colyton) DEV and Conington CAM.
[106] DBGlo 1, 11.

[107] SJ 30 37.
[108] White. R. In Lafflin 2001.
[109] SJ 480 099.
[110] SJ 4444.
[111] SJ 444 140.
[112] Patterson 1799: p. 227.
[113] ULAS. Dr Patrick Clay
[114] Brian Rich, Community Education Officer in this area, confirmed this proposed routeway.

(Grange), in the parish of Claverdon, does not appear to be sited on or near an identified Roman road, although the long-distance ancient road on which it does lie might have been Romanised. Wooton Wawen, the caput of this royal estate, lies close to the Roman road that ran south from Birmingham to Stratford upon Avon.

Kineton Green (Solihull) lies in the parish of Solihull, five miles south-east of Birmingham in the west of the county, on the boundary between Worcestershire and Warwickshire. A Roman road, known locally as Monkspath Street, leaves the Roman fort at Metchley, Edgbaston, Birmingham, in a south-easterly direction. Kineton Green is sited on this road which forms part of the boundary of Solihull follows this street. The line of this road, which is represented broadly by the present-day A34, continues on in the general direction of Henley in Arden, Wootton Wawen, and Stratford upon Avon. The true line is understood imperfectly, and it is only because of the tireless commitment of the Birmingham Roman Roads Study Group, which began life as a University of Birmingham Adult Education class, that the line is understood at all, particularly where it runs through the suburbs of Birmingham.[115] This is the third example in this study of how focused, detailed research, undertaken in places where there is some indication that there is might be some potential, has led to the retrieval of significant corroborative evidence (see White in Shropshire, and Clarke in west Hampshire (above).

The first appearance of Kineton Green (Solihull) in the record is in 972 as *Cinctun(es) broc*, in the bounds of a land grant of Edgar to Pershore Abbey. This charter gives Kineton Green a royal connection, but it has not been possible to suggest the royal estate of which it would once have been a component part. In DB it is listed independently as *Cintone*, where there was one manor of two hides held TRW from William son of Corbucion by Aelmer, and TRE by Thorkel who held it freely. It is also listed in the Worcestershire DB (see below).

Kington Grange (Claverdon), eight miles south of Kineton Green, lies in the parish of Wooton Wawen, two miles off the continuation of Monkspath Street discussed above. At Monkspath Hill this proposed Roman road turned south towards Hockley Heath, Henley in Arden, Wootton Wawen and on to Stratford upon Avon. The Roman line is secure as far as Monkspath Hill, thereafter it is less secure. Ecclesiastically Kingston (Grange) is the daughter of Claverdon, which originally would have been a daughter of Wooton Wawen, the estate centre to which it must once have been attached. Steven Bassett has established that the extensive parish of Wootton Wawen reflects broadly the territory of the Anglo-Saxon tribal group known as the *Stoppingas*. Kington appears in DB as *Cintone*. TRW it was held by the Count of Meulan and TRE by Brictnoth, 'a free man'. The *villa regalis* of which Kington Grange was a member is discussed in Chapter 4. No Roman road has been identified here but Wootton Wawen lies close

to an ancient route-way between south Birmingham and Stratford upon Avon.

Kingston Farm (Chesterton), which today is represented by a farm name in Chesterton parish, lies on the Fosse Way. Five miles to the south, and also lying within a mile of the Fosse Way, is Kineton, sited three miles or so from the known *villa regalis* of Wellesbourne. The extent of this estate has not been established securely. It is possible that the territory of the *Stoppingas* might extend as far as Kineton, Wellesbourne, and Kingston (Chesterton), which is the north-eastern boundary of the ancient diocese of Worcester which follows broadly the boundaries of the Anglo-Saxon kingdom of the *Hwicce*. The parish boundaries of Chesterton lie across the Fosse Way (M 5d) which cuts through the territory of the putative Wellesbourne estate, suggesting that it might have existed as a land unit before the road was constructed. A Roman small town, apparently walled (as the name Chesterton suggests), lay here on the Fosse Way. The outline of the town can be seen in the fields beside the Fosse Way. Excavation has revealed that the gates of the town were fortified, and this, together with the possibility that it was walled, suggests higher status, an official *mansio* perhaps, than most Roman small towns, the majority of which were unplanned and undefended.[116] This is one of six Kingstons in the corpus that are closely associated with Roman small towns, which Charles Phythian-Adams notes were often sited where major Roman roads crossed ancient administrative boundaries, as is the case with Kingston Farm (Chesterton).[117]

Kingston Farm (Chesterton) is first recorded in 1279 as *Kyngeston*. Chesterton, however, is listed. There were five small manors: the largest was three hides, the smallest a half; they all had different and minor land-holders. One manor has no information TRE, two had one holder, and two had three, one of which was held by three thanes who held their lands freely. None of the manors were royal at DB and it has not been possible to establish any royal connection at all for this place.

Kineton lies a mile and a half off the Fosse Way, five miles south of Kingston Farm (Chesterton). A direct road links Kineton to the central place of the *villa regalis* of Wellesbourne, five miles to the south-west along the Fosse Way. Although the king's hall could, theoretically, have been sited almost anywhere within the royal *estate,* its most likely position would have close to the church and the place within the estate to which the name became attached.

Kineton is first recorded in a charter of Edgar in 969, in which he granted to Ælfwold, his faithful minister, 10 hides at *loco qui vulgari Cyngtun dicitur* 'the place that is commonly called *Cyngtun*'. The bounds of the charter contain this reference to Wellesbourne: *ðis synt ða lond gemæra into cyngtune of weles burnan*, 'this is the land

[115] Leather 1994: p. 103.

[116] Burnham & Wacher 1990: p. 250.
[117] Phythian-Adams 1977: pp. 77–8.

that is the boundary of *cyngtune* and *weles burnan'*,[118] By DB the land at Kineton, which 80 years earlier had been granted away, was back in the hands of the king. *Quintone* (Kineton) and *Waleborne* (Wellesbourne) are listed as 'the manor and the outlier together'. Both were held TRW and TRE by the king. The hidation of the manor was low, just three hides, yet the population was sizeable with 93 villagers, 18 smallholders, with 39 ploughs and five slaves; 39 ploughs is an exceptionally high number. In 1220, Kineton was granted a market charter, although it is possible that there may have been an earlier prescriptive market here from when Kineton was probably the collecting centre for renders to the king.[119] Kineton, a daughter of Wellesbourne, is now a parish in its own right, although its church has the same dedication, St Peter, as the mother church of Wellesbourne. The association between Wellesbourne, Kineton and Kingston Farm (Chesterton), which mirrors closely the configuration of the Wiltshire group of West Kington, Kingston (St Michael) and Chippenham, is examined in Chapter 4.

There are two Kingstons in Worcestershire: Kington, which lies nine miles east of Worcester and eight miles west of Alcester on the present-day A422 road, and Kineton Green (Solihull), which lies on the boundary of Worcestershire and Warwickshire and is listed under both Worcestershire and Warwickshire. As late as Domesday many county boundaries, particularly in wooded areas, were often still ill-defined. As Kineton Green (Solihull) is an ecclesiastical daughter of Solihull, and is now firmly in Warwickshire. It is analysed here under that county.

Kington lies centrally in the county, nine miles east of Worcester and eight miles west of Alcester on the present-day A422 road. No Roman or other ancient routeway has been identified here, although the present-day road from Worcester to Alcester, which crosses the southern part of the parish, is clearly following an ancient line eastward to the Roman Ryknield Street and from there on to Stratford upon Avon. Even a cursory examination of the map suggests that, with the extensive network of Roman roads and settlements in this area, a road would not be unexpected here. Perhaps, as has turned out to be the case with Kinton in the parish of Great Ness, Shropshire, the presence of this Kington adds strength to this suggestion (see above).

Kington is first recorded in 930 as *Cyngton*, in a land grant of Æthelstan to Abbot Cynath of land *æt pidwellan*.[120] The boundary clause of this grant survives and has been identified as the parish of Kington, whose present-day boundaries follow almost exactly those of the boundary clause. In 1002 the estate, now called *æt Fleferht* (Flyford), was leased for a second time, this time by Æthelred to Archbishop Ælfric.[121] The bounds also survive, unchanged from the earlier grant. This estate of *æt pidwellan* was

named after the River Piddle. Was the Kingston name coined because of the need for the land to be identified for the charter or was it already known by that name. Certainly, by DB this area of land had become known as *Cyngton*. Watts is of the opinion that this came about because the descriptive term royal manor had become current. However, if Watts's reasoning is correct then we would expect that given the quantity of land grants issued by the king, there would be hundreds of places known as Kingston. A more probable explanation is that this estate was already a Kingston, with the name having fallen out of use when its founding function had ceased to be. When in 930 the estate was delineated as a discrete unit and an identifying name was needed, Kingston might have been waiting its resurrection. By DB *Chintune* was no longer in the king's hands, neither was there any hint of its royal past. It was held TRW by Roger of Lacy, and TRE by Eilaf and Tori, who 'held it as three manors and could betake themselves where they would'. There were also two men-at-arms on the manor. Kington is now an independent parish, its original ecclesiastical connection uncertain. We know it was royal land at the time of Æthelstan, but it has not been possible to establish of which royal estate it was once a component part.

Group 3 Counties lying between Watling Street and the Mersey/Humber Line plus East Anglia

Kingstons are sparsely represented in these counties. These were regions of Scandinavian settlement which may, in some way account for this.

Leicestershire, **Congerstone,** the sole Kingston in Leicestershire, lies in the south-west of the county, three miles north-west of Market Bosworth, and four miles from the Roman Watling Street, which here forms the county boundary with Warwickshire (M 1g). Congerstone does not appear to be sited on any significant, immediately identifiable, long-distance routeway. However, Lewis's map of 1830 places Congerstone on a proposed long-distance route that entered Leicestershire in the north-east of the county from Saltersford, Grantham. This road intersected Ermine Street (M 2c) at the Fosse Way at Six Hills, then taking a south-westerly line to Barrow on Soar where it crossed the River Soar. It continued through Charnwood forest to Markfield, Thornton, Bagworth, Barton in the Beans and Congerstone. Although the exact line beyond Barrow on Soar as it crossed Charnwood Forest is almost impossible to identify with the line suggested by Lewis, it is considered to be broadly correct.[122]

---

[118] Wellesbourne also featured in an earlier charter of 840, issued from *Wassanburna* by Berhtwulf, king of Mercia. S 192.
[119] Charles Phythian-Adams pers. comm.
[120] S 404.
[121] S 901.

[122] Peter Liddle, County Archaeologist for Leicestershire, considers the Lewis route to be broadly correct. He notes that there is growing evidence of Roman activity at Thornton. A second possible line for the proposed road after it leaves Charnwood Forest is at the point where the Lewis line crosses the present A50 at Stanton under Bardon. The road turned due west towards Ibstock where, at the church, it follows a now indeterminate line towards Odstone and Congerstone. (Peter Liddle (pers. comm.); Lewis 1830: no page numbers.

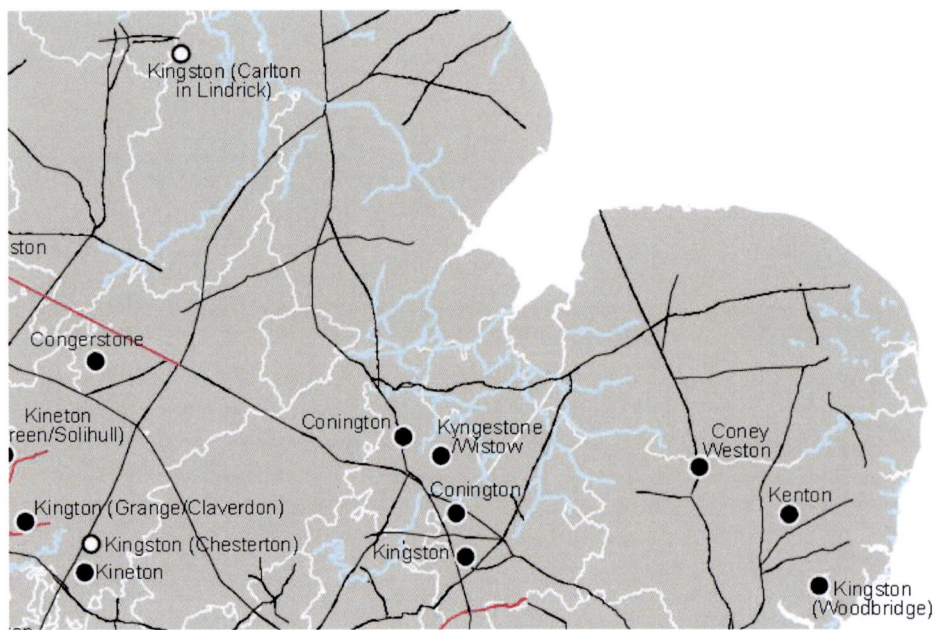

Figure 7: Leicestershire, Nottinghamshire, Huntingdon, Cambridgeshire, Suffolk.

Peter Foss has argued convincingly that Congerstone was a component part of a Mercian royal estate centred on Market Bosworth.[123] The south-eastern boundary of this proposed estate is defined broadly by the line of the Roman road, known locally as the Fenn Lanes. This ran south-westwards from Leicester to Mancetter, the Roman small town of *Manduessedum* on Watling Street (M 57b).

Congerstone first appears in the record at DB as *Cuningestone*, a Scandinavianisation of the OE *Cyningestun*. There were two manors here, neither of which was in royal hands TRW; and no TRE information is given for either manor. At DB Congerstone possessed the only mill within the Bosworth estate. It is possible that Market Bosworth might have been the central place of an early Anglo-Saxon small kingdom (see below).

In Nottinghamshire, **Carlton in Lindrick**, has one Kingston, now completely subsumed into Carlton, where it survives as the name of a street on a small housing estate in North Carlton. Both Carlton and Kingston lie on the present-day A60 road between Worksop and Blyth. No Roman road has been confirmed in the immediate area of Carlton, although a Roman villa site has been identified two miles north at Oldcoates, on the same road as Carlton and Kingston (A60). Oldcoates also lies on the line of the Roman road which crossed the county from Rycknield Street in the west, linking up with the Roman road from Lincoln to Doncaster in the east (M 58e). The line of this road is hard to establish along much of its length because of the destruction caused by heavy industry. At Oldcoates, where there was less heavy industry, a pronounced *agger* can be seen clearly in the fields running for three-quarters of a mile along the north side of the present Firbeck to

Oldcotes road.[124] The presence here of Kingston, Carlton and a Roman villa site, located on a minor Roman road which joins a major Roman through-road just two miles or so distance away, is similar to Kingston locations observed elsewhere in the corpus. This might indicate that there could have been a royal estate, as yet unidentified, somewhere in the area. It has not been possible to uncover any evidence of this or to propose a possible estate centre.

Kingston (Carlton in Lindrick) is first recorded in 1308 as *Le Kynggeston*, and by 1356 as *Kengeston in Carlton*. At DB Carlton is listed as having one manor which was divided TRW between the king and Roger de Busli. There is no TRE information. The king's part of this manor is probably represented by the Kingston housing estate in North Carlton. This gives Kingston a royal connection no later than DB.

Cambridgeshire, Huntingdonshire, and Suffolk

Two Kingstons are found in Cambridgeshire, two in Huntingdonshire, and three in Suffolk.

Kingston CAM is an ancient parish with a church whose structure dates in part from the twelfth century, an early date for this region of Cambridgeshire. It first enters the record at DB where it is recorded as *Chingestone*. There were six manors here held by six different landholders. One manor was held by the king both TRW and TRE, two were held TRE by Earl Waltheof, and two were held TRE by freemen. The 14 Freemen who held the sixth manor TRE owed particular responsibilities to the ing; 10 of the freemen who held land 'of the King's jurisdiction' were obliged to provide '7 cartages and 3 escorts' presumably for the king (or his representative) when he was in the area.

---
[123] Peter Foss 1998: pp. 83–106.

[124] Margary 1957: vol. 2, p. 145.

This obligation is similar to that which applied in several other DM manors.

Conington CAM is sited on the Roman road from Godmanchester to Cambridge in the angle formed where it branches off Ermine Street (M 24). The north-east boundary of the parish takes the line of the Godmanchester to Cambridge road as a boundary, and the north-west parish boundary follows the county boundary of Huntingdonshire.

Conington CAM is first recorded in 975 as *æt Cunningtune* in the will of Ælfhelm. At DB there were three manors, recorded variously as *Contone, Cunitone*, with three different landholders; TRE information is given for only one of the manor, that which was held by 'three Freemen of King Edward'.

Huntingdonshire, ***Kyngestone*/Wistow** lies three miles south of Ramsey close to the fen edge; the surrounding area lies within the Bedford Middle Levels. No important Roman road is known here, although the road that connects Ramsey with Godmanchester on the Great Ouse, and on which *Kingestune*/Wistow stands, is clearly ancient. It was turn-piked in the eighteenth century, a confirmation of some degree of antiquity. On the first edition of the six-inch to the mile OS map, a 'Roman camp' is marked at Bury on this road, immediately to the north of *Kingestune*/Wistow. This feature can no longer be seen on the ground. The nearest major Roman road is Ermine Street (M 2b), six miles to the west. The Roman camp at Bury, the presence of a Kingston, and the straight road suggest that this line could be a minor Roman road. Here, however, on the fen edge, almost all roads are straight.

In almost every respect *Kyngestune*/Wistow presents a significantly different picture from the other three examples in this group. Today, the only evidence for the earlier existence of *Kyngestune* is a lane known as 'Kingston Way' on the west side of Wistow church. Watts suggests that in this instance the name Wistow OE *wīc-stōw* may be referring to the site of a royal house or palace.[125] This is a complex argument which is discussed in full in Chapter 4.

Conington Huntingdonshire, is an ancient parish which enters in the record in 957 as *aet Cunic tune*, in an authentic charter of Eadwig. The name occurs in 1017 in the will of *Mantat*, an anchorite, who bequeathed land at *Cunintun* to the 'priests and deacons who have served me all my life'. She also bequeathed lands at Twywell to Thorney, where she 'wants her bones to lie'. Conington is recorded at DB as *Coninctune*. It was held TRW by Countess Judith and TRE by Thorkell. Six hides of this land belonged to St Mary of Thorney, and it was held by Thorkell from the Abbot. This is probably the same land that was bequeathed by the anchorite *Mantat* in 1017.

There are no Kingstons in Norfolk. Suffolk, in comparison, has three, none of which seem connected to each other in any way.

Kingston (Woodbridge) lies on a small promontory of slightly elevated ground on the west bank of the River Deben. Across the river, is Sutton Hoo, the burial ground generally accepted burial of the royal house of the *Wuffingas*, the kings of East Anglia who ruled between the fifth and seventh centuries. The river would have been an important routeway allowing easy access into the heart of the kingdom where, Rendelsham, the once presumed, and now almost certain, centre of their royal power, is lies four miles up-river from Kingston, at a place described by Bede as 'the king's country seat of Rendelesham' (below, Chapter 4).[126] A small connection, but worth noting is that the church at Rendlesham and the church at Kirknewton NBM, which stands adjacent to the site at Yeavering of the *villa regalis* of the kings of Bernicia, the central place of royal power in seventh-century Northumberland, are both dedicated to St Gregory. No Roman roads have been identified here, although there is evidence of Roman activity in the immediate area. A temple to *Mars Coroiacus* was found in the neighbouring village of Martlesham, and there was a late Roman fort at Walton Castle close to the mouth of the Deben on the south side. The nearest Roman road is five miles north of Kingston (M 340). There is a direct route, now a minor road, north from Woodbridge that broadly follows the river. Kingston lies half a mile east of this road. The road out of Woodbridge to the south leads to Felixstowe.

Kingston (Woodbridge) first enters the record in 1042 in a writ of King Edward to Ely Abbey, confirming privileges at *Kingestun*. *Oddebrug* 'Woodbridge' is listed in the same writ; 44 years later at DB, Kingston was not listed independently, subsumed no doubt into the entry for Woodbridge where seven manors are recorded TRW comprised largely of freemen. No TRE information is given for any of the manors.

Coney Weston lies on the River Waveney, which for much of its length is the county boundary with Norfolk. Two Roman roads cross this parish. To the south of Coney Weston, two miles north-east of Ixworth, the Roman road from London to Norwich divided. The left fork, known for much of its length as the Peddlars' Way, continued in a northerly direction, crossing the western half of Coney Weston parish. The right fork took a north-westerly direction and crossed the east side of the parish on its way to *Icenorum* Norwich (M 331; 33a). Coney Weston was recorded as *Cunegeston* in a writ of King Edward; this onfirms its royal antecedents. At DB Coney Weston was held both TRW and TRE by St Edmunds. The entries for Hepworth, Hopton, and (Market) Weston record that 'service was due in Coney Weston'.

---

[125] Watts 2004: p. 689.

[126] *HE* iii, 22.

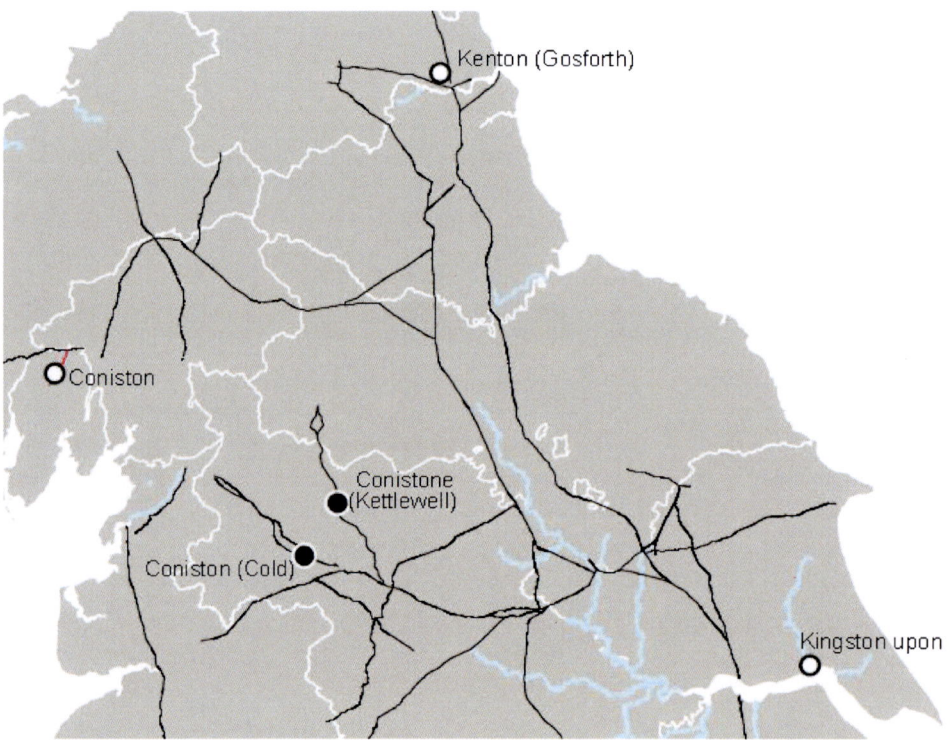

Figure 8: Lancashire, Yorkshire West Riding, Yorkshire East Riding, Northumberland.

Kenton lies adjacent to Debenham. Although a question has been raised concerning whether the first element could possibly be the OE male personal name *Cena,* Kenton has been included in the corpus, as the consensus amongst place-name scholars is that the balance of probabilities is towards the first element being 'king'. The River Deben rises in the south-west corner of the parish of Kenton two miles off the Roman road to Dunwich, a branch of the Colchester to Norwich Roman road at Baylam (M 34b).

Kenton is first recorded in DB as *Chenetuna* where there were three manors, one held by St Edmunds and one described as an outlier of Debenham. Kenton is a neighbour of the parishes of Earl and Monk Soham, where in places the line of the Roman road can be seen clearly. This connection with the Sohams might have significance in the light of their being liable for the *firma unius noctis*. It has not been possible to establish any link between Kenton and the Sohams but a Kingston sited in close association to an estate liable for the *feorm* is an association that is seen frequently in ancient Wessex. This is explored in Chapter 4.

Group 4 Counties North of the Humber/Mersey Line

Only five Kingstons lie north of the line between the Mersey and the Humber: one in Lancashire, two in the West Riding of Yorkshire, one in the East Riding, and one in Northumberland.

The Yorkshire West Riding and Lancashire examples may be associated in some way with putative early Anglo-Saxon/Scandinavian kingdoms.

Coniston Lancashire lies at the head of Coniston Water. A packhorse road ran north from here for three miles to join the Roman road to Ravenglass, via the Hard Knott pass to Ambleside (*Galava*) and Kendal (M 740). This is the same road on which Coniston Cold in the West Riding of Yorkshire lies. The copper ore mined here was considered to be of the finest quality, and initially, as many of the seams could be accessed from the surface, it was easy to extract. No evidence of the ore being extracted prior to the late sixteenth century has survived as each new layer of mining destroys the ones before. Eric Holland, the mining historian, is of the opinion that not only was it unlikely that the Romans would have ignored these fine surface deposits, but there is evidence of mining here in the Bronze Age.[127] The copper ore would have been taken away by packhorse up to the Roman road or by boat down Coniston Water to where the River Crake meets the coast.

Coniston is first recorded *c.* 1157 as *Coningeston,* ecclesiatically it is one of several chapelries of Ulverston. Anglian names are rare in this corner of the county but the first element of the name is the Scandinavianised form of OE *cyning,* Ekwall has suggested that the name might not be a scandinavianisation of OE *cyningestūn* but could have been coined at a later date, as *kunungstūn* in Old Norse, preserving the memory of a small Scandinavian mountain kingdom'.[128] We cannot know if Ekwall is right but, in any case this argument does not work philologically as the early forms of the name do not allow a distinction to be

---

[127] Eric Holland, 1986; Cumbria Amenity Trust Mining History Society, www.catmhs.org.uk
[128] Ekwall 1922: p. 215.

made between a name that is Scandinavian and one that has been scandinavianised.

Kingston upon Hull lies on the north bank of the Humber estuary on ground that is low-lying, and agriculturally favourable.[129] In 1292, Edward I exchanged with the monks of Meaux lands he held in Wawne and Wilsby for *Wyke*, for the purpose of securing the port which was renamed *Kingestonam super Hullo*. The charter recording this exchange is preserved in the Guildhall of the city of Hull.

The name *Wyke* is either OE *wīc* 'a dairy farm, a trading place', or ON *vik* 'a creek, an inlet'. The name of the parish in which Wyke lay was Myton, OE *mȳðe tūn,* the 'settlement at the confluence of the Hull and the Humber'. At DB *Mitun(e)* was an outlier of Ferriby, held by Ralph of Mortemer TRW and by Eadgifu (DBYOE14e 15).

Yorkshire West Riding, **Coniston (Cold)** in the West Riding of Yorkshire lies between Skipton and Settle on the line of the Roman road which crossed Yorkshire and Lancashire from Tadcaster, Ilkley, Skipton, Kendal and Ambleside (*Glava*) to the coast at Ravenglass (M 740). Some stretches of this road are still unclear, but there is no disagreement as to its broad direction. At Gargrave, Coniston's immediate neighbour and ecclesiastical mother settlement, a Roman villa site has been identified and a stretch of the cobbled surface of the Roman road has been seen, leaving no doubt as to the true line of the road. As is the case with Coniston LNC the name is the Scandinavianised OE *cyning*. Coniston is first recorded at DB, spelt variously as *Coninestone and Cuningestune,* with *Coneghestone Calde* first recorded 1202. There were four manors at DB; two held TRW by William of Percy and TRE by Bjornwulf, one third was held TRW by Bolton Abbey with no TRE holder given. No land holder is given for the fourth manor and, apart from the name, it has not been possible to establish a royal connection.

Conistone (Kettlewell), another Scandinavianised OE *cyning* name, lies on the road that ran south from Brough by Bainbridge (*Virosidum*) to meet the Roman road from Ilkley to Settle (M 722; 72b). This road, which takes the only line possible through a difficult landscape, was used and almost certainly improved by the Romans. At Threshfield, two miles south of Conistone (Kettlewell), the direction of the road onwards is uncertain. It could have turned to the south-east to join the M 722 at Addingham, two miles west of Ilkley, or have taken a south-westerly line to Gargrave and Coniston (Cold), which also lie on M 722. Conistone (Kettlewell) to Addingham is ten miles; Addingham to Conistion (Cold) is also ten miles, as is Coniston Cold to Conistone (Kettlewell). These roads can be seen clearly on Bacon's 1891 map of Airedale.[130] This ten-mile pattern could be significant, mirroring as it does similar patterns that have been observed in Wessex, Gloucestershire, and hinted at in other southern counties.

Both of these Kingstons lie in the British kingdom of Craven whose territory was the upper dales of the rivers Wharfe, Ribble and Aire, and which was still a sizeable district at the time of DB.[131] These Kingstons must be associated in some way with the district of Craven, but it has not been possible to establish what that relationship could have been.

Conistone (Kettlewell) is first recorded in DB as *Cunestune*. In 1285 it is recorded as *Conyston in Kettlewell*, presumably to differentiate it from Coniston (Cold). There was one DB manor here which TRE was the 'Land of the King's Thanes', giving it a royal connection. The church, which is a chapelry of Burnsall, has some Anglo-Saxon surviving structures. Other daughters of Burnsall are Thorpe, Hartlington, Appletreewick and Drebley.[132]

Northumberland, **Kenton (Gosforth)**, the most northerly example of the corpus, lies two miles north of Newcastle upon Tyne, and is one of several daughters of Gosforth whose parochial lands lie across the present-day A1, which is the line of the Roman road from London to the north. This road approached Newcastle from the south via Stamford Bridge and Durham, where there was a connecting link just north of Binchester, and Chester le Street (M 80a, 80b). At Gateshead the road crossed the River Tyne on the *Pons Ælius* (Newcastle). It has now been established that a road, in line with Gateshead and the bridge, continued on north of Hadrian's Wall, taking a straight line out of Newcastle, through Gosforth and Wideopen to Seaton Burn where it joined the line of the present A1. This road, now classified as the B1318, can be seen clearly marked on the first edition of the six-inch to the mile OS map. The road continues northward to join the Roman road from Corbridge to Berwick-on-Tweed (M 67). Kenton appears in the record for the first time in 1255 as *Kynton* and *Quenton*.

Having established and reviewed the patterns of distribution, and the historical and archaeological sources of all the names in the corpus, certain recurrent features shared by many of the Kingston-named places have emerged. Analysis and interpretations of these patterns is discussed in Chapter 4.

---

[129] Whaley 2006: pp. 80–1.
[130] Bacon 1891: Map of Airedale.

[131] Wood 1990: pp. 1–20.
[132] Raistrick 1948: p.14; p. 22.

Chapter 4

Interpreting the Patterns

The previous chapter outlined the evidence for the Kingstons in the broad context of their geographical location, relationship to long-distance Roman roads or other major ancient routeways, and the wider landscape. The documentary evidence for each name was discussed: early history, archaeology, royal connections, ecclesiastical status, appearance in Domesday Book, together with any other relevant information, was presented and discussed. From this, certain patterns and associations emerged.

A royal connection has been established for all the names in the corpus except for five examples, with the majority of the Kingstons displaying distinct distributional patterns that suggest their siting was purposeful, raising the question as to what their function might have been, what processes led to their being founded, under whose authority, and when. Overall, there is a pronounced distributional bias towards Wessex, and the kingdoms of the *Hwicce* and the *Magonsæt*, with the 'road/string' distributional pattern in expanded Wessex and the South West Midlands, particularly the kingdom of the *Hwicce*, showing a distinct association between the Kingstons and major long-distance Roman roads and ancient routeways. In the main the Kingstons are less likely to be found in areas of pronounced Scandinavian settlement.

Kingstons: the royal connection

The name itself is evidence enough that at some time in their past the Kingstons must have been royal holdings of some kind. A direct royal connection for over half of the names in the corpus has been established, and a connection by association for almost all of the others. In only five cases has it not been possible to confirm a royal history of some kind. What was the nature of these connections and were they the central places of *villæ regales* as has often been asserted?

Bede names five *villæ regales* and makes reference to several others without naming them specifically. Three were in Northumberland, a reflection perhaps of Bede living all his life in the north-east. *Bebbanburgh* 'Bamburgh' is described by Bede as a 'royal city', *Ad-Gefrin* 'Yeavering' he calls a 'royal residence'. *Mælmin*, thought to be Millfield, lies two miles to the north of *Ad-Gefrin*. This was built as a replacement for *Ad-Gefrin* after it was abandoned.[1] Two *villæ regales* lie beyond Northumbria. The site of *Campodunum*, which Bede makes clear is in Yorkshire, is still uncertain but is generally thought to be in the West

Riding. Saint Paulinus built a church here where King Edwin had a 'royal residence'. The fifth is Rendlesham in Suffolk, 'the king's country seat'. The king was Rædwald, the early seventh-century king of the East Angles, who might be the king buried in the magnificent ship burial at Sutton Hoo.[2]

At Bamborough recent excavations have uncovered the site of the royal hall and the excavations at Yeavering revealed the royal compound within which, in addition to structures which were royal halls, there stood a unique amphitheatre-like structure which might have been a stage. The missionary Paulinus spent 36 days baptising converts in the river Glen which runs close by.[3] It is not too fanciful to imagine Paulinus preaching the gospel from this structure.

Since 2008, Suffolk County Council Archaeological Service has been coordinating a programme of survey and investigation at Rendlesham. Several survey techniques have been employed, including systematic metal detecting, geophysical, topographical, and geochemical surveys, air-photo plotting, and targeted small-scale excavation. The results so far have been spectacular, revealing Rendlesham almost certainly to have been the *villa regalis* recorded by Bede. The site, which spans the fifth to eight centuries, appears to have been at the peak of its importance between the early-middle sixth century until the second quarter of the eighth century, when it covered an area greater and richer than any other settlement known from England at the time. 'It was an important settlement where kings feasted their followers, skilled metalworkers produced luxury goods of the highest social order; foreign imports were traded, and large quantities of coinage changed hands'.[4] To date this is the most productive site for gold coins in England. Aerial photographs taken in 2015 revealed cropmarks that seem to represent the footprint of a rectangular timber building, measuring 23m by 9.5m which Christopher Scull, the principal investigator, thinks is the site of the royal hall. Plans for the excavation of the site to confirm this are in preparation.[5]

Peter Sawyer has identified almost two hundred pre-Conquest *villæ regales*.[6] Many have developed into

---

[1] *Bebbanburh HE* iii, 16; *Ad-Gefrin HE* ii, 14; *Mælmin HE* ii, 15.

[2] *HE* iii, 22.
[3] *HE* 2. 9.
[4] Chris Scull, presenting the results of archaeological excavation at Rendlesham, 2008-14. Bury St Edmunds, 24 September 2016.
[5] Christopher Scull, Faye Minter, Judith Pluvier, 'Social and economic complexity in early medieval England: a central place complex of the East Anglian kingdom at Rendlesham, Suffolk'. *Antiquity* 90 2016.
[6] Sawyer 1983: 289-99.

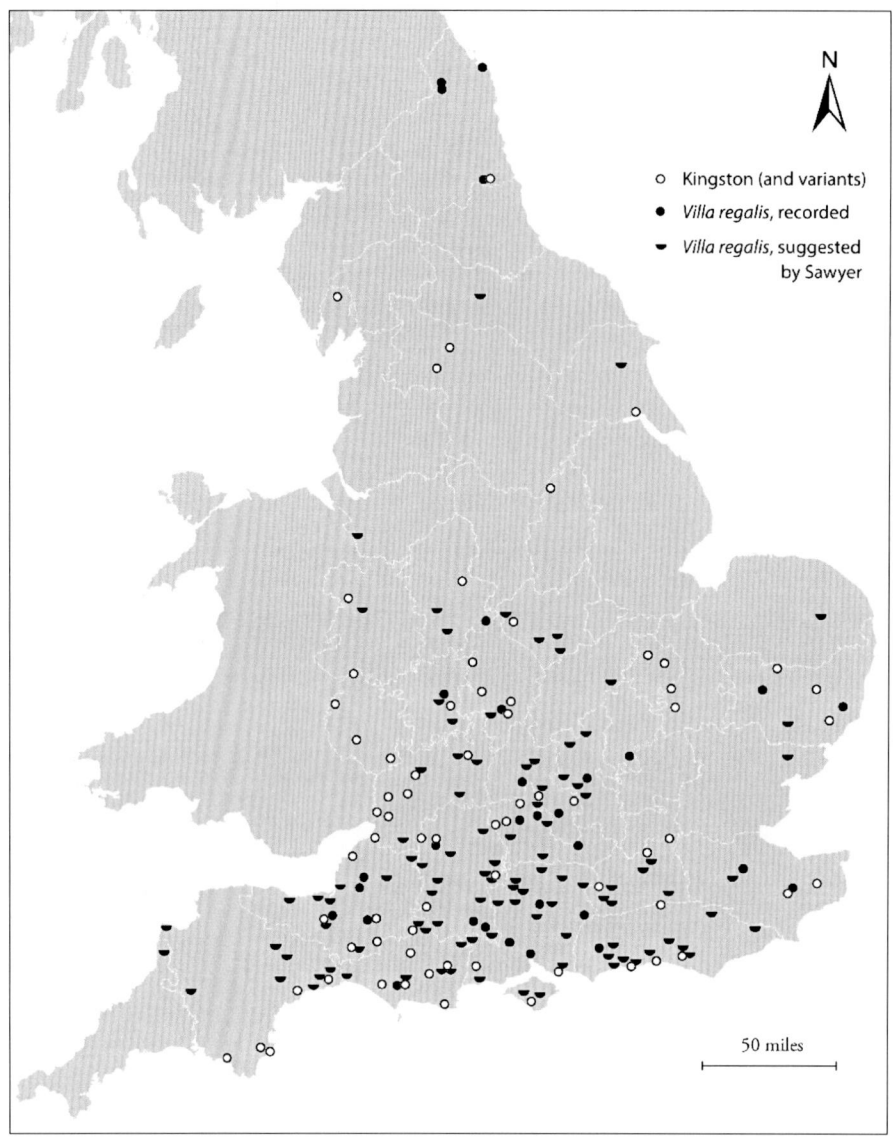

Figure 9: Sites of *Villæ Regales* with Kingstons superimposed, differentiated between those recorded by DB, or earlier, and those recorded for the first time post DB. (Based on Sawyer's list.)

important places that have endured over time, others are known, but have not survived, and at least another 40 are known by name but not by location.

The built structures of the early/mid-Saxon period would have been constructed in wood, leaving little or no trace in the landscape. The list shows that, even allowing for the documentary evidence presenting a skewed picture, a network of *villae regales* extended across England. Sawyer asserts that it is in the study of royal halls and what happened in them that we come closest to the realities of early medieval kingship, with the royal residence being the key site in Anglo-Saxon systems of administration. It was the at the *villa regalis* that contemporaries witnessed the routines of royal power, routines that included the noble pursuit of hunting as well as the celebration of solemn festivals, and discussions, both private and public, in great assemblies. Some of these royal estates will have had great mead-halls like *Heorot,* the 'Hall of the Hart'; with all it represented, it was both literally and metaphorically the most important

place on any *villa regalis*.[7] Not all royal residences would have been as spectacular as *Heorot*, and although many will have been relatively modest hunting lodges, they would still have been adorned with the visible signs of royal power and authority. Some estates may not have had permanent residences on all his estates, and we know that the accommodation at some assemblies was often in tents. As kingdoms expanded the king might not even have visited all of them.[8]

Were the Kingstons *villæ regales*?

Sawyer's list of *villæ regales* shows beyond dispute, that with the possible exception of Kingston upon Thames (see below, Chapter 5), the simple answer to this question is *no*, although they do appear to have been significant members of these royal estates. It is unlikely that all the activities relating to the administration and day-to-day running of an

---

[7] *Beowulf* Lines 74-79.
[8] Sawyer 1983: p. 286.

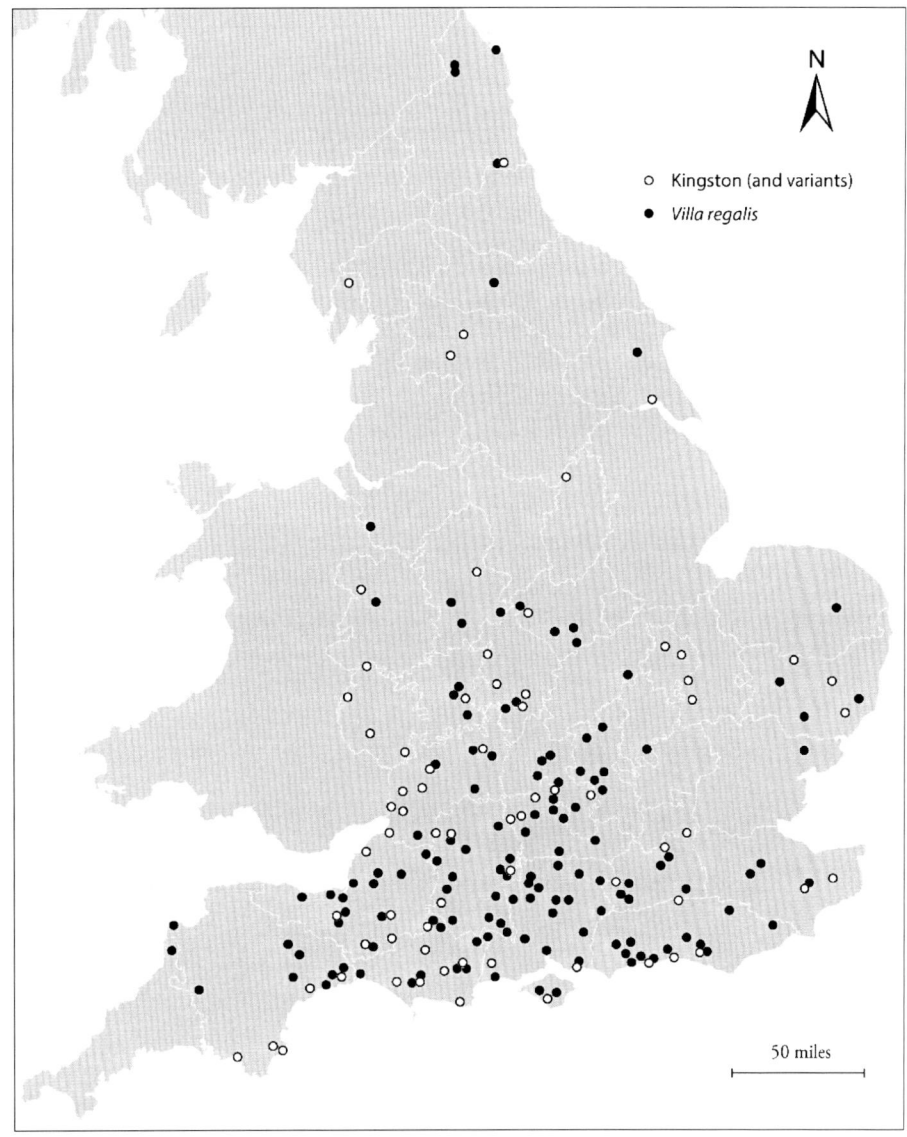

Figure 10: Sites of *Villæ Regales* with Kingstons superimposed, differentiated between those recorded by DB, or earlier, and those recorded for the first time post DB. (Based on Sawyer's list.)

estate took place close to the hall. There would have been 'archipelagos' serving specialist functions across the estate lands, with a Kingston being one of these 'islands'. The Kingstons were plainly not royal estate centres, although their function will have been related to their position within the royal estates. An examination of the four appearances in the documentary record (other than DB) of the OE term *cyninges-tūn* might take us closer to what their function might have been. Sawyer does not discuss what the relationship between the *villæ regales* and the *cyninges-tūn*s in the record might have been: this is a knotty problem but it has to be tackled in order to move towards an understanding what Kingstons might have been.

Can anything be extracted from the two instances of the term *cyninges-tūn* in the laws of the early Anglo-Saxon kings? The first appearance of the term is in the late sixth-early seventh-century laws of King Æthelberht of Kent who legislated as 'King of the Peoples of Kent'. This is the first extant English document written in the vernacular.

Ch.§5, the fifth law states: *Gif in cyninges tune man mannan ofslea, L scill' gebete* 'If one man slays another on the king's premises he shall pay 50 shillings compensation'.[9] That is in addition to the customary payment.[10] The second appearance of the term is about 250 years later in the late ninth-century laws of King Alfred where Ch.1§2 states that one who breaks an oath will, *beo feowertig nihta on carcerne on cyninges-tūn,* 'Will remain forty days in prison *on* (or *æt,* 'at') *cyninges-tūne* and undergo there whatever penance the bishop prescribes for him'.

The use of the term in the laws is a clear indication that both the term and its physical manifestation would have been understood by all. The precise meaning of the term is not now immediately plain. Æthelberht's law seems to equate

---

[9] Attenborough 1922: pp. 4–5, translates *cyninges tune* as the king's premises, a term chosen no doubt because its precise meaning in this context is unclear.
[10] Lieberman 1960: vol. 1, p.3.

cyninges tūn to a place, although it is not clear what this unit was. *Cyninges tūn* could have been used generically meaning the whole royal estate, or be referring to a specific named compound within it. *Tūn* in place-names refers to a particular, demarcated place, an 'enclosure' of some sort within which there would have been built structures of some kind. Alfred's law could carry two meanings. It could be referring to the prison where the oath-breaker will be *on carcerne* 'imprisoned', located somewhere within the lands that comprised the *villa regalis*; or to a specific place known as a *cyninges-tūn* within the royal estate. The term *cyninges-tūn* itself, and its immediate legal context, is of limited use in determining what it signified. It is, however, not unreasonable to assume, cautiously, that other terms for the king's premises in the laws might help us decide, if nothing else, what a *cyninges tūn* was *not*. Ine's law 6 § 1 refers to fights *on cyninges huse* 'house'; the laws of Hlothhere & Eadric 7§ and 16§ refer to the *cynges sele* 'hall/palace', and Alfred 7 § 1 refers to the *cyninges halle* 'hall'. These highly specific terms seem to be referring to built structures of some sort with the implication that the *cyninges-tūn* was something other than the central place on a *villa regalis* where the king's hall lay. The views of scholars of the period might be helpful here. Finberg states:

> Justice would be done at the nearest cyningestun – we shall hardly be coining a word if we call it a 'Kingston' – one of those domains which the king owned in every shire. The 'Kingston', managed for him by a reeve, was the fundamental unit in the old English organisation of justice and finance …there would have been a prison, a public court, and a place where renders to the king would be collected.[11]

James Campbell is of the opinion that we can be reasonably certain that in much of early England the organisation of dues and services for the ruler was systematic, methodically integrating settlements to their respective *villae regales*.[12] The main unit in such a system would have been sizeable, no less than a hundred square miles, centred on the site of the king's residence on the estate, to which all, or most, people in the area owed something, including the renders in kind which provided for the king and his retinue as he moved around his kingdom. This is evidenced from the late seventh century onwards by charters that suggest settlements were assessed in hides and that if there were lands within such an area which were particularly bound to and exploited by it, they probably formed a kind of archipelago.[13]

The third occurrence of the term *cyninges tūn* is in the entry in the *Anglo Saxon Chronicle* for the year 787 regarding the arrival of three ships of Northmen:

> There came for the first time 3 ships and then the reeve rode there and wanted to compel them to go to the

cininges tun because he did not know what they were; and then they killed him. These were the first ships of the Danish [Viking] men from Hordaland [the district around Hardranger fjord in west Norway] which sought out the land of the English race.[14]

This is the first recorded Viking attack of its kind on the English mainland, six years before the attack on Lindisfarne in 793. Although the *ASC* does not record where the Vikings landed and the reeve was assassinated, we are fortunate that Æthelweard, a West Saxon ealdorman writing in the late tenth-century, made a Latin translation of the *ASC* in which he included material that had not been entered previously in any of the surviving English versions. He augments the brief entry in the *ASC*, writing of the event:

> A reeve was called Beaduheard, being in oppido quod Dorceastre, learned that a small fleet of Northmen had arrived at Portland, he went to the harbour with a few men assuming the arrivals were merchants rather than marauders, and spoke to them haughtily. He gave orders that they should go with him ad villam regiam, whereupon they killed him and his companions on the spot.[15]

This reference is helpful but ambiguous. The reeve rode out from the *oppido* of Dorchester, but for the place to which he intended to take the Northmen Æthelweard he uses the term the *villam regiam*, one of several terms used in the documentary sources for *villa regalis*. The term *cyninges tūn*, as has been demonstrated, is more likely to have been referring to the Kingston, not a *villa regalis*, which, although associated with Dorchester, was in some way a distinct and separate place. At this time, and in this context, *oppido* would have carried the restricted meaning of being the main, and most important place, in a large administrative area. The reeve's intention would not have been to take the northmen inland to bring them before the king, but to take them to the place on the royal estate where they could be vetted and recorded. Although the relationship between the *oppido* and the *villam regiam/cyninges tūn* is not clear, what is clear, is that Æthelweard is referring to two physically separate places,

Two possibilities suggest themselves as to where this *villam regiam/cyninges tūn* might have lain. On the east coast of Portland a 'King's Pier' is recorded on modern maps: earlier maps record this as 'Kingston Pier'.[16] The notes that accompany the Dorset map in Lewis's *Atlas* of 1833, state: 'The most extensive [of the piers on Portland] are those called the "King's piers at Kingston".'[17] There are no earlier forms of the name, so whether this was a Kingston or not cannot be confirmed. If one of the functions of a Kingston was to control and monitor *æltheodige mæn* 'foreigners, strangers', unknown travellers and incomers,

---

[11] Finberg 1972: pp. 482–99.
[12] Campbell 1979 (b): p. 11.
[13] Campbell 1986: p. 109.

[14] *ASC* A 787, *ASC* E, *ASC* F.
[15] Æthelweard: p. 27.
[16] This pier is used for the shipping of stone.
[17] Lewis 1833: vol. 2 (the atlas is not paginated).

in accordance with the laws this would have been an ideal place from which to control and monitor arrivals by sea.

The other candidate for Æthelweard's *cyninges tūn* is Kingston Maurward, sited two miles from the east gate of Dorchester on the Roman road that crossed central Dorset. John Blair has suggested the possibility that this Kingston might have been the *cyninges tūn* to which the reeve would have taken the Vikings. Its neighbour, High Burton, is a classic *burh-tūn*, affording high and wide views of Dorchester, Poundbury and Maiden Castle, with Kingston on the lower level controlling the road, together functioning as complementary adjuncts to an important centre.[18]

The weight placed upon control of the roads, and the conduct of travellers, is stated plainly in the laws of Kings Ine (of Wessex), Wihtred (of Kent),and Alfred (of Wessex):

Ine 1 § 25: [*Be cypmanna fare uppe land*]

Gif ciepemon uppe on folce ceapie, do Þæt beforan gewitnessum.

If a trader makes his way into the interior of the country and proceeds to traffic he shall do so before witnesses.

Ine 20: Gif feorcund mon odde fremdebutan wege geond wudu gonge7 ne hrienne ne horn blawe, for deof he bid to profianne, odde to sleanne odde to aliesanne.

If a man from afar, or a stranger, travels through a wood off the highway and neither shouts or blows a horn, he shall be assumed to be a thief, and as such may be either slain or put to ransom.

Wihtred 1§28 is almost identical to that of law §20 of Ine.

The laws of Alfred, which are in part the laws of Ine, express the same intention:

Alfred Ch § 34:

[*Be cypmannum*]

Eac is ciepemonnum gereht : da mende die hie up mid him læden, gebrengen beforan kyninges gerefan on folcgemote, 7 gerecce hu manige para sien ; hie nimen pa men mid him pe hie mægen eft to folcgemote to ryht brenegan........

[With regard to traders]

It is decreed: they shall bring before the king's reeve, at a public meeting, the men they are taking with them up into the country, and declare how many of them there are; and they shall take with them only such men as they can bring to justice again at a public meeting.

The application of the laws and regulation of travellers who passed through the realm, from both within, and from without, the *æltheodige mæn* 'foreigners', 'strangers' would have been ineffectual if they had not been confined to the highways. The law states that the king's reeve was charged with undertaking this routine, no doubt a time-consuming administrative task. Beaduheard rode out to Portland from the *oppido* of Dorchester, which was probably his base, with the intention of taking the Vikings to the *villam regiam/cyninges tūn*. If the laws relating to the roads were to be enforced there would have to have been designated king's officers patrolling the highways. The reeve was the most important administrative officer on a royal estate, usually a high-ranking nobleman who would certainly not have undertaken a humble routine task himself. We can only speculate on the detail of how the laws were applied and where, but it would seem to be unlikely that the general mass of travellers and traders would have been required to register at the place on *villa regalis* where the king's hall stood. Was it to a Kingston they reported?

Slight as these early documentary sources are, nevertheless, some conclusions can be teased-out of them. Kingstons were not the central places of *villæ regales*, although several appear to have purposefully sited close to these centres to serve them in some specific way. The laws of both Æthelberht and Alfred intimate that a *cyninges-tūn* was a particular place whose function was that of the application of the law of the kingdom. What cannot be said with certainty is whether the *cyninges-tūn* of the laws can be linked securely with the Kingstons. Finberg links the function of a *cyninges-tūn* not only with justice, but also with renders to the royal estate. In the light of this, is there any evidence as to the possible role the Kingstons might have played in the system known as the *firma unius noctis*?

Kingstons and the *Firma Unius Noctis*

The *Firma Unius Noctis* (the *feorm*)'farm of one night' was essentially a form of tribute which sustained the royal estate structure. It was a system for provisioning and generally supporting Anglo-Saxon kings and their retinues through levies of food and other goods, in short, the product of the lands over which they ruled. There does seem to be an historiographical consensus that a primitive natural economy lay behind the system and that its traces can be seen in DB. Itineration was the economic basis of kingship.[19] To survive, the king and his retinue had to keep on the move. Lavelle observes that although the precise nature and practice of the *feorm* remains elusive, it was clearly a fundamental feature of kingship. The renders were delivered to the *villa regalis*, probably to a specific location within the territory of the estate designated for the purpose of collection. The oversight of and responsibility for this process was the royal reeve. Most of the documentary

---

[18]   John Blair, pers. comm.

[19]   Lavelle 2007: pp. 15–16.

evidence relating to those royal manors known to have been liable for the *feorm* is derived from DB. It is not easy to establish the detail of these manors and their earlier connections, as the arrangements for the collection of and liability for the *feorm* were restructured in the later Anglo-Saxon period.[20]

At DB King Edward held the largest estate in the land. Only Cornwall, Essex, Cheshire, and Lincolnshire were without royal lands. There is evidence, albeit much of it slight, of the existence of the *feorm* in all the DB circuits, with the foremost evidence concentrated in ancient Wessex where an extensive proportion of the *terra regis* is recorded as being liable for the *feorm*. The evidence for the counties outside Wessex is less clear and more diverse. Sussex has three examples and Surrey three, one of which is Kingston upon Thames. The payments for Oxfordshire were expressed in DB as a payment from the whole county; Berkshire shows no traces, but Pauline Stafford is of the opinion that this is a reflection of the caprice of the compilers of DB.[21] The evidence north of the Thames is varied, patchy, and often difficult to interpret, largely because the local circumstances of different circuits determined the details of what was recorded. Gloucestershire shows evidence of the West Saxon system of large-scale organisation of the *feorm* alongside limited specific renders which are more characteristic of the areas north of the Thames. There is evidence in eastern England of organised food renders most of which had been commuted to either cash payments or standard payments in kind. Pauline Stafford notes that, 'ancient features, old organisation, and regional variations all have played a part in the formation of the structure of royal estates in 1066 to such an extent that it is often difficult to sort out which elements of their organisation should be attributed to which'.[22] This cautionary note must be borne in mind when determining whether or not the Kingstons may have had a role in the management of the *feorm*, particularly in the light of the considerable DB evidence that many of the dues seem to be the result of both recent, and, in some cases, even earlier reorganisation.

There are 11 counties where Kingstons are found and where there is evidence for the *feorm*.[23] These are the 'core' counties of Ancient Wessex (the Devon evidence is recorded in the Exon DB only), Cambridgeshire, Huntingdonshire and Sussex. The lands of the *ing* in Wiltshire, Somerset, and Dorset show the clearest evidence of the *feorm* having been rearranged into an orderly system; the royal lands added post-Conquest do not have the same orderliness. The systems in these counties differ from each other. In Somerset and Dorset the groups of manors, which themselves comprised sub-county land units, are grouped together for payment, an in Somerset groups of two or three large manors are linked; whereas

in Wiltshire the *feorm* is laid on large single manors and their surrounding lands. The royal manors in Hampshire do not seem to have undergone a systematic rearrangement, although there is evidence in some of them of their being liable for the *feorm*. The extensive royal lands in Devon show only slight evidence of reorganisation.

The diverse methods of recording liability for the *feorm*, its varying reorganisation, and the liable units seldom being compact territories, make it hard to establish any secure connection between the Kingstons and the various liable land units, although there are hints, in parts of Ancient Wessex, that there could have been an association. Four of the seven Dorset Kingstons are sited in close association to manors dominated by *feorm* organisation. These are: Kingston (Lacy) with Wimborne Minster, Kingston (Winterborne) with Bere Regis, Kingston (Maurward) with (Fordington), and Kingston (Magna) with Gillingham. Lavelle is of the opinion that the Dorset estates as they appear in DB were almost certainly reorganised in the late Anglo-Saxon period, and are not cohesive enough territorially to represent the ancient units.[24] In Wiltshire none of the Kingstons show a connection with the *feorm*, neither were there any connections in Hampshire, Devon, Sussex or Berkshire. The sole inference that can be drawn safely from this late evidence is that there is a hint that four of the Dorset Kingstons might have had a role in the provisioning of the king in this way in the late Anglo-Saxon period. There is no evidence that they, or any of the other Kingstons, had such a rôle in earlier times.

Kingstons sited in an apparent direct relationship *villæ regales* named as such in the record

Five *villæ regales* that are described as such in the record, and from which charters were issued, have a Kingston sited immediately adjacent or close by. Although the precise nature of these relationships remains elusive it is, nevertheless, highly probable that a functional relationship of some kind was the case. Of these, Chippenham, Somerton, Taunton, and Dorchester are in Ancient Wessex; Wye, the fifth, is in Kent. It is worth exploring these in a little more detail.

Chippenham WLT is indisputably an important early Anglo-Saxon *villa regalis*. It is listed in the will of Alfred;[25] three charters of Æthelstan, his grandson, and a charter of Emund, were issued from here.[26] At DB it was held by the king both TRE and TRW, and was liable for the *feorm*. Haslam suggests that the topography of the town, with its market place, minster church, and enclosed and possibly fortified area for the royal residence, may date back to the eighth century.[27] Kington (St Michael) lies on the northern boundary of Chippenham.

[20] Stafford 1980: p. 491.
[21] Stafford 1980: p 494.
[22] Stafford 1980: p. 494.
[23] These are: Devon, Somerset, Dorset, Wiltshire, Hampshire, Sussex, Gloucestershire, Herefordshire, Shropshire, Cambridgeshire, Huntingdonshire and Suffolk.

[24] Lavelle 2007: p. 36.
[25] S 1507.
[26] S 405, S 422, S 423, S 473.
[27] Haslam 1984: pp. 132–136.

Somerton, also in Wiltshire, is first recorded in the *ASE* under the year 733 as *Sumur tūn*.[28] This is a tribal name, the OE *sumor* + *tūn*, 'summer settlement', the *tūn* of the *Sumortūn-sæte* 'the people who live at or who are dependent upon Somerton'.[29] It is from here that the shire takes its name. Notwithstanding its being a royal holding of undoubted importance, Anglo-Saxon Somerton differs markedly from Chippenham in that there is no evidence of an urban nucleus or indeed any proto-urban activity[30] Michael Aston sees Somerton as essentially a large agricultural holding that kings clearly liked to visit.[31] Several charters were issued from here and the Witan, the royal council, gathered here on at least one occasion.[32] At DB Somerton was held by the king TRE and TRW, and was liable for the *feorm*. Keinton Mandeville lies immediately adjacent to Somerton on the Fosse Way.

The third example is **Dorchester**, an important Romano-British town which John Blair (amongst others) suggests may have continued in use as a central place of importance right into the Anglo-Saxon period when its appearance in the record reveals it to be an important royal centre.[33] Of the four Dorset boroughs listed in DB it was the largest, and was held both TRE and TRW by the king. It had a mint, two moneyers, and was liable for the *feorm*. Kingston (Maurward) lies a mile from the east gate of the Roman town.

Of the five *villæ regales* in this group only Dorchester was a Roman settlement. Its neighbouring Kingston (Maurward/Stinsford) differs from the other Kingstons in this group, in that it is also part of a road/string system. Ecclesiastically, Kingston (Maurward/Stinsford) is a daughter of Fordington (the mother church of Stinsford), which lies immediately outside the east gate of Dorchester and which, Keene has suggested, is the site of the first Anglo-Saxon royal residence, not inside the walls of the Roman town as has generally been thought to have been the case (see chapter two).[34] If Keene is correct in his suggestion then the association of Kingston (Maurward/Stinsford) is more likely to have been with Fordington than Dorchester.

Taunton SOM, now the county town, is the fourth example of a known major *villa regalis* with a Kingston sited immediately adjacent. It enters the record for the first time in an enigmatic entry in the *ASE* for the year 722: 'Queen Æthelburh [King Ine's wife] threw down Taunton, which Ine built earlier'.[35] Taunton is the OE *tūn* 'estate', 'settlement', on the River Tone;[36] the evidence for its being an eminent Anglo-Saxon centre is considerable. Royal charters were issued from here,[37] and at DB it was held

both TRW and TRE and by the king. Kingston (St Mary) lies immediately adjacent to Taunton on the north.

Wye, the only one of this group that is found outside Wessex, is first recorded in 762 as 'the royal *villa regia* of Wye'.[38] The name, which is the OE *wīg*, *wēoh* 'a pagan shrine', might preserve the earlier British name of the River (Great) Stour the *Ụīsa*.[39] Three kings issued charters from here. The name, which derives from *Wiware*, the name of the local Anglo-Saxon tribal group, occurs in the phrase: *on Weowera wealde* 'the forest of the *Wiware*',[40] and *uueowera get* 'the gate [of] Canterbury] of the *Wiware*'. As late as 849 this term was still being used as the name of the gate.[41] Wye lies on the ancient route-way that crosses the North Downs; this is bisected by the Roman road from Canterbury to the Weald. At DB Wye was held both TRE and TRW by the king. There is a reference within the lathe to customary dues for carts, eels, yokes, and two escorts whose lands lay in Wye: 'Men from these lands guard the King at Canterbury or at Sandwich for three days if the king comes there'. Kennington lies next to Wye on the south-west on the Roman road from Canterbury to the Weald.

The primary connection of Kington (St Michael) Chippenham and Kingston (St Mary) Taunton appears to be with their neighbouring *villæ regales*, whereas Keinton (Mandeville) (SOM) and Kennington (Wye) (KNT) are adjacent to both their neighbouring royal centres, and also to Roman through-roads. There is no hint that Kennington (Wye) was part of a road/string system, but there is with Keinton (Mandeville) which lies on the Fosse Way with Kingstone (Ilminster), lying 20 miles to the south and on the Fosse Way.

This pattern can be seen at Wellesbourne WAR where Kineton lies adjacent to Wellesbourne with Kingston (Chesterton) located five miles away on the Fosse Way, but still within the bounds of the *villa regalis*. This estate of Wellesbourne, from which Berhtwulf (in 840) and Burgred (in 862) issued charters,[42] may represent a small early Anglo-Saxon petty kingdom.

Did these '*villæ regales*/adjacent-Kingstons' differ from Kingstons which stood adjacent to other clearly important central places, but which were not described expressly as *villæ regales*? Places such as Kingston (Lewes) SSX, Congerston (Bosworth) LEI and *Kingeston*/Wistow HNT appear in all essential respects to have been the same as, or similar to, the five royal estates discussed above. The mostly likely explanation is the custom and practice of the various scribes. How the road/string Kingstons compared with the Kingstons discussed above, is discussed below (this chapter).

---

[28] *ASC* A 733.
[29] *CDEPN* p. 559.
[30] Aston 1984: p.186.
[31] Aston 1984: p. 186.
[32] S 329, S 549, S 832a, S 1055, S 5119, S 1535.
[33] Blair 1999: p. 144.
[34] Keen 1984: pp. 206, 229.
[35] *ASC* (A), *ASC* (E) under the year 722.
[36] Watts 2004: p. 602.
[37] S 254, S 310, S 443.

[38] S 25.
[39] Watts 2004: p.706.
[40] S 1180.
[41] S 296.
[42] S 192, S 209.

Kingstons and small, early 'kingdoms'

There are two competing views with regard to the origins of the Anglo-Saxon kingdoms. One is that there was an almost complete breakdown of what had gone before, the other that there was a considerable degree of continuity. There are powerful arguments on both sides which need to be borne in mind, but the task here is small and specific. It is to take all the available evidence relating to the place-name Kingston and its context to uncover what it might reveal about the emerging political structures and organisation of early/mid-Anglo-Saxon England. By the time of Bede the major kingdoms of the seventh century were identifiable. He also recognised the smaller tribal units, petty kingdoms, which he referred to as *regiones* or *provinciæ*. It is from the fusion of theses tribal territories that in many areas of England the larger kingdoms emerged. It is clear from Bede that the processes of kingdom formation were still taking place as he wrote.

These tribal territories are listed in a remarkable document known the *Tribal Hidage*. It is written in OE, is of unknown origin, and could date from the seventh century. There is still considerable debate as to the date of this document and to whom the tributes were due. Its unique value is that many of the names listed are those of the minor tribal proto/petty-kingdoms.

There have been several attempts to map these territories, the most widely accepted is that drawn by Cyril Hart. This was used as the base of this simplified version of the map (Fig. 2) on which the seventh-century expanded kingdoms and the Kingston place-names have been superimposed.

Mapping the places listed in the Tribal Hidage document, and superimposing the seventh-century kingdoms and the Kingstons, shows six of the Kingstons lying in these putative early kingdoms. Although the evidence for this is admittedly scanty it is, nevertheless, worth exploring. If a pattern can be established which shows a close association between some Kingstons and early land units it offers the potential of unlocking the original purpose of places named Kingston.

The Stoppingas

Kington (Grange/Claverdon) WAR lies in the extensive *parochia* of Wootton Wawen, which Steven Bassett has shown to be broadly co-terminus with the territory of the early Anglo-Saxon proto-kingdom of the S*toppingas*.[43] The chief evidence for this is the foundation charter for the church at Wootton Wawen.[44] This charter, issued between 716 and 737 by Æthelbald, king of Mercia and the South Angles, relates to the foundation of a church *in regione quæ antiquitus nominator* 'in a *regione* known in antiquity

as *Stoppingas'*. Bassett offers three possible explanations for the presence of Kington (Grange/Claverdon) within this kingdom. The name might have been attached to a 'toe-hold' of once-royal land reserved by the king for himself after he had granted away the rest of the *villa regalis*; it could have been the site on the estate where the renders to the king were collected. Bassett thinks that it might have been the site of the royal residence, but in the light of recent research this now seems to be unlikely.

Kingestune *(Wistow)* HNT

Kingestune/Wistow presents an intriguing picture. The first reference is in a charter of King Edgar, issued in 974: *Kingeston id est Wistowe cum Raue*, and *Biri Berewycis* '*Kingestune* that is Wistow with the Berewicks of Raue and Bury'.[45] The charter may be spurious but the names are not in dispute. The element *wīc*, which is a loan word from the Latin *vicus*, is OE for 'dwelling', 'a building', 'a collection of buildings for special purposes'. For *stōw*, Smith offers, 'a place', 'a place of assembly', 'a holy place'. Generally, although not exclusively, its use seems to have been confined to special or noteworthy places.[46] A charter of 1062 from the King to Ramsey Abbey confirms a grant of land at *Kingeston cum Raffleya* and *Byri berewicis suis*, but with no reference to Wistow.[47] At DB, less than 20 years later, Wistow is listed, with a church and priest, which is what would be expected if Wistow was the central and most important place within a wider royal estate. If this was the case it is puzzling that Wistow was not mentioned in the charter of 1062; as late as 1253 there is one final reference to *Kingeston*, confirmation that the name was in use until at least that date. Although the references to *Kingestune* and Wistow are ambiguous, it can be said with confidence that in some way they were closely connected. The element *wicstow* 'a building/collection of buildings for special purposes', is a fitting description for the central place where the king's *aula* 'hall' would have stood on the *villa regalis*, with its associated site close by. Less than a mile north of Wistow there is a 'Kingsland Farm' could this be the site of *Kingestune*? At DB *Kingestune* is not listed but Wistow is, held TRW by Ramsey Abbey; no TRE information is given, but it is unlikely to have been any landowner other than the Abbey.

Kingeston/Wistow might have been the central place of one of the early Anglo-Saxon proto-kingdoms, listed in the Tribal Hidage and mentioned in Bede. It lies just south of the Wash in Huntingdonshire, where several other folk groups listed in the Tribal Hidage are thought to have been located. As already mentioned there have been several attempts to map these tribal peoples and their territories; there is broad agreement as to where the larger kingdoms with the highest assessments lay, but the position of the

---

[43] Bassett 2007: pp. 115–142. The name is either 'the people of the bucket-shaped hollow', which describes the natural topography of the district, or '*Stoppa*'s people'.
[44] S 94.

[45] S 798.
[46] Smith 1956: vol 2, p. 158-161.
[47] S 1030.

smaller kingdoms with lower assessments is less clear, particularly in the area south of the Wash.[48]

Kingestun/Wistow seems to be sited in the territory of the *Hurstingas*. East of this (putative) land unit lies the proposed territory of the tribal group the *Suð* 'south' *Gyrwe,*

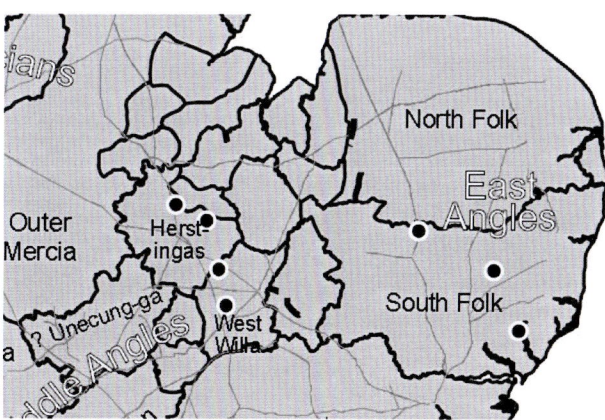

Figure 13: The territory of the *Hurstingas*: detail from Fig. 2 map of the Tribal Hidage.

Figure 11: The Hundred of Hurstington, Huntingdonshire. Robert Blome 1673/4.

Figure 12: The Hundred of Hurstington, Huntingdonshire with the georetrivication map of the outline of the Domesday Hundred superimposed as a red line.

known to Bede as the *Gyrwas*.[49] Bede records that in 660 a daughter of Anna, King of the East Angles, had been the wife of Tondbert, *princeps* of the South *Gyrwas*, before she married King Egfrid. Barbara Yorke suggests that Tondbert might have been a quasi-independent ruler who controlled a relatively small *provincia* or *regio* characteristic of the pre-kingdom Anglian, Saxon and Jutish confederations.[50] Was Wistow a kingdom similar to that of the North and South *Gyrwas*, with a royal residence and an adjacent *Cyningestune*? The Tribal Hidage assessment of the *Hurstingas* as 1,200 hides is the same as the combined hidage of the North and South *Gyrwas*.

Within Hurstington Hundred there is no candidate other than Wistow that could be the central place of the *villa regalis*. The traditional hundredal meeting place was Abbots Chair in the parish of Woodhurst, but this is unlikely to have been the site of the royal hall.

The Isle of Wight: The kingdom of the *Wihtgara*

A tentative suggestion, but worth consideration, is the possibility that the Kingston on the Isle of Wight served its Kingston function within the kingdom of the *Wihtgara*. There is indisputable evidence of an early Anglo-Saxon royal presence on the island. The *ASC* records that in the year 530, Cerdic and Cynric obtained possession of the island 'slaying many men at *Wihtgarabyrig*, the stronghold of the people of *Wiht*'.[51] This date is perhaps too early to inspire confidence in the reliability of this report, but later references can be trusted. The *ASC* A records for the year 661 that: 'Wulfhere, Pend's offspring raided on Wight putting it under the control of King Æthelwalh of the South Saxons'. The overlordship of the island then passed into the hands of King Cædwalla of Wessex who, with an act of ethnic cleansing, slaughtered the king, his brothers, and most of the inhabitants of the island 'replacing them by settlers from his own province'.[52] Barbara Yorke thinks that

---

[48] Courtney 1981: p. 92, Fig 6.1; Blome 1673.

[49] Bede iv 19.
[50] Yorke 2009: p. 91.
[51] *ASC* A 530.
[52] *HE* iv 16.

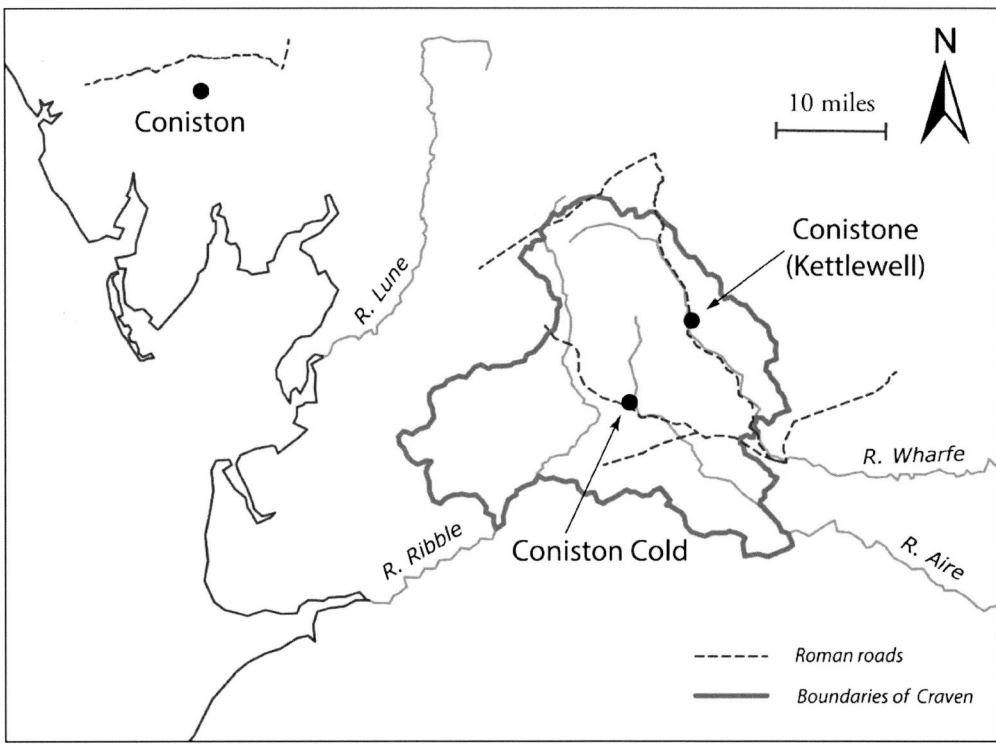

Figure 14: Kingstons in the Kingdom of Craven.

the island was a self-governing area of some significance before Cædwalla.[53] As noted above, the most likely royal central place on the island is in the Carisbrooke/Bowcombe area, with recent archaeological evidence confirming this.

(Market) Bosworth/Congerstone Leicestershire

Peter Foss has argued persuasively for Market Bosworth being the central place of a Mercian *villa regalis*.[54] He has defined the estate boundaries in the south-west as following the Roman Watling Street (M 57b), and the south-east as the Roman road, known as the Fenn Lanes, that ran south-west from Leicester to the small town of *Manduessedum* (Atherstone) on Watling Street. The northern boundary is less secure. Foss describes this territory as a 'discrete multiple (or composite) estate' with (Market) Bosworth as the central place with apendant areas/settlements at different locations within the estate lands, linked in significant interactive social and economic relationship to the focal point. Cox suggests that this putative royal estate may have developed subsequently into a 'small hundred' which was subsumed later into the Danish wapentake of Guthlaxton.[55] Foss sees Congerstone, which lies centrally in this estate two miles north-west of Market Bosworth, as possibly the place on the estate where royal food renders were gathered and where the reeve of the royal estate presided over the proceedings.

Conistone (Kettlewell) and Coniston (Cold) YOW

These two examples of the name Kingston, Scandinavianised to the OD *cung,* in the West Riding of Yorkshire, present hints of an earlier royal history. Both lie on major Roman roads within the Anglo-Saxon (and probably British) kingdom of Craven.[56]

The earliest reference for this kingdom is in DB where it is recorded as *Crave* or *Cravescire*, the name of a district that extended across the upper dales of the Rivers Wharfe, Ribble, and Aire. The towns of Settle, Skipton, and Keighley lie within it. It has been suggested that there might have been two separate shires within this kingdom, but their boundaries have not been identified satisfactorily. The presence within the kingdom of two Coniston(e)s might support this suggestion. *Craven* seems to have remained independent until the 670s, when it was subsumed into Northumbria under Kings Ecgfrith, and Ælwine.

Coniston (Kettlewell) is listed in DB under Land of the King's Thanes, giving it a royal connection. Conistone (Cold) is not listed. It is a chapelry of Burnside, neither of which present any evidence of their being significant central places. Little more can be said other than to note some similarities to the other Kingstons in this section that might have stood within small, early Kingdoms.

---

[53] Yorke 1989: p. 89.
[54] Peter Foss 1998: pp. 83–106 and Chapter 2 above).
[55] Cox 1971: p. 536.
[56] Wood 1990: pp. 1–20.

Kingston Kent: the Bourne people

Alan Everitt has described an early royal Jutish riverine estate in Kent, which he has identified as that of the 'Bourne' people Bourne being an early alternative name of the Little Stour river. This land unit comprised nine or ten parishes, four of which are still called Bourne.[57] Along with five, or perhaps six, others,[58] it has an area of about 21,000 acres, which is similar to that of Everitt's proposed Wimborne people in Dorset. Everitt sees Kingston as a subsidiary settlement of Patrixbourne which came to be called Kingston. He points out, however, that the place-name element *tün* was identifying a royal pasture farm and not a 'king's town or *villa regalis*'.[59] It is surprising that Everitt accepts, without further questioning, the place-name element *tun* as a suitable element for pasture land, although he is clearly puzzled by this. However, the telling point here is that he states categorically that although Kingston itself is not a *villa regalis* it lies next to the royal central place of Wickhambreaux towards the south-western boundary on the Dover to Canterbury Roman road which crossed the territory of the Bourne people. With the exception of Bridge, sited two miles further along the road to Canterbury, Kingston is the sole place sited on the road in a stretch of ten or eleven miles.

These six examples of Kingstons lying adjacent to the central places, where the king's hall might have stood, on a estates that present most of the defining characteristics of known *villæ regales*, but are not specifically described as such in the documentary record, appear to be, in almost every respect, the same kind of place. The cumulative evidence of both groups points convincingly to the Kingstons having a close association, and a specific function, within royal estates. In many ways, given an itinerate kingship and the *firma unius noctis*, this is not surprising; what is surprising, and heretofore unnoticed, is the close association, and pattern of distribution between some Kingstons and major Roman and ancient long-distance roads.

Kingstons: the road connection

After the shadow-chasing of the previous sections, it is something of a relief to return to the unexpected regular road/string distribution pattern of the Kingstons that emerged by the simple act of mapping them. They had been hiding in plain sight. By far the greater majority of road/string Kingstons are found in greater Wessex and the lower River Severn valley, although there are hints that this pattern might have been present elsewhere in England. The long-distance salt-ways do not appear to have been part of the system of which the road/string Kingstons were part, although the reasons for this are unclear. As already discussed, the Kingstons were connected in some way with the exercise of royal authority within the administrative

structure of a *villa regalis*, but the distribution pattern of the road/string Kingstons points to the possibility of a further purpose related to the control of the major roads within the kingdom.

At the time the Kingstons were founded, the roads on which they stood would still have been pronounced features in the landscape. It is all in the name. They were the 'high' ways, no doubt much decayed but still a serviceable resource to be exploited, particularly given the poor condition, especially during the winter months, the other trackways and footpaths would have been in.

The close connection between 70 per cent of the Kingstons and major Roman roads, and a further 15 per cent with Romanised ancient/long-distance routeways, is so pronounced that their condition needs further exploration. A short discussion on their likely condition after the end of the Roman administration is offered as a preliminary.

Anglo-Saxon settlement and the Roman road system

By the end of the first century the Romans had constructed a network of roads for military and commercial purposes, built to the highest standard of Roman road engineering, linking the military structures and towns of Roman Britain. The military roads, and those constructed for economic reasons associated with the post-conquest exploitation of Britain, were the most highly engineered and the most important. Branching off these roads were smaller roads and tracks, linking extensive rural settlements with the main arteries of Roman trade. This process included in some places the 'Romanisation' of ancient route-ways. Along much of its length the Icknield Way/Ridgeway is such a road. Kingstons Blount OXF, Lisle, and Winslow BRK lie on it.[60] The *Cursus Publicus*, the Roman imperial postal system, connected to the administration of the entire Roman Empire, was dependent upon this network of roads along which, at approximately ten mile intervals, there were *mutationes* 'horse-changing stations', and wayside *mansiones* 'travel-lodges', to service the officials who used the system. In addition to these official posting stations, a network of unofficial, unplanned settlements (archaeologically categorised as 'Roman small towns'), which were both urban and semi-urban, grew up along the roads. These settlements were informal and played no part in the official *mansione* system. Six Kingstons are sited adjacent to these Roman small towns (see below).

The road system appears to have functioned fully right up to the end of the Roman administration in the early decades of the fifth century. It seems that its end was abrupt, as was the systematic maintenance of the roads. There is almost no archaeological evidence to suggest that the roads continued to be maintained and the slight evidence there is, is hard,

---

[57] Littlebourne, Bekesbourne, Patrixbourne, Bishopsbourne.

[58] Wickhambreaux, Ickham, Bridge, Barham, Kingston, and probably Stodmarsh, together with parts of Denton and Wootton.

[59] Everitt 1986: pp. 79-83.

[60] The Icknield Way which begins near Wells next the Sea NFK runs via Swaffham, Newmarket, Luton and Goring, where it crosses the Thames. From here onwards it is known as The Ridgeway. After Goring it runs along the northern edge of the Berkshire Downs towards Swindon, Avebury and Salisbury Plain.

if not almost impossible to date.[61] The robust character of most of the roads, particularly the military roads, was such that, although they were much reduced from their former glory, the in-coming Anglo-Saxons would have found to be highly visible, and largely useable. Watling Street must still have been a major, recognised landmark in the later ninth century for it to have been used by King Alfred as the line of demarcation between Alfred's kingdom and the Danelaw. Perhaps he and Guthrum, the Viking leader, stood together somewhere on this road and made their agreement. Anne Cole has discovered evidence for the Roman roads south of York still being serviceable as late as the eleventh century.[62] David Pelteret is of the opinion that we can only make sense of the inter-tribal warfare of the Anglo-Saxons by hypothesising the existence and use of these roads.[63] They were convenient, ready-made structures for penetrating, controlling, and administering the countryside. The major roads would have stood at least a metre or more above the level of the surrounding country, some were even higher, as already mentioned recent excavations in Puddletown Forest DOR revealed a road would have stood at least three metres high in places. They were, literally, the 'high' ways, offered reliable, relatively speedy, and convenient access throughout the year.[64] The work of Barrie Cox on the early habitative place-name element *hām* in the Midlands and East Anglia, confirms that the Roman roads must have been obvious and serviceable. He sees the incomers largely from the east, arriving by boat, sailing up the rivers, and then using the roads they found waiting to penetrate further inland. The frequent occurrence of settlements containing the element *hām* lying within three miles of a Roman road adds strength to this proposition.[65] The founding of the Kingstons along many of these roads further evidences this.

The concept of the king's highway is found in all the early law codes, with wrong deeds done on these roads attracting more severe penalties than on others. Important as they were there is no trace in the documents of any requirement to repair roads then. The only evidence for any systematic use of them are the Kingstons. There are references to roads in the bounds of 13 seventh- and eighth-century royal charters; they are described variously as *via publica, strata publica, þeodweg,* and *folcesweg*).[66]

It would have been almost impossible to govern even a small kingdom without a system of communication. The day-to-day administration of an itinerant king and court, the collecting and recording of the produce of the *firma unius noctis*, and the application of the laws, would have been a massive undertaking, and all taking place with endemic warfare as the norm. The roads were essential. They would have been used daily by the king's riders, escorts, messengers, horses, baggage trains, pack and farm animals, the list is endless and would have had a punishing effect on the roads. There was of course the *trinodus necessitas* but that did not apply everywhere and was mainly related to bridge-work.

Pelteret's evidence demonstrates that the Roman roads not only formed the basis of the Anglo-Saxon road network, but were also used by the Vikings. By the ninth and tenth centuries many of the roads might not have been usable as such, but they would still have been recognisable earthworks that could be followed for miles across the landscape enabling the Vikings to gain control. It is Pelteret's view that the absence of these roads from articles and textbooks on Anglo-Saxon history lies, not in the paucity of the material, but in the failure to look for topographical explanations for significant political, social and cultural developments in Anglo-Saxon history. This Kingston research offers a response to these (justified) observations.

The 'road/string' distribution pattern

The mapping of this group of Kingstons revealed this strikingly distinct pattern of what appears to be deliberate triangulation in their positioning. Patterns of names emerge quite readily; the hard task is uncovering their significance.

The road/string pattern of Kingstons which lie between Badbury Rings in Dorset and east Devon is the most distinct example of this phenomenon. As already noted, for almost all of its length across the county this line is remarkably prominent, less so towards the west, largely because the underlying geology is different, making the line much more difficult to trace. This road is the 'spine' on to which Kingston (Deverill) in south-west Wiltshire and Kingston (Ringwood) in west Hampshire are aligned in what has to be a planned association. Kingston (Corfe) also looks as if it was also part of the pattern. Kingston (Hazelbury Bryan) completes the triangulation in the centre, holding them all together. To complete the Kingston system along the 'spine' to the west, two more Kingstons could be expected; one between Kingston (Russell) and Kingston (Colydon), and another to the east of Exeter. Kingston (Colydon) is sited at the point where the lower Fosse Way and the Dorset Roman road meet, and there are hints that the road/string system might have extended from Colyton up the Fosse Way to Keinton (Mandeville). The map of the lover Fosse Way shows this pattern clearly. There is no known historical reason to link north-east Warwickshire with Wessex, but a hint of this pattern can be seen further along the Fosse Way in Warwickshire.

[61] Taylor 1979: pp. 41–7; Nicholas Cooper of the School of Archaeology and Ancient History in the University of Leicester has been endlessly patient with my many queries relating to Roman Britain.
[62] Cole 2010: pp D, Phil. Thesis, Oxford and pers.comm.
[63] Pelteret 1999: p. 395.
[64] Pelteret 1999: p. 395.
[65] Cox 1971–1.
[66] Brooks: 2002, fn., p. 9. For the *via publica* in charter boundaries see S 100 AD 716 x 757 (Yeading MDX); S 165 AD 811, (Borstall KNT), S 262 AD 766 for 744 (on River Wellow SOM), S 268 AD 801 (Crux Easton MDX). For *strata publica* see S 9 AD 686 (Stodmarsh KNT); S 73 AD 681 (Long Newton WLT); Tetbury GLO); S 178 AD 815 (Faversham KNT); S 187 AD 823 (Canterbury KNT); S 1203 (Ham, Romney Marsh KNT); S 1209 AD 939 (Canterbury KNT); S 1266 AD 824 (Eythorne KNT); S 1267 AD 826 (Doddingland, Margate KNT); S 1288 AD ?905 or ?920 (*Wærincg mersc* KNT).

Figure 15: The location of the Dorset Kingstons and immediate neighbours, with the suggestion of triangulation in their planning.

The lower Severn Valley of six Kingstons sited along the lower Severn valley present a remarkable precision in its planning, as distinct as the Dorset system. This is essentially the southern region of the kingdom of the *Hwicce*. There is also a hint of planning in the territory of *Magonsæte* with the Kingstons sited on the western boundary.

The east and west bank Kingstons might have been connected via a ferry from Newnham to Arlington. The Romans had a ferry here and there are several medieval references to one. Further south there was a ferry from river from Aust to Beachley, close to where Offa's Dyke reaches the sea , and where Sedbury, one mile north of Beachley is the (presumed) site of a Kingston which lay in the parish of Tidenham.[67] The ferry at Aust was accessed by a Roman road that struck off west from the Gloucester to the Kings Weston road, mid-way between Kings Weston and Thornbury. This is a short crossing which saves at least 100 miles. Assuming that there was a ferry here, all these lower Severn valley Kingstons were linked together. It would not have been a surprise to find a Kingston at Newnham, nine miles from Kingston (Aylburton): none has come out of hiding in spite of serious searching but there is cause for optimism. Newnham itself is an intriguing name in this context, with the hint that it could have replaced an earlier name. Glimpses of other possible road/string systems can be made out in Sussex, Cambridgeshire and Huntingdonshire. There can really be very little doubt that these road/string configurations were planted in the landscape, on interdependent sites but not intervisible.

Kingstons and Roman small towns

Within the road/string patterns there is a sub-set of six Kingstons sited immediately next to, or possibly on, the site of what archaeologically, are defined as Roman small towns. If Kingston (Maurward Stinsford), lying outside the gates of the *civitas* capital of Dorchester, is included, they make up 10 per cent of the corpus. Roman small towns

were numerous, and more are being recognised now we know what to look for. Although they are usually found sited roughly ten miles or so apart, this distance is not fixed as is the distance between the official *mansiones* of the *cursus publicus*. They were informal settlements, not part of the Roman system of road administration, although there is some evidence that they may have been subject to some sort of official oversight. They were of varying size, unplanned in the main, without the public buildings of the larger towns and cities, with built structures made of wood. Stone is seldom found on these sites, although at Kingston (Chesterton) WAR a building interpreted as a gate-house, had stone footings, the earthworks of which can be seen clearly in the fields alongside the present line of the Fosse Way. West Kington WLT presents a similar pattern lying next to the small Roman town of Nettleton Scrubb on the Fosse Way. Excavations here have shown that this site began life as a Romano-British temple which, by the third century, had developed into a small town associated with the production of pewter. This site lies on a Romano-British tribal boundary.[68] Kinton (Leintwardine) HER lies next to *Bravonium*; Kingstone (Weston under Penyard) HER adjoins *Ariconium,* a centre both for iron production and the administration of the iron industry in the region. Kings Weston GLO lies beside the Roman port and small town of *Abonæ*, Kingston (Lacey) DOR is sited at *Vindocladia*, Badbury Rings, and Kingston (Maurward/Stinsford) DOR lie next to the *civitas* capital Dorchester.

This distribution pattern could have its own significance, but it the more likely explanation is that, within a system of places lying nine/ten miles distance apart, based on the Roman road system, these points will coincide on occasion. In addition there would have been milestones and various other Roman structures along the roads, presenting a ready-made foundation on which to base the Kingston road/string system.

---

[67] Rivet and Smith 1979: p. 177.

[68] De la Bedoyere 1991: p. 188.

Radmanni, radchenistri and carting obligations in Domesday England

Having established the close association of Kingstons with major Roman long-distance roads, the riding, escort, and carting duties, which are listed in some DB entries, suggest that there might be a Kingston connection. The five English shires of the Welsh border formed a distinct region with common features, which distinguished them from the other English shires. One of these distinguishing characteristics is the presence at DB of *radmanni, radchenistri*, radcaiit, 'riding men'. They are listed only in rural areas, and were closely connected with the cultivation of the soil. Although they were of free status and they all held land, most entries record that they also had manorial obligations. They are generally thought to have been an Anglo-Saxon institution, a particular type of *thegn*, that carried over into the new political and social structure of Norman Britain. Although here is no direct evidence, their location, and the nature of the society in which they were embedded, suggest they were a type of frontier militia rendering escort duties and messenger services for the king or lord. There was also a class of men known as *hevewarda*; these were bodyguards who had local obligations to guard the king when he passed through the region. They were the 'heavy gang', whereas the escorts would have been men of noble status, *thegns*, who accompanied king. There are also references in DB to *cartage avera*, the obligation to provide horses or mules for use by the king.

That the riding men were a frontier phenomenon is confirmed by there being only eight listed in DB on manors outside the frontier counties. Of these, seven are in Hampshire, on three manors, and one in Berkshire. Mapledurham in east Hampshire was one of these manors. It was held by the king TRW and by Wulfeva TRE. *Duo rachenistre* are listed here, 'they were not free to leave'.[69] In west Hampshire, one *radchenist* with half a plough is listed in DB under the entry for Ringwood, which was held TRW by the king and TRE by Earl Tosti.[70] The first element of Ringwood is the OE *rimuc*, 'an edge, border, boundary, ridge' + *wudu* 'wood', 'the boundary wood'. Both Ringwood and Mapledurham lie on boundaries. The Kingston sited in Ringwood lies at Watton's Ford right on the boundary. Ringwood, which is now an independent parish with chapelries of its own, was in origin part of the extensive *parochia* of Twynham (Christchurch), its neighbour on the south, where at DB '4 *radchenistri* with 2½ ploughs' are listed. Twynham was held both TRW and TRE by the king and was liable for the *firma unius noctis*. The eighth riding man is found in the manor of Goosey in Berkshire. Here at DB, 'one *racheneste* with his plough' was listed. The manor was held by Abingdon Church which 'had always held it'.[71] Goosey is a detached member of the Hundred of Marcham which is the DB hundred in which Kingston (Bagpuize) is sited. This link is so extended

and tenuous, it would seem unlikely that it holds any significance. The DB entries for these three manors offer no insight into the presence of the riding men. The location of the Hampshire examples are boundary parishes, but why so few in the whole of England. Twynham, Mapledurham and Ringwood were all in royal lands at DB, and the holdings of the church at Abingdon would of course have been in origin royal. Everitt has suggested that the Christchurch/Wimbourne (Minster) area was the core of an early small kingdom; these riding men may hark back to these earlier times.

Five Kingstons lie in manors where the DB entries make explicit reference to cartage, or escort duties. Four are found in frontier counties. At Kingstone (Thruxton) HRE, which was held by the king TRE, a wood, known as *Triueline*, lay within the manor and 'paid no customary dues except hunting rights, and the villagers who lived there before 1066 carried the produce of the hunt to Hereford [which lies five miles to the east] and did no other service, as the Shire states'.[72] At Leintwardine HRE, where there is a Kingston, there were two riders on the manor that was held TRE by the king. An additional note states: 'When the King left the City [Shrewsbury] the Sheriff sent him 24 horses from Leintwardine and the King took these as far as the first manor in Staffordshire'.[73] The DB entry for Thornbury GLO, lists 14 *radchenistre* holding 21 ploughs. There is a Kingston in this parish. Thornbury was held TRE by *Brictric*, a thane of King Edward. This is the same Brictric who also held Temple Guiting (a manor with a Kingston), where on two manors there were nine riding men. At Kingston CAM, the sole non-frontier example, on one of the six manors listed, there were 10 freemen who had to find '7 cartages and 3 escorts'. On all of these manors all the riding men had land to farm, free of dues. Presumably they worked their land until they were called upon to undertake their riding duties. The pattern of a distance of nine to ten miles between them is a classic distance for a fast ride on one horse before a change would be needed, suggests that the Kingstons could have been be connected with riding duties, although it has to be concluded that the DB evidence relating to riding men does not really add anything to our understanding of the Kingstons.

The Wessex bias is observable not only in the distribution of the road/string Kingstons, but also more generally, as can be seen clearly on the Base map (Fig. 1) Eighty per cent of the corpus of Kingston names lie in core Wessex, expanded Wessex, and the kingdoms of the *Hwicce* and *Magonsæte*. This is where the answer might be found. The road/string system does not have to have been devised in these regions, but the accumulated evidence to date indicates strongly that this is where it was developed.

---

[69] DBHa. 1, 8.
[70] DBHa. 1, 30.
[71] DBBrk. 7, 23.

[72] DBHe 1,3.
[73] DBSa: C10. The Leintwardine DB entry is listed in the Shropshire folios (DBHe ES 1 C 10). They were later transferred to the county of Herefordshire.

Expanded Wessex: origins and chronology of the kingdom of Wessex and its kings

The name alone is evidence that Kingstons were royal in conception; only a king would have the power to impose such a comprehensive system of control across such a far reaching land area. An investigation of the infrequent occurrence of the name in counties north and east of Watling Street, and its total absence in others, might help tease out the answers.

Of all the names in the corpus 33 per cent are found in the 'core' lands of ancient Wessex – Dorset, Hampshire, Wiltshire, Somerset and Devon. A further 13 per cent lie in counties with which Wessex had close pre-seventh-century tenurial links – Berkshire, Surrey, and Oxfordshire. Another nine per cent are found in the counties over which Wessex had established dominion by the later years of the seventh century – Sussex and Kent, bringing the total number of Kingstons in this group to 55 per cent.

What shift in the political landscape brought about such a preponderance of Kingston names south and south-west of the Thames. Does the early history of the Anglo-Saxon tribal group the *Gewisse*, and the expansion of their kingdom of Wessex from the early sixth to eighth centuries, hold the key? Reliable written sources are virtually absent until the mid-seventh century at the earliest, after which the establishment of religious houses and their written records led to a gradual increase in documentation.[74] The major documentary sources for this period are the *Anglo-Saxon Chronicle* and Bede, both of which present problems of interpretation and chronology. There is also other source material which can be flimsy and often opaque but we must be grateful for the testimony of these resources as they provide a framework of events and other information around which other evidence can be constructed, and we would be lost without them.[75] All this early material has to be used with caution. Barbara Yorke reminds us that the *Anglo-Saxon Chronicle* recounts how the West Saxons of the ninth century saw, or wished to see, themselves and the origins of their kingdom, not necessarily how it actually was.[76] Bede, who unfortunately for us had little information about Wessex, nevertheless records that the West Saxons were 'anciently known as the *Gewisse*'.[77] A small enough point, but without which there is no other way we would have known this. Archaeological evidence is always patchy, particularly for this early period, but enough has emerged to confirm that the upper Thames valley, the Cotswolds, and possibly northern Hampshire were the sixth-and early seventh-century heartlands of this group, whose military conquests eventually brought political unity and a common institutional framework to Wessex.[78]

Documentary references for Wessex

The earliest reference is in the *ASC* **A 556** which states: 'Cynric and Ceawlin fought against the Britons at Barbury [WLT]. Cynric and Cerdic landed on the Hampshire coast, conquering all the surrounding area and the Isle of Wight'. This account conflicts with Bede, who claims that the Isle of Wight and the Hampshire coast opposite were settled by Jutes.[79] 'Ceawlin succeeded to the kingdom in Wessex', *ASC* **A 560**. His reign was long. The claim that he reigned for 32 years from 560 to 592, is regarded as essentially reliable. He and his brother Cuthwulf made conquests in Gloucestershire, where seven Kingstons are found, and Somerset, where there are four Kingstons. Ceawlin, and his brother Cutha were also active in Kent. The *ASC* **A 568** records: 'Ceawlin and Cutha [his brother] fought against Æthelberht [King of Kent] and drove him in flight into Kent'.[80] Presumably Æthelbert, had been pushing westwards outside the boundaries of his own kingdom. *ASC* **A 571**: Cuthwulf fought against the Britons at *Biedcanford* [unidentified] and took 4 *tunas* 'major settlements' Limbury, Aylesbury, Benson, and Eynsham; and in the same year he passed away.

ASC **A 577**: Cuthwine and Ceawlin fought against the Britons, and they killed 3 kings'…in the place that is called Dyrham' [Gloucestershire], 'and they captured three of their *cæstro* [cities], Gloucester, Cirencester and Bath'.

Caroline Heighway notes that the earliest Anglo-Saxons to the west of the Severn in Shropshire and Herefordshire, were late arrivals, with the Anglo-Saxon presence in that area dating from the 577 battle, the first recorded occasion of an approach to the British lands in the west.[81] Dyrham, a high point from where the Severn valley can be seen, lies five miles west of the Fosse Way. West Kington WLT lies on the Fosse Way, four miles east of Dyrham. The three *cæstro* lay in the territory of the *Hwicce*, where 12 Kingstons lie.[82] This was now open for the invaders to separate the 'North' Welsh from the 'West' Welsh.[83] The general consensus is that the valley of the lower Severn first came into English possession as a result of Ceawlin's victory at Dyrham. It is worth highlighting at this point that the origins of the road/string Kingstons could reach back this far, as Ceawlin and his successors held this country for 50 years until 628, when it seems that an 'agreement' (almost certainly a defeat) was made between Cynegils of Wessex and Penda, which led to Penda gaining Cirencester and the lands along the Severn.[84] Five years later, Penda became king of the Mercians. These 50 years are a blank are about which almost nothing is known. The Gewisseans and the Hwicceans were wrestling with the same problem

[74] Dumville 1985a: pp. 21–66.
[75] Yorke 1999: pp. 25–29.
[76] Yorke 1989: p. 84.
[77] *HE* 3 vii.
[78] Yorke 1995: p. 52.

[79] *HE* i, 15.
[80] The dates for Æthelberht of Kent are uncertain: death in 616 is secure but his birth not so. It may have been as early as 560 or as late as 590.
[81] Heighway 1989: p. 172.
[82] Sims-Williams, amongst others, is of the opinion that this event probably took place much later and was attributed subsequently to 577.
[83] Swanton 1996: p. 19 fn15.
[84] Stenton 1971: pp. 44–5.

−the take-over of the British kingdoms. Might they have cooperated in some way? If they did it would have to have been before the rise and dominance of Mercia.

ASC **A 584**: 'Ceawlin and Cutha fought against the Britons at the place which is named Battle Wood [this is *Fethanleagh*, a lost name in Stoke Lyne, OXF], and Cutha was killed; and Ceawlin took many towns and countless war-loot, and in anger turned away into his own territory'. *ASC* **A 592**: 'Here there was a great slaughter at Woden's barrow [Alton Priors WLT], and Ceawlin was driven out'.[85] *ASC* **A 593**: 'Ceawlin, Cwichelm and Crida perished'. <u>Bede</u> *HE* Ch. 5 records that 'Ceawlin was the second king to hold sway over all the provinces south of the river Humber'. *ASC* **A 597**: 'Ceolwulf began to rule in Wessex, and he continually fought against the Angle race, or against the Welsh, or against the Picts, or against the Scots'. It may have been Ceolwulf who fought King Meurig of Gwent at Tintern. This was when Oudoceus was bishop of Llandaff.[86] *ASC* **A 607**: 'Ceowulf fought against the South Saxons'.

ASC **A 611**: 'Cynegils succeeded to the kingdom in Wessex and held it 31 years'. *ASC* **A 614**: 'Cynegils and Cwichelm [his son] fought on *Beandun* [Bea's Mount, unidentified] and killed 2 thousand and 65 Welsh'.

From Cynegils onward we are on safer ground. Literate clerics recorded events with an accuracy which means that most dates are reliable to within a year or two. West Saxon history can, therefore, be dated with greater certainty from this point.[87] The processes that led to the *Gewissæ* becoming one people seem to have begun by the time of Cynegils. These early kings recorded in the Chronicle must represent, in the main, the ramified descendants of an earlier royal kin group from which petty kings emerged: some through inheritance, some by agreement, even election; others almost certainly through murder and battle. Cynegils was baptised in 635 with Dorchester as the seat of the bishop, and the *Gewisse* 'joined the European club of civilised peoples'.[88] West Saxon territory now extended across Oxfordshire, north Berkshire, Wiltshire, Dorset and north Hampshire; ten Kingstons are sited within this territory.

This new political order, so recently achieved, was short-lived. There was rivalry between the *Gewissæ* and the British, and with the Mercians under Penda, for territory in Gloucestershire and the Severn valley, an area in which seven Kingstons are found. In 628, Cynegils and Cwichelm fought an inconclusive battle at Cirencester against Penda, after which, 'they came to terms'. *ASC* **A 628**. Barbara Yorke presumes that the terms favoured Mercia as it was they who went on to overrun the territory of the *Hwicce*, a hybrid group whose territory is broadly represented by Worcestershire, Gloucestershire and Warwickshire. *Hwiccian* land had passed from the West Saxons to Mercia.[89] The loss of their lands north of the Thames and Avon, probably taken by Ceawlin in 577, caused the Wessex kings to adopt a more southerly focus, and driving them into alliances with other enemies of the Mercians. The *ASC* **A 643** records that 'Cenwalh succeeded [Cynegils] to the kingdom of the West Saxons, and held it 31 years, and ordered the church at Winchester to be built'. By 645 (*ASC* **A 645**) Cenwalh had been driven out by Penda into exile into the kingdom of the East Angles, leaving Cuthred, a kinsman, to act as a sub-king under Penda during the three years of his banishment. On his return in 648 Cenwalh made a grant to Cuthred of 3,000 hides of land, the size of a small kingdom, near Ashdown BRK.[90] Kingston (Lisle), Kingston (Winslow), Kingston (Bagpuize), and possibly Kennington, all lie within this territory. It was at Wantage, within this territory that Alfred the Great was born.

Cenwalh continued his advance to the south west. The *ASC* **A 658** records: 'Cenwalh fought against the Welsh at *Peonnum* and drove them in flight as far as the [River] Parret in Somerset'. At that time, the Parret, which crosses the Somerset wetlands, was a major physical obstacle and boundary. The precise location of the battle is not known. Barbara Yorke is of the opinion that on balance the most likely site is Penselwood 'the head of Selwood', close to the meeting point of the boundaries of Wiltshire, Dorset, and Somerset.[91] This is the same place where, in 1016, a major battle between Edmund Ironside and the Vikings was fought. The *ASC* **A 661** records Cenwalh fighting again: 'At Easter [Cenwalh] fought at Posent's stronghold; and Wulfhere, Penda's offspring raided as far as Ashdown and on Wight, and gave the inhabitants of Wight to Æthelwald, king of the South Saxons'. Posent's *byrg'* 'stronghold', has yet to be identified securely. Posbury in Devon and Pontesbury south-west of Shrewsbury have been suggested as possible candidates.[92] In 660 Cenwalh divided the kingdom into two dioceses. The West Saxon see was transferred from Dorchester on Thames to Winchester, where he built a new minster.[93] This move was most probably brought about by the southward expansion of Mercia, leaving Dorchester exposed and vulnerable on the north side of the Thames. The *ASC* **A 672** entry records: 'Cenwalh passed away', after a lifetime of fighting on all fronts.

There is no doubt that Cenwalh was a major leader who wielded aggressive power and influence, and upon whose achievements his successors would be able build. He created a personal hegemony which, for reasons that are not clear, was not transmitted to a sole successor. His power and influence must have been remarkable as, for a year after his death, in what was almost certainly an unprecedented move, his widow, Seaxburh, ruled for one year after his death. For the following nine years, as Bede

---

[85] This tumulus, now known as Adam's Grave, at Alton Priors WLT, is a prominent long barrow on the north downland of the Vale of Pewsey, close to the Wandsdyke.

[86] *Liber Landavensis*, Ch. 4 sec 3, referenced in Walters 1992: pp. 124–5.

[87] Dumville 1985: p.x.

[88] Blair 1994: p. 41.

[89] Yorke 1995: p. 57.

[90] *ASC* A 648.

[91] Yorke 1995: p. 53 and fn7.

[92] Swanton 1997: fn. 6, p. 32.

[93] *HE* iii, 7.

notes: 'sub-kings divided up the kingdom and ruled the various parts'.[94] We know the names of two, possibly three, of these sub-kings. Æscwine, ruled for some of these years, followed by Centwine,[95] who Barbara Yorke thinks may have been powerful enough to suppress the under-kings.[96] There is also the possibility that Cenred, King Ine's father, more of which below, was one. Sawyer considers that Bede under-records multiple kingship and that it was common, almost the norm, in the seventh century. He interprets the multiplicity of kings as revealed in the *ASC* as an indication that there were probably several kingdoms, each with their own 'royal' families, who were probably of the same kin, and had the same forebears.[97] These provinces, or small kingdoms, were almost certainly the later shires of Wessex, and it was not until the later seventh and early eighth centuries that overlordship was ever held for long by any one of the constituent dynasties. Although the record is patchy, it can be seen that as the seventh century advanced there was a gradual coming together of the sub-kingdoms of the West Saxons, but there was still much to be done.

The *ASC* A 685 records: '*Cædwalla* began to contend for the kingdom'. Cædwalla, son of Cenberht, a (presumed) sub-king under Cenwealh, emerged as king after a period of exile in the weald of Surrey, and Sussex. His exile must have been associated with the ten unstable years that followed the death of Cenwalh. He seems to have burst on the scene, from nowhere we can identify, and began to wage war against the rulers of Kent, Surrey, and Sussex, to bring them under his overlordship.

His reign was short, just two years, but his impact was huge. With his brother Mul, he 'ravaged Kent and [the Isle of] Wight', killing the males of the royal house, seizing them from Wulfhere (son of Penda) of Mercia who, after overpowering them in 661, had given them to Æthelwealh, king of the South Saxons, along with the Jutish territory of the *Meonwara*, on the mainland opposite the Isle of Wight in south Hampshire.[98] Cædwalla granted 600 hides on the island to Wilfred (later Saint). Æthelwealh had military ambitions towards Kent which he may already have held under Wulfhere.[99] Cædwalla thwarted these ambitions. He killed Æthelwealh, established control over Kent, and put his own brother Mul on the throne. The following year, as a result of an uprising in Kent, Mul and his men were killed. Cædwalla attacked Kent and was, again, successful. In the last weeks of his reign, although still a pagan, Cædwalla granted sixty hides at Farnham SUR for the building of a minster,[100] evidence that Surrey, or at least this south-western part, was under Cædwalla's control: he must have recaptured it from Æthelred, Wulfhere's successor.

It is unlikely that he recovered all the original *Gwissean* lands as Surrey was frequently passed from one lordship to another in these years, as had neighbouring Berkshire.[101] These were the 'debateable lands' so frequently did this happen. The original extensive *parochia* of Farnham is probably represented by the 60 hide land grant. Kingston (Seale), adjacent to Farnham on the east, is an ecclesiastical daughter of Farnham. Bede records that when Cædwalla abdicated in 688 he had 'ruled the West Saxons most ably for two years, having lived for about thirty years'.[102] He went to Rome where, within days of his arrival he was baptised, dying a few days later still wrapped in his baptismal robes. He had launched the Wessex domination of Kent, Sussex, Wight and the Jutish parts of Hampshire, thereby giving the West Saxons direct access to the sea, but the original tribal lands remained still in Mercian hands. This scene was now set for Ine to step centre stage.

The major events of the reign of Ine of Wessex 688–726

Ine, successor to Cædwalla, is considered by Stenton to have been the most important king of Wessex between Ceawlin and Egbert; he is also the first true king of Wessex. His name is a diminutive of a longer name, probably Cenwine or Cuthwine, the latter, it has been suggested, might have been the brother of (St) Aldhelm who Ine appointed as the first bishop of Selwood. [103] Little is known about his background. Bede has little to say, mentioning only that he was 'of the blood royal' and that he held the province of the South Saxons in subjection for several years.[104] Early sources agree that Ine was the son of Cenred, a sub-king of Wessex, probably one of the petty kings noted above, who had ruled during the ten years following the death of Cenwealh. Cenred appears in several spurious charters, described in some of them as *rex*.[105] In a charter of 670, which is generally considered to be authentic, he granted 30 hides of land at Fontmell Brook, Dorset, to Abbot Bectun, a hint perhaps that Dorset might have been his territory, although this is not one of the charters in which he is described as *rex*.[106] Ine had a brother Ingild (an ancestor of King Alfred), and sisters Cwenburg and Cuthburg, the latter had been wife Aldfrith king of Northumbria, and for whom Ine founded a convent at Wimborne Minster when the marriage ended. Cenred was still alive when Ine drew up his law code (see below), in the prologue he acknowledges his father's advice. Perhaps they even reigned jointly for a time. Although multiple kings occur frequently in early Wessex there is no other English parallel to that of Ine and his father, a confirmation that kingship in Wessex was personal, not hereditary.

Ine inherited a kingdom which extended into Sussex and Kent. It did not include the *Gewissæn* heartlands which Ine was never able to regain. He must have made peace with

---

[94] Kirby 1991: pp. 50-51.
[95] Centwine, described as Saxonum Rex, issued an authentic charter in 682 of land near Quantock Wood and at *Crycbeorh* (probably Creechbarrow Hill). S 237.
[96] Yorke 1995: p. 82.
[97] Sawyer 1978: pp. 48–9.
[98] *HE* iv, 16.
[99] Wulfhere of Mercia had already granted the provinces of the Isle of Wight and the *Meonwara* to Æthelwalh.
[100] S 235.

[101] Stenton 1934: p. xv.
[102] *HE* v, 7.
[103] 560-92, or 571 (or 581)–88; Stenton 1971: pp. 71–73.
[104] *HE*: v, 7.
[105] Attenborough 1922: p. 183.
[106] S 1164.

Kent, as in 694, Wihtred, King of Kent, paid the *wergild* owing for Cædwalla's brother Mul who had been murdered during the Kentish rebellion of 697. There must also have been a considerable degree of co-operation as the respective laws of both kings mirror each other in large part.

In 674, Wulfhere, king of Mercia, confirmed at Thame a 672 charter of Frithuwold, *subregulus* of Surrey, confirming a date after which Surrey must have come into West Saxon hands.[107] This charter granted to Bishop Erconwald and to St Peter's, Chertsey, 200 hides at Chertsey, Thorpe, with 10 hides by the Port of London. This latter grant gave Ine a land-holding of prime importance, well beyond the core lands of his kingdom. The London connection is confirmed further by Ine's acknowledgement in the prologue to his laws of the advice of Erconwald Bishop of London whom he calls 'my bishop'. The diocese of London was transferred to Winchester in 705, and Ine founded a second West Saxon bishopric at Sherborne, to serve the lands west of Selwood forest. Ine's control of Surrey is confirmed further by a papal privilege of 708 (x 715)0, which locates the Surrey minsters of Bermondsey and Woking '*in provincium West Saxonum*'.[108]

Bede records that Ine held Sussex in subjection for 'several years' and yet, when Ine exiled the ætheling Ealdberht, he sought refuge in Surrey and Sussex (probably the Weald), after which Ine 'fought the South Saxons again'.[109] This would seem to suggest that Ine's control over these territories must have been partial. Subsequently Ine invaded Sussex yet again, this time killing Ealdberht. Ine's relationship with Sussex was complicated, muddied perhaps by kin connections. In 692 a charter of Nunna, described as 'King of Sussex', is witnessed by *Coenredus* described as *rex Westsaxonum* and also by Ine, with no designation.[110] In spite of the sporadic warfare between Ine and Nunna, they are recorded as campaigning together in the west against the British kingdom of Dumnonia: 'Ine and Nunna, his relative, fought against Geraint, king of the Welsh'. These are the West Welsh of Devon and Cornwall.[111] Ine advanced down the south-western peninsula, pushing back the boundary of the kingdom of Dumnonia as far as the River Hale in Cornwall where his campaign failed. He withdrew and seems not to have tried again.[112] The River Tamar was now the furthest extent of his kingdom in the south-west.

Ine's next appearance in the record is in 715, where the *ASC* A records: 'Ine and Ceolred [of Mercia] fought at Woden's Barrow' [Wiltshire], which is where Ceawlin had been defeated by the Mercians in 592. There are indications in the record that during the final years of Ine's reign there

was internal unrest and dissention. In 721 he killed the ætheling Cynewulf, and in 722 the *ASC* **A 722** records an enigmatic event that could be interpreted as evidence of turbulence within the ruling family: 'Queen Æthelburg [wife of Ine] threw down Taunton which Ine built earlier'. Presumably these were fortifications, a burh, she destroyed. The implications of this incident are intriguing, but at least it provides us with a *terminus post quem* for the foundation of Taunton, and by association perhaps for Kingston (St Mary) which lies next to Taunton in the north.

The law codes of Ine and the governance of the kingdom

The date that Ine began to formulate his law code falls in all probability between 688, the year he became king, and 694. If it was the earlier date, the swiftness of the move suggests that he had begun his planning before he acceded the throne. In the preamble to his laws Ine states:

> I, Ine, by the grace of God king of Wessex, with the advice and instruction of Cenred, my father, of Hedde, my bishop, and of Erconwald, my bishop, and with all my *ealdormen* and the chief councilors of my people, and with great concourse of the servants of God..., so that no *ealdorman* nor subject of ours may from henceforth pervert these our decrees.[113]

The observed changes of Ine's reign indicate that he was a strategic thinker who understood the importance of strong law and order in the achievement of peace, unity and, presumably, prosperity to his kingdom. The publication of the code of laws would have been a powerful instrument in the support and creation of a single, structured and governable kingdom, and a sound basis for further expansion.[114] The law code was completed by 694 at the latest, and in the following year the law code of King Wihtred of Kent appeared. Some of the laws in the two codes are similar, some even identical, pointing to communication, even co-operation, between the two kingdoms. The motivation for this alliance might have been, at least in part, to present a united front against Mercian expansion into southern England. For Ine, there would have been the additional benefit of now being able to concentrate on his westward campaigns without fear of attack from the east.

It is in Ine's laws that the first reference to ealdormen and their shires appears; these were almost certainly the petty kings, the *sub-reguli* of sixth- and seventh-century Wessex who never again appear in the record.[115] The prologue to the laws states that the just laws and just decrees had been

---

[107] S 1165.

[108] Birch 1885–1893: vol. 1, pp. 196–7, no. 133.

[109] *HE*: iv 16; *ASC* A 722; *ASC* A 725.

[110] S 45.

[111] *ASC* A 710.

[112] The *Annales Cambriae* record three battles in 722, the River Hayle in Cornwall, the battle of Garth Maelog and the battle of Pencon 'among the south Britons', and notes that the British were victorious in all three. None of these are mentioned in English records.

[113] Attenborough 1922: p. 37.

[114] Loyn, 1960: p.81. xxx Loyn summarises this as follows, 'Kings were not motivated by an innate sense of justice and a desire for orderly government; they were primarily interested in a strong law and order because it brought peace and unity to their realm, gave them military strength, and produced a steady flow of income into the royal chamber.'

[115] Laws of Ine. The prologue refers to 'my ealdormen'. Chap 8, 'If anyone demands justice in the presence of any 'shireman' or of another judge...'A shireman is presumably an ealdorman. Keynes in BEASE, pp. 420–22.

established and ensured throughout the nation, 'so that no *ealdorman* nor subject of ours may from henceforth pervert these our decrees'.[116] There was now only one king in Wessex. Barbara Yorke, who describes the creation of the ealdormen 'as the fate of lesser kings',[117] is of the opinion that the office of ealdorman was a carefully created invention by Ine, and that it was he who was almost certainly responsible for the division of Wessex into the shires of Hampshire, Wiltshire, Dorset, Somerset and Devon. The present-day county boundaries follow broadly those of the seventh-century shires, which in turn may, in large part, reflect earlier land units.[118]

The laws reveal that Ine supported, and sought the support of the church. Thirteen charters promulgated by Ine survive, 11 of which relate to the founding and support of minsters.[119] The nunnery he founded at Wimborne (Minster) DOR on a pre-existing Roman structure, probably a villa, was newly created for his sister, Cuthburh, (*ASC* **A 718**). This marriage to the ruler of a major kingdom underlines the status of Ine's family. The division in 705 of the bishopric into Winchester and Selwood, and his subsuming of the bishoprics of Sussex and the Isle of Wight, further confirms Ine's power, and strategic mind.

The foundation of Hamwīc

The other notable national development that dates from Ine's reign was the development in the late seventh/early eighth centuries of trading emporia that began to develop along the east and south coasts of England. They arose as a response to commercial growth in north-western continental Europe, fuelled by the state-building ambitions of eighth-century kings to accumulate wealth by taking control of, and increasing the trade in, high prestige, often exotic, goods. Blair notes that by *c*700 each of the four dominant kingdoms had a major port or *wīc*:[120] *Lunden wīc* London for Mercia, *Yppeswic* Ipswich for East Anglia, *Eoforwīc* York for Northumbria and *Hamwīc* for Wessex on the west bank of the River Itchen. The siting of a trading centre on the Solent demonstrates the confidence of the West Saxons that they had complete control over southern Hampshire, perhaps even all of the shire, and the Isle of Wight. Although there is no direct evidence linking Ine to *Hamwīc* it is unlikely, particularly in the light of the recently revised date of the settlement at *Hamwīc*, that he was not the instigator of the venture. There are no other candidates. The creation of a planned hundred-acre development, with a population of over 5,000, on a site with no previous occupation, could only have come into being with royal command. Since the 1940s there have been several large-scale excavations on this site, making *Hamwīc* probably the best understood of the English *wīc*s. All the excavations have dated the foundation of the trading centre to the early years of the eighth century.

However, more recent excavations undertaken between 1998 and 2000, prior to the building of a new stand at the Southampton football club, have revised the date of the inception of *Hamwīc* to the earlier date of the final years of the seventh century, a date similar to those of London and Ipswich. A cemetery was excavated which contained a high proportion of exceptionally richly-furnished graves, many with high-status weapons, with several graves having more than one weapon, and one with four. Many graves contained gold objects and pieces of fine, intricate jewellery. Both Alan Morton and Helena Hamerow have suggested that these graves could have been associated with the ruling dynasty who founded *Hamwīc*, and that the founder, because of the secure dating sequences, must have been Ine.[121] All the artefactual evidence corroborates the earlier dates, placing the cemetery at the foundation of the settlement. The cemetery, and the adjacent domestic site on the north-eastern edge of the *wīc,* might have been associated with a (proposed) late seventh-/early eighth-century *villa regalis* that had either been newly established close to the trading centre but separate from it, or it might have been in existence prior to the foundation of *Hamwīc*. Could it have been the periodically used residence of the itinerant king?[122]

The archaeology of this site is subtly different, both in layout and surviving material from the rest of *Hamwīc*. The current consensus is that *Hamwīc*, with its grid pattern of gravelled, well-maintained streets, planned from its inception, points to an overall controlling authority. The increased political stability of Ine's long reign would have offered a secure environment where a population, which may have been as many as 5,000 artisans and traders, could thrive. Hodges, writing before the football stadium excavations in 2000, had already stated that *Hamwīc* was almost certainly a reflection of Ine's personal status.[123] The names *Hamwīc* and *Hamtūn*, which co-existed throughout the life of the settlement, probably reflect the differing functions of trade and administration, and may have applied not just to the settlement but to the whole peninsula.[124] Hodges suggests that, strictly speaking, *Hamtūn* should prevail as that is how the West Saxons would have referred to it, whereas *Hamwīc* was the seldom-used Carolingian name for the settlement.[125]

Ine abdicated the throne in 726 to go on pilgrimage to Rome, as his predecessor Cædwalla had done before him. As far as we can tell, as was the case with Cædwalla, Ine does not appear to have recovered the ancestral *Gewissean* lands in the upper Thames valley; nonetheless he left a politically highly developed kingdom which stretched south from the Thames and Avon, and west from the borders of Kent to the Tamar.

---

[116] Laws of Ine, prologue.
[117] Yorke 1999: p. 251–2.
[118] Laws of Ine 36.1: 'If he is an ealdorman he shall forfeit his shire'.
[119] See Appendix 1, this volume, for details of these charters.
[120] Blair 2001 p. 451.

[121] Hamerow 2004: *British Archaeology* 54; Alan Morton, Southampton City Senior Planning Archaeologist, pers. comm.
[122] Hamerow 2002: *British Archaeology* 66.
[123] Hodges 1982: p. 44.
[124] Rumble cc: xx.
[125] Hodges 1989: pp. 67–9.

If the Kingstons formed part of a network of administrative sites within Wessex, how did they fit into that kingdom's evolution? Their spread and their planned siting points to a period in the history of the kingdom when there was a strategic guiding hand at the helm, a hand sufficiently strong to implement the rolling out of an extended system of Kingstons, all performing the same, or similar functions. This might not have been implemented and driven by one king. It might have been a much wider movement reflecting the changing nature of kings and their kingdoms. As they became more powerful and wealthy, they would have needed a more sophisticated system of management (Chapter 5).

Kingstons Sited in the Severn Valley and the West Midlands

The 17 Kingstons which lie in this region comprise 25 per cent of all Kingston-names; 12 are found in the territory of the *Hwicce*, four in the territory of the *Magonsæte*. One,

Kinton, lies just over the boundary into Shropshire, close to the north bank of the River Severn, in the territory of the *Wrocensæte*. It is uncertain in which kingdom Kingstone STF lay prior to its becoming part of Mercia. This group, together with the 55 cent of Kingstons in Greater Wessex, accounts for over 80 per cent of all Kingston names.

The Hwicce and the Magonsæte

The Hwicce

There is precious little evidence as to the origins of these people; their name is unclear and no king-lists or genealogies survive. The balance of probabilities is that they are the *Hwicna*, a tribal group assessed at 7,000 hides in the Tribal Hidage. They may have been an amalgamation of several small tribes, possibly of both Angles and Saxons, who moved into territory they had conquered from the Britons and who came together under the ruler of one of them, the leader of the *Hwicce* perhaps, whose territory was centred

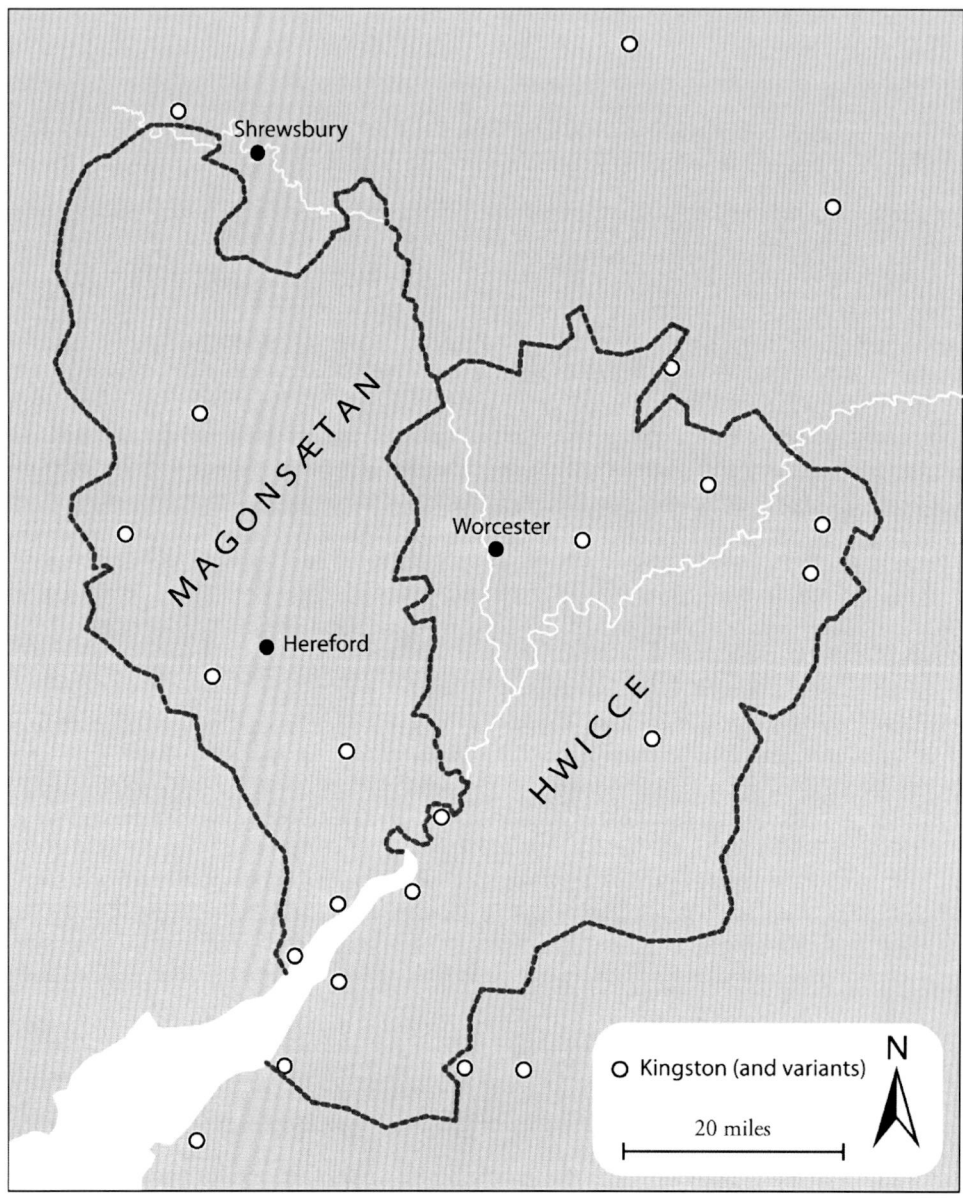

Figure 16: The territories of the *Hwicce* and the *Magonsæte*.

on Winchcombe GLO.[126] Della Hooke considers that they evolved out of the territory of the late Iron Age tribal group the *Dobunni* and that their focus of rule may have been forced northwards from Cirencester by pressure from the West Saxons in the later years of the sixth century.[127] Their boundaries, which were broadly those of the old diocese of Worcester, created by Archbishop Theodore in 679 or 680, comprised Worcestershire, except for the north-western tip, the south-western half of Warwickshire, Gloucestershire (excluding the southern part of the Forest of Dean, which remained in Welsh control until the 700s) and the area north of the Avon in the neighbourhood of Bath.[128] The West Saxons fought against Penda at Cirencester in 628, after which in all written sources the *Hwicce* are designated as being subordinate to Mercia.[129] This continued until Æthelred submitted to the overlordship of King Alfred in the early 880s.[130] It is not absolutely clear whether, before the battle at Cirencester, the *Hwiccian* royal dynasty was connected to Wessex or to Mercia, although the consensus is that it was not Mercia. There is a reference in Bede, relating to the years 680-81, where he records that the South Saxon queen, Eabæ, daughter of the first recorded king of the *Hwicce*, had been baptised in her own province of the *Hwicce*.[131] This suggests a political link between the two kingdoms which might illuminate the connection in the late seventh century between Mercia and the South Saxons, which both Cædwalla and Ine sought to sever (see below). By the tenth century the *Hwiccian* province had been divided between Worcestershire and Gloucestershire, a few small land holdings were in Warwickshire and in the, now lost county of Winchcombeshire. There are hints here of some connection with Wessex, more of which below.

The Magonsæte

It is possible that the territory of the *Magonsæte* may have been settled by Saxon groups who migrated northwards from the territory of the West Saxons and the *Hwicce*. Their territory, the western boundary of which follows broadly the line of Offa's dyke, corresponds to the boundaries of the diocese of Hereford, centred on Kenchester. Five miles west of Hereford is the Roman small town of *Magnis*, from which the people-name is derived. By the beginning of the eighth century both the *Hwicce* and the *Magonsæte* were subordinate to Mercia.

The boundaries of the *Wrocensæte* lay within Shropshire and are listed in the Tribal Hidage. No royal line is known and they had no separate bishopric, becoming part of the diocese of Lichfield when they were subsumed into Greater Mercia. Kinton near Great Ness lies in their territory, four miles from Wroxeter, the Roman civitas capital of *Viriconium*. As with the *Hwicce* there are hints of contact with Wessex.

Around 14 per cent of the corpus of Kingstons is found north and east of Watling Street, and south of the line between the Mersey and the Humber. Half of these lie in close association with Roman roads, and the other half are located on significant through roads or rivers. This suggests that in some essential respect the histories of Kingston-places throughout England must, despite the south-west bias, be in some way comparable. Significantly perhaps, they lie, in the main, outside the main areas of Scandinavian settlement.

Of the 14 names in the group, six have been 'Scandinavianised': Congerstone LEI, Conington CAM, Conington HNT, Coniston (Cold) and Conistone (Kettlewell) YOW, and Coniston LNC. This does rather presume a pre-Scandinavian foundation date. Except for Coniston LNC they are all listed in DB, although ecclesiastically they are all daughters in origin, as is the case with all the Kingstons with possible exception of Kingston upon Thames. Ekwall considers that Coniston LNC may have started life as a small Scandinavian mountain kingdom.[132] The two Yorkshire examples, which are sited within 10 miles of each other on Roman roads near the source of the rivers Warfe, Ribble and Aire, are, as noted above, sited within the Anglo-Saxon, possibly British, kingdom of Craven.

Cambridgeshire and Huntingtonshire

The cluster of four examples in mid-Huntingdonshire and west Cambridgeshire is found in an area within the Danelaw, which seems to have experienced less Scandinavian influence than the surrounding areas, giving a better chance of the OE name surviving. Coningtons HNT and CAM share many similar characteristics, notably their situation on major Roman roads, with the 20 miles that separate Conington HNT and Kingston CAM on Ermine Street hinting at the road/string pattern seen in Greater Wessex and the lower Severn valley. All except *Kingestune*/Wistow are listed in DB. Conington CAM and both the Huntingdonshire examples feature in pre-DB royal charters, but only Kingston CAM had royal connections at DB, where two of the six manors listed were held TRE by the king and where special riding duties are listed. *Kingestune*/Wistow presents significantly different characteristics from the others in this group. It is possible that something different is going on here, a history that might differ from the others in some essential regard. The possibility that this cluster could be related in some way to the movement north of Edward the Elder and his sister Æthelflæd has been considered.

Suffolk

The three Kingstons sited in Suffolk are all found within the southern part of the kingdom of the East Angles; Kingston (Woodbridge) and Kenton both lie in relationship to the River Deben: Kenton is close to the source, and Kingston

---

[126] Bassett 1989: p. 6.
[127] Hooke 1992: p. 48.
[128] The Forest of Dean may have been part of Wales at this time.
[129] Hooke 1985: p. 47; Yorke 1999: p. 246.
[130] Stenton 1971: pp. 324–30.
[131] HE iv, 13.

[132] Ekwall 1979, 4th edn: p.120.

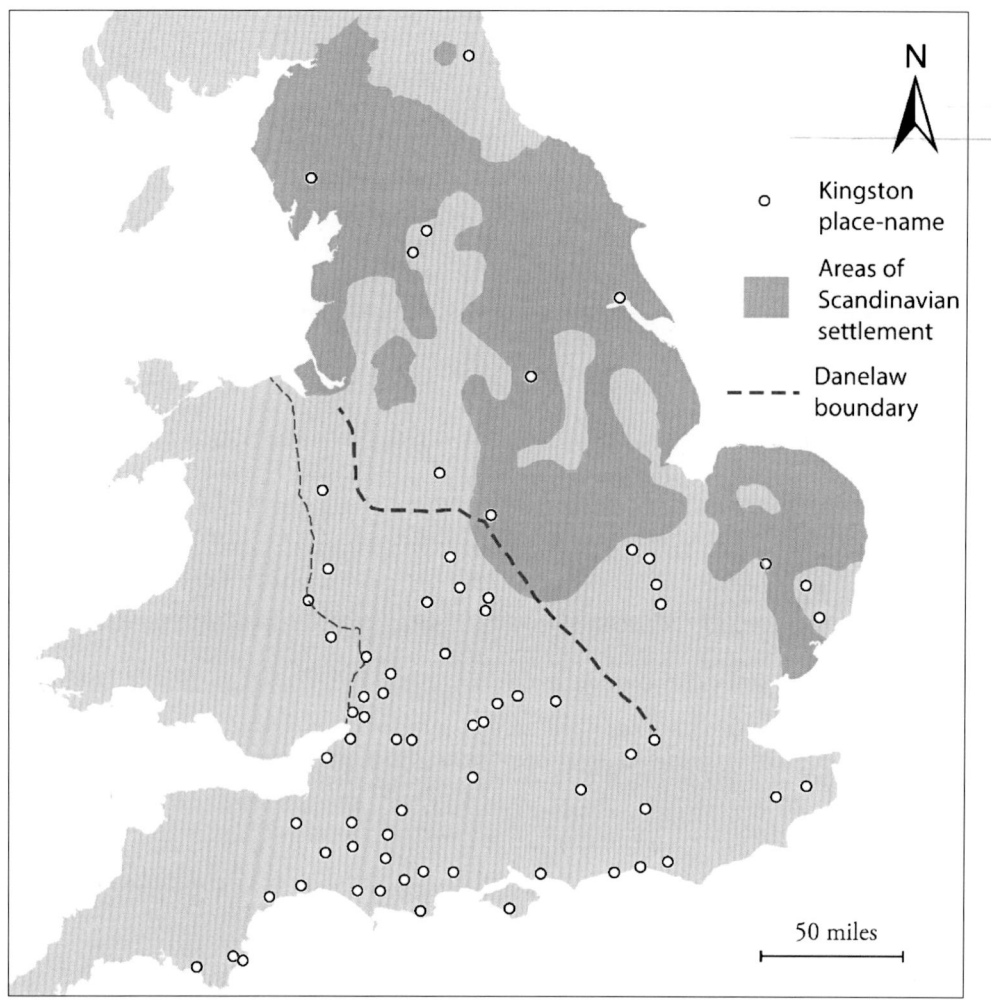

Figure 17: Kingstons in the Danelaw.

(Woodbridge) sits on a small promontory at a point where the river narrows. The effects of silting have modified the river to such a degree that very little can be said with any confidence in regard to how it would have been in the early to mid-Saxon period when Sutton Hoo, which lies immediately opposite on the other bank of the river, was in its prime as the burial ground of the kings of the *Wuffingas*.

It has not been possible to make any connection between the organisation of the early kingdom of the East Angles and these Suffolk Kingstons which are found within it. There was Scandinavian settlement in this corner of Suffolk but as might have been the case with the four Kingstons in Huntingdonshire and Cambridgeshire, it might have been lighter than other areas of East Anglia. Coney Weston is the only one of the three examples with the most significant Kingston characteristic - the long-distance Roman road between London and Norwich which runs through the centre of the present-day parish.[133]

Congerstone LEI and Kingston (Carlton in Lindrick) NTT, and Kingstone STF all lie within Greater Mercia,

with Kingstone STF being the only one sited on a major Roman road. Congerstone and (Carlton in Lindrick) lie on ancient through-routeways. As already noted, Peter Foss has demonstrated convincingly that Congerstone was a component part of an Anglo-Saxon royal estate centred on Market Bosworth, whose boundaries on the south follow the line of the Roman Watling Street that forms the boundary with Warwickshire. The boundary on the west is Staffordshire. This estate might represent a small Middle Anglian kingdom such as the kingdom of the *Stoppingas*, which also was subsumed into Mercia, It has not been possible to establish contexts for either Kingstone STF or Kingston (Carlton in Lindrick) NTT further than that which has been offered above.

The Viking settlement north of Watling Street created an almost total re-assignment and re-structuring of landscape; this was also a time when changes in farming practices began to change; along with an increased shift towards nucleated settlements.[134] If the original purpose of the Kingstons was now redundant, and their position on the major roads were not settlement sites of choice, they would simply have languished and faded away, a process hastened by the changes in overlordship. Where

---

[133] I am grateful to Dr Sam Newton, of Wuffing Education, for generously giving his time to discuss the possible significance of the Kingston names in Suffolk.

[134] Cullen *et al* 2011: pp. 111-37.

the Scandinavian settlement was less dominant it would be expected that, had they existed, more Kingston names might have survived. Peter Liddle, county archaeologist for Leicestershire, a county where the place-name evidence suggests sizeable Scandinavian settlement, has been running a 35-year community archaeology programme of extensive, and intensive, field-walking across the county. Over these decades, and with hundreds of field-walkers having involved over the years, not a single settlement site, which contained the element *tūn*, has been identified and confirmed, in the documentary record. Liddle is of the opinion that if Kingstons had existed in any numbers within the Scandinavianised areas of the country, they would have come to light. He rejects the theory that they were once there, across-the-board, but are now lost.[135] If we accept this, the reasons for the existence of the names found north of Watling Street have to lie in other aspects of their own individual histories. Given the scarcity (and vagaries) of the evidence, conclusions can be only tentative.

Some kind of royal connection has been identified for almost all the Kingstons. It can be assumed, relatively confidently, this will have been the case for those for whom a connection has not been established. That they fulfilled legal and administrative functions seems indisputable. If they were not places where some aspect of royal authority was enacted, what were they? The written record offers no direct, secure help here.

The evidence so far?

The Kingstons were largely a major long-distance Roman road and ancient trackway phenomenon with many of them standing at regular distances of nine to ten miles apart along these roads. These road/string Kingstons are restricted geographically to Wessex and the lower Severn valley. To a lesser extent in the south west Midlands, and a hint in Sussex, this bias is evident, not just for the road/string Kingstons, but for the corpus as a whole. There is some evidence for the 'original' Kingstons serving a function within some of the small, early petty kingdoms. Circumstantial evidence suggests a time-frame within the long eighth century, and within that frame, the possibility that Ine of Wessex, whilst not necessarily the originator of the Kingston 'concept', could have exploited its potential in an attempt to secure the newly acquired British kingdoms, and block the territorially ambitious Mercians from bringing the south-eastern kingdoms under its overlordship.

These hypotheses - and they can only be hypotheses - are explored further in chapter five. Before this, however, the 'problem' of Kingston upon Thames has to be addressed. Is this Kingston the exception to the rule, or is it the rule?

---

[135] Peter Liddle, County Archaeologist for Leicestershire, pers. comm. Liddle pointed out the lack of secure evidence either way.

Chapter 5

Kingston upon Thames

Kingston upon Thames is unique in the corpus of Kingston names in that it appears to meet almost all of Sawyer's criteria for being a *villa regalis*.[1] Its first appearance in the record is November 838 in an authentic charter of Ecgberht King of Wessex, issued from [*v*]*illa famosa loco quæ appeletur Cyninges tun in regione Suðregiæ* 'the well-known/famous place which is called *Cyninges tun* in the region of Surrey'.[2] The occasion was a meeting of the king, his son Æthelwulf, and Ceolnoth, Archbishop of Canterbury. Its purpose was of profound political significance, perhaps the most momentous in the history of the West Saxons to that date, the signing of an agreement whereby all the kingdoms south of the Thames that is Kent, Surrey, and Sussex, together with Essex would thenceforth be within the realm of the West Saxons. Catherine Cubitt considers this meeting not to have been a synod of the whole Southumbrian church since it was attended only by the archbishop and the bishops of Winchester, Sherborne, Rochester, and Selsey, with only one bishop coming from outside Kent and Wessex.[3] There were 18 other signatories to the agreement, all of whom were senior clerics. At the same meeting, Ecgbert restored to Christ Church, Canterbury, land at *Mallingum* which had been confiscated by the West Saxons when they overran Kent in 831. The community at Christ Church promised that in return for the restoration of their lands at *Mallingum*, they and their successors would be loyal to the West Saxon kings and their heirs.[4] The agreement and the land grants were confirmed the following year by Æthelwulf (Egbert having died soon after the earlier meeting) at a council held at the royal *villa regalis* of Wilton, and again, later in the same year, at a full synod held at the unidentified *villa regalis* of *æt Astran*, with all the bishops south of the Humber in attendance.[5]

A hundred years were to pass before any other further charters were issued from Kingston upon Thames, after which, between 943 and the early eleventh century, five were issued.[6] By 925, *Cinges tun(e)* had become so celebrated

that Æthelstan, son of Edward the Elder, and grandson of Alfred, chose to be consecrated there in a ceremony conducted by the Archbishop of Canterbury, who devised a new coronation ritual where, for the first time, the king did not wear a helmet, but a crown.[7] Æthelstan might have chosen Kingston for its symbolic association with Egbert and the agreement of 838. David Hill is *mystified* by the lack of any explanation for the *apparent* insistence on the part of kings successive to Æthelstan that they be consecrated there.[8] Swanton, who is also puzzled, thinks that Kingston upon Thames possibly went on to become the place where coronations took place because of Æthelstan's standing and reputation.[9] Keynes broadly concurs with Hill, and Swanton.[10] It has become received opinion that four other Anglo-Saxon kings were crowned here: Edward the Elder (902), Edmund (Ironside) (940), Eadred (946), and Edwig (950). The origin of this claim seems to be Ralph de Diceto, a twelfth-century dean of St Paul's, London, who places seven Anglo-Saxon coronations here. He seems to have been his own source for these assertions. There does not seem to be any secure supporting evidence for this claim and yet nineteenth-century historians seem, in the main, to have accepted de Decito's assertions uncritically, as if he were a contemporary source.[11]

At the time of the Domesday survey Kingston upon Thames is listed seventh in the king's holdings in Surrey. It was held both TRE and TRW by the king and was head of its own large hundred whose territory extended from Kew in the north, to Hook in the south, and from East Molesley in the west to Malden in the east. Of the 14 DB entries for Surrey under the Land of the King, Guildford is listed as the pre-eminent place. Kingston upon Thames is seventh in the list and yet it answered for the highest number of hides and was the most populous manor in the county.[12] The present church of All Saints contains a fragment of a late tenth/early eleventh-century stone cross-shaft, suggesting the presence of an earlier church which Blair thinks might have been an early minster church serving all of Kingston Hundred, including Elmbridge.[13]

There will have been compelling reasons behind the choice of place for the signing of the 838 agreement. Its central location within the realm, and the accessibility afforded

---

[1] Sawyer 1983: pp. 273–99.

[2] S 1438.

[3] Catherine Cubitt 1995: fn. 8, p. 237.

[4] Brooks discusses this and two other charters, issued at about the same time, in the context of the wider relationship between the West Saxon dynasty and the church at Canterbury in *The Early History of the Church at Canterbury,* 1984: p. 145–6.

[5] S 281.

[6] Æthelstan, *Æthelstanus rex totius Britanniæ,* in 943 for 924 x 939, from '*in villa uæ dicitur Kingeston*'. S 450; Æthelstan, *Æthelstanus rex totius Britanniæ* in 933, from '*in regali villa que anglice Kingestone vocatur*'. S 420; Eadred, *Edmundi regis qui regimina regnorum Angulsaxna & Northymbra,* 946, from '*in villa quæ dicitur regis Cyngestun tun*'. S 520; Edgar, *Eadgar rex Anglorum*', 951 (for ?959) from '*in notissimo loco qui dicitur Cyngestun*'. S 1450; Cnut, *Cnut rex* early eleventh century, issued from '*in Suðrie apud Kyngestune*'. S 981.

[7] The place was almost certainly present-day Kingston upon Thames.

[8] Hill 1981: p. 85.

[9] Swanton 1990: p.104, fn. 10

[10] Keynes 1999: p. 272.

[11] Quoted in W. Stubbs (ed.) 1876 pp. 140–8, 235–7; 'More on Saxon Kingston' in *London Archaeologist,* vol 8. no. 12, p. 335.

[12] DBSr. 1:8.

[13] Blair 1991: pp. 99–100.

by both river and road must have influenced the choice. The Thames, which for so long had been a frontier zone, was now peaceful. Mercia was no longer a threat, largely because of the military successes of Egbert himself who now controlled the river on which *Cyninges tūn* lay, sited strategically at the highest tidal point and the first good fording place above London. It was a natural intersection for river and road, although there is no evidence for a bridge here before 1170.[14] The precise level or width of the river at this point in Roman and Saxon times is uncertain, although the excavated evidence indicates that the twelfth-century river would have been significantly lower than it is today, and between 30-60m wider. There is the possibility also that this site had long been regarded as sacred (see below).

Between 1998 and 1999, large-scale archaeological excavations at Charter Quay were undertaken in the part of the town which straddled the surviving south arm of the Hogsmill.[15] These revealed that in the twelfth and thirteenth centuries the river was a substantial watercourse with a 20m wide mouth at its confluence with the Thames. The name of the river along this stretch at this time was the *Lurtebourne*, the first element of the name being the OE *lurte* 'filthy'. The current name is associated with Jon Hog, the owner of a large mill that stood here at the turn of the twelfth century.

Hawkins suggests that during the Roman period we should visualise the area of modern central Kingston as a low-lying area dissected by numerous river and stream channels flowing into the Thames, with three areas of slightly higher ground forming 'islands' of gravel, the whole area being subject to flooding and bank erosion. There is evidence that this may have worsened in the post-Roman period. In short, this was an unstable riverine environment.[16] The Geological Survey map shows river gravel (Kempton Park Gravel) covered by 'brickearth' (Langley Silt), but does not depict these emergent gravel 'islands'.

Kingston Hill and Coombe Hill

These 'hills' rise from 10m to 50m AOD just under a kilometre east of Kingston town centre. Between these hills a small number of *coombes* cut into the high ground between 15m and 30m AOD. This is an area of a natural spring line. Many Roman finds were recorded from the base of these hills during the sixteenth to eighteenth centuries, and recently it has been suggested that the Coombe Hill finds might represent a temple. Hawkins is of the opinion that the spread of finds here from several locations suggests a complex landscape of Roman activity both sacred and domestic.[17] Roman occupation from the first to fourth centuries has been revealed at Skerne Road, Clarence Street, and Orchard Road. This is largely domestic, but the fill of one large pit contained partially articulated cattle

and horse skeletons which may indicate ritual activity. Hawkins suggests that this possibility gives an additional context to the assemblage of 355 coins, jewellery, lead strips (possible votive), smelting waste, a large quantity of iron nails, animal bones, and part of the skeleton of a horse or a cow. A further hint that this area may have been regarded as sacred is a further reference in Aubrey to a special spring of which he states: 'about a mile from the Bowling Green at the West End of the town is a spring that is cold in summer and warm in winter, it bubbles up and is called the Seething-Well. The inhabitants thereabout do wash their eyes with it, and drink of it'.

Hawkins is of the opinion that the central Kingston area was probably not much more than a riverside hamlet, with its economy based on agriculture and stock-raising appropriate to the generally heavy soils there. There was certainly no substantial Roman settlement at Kingston.

Anglo-Saxon Kingston upon Thames

Anglo-Saxon Kingston throughout the Saxon period comprised a large but relatively low-lying gravel island surrounded on all sides by watercourses. It was not until the excavations at South Lanes in 1996 that a further hitherto unknown gravel island, smaller than Central Island but

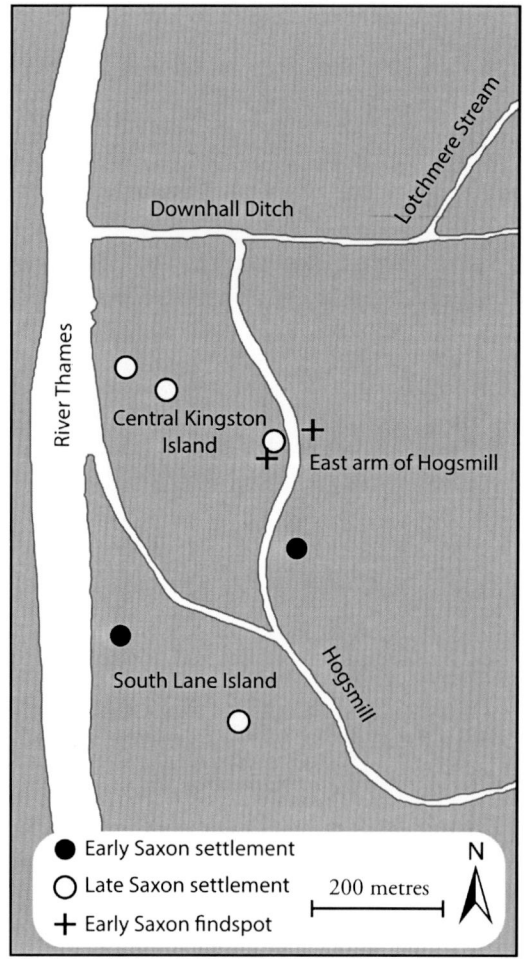

Figure 18: Sketch map of the gravel islands, Kingston upon Thames.

14 Potter 1988: p. 140.
15 Andrews *et al* 2007: pp. 199–203.
16 Hawkings 2007: p. 201.
17 Hawkins 2007: p. 201.

slightly higher, was revealed and examined. This turned out to be a pre-700 Anglo-Saxon domestic site, as evidenced by weaving, antler work, and pottery, all associated with a post-and-hole construction of a hall building which was probably a farmstead. This building was abandoned by about 700 when the focus of activity reverted to the Central Island, where only slight evidence of Saxon occupation was retrieved during excavation, and nothing at all of the high-status structures or small finds that might have been expected at the central place of a royal estate. Nothing Saxon came from the market frontages either. The reasons for the shift back to Central Island and the building of a church there has not been established. There is no evidence either that this could have been the site of a Saxon *burh*. Between the ninth and eleventh centuries such settlement as there was lay to the north of the church. Frustratingly, and perhaps significantly, no conclusive evidence emerged that there was anything remarkable about this place from the ten-year extensive research and excavation project, and certainly nothing to suggest that this was a place where Anglo-Saxon kings would choose to be anointed.

An intriguing mid-nineteenth-century archaeological recovery resulting from the dredging of the Thames, close to the mouth of the Hogs Mill river, might offer an insight into the significance of this place. A hoard of eight early sixth-century gold coins of the Emperor Justinian I came up from the river bed. These coins are now lost but by a happy chance their descriptions have survived.[18] A list of all finds of gold coins from the late fifth to eighth centuries has been compiled by the numismatist J. Rigold who considers this hoard to be important.[19] Cohen suggests that the Thames itself might even have been regarded as sacred and perceived as a metaphysical border of sorts.[20] Hines is of the opinion that its deposition at Kingston certainly represents *significant* activity along the river in this period, although he does not infer the presence of any specific type of site.[21] This, along with the other evidence discussed above, suggests that the Thames and its tributary the Hogs Mill, here at its highest tidal point, was possibly fordable. Aubrey records of Saxon Kingston that 'its ancient name was Moreford... but the Saxon kings making it sometimes their place of residence occasioned the name Kingston to be given it'.[22]

A note on the 'lost' *villa regalis* of *Frœricburna*

There is in Surrey an unidentified Anglo-Saxon *villa regalis* from which at least two, and probably three, charters were issued. The earliest of these is an undated charter of Offa, *rex Merciorum*, granting 20 hides to the church at Woking, issued from *in regione Suthregeona villa regali nomine Frœricburna*,[23] '[in] the region of Surrey [the] royal estate named *Frœricburna*'. The date

cannot be ascribed securely to any particular year within Offa's long reign although Margaret Gelling has suggested that it is likely to be between 775 and 796.[24] The second appearance in the record of this royal place is in 838, when Egbert King of Wessex issued a charter from, *in [v] bica sic regali que dicitur Frœricburna*, 'the royal estate called *Frœricburna*', granting land in Kent to Bishop Beornmod.[25] The long list of signatories suggests that this was a major gathering; it is also noteworthy that 838 is the same year as the momentous meeting held *æt Cyningestune* between Egbert and the Archbishop of Canterbury. There is a third reference in 861, 23 years later, to what must have been *Freoricburna* in a charter of Æthelberht, king of Wessex and Kent, promulgated from '*in loco preclaro qui nominator Fregetburna an hsuðrium*' (Surrey).[26] The form *Fregetburna* is not an obvious development of the two earlier forms of the name, but the close similarity to the two earlier charters, its location in Surrey and subsequent disappearance from the record, suggests that it was probably the same place. The scribe who rendered Surrey as *hsuðrium* would have been perfectly capable of making a hash of *Frœricburna*! All three charters are considered to be essentially authentic.

Freoricburna/Frœricburna and *Cyninges tūn* could both have been component members of the same royal estate, the caput of which, theoretically, could have lain anywhere within its land area. There is no doubt that the place known as Kingston upon Thames stands on its historical site and there is no evidence that its name has changed. Is it possible that in origin this Kingston was essentially the same as, or similar to, the other 69 Kingstons in the corpus. All were deliberately founded with the specific purpose of imposing some aspect of royal power, lying close to but separate from where the king's hall would have stood. As London and the river grew in economic importance so did Kingston, with the focus of the estate no longer being the old royal centre of *Freoricburna* but the thriving quayside of Kingston. If this were the case it is easy to see how the generic term *Cyninges tun* and Kingston became confused, merged, and eventually conflated. The survival of the name *Fregetburna* more than 20 years after the 838 meeting between Egbert and the Archbishop supports this suggestion. Like Aubrey, John Blair has suggested that the name Kingston might have replaced an earlier name.[27] He is largely right in this but what this research has revealed is that *Frēoricburna* might have been subsumed into Kingston.

The villa regalis *of* Frēoricburna/Frœricburna *and the Hogsmill/Lurtebourne valley*

The second element of the name *Frēorichburna* is the OE place-name element *burna* 'stream', a term most commonly used of watercourses which are not substantial enough to qualify for the term *ēa* which seems largely to

[18] Hines 2004: p. 94.
[19] Rigold 1975: pp. 653–77.
[20] Cohen 2003: p. 18.
[21] Hines: p. 94.
[22] Aubrey vol I, pp. 18-21.
[23] The name is spelled variously as *Frēorichburna* or *Frœricburna*'.

[24] S 144; Gelling 1979: p. 153.
[25] S 280. *Bica* is a misspelling of *vica*.
[26] S 330.
[27] Blair 1991: pp. 99–100.

have been reserved for major rivers. The distributional bias of *burna* is towards chalk country which produces clear streams.[28] The term *burna* was current at the earliest date of English speech, remaining current in the areas where it was in common use. These were largely south of the Thames. The first element of the name is OE *frēorig* 'freezing, cold, chilled', and by extension the term can refer to the emotions, cold (with fear), sad, anxious. The latter meaning is unlikely to have applied in this case. *Burna* is common and easily understood. In contrast, *Frēorich* is rare and on first consideration puzzling. Its rarity in place-names offers no comparisons on which to draw.

Can we get behind this obscure, descriptive term? It is unlikely that the term was used literally as the name would have applied on rare occasions only. It could, however, have been used for a watercourse or spring that was exceptionally cold. The Hogsmill rises from a spring at Ewell in the lake in the grounds of Bourne Hall, a name that itself reflects its possible earlier incarnation if we suppose that the Hogsmill equates with *Frēorichburna*. Ewell is OE *æwell*, 'spring', 'spring that gives rise to a watercourse'. John Aubrey, the antiquarian historian of the County of Surrey, describes the spring as the 'most plentiful spring, the head of a crystal brook'. John Tolland, an informant of Aubrey, comments: 'the spring at Ewell is of such crystaline purity and cleanliness that Queen Elizabeth of famous memory would daily send for it for her own use when she was staying at nearby Nonsuch Palace'. The spring here at Ewell, which seems to have been venerated and celebrated in both Roman and pre-Roman times, lies on Stane Street, the major Roman road which ran from London to Chichester. As the road approaches Ewell, it deviates from its straight alignment to make a double bend that is not required by the local topography. A possible reason for this might be the need (or wish) to respect a Romano-British temple, which it is thought stood in the vicinity of the spring.[29] David Bird concurs with this suggestion and notes that an examination of several other sites in Roman Britain and other provinces provides supporting evidence that roads may be affected by the existence of religious sites, and that sometimes roads were deliberately laid out to point directly at, and then bend round, sacred sites.[30] No evidence for this proposed temple at Ewell has been identified archaeologically, although a series of votive shafts containing the bones of hares and other offerings has been excavated close by, and when the lake at Bourne Hall was drained the sacred nature of the site was confirmed both by the quantity and nature of the finds that were recovered from the lake-bed.[31] Bird says that we should be starting to think about Ewell as rather more than just another roadside settlement, but potentially more like the complex at Springhead, Kent, where the Roman Watling Street goes through a marked doubled

bend as it passes through a complex of temple sites.[32] If Bird is right, Ewell has a treat waiting should there ever be a need to excavate the centre of the settlement.

It was long observed that the temperature of small (less than 15km) tributaries of the Thames that are chiefly fed by head-springs, such as the Hogsmill and Wandle is controlled by the temperature of the springs for the whole of its length. Measurements taken long the course of the Hogsmill in 1894 showed that the river was 4 degrees colder than the Thames. However, it was calculated that if the river was not influenced by mill-ponds, the temperature difference would be nearer to 8°.[33]

The River Hogsmill, which was not recorded by that name until 1535,[34] flows north to Kingston upon Thames through land that is mainly low-lying London Clay to (Old) Malden, where there is an ancient church and where Roman structures have been identified. When the river lost its original name the 'freezing-cold-burn' is not known, and is unlikely ever to be so. However, we do know that the earlier name of the lower reaches of the Hogsmill was *Luertebourne*. It is not uncommon for the name of a river to change when it flows across a different geology, and this appears to have happened here. The first element of the name *leurte* is the OE 'filthy', a fitting name for the water course at this point as it regularly becomes 'flashy' after rain, causing debris to be pulled into the stream.[35]

Holy springs at both the source and mouth of the river may have led to the whole valley being regarded as hallowed, with something of this persisting long after any evidence of sacred structures had gone. It is perfectly possible that this could have been a factor in Egbert's choice of place for the signing of an agreement that proclaimed his imperium over all the lands south of the Thames, as the choice of sacred sites as meeting places was a widely recognised practice at this time.

The site of the royal residence of Frǣricburna

In general the evidence suggests that most pre-Conquest kings, particularly in the early/mid-Anglo-Saxon period, seem to have preferred rural estates for their residences.[36] Royal assemblies were occasionally held in the newly emerging towns but in the main they seem to have been held in the king's hall at the *caput* of a rural estate. Hunting,

---

[28] Gelling and Cole 2000: pp. 9-11.
[29] Orton 1997: pp. 89-122.
[30] Bird 2002: p. 44.
[31] Jeremy Harte, Curator of Ewell Museum, pers. comm.

[32] Springhead, Kent, lies at the source of the River Ebbsfleet, where in ancient times there was a pool formed by eight natural springs. A two-year excavation was undertaken here by Wessex Archaeology in advance of the construction of the Channel Tunnel. The site was a huge (30 acres), multi-period, stratified, and well-preserved area. It was sacred to the Celts who began settling there around 100 BCE. Ten temples were unearthed and a 600m ceremonial way was identified. The Romans were also drawn to the religious significance of the site, they called it *Vaginacis/Vaginacae* 'the place of the marshes'. The road to London (known later) as Watling Street was constructed through the centre of the site.
[33] Guppy 1895: pp. 1-11.
[34] A Jon Hog had a mill on the *Lurtebourne* in Kingston in the twelfth century.
[35] Gelling and Cole 2000: pp. 6–11.
[36] Sawyer 1983: p. 277.

after all, was paramount. This being the case, perhaps we should be looking somewhere other than a busy quay on the banks of a major river for the site of the king's hall at *Frēoricburna*. In theory, this could have been almost anywhere within the putative estate.

Although the evidence for reconstructing the extent of the land unit that was *Frēoricburna* is largely circumstantial, it is possible to suggest some of its component members. The Domesday entry for *Chingeston* points to its being a substantial place, head of its own Hundred and second only to Guildford in population size. The component members of the hundred were Petersham, Ham, Coombe, 'Immerworth', Thames Ditton, Long Ditton, Tolworth, Malden, Chessington, and Claygate. Ewell was not in Kingston Hundred, although it was held by the king both TRE and TRW. The present-day village of (Old) Malden overlooks the Hogsmill river midway between Ewell and Kingston on land that topographically commands a prominent vantage point, being the only stretch of the river that is overlooked by a 'cliff'.[37] The church is ancient, and Iron Age and Roman finds indicating settlement have been found here.[38] The name Malden identifies a feature of special note, although what this was is inknown. The first element, the OE *mæl* 'monument', 'a sign', 'a cross' is rare in place-names, with only three other examples of the element + *dūn* in England.[39] The second element of the name is the OE *dūn* 'a hill', an 'expanse of open hill-country', 'a low hill with a fairly level and fairly flat summit' offering a good settlement site for settlement in open country. It seems to have been applicable to anything from a slight gentle slope to a high mountain. There are three landholders listed in the DB entry for Malden, the Archbishop of Canterbury, who held it both TRE and TRE; Robert of Wattewille held it from Richard TRW with the king holding it TRE; the third was in dispute, remaining 'exempt in the King's hand'. Ewell at the head of the river, Malden in the centre of the valley, and Kingston at the confluence of the Hogsmill and the Thames, were all in the hands of King Edward before the Conquest, a strong confirmation of its earlier royal past. It might be significant that the ancient parishes of Cheam, Malden, Merton and Morden, and the hundreds of Copthorne, Kingston, Brixton, and Wallington all converge on a square piece of ground called Hide Hill in Malden parish, east of Motspur Park. It is tempting to interpret this as *Moot*spur, which would be fitting; it does, however, relate to a person named Mot whose presence from the fourteenth century is attested. On early maps it is called Motes Firs Ferm and Motts Furse Farm; also, the uniform presence of 's' following the name indicates a genitive form from a personal name. Additionally, *mōt* as a place-name is only found in compounds. This still leaves this one-hide farmstead stranded in an odd relationship to the various boundaries that meet at this point. The squareness of the

field as shown on the map is deceptive: it is not man-made as it appears to be. A close examination of the contour line shows it to be a modestly upstanding, sharply angular topographical feature. We must look beyond the surviving documents to a more remote, undocumented period, for an explanation of this enigmatic parcel of land.

If Kingston upon Thames is the *cyninges tūn* of the charter, it is the only one in the corpus of 70 Kingstons that was a *villa regalis*. It is also, the only known *villa regalis* out of over 200 other known *villæ regales*, that is simply called *Cyninges tūn*, all the others having their own identifying names, the greater majority of which are derived from topographical features. The 838 charter cites the meeting place as '[v]*illa famosa loco quæ appeletur Cyninges tune in regione Suðregiæ*' – the 'famous/celebrated' estate called *Cyninges tune* – not *villa regalis*, or one of the other terms used in the written sources to describe a royal estate. There is a distinct possibility that *Cyninges tun* and *Frēoricburna* might have been one and the same place, and the freezing cold burn is the Hogsmill/*Lurtebourne* river. Or, and this is the more likely, *Cyninges tune* was a specific place within the estate serving a purpose related in some way to the exercise of royal power, with the central place within the estate lying elsewhere.

The meeting in 838 took place in November, a difficult time to travel when the roads, such as they were, would have been hard to negotiate. The attendees would have made their way there via the River Thames or the Roman road from Chichester to London. If the latter, at Ewell, they would have turned north into the valley of the freezing cold burn. Those arriving by boat would have landed at the place called *Cyninges tun* and from there would have made their way to the royal place. Might there have been confusion when the scribe recorded the event later? Also, two meetings of the king's council, held in Surrey in the same year, with the archbishop present at both events, raise the question that there might have been only one event. *Frēoricburna* appeared in the record for a third (and final) time in a charter of 861, issued by King Æthelberht from '*in loco preclaro qui nominator Fregetburna an hsuðrium*', the celebrated place that is called *Fregetburna* in Surrey. Although the first element *freget* is not an obvious, or expected, linguistic development from the two earlier forms of the name it is, nevertheless, a distinct possibility.

This writer is not the first to question what the name *Cyninges tūn* signified in the charter. Swanton, Keynes, Hill, and Blair have all expressed disquiet, with Blair raising the question that *Cyninges tūn* might have replaced an earlier name. Clearly something is not quite right here. The answer might lie in the simple explanation that the scribe muddled the name Kingston with the generic term *cyninges tūn*. It is not unreasonable to conclude that there is a distinct possibility that in origin Kingston upon Thames began life serving the same, or similar, purpose as the rest of the Kingstons in the corpus.

---

[37] I am deeply indebted to David Bate, of the British Geological Survey, who gave generously of his time, not only in sourcing geological maps, but also walking and surveying the area with me, in pursuit of the site of the caput of *Frēoricburna*.
[38] Hawkins 2007: p. 203.
[39] Maldon Ess; Mauldon Bd; Meldon Nb.

Chapter 6

What Was a Kingston?

Can the question 'What was a Kingston?' now be satisfactorily resolved: and can we derive history from place-names? The paucity of both documentary and archaeological evidence for the early/mid-Anglo-Saxon period makes a clear-cut answer not possible; its precise function must remain partial at best. The employment of an interdisciplinary, holistic, and detailed methodology has made it possible to suggest what Kingstons *might* have been, and to propose a possible origin and purpose for their foundation. Stuart Brookes has compared the distribution and significance of the Kingstons with the common Scandinavian place-name *Huseby*, making it possible to place the Kingston phenomenon in a wider setting, beyond our shores, both spatially and over time.[1] The place-name *Huseby* has recently been the subject of a conference, held in Copenhagen at the National Museum. It is remarked upon here as significant parallels have emerged to similar changes, identified in England, between the years 650 and 850. The themes covered were: the current status and evidence for the dating of the foundation of *Husebyer*; the origin of the, presumed, *Husebyer*-system; explanations for the uneven distribution of the name; and the identification of *Husebyer* across Scandinavia, including Orkney. Research to date has yielded several common themes associated with the broader processes of royal territorialisation, including the expansion of kingdoms, with the consequential need to bring to bear control over communications, taxation, collection of tribute, and the imposition of lordship over the newly-acquired territories and their leaders.

What Kingstons were *not*

By establishing what a Kingston was *not* we might see more clearly what it *might* have been. Kingston is a common name, apparently straightforward, but one which on closer inspection defies easy understanding. Prior to this research, no systematic, detailed research had been carried out into what the name might have signified. The research that had been undertaken was good, and the right questions were beginning to be asked, but, as Duncan Probert, one of the earlier researchers concluded, only a wide-reaching research project could tease out the deeper subtleties of the name;[2] and to challenge the untested assumption that the *cyninges tūn* of the 838 meeting between Ecgberht, King of Wessex, and the Archbishop of Canterbury was a *villa regalis*, whose defining name was *cyninges tūn*. The discussions in the previous chapter point to the generally held assumptions regarding the name being misguided.

It now seems not unreasonable to suggest that the '*famosa*' *villa regalis* of the meeting was not the present-day Kingston upon Thames but the heretofore unidentified *villa regalis* of *Frēorichburna*.

Kingstons were *not* centres of royal power, mother parishes, *burhs* (Alfredian or otherwise), execution sites or meeting places, although two were adjacent to known mustering points. They were not liable for the *firma unius noctis* or the *trinoda necessita*, and few developed into settlements of any significance. They do not seem to have been associated directly with the control of natural resources; neither, with the sole exception of an early Anglo-Saxon brooch of outstanding craftsmanship, excavated at Kingston in Kent, has any significant archaeological evidence of Anglo-Saxon activity been unearthed at, or even close to, a Kingston. This includes Kingston upon Thames where 10 seasons of archaeological excavation produced only a small quantity of early Anglo-Saxon domestic finds.

Can we take things one step further without, to quote Margaret Gelling, 'offering desperate solutions to difficult problems which readers might reject on the grounds that they outraged common sense'?[3] Gelling herself conceded that some of her own conclusions were sometimes 'desperate'. She was, at the time, struggling to explain the problems associated with the use of British and Welsh sound-changes in determining the date at which English settlers might have adopted a Welsh name! This confession from one of the leading place-name scholars of the twentieth century has encouraged this writer to put forward some suggestions which, whilst not open to proof, are, nevertheless, possible, and which, it is hoped, do not outrage common sense. In other words, are there any factual statements that can be made about the term *cyninges tun(e)* and the Kingstons?

What Kingstons *might* have been

It seems relatively safe to make the following points. The term *cyninges tūn* was well known and in use no later than the earliest years of the seventh century, where it appears in the laws of Æthelberht of Kent, providing a secure *terminus ante quem* for its existence. The precise meaning of the term, as used in the laws, is not clear. It could have been referring to the area that comprised the entire *villa regalis*, or to a precise location within the estate where a specific function or functions relating to the administration of royal power took place. What the term meant on the ground

[1] Brookes 2016: pp. 107-18.
[2] Probert 2008: p. 22.

[3] Gelling 1997: p. 105.

might have differed depending on whether it was sited in relation to the king's hall on a royal estate, or, probably at a later date, to a road/string Kingston.

What *can* be said with confidence is that the distributional patterns of the Kingstons cannot have been random, there has to have been a purposefulness in their positioning. The three separate statistical methods applied to the data confirm this uniquivally: the road/string Kingstons must have been related to communication and control, predicated on the existing network of long distance Roman highways, and other ancient routeways, still visible in the landscape.

The distribution of the name indicates that our understanding of what they were lies in greater Wessex and to a significant, but slightly lesser degree, the territory of the *Hwicce*. The importance of the control of the roads, and the conduct of travellers, is confirmed in the law codes of all the early Anglo-Saxon kings. Travellers both from within the realm and from without were confined to the highways, with harsh penalties, including death, exacted on any who strayed off the road without blowing a horn and calling out.

> *Gif feorcund mon oððe fremde butan wege geond wudugonge ne hrieme ne horn blawe, for ðeof he bid to profianne, oððe to sleanne oððe to aliesanne.*

'If a man from afar, or a stranger, travels through a wood off the highway and neither shouts nor blows a horn, he shall be assumed to be a thief, and as such may be either slain or put to ransom'.[4]

In the absence of documentary evidence, we can only speculate on the detail of the day-to-day management of the laws relating to the roads. For reasons of security, if nothing else, it is unlikely that the general mass of travellers and traders, passing up and down the highways, would have been required to report to the place within the *villa regalis* where the king's hall stood. In general, this place on most royal estates seems to have been located two to three miles or so off a major road. Common sense suggests that the place of registration would have lain at a remove from the royal hall, and on or close to a road, this latter applying only after the road/string Kingstons were established. Prior to this travellers must have had to report to the site of the Kingston within the lands of the *villa regalis*.

What might a traveller have found when arriving at these proposed check-points? Something similar to to the check-points that abounded in post-war, Cold-War Europe is the most probable. Such a system would not have come as a surprise to the road-users of Anglo-Saxon England. Its name is unambiguous, its purpose known and understood. This is a 'Kingston', where 'Kingston things' happen. There might have been a moveable barrier or gate across the road, manned by the king's officers, the *hevewarda* 'heavy guard' perhaps, that are recorded on some Domesday

manors. There might have been a few wooden buildings for the use of the guards; maybe a designated room for the king's reeve. Doubtless there would have been stabling, paddocks, and general facilities for the grooming and care of horses. There may have been a temporary lock-up where offenders were held before being transferred to a less accessible part of the estate. A roadside check-point would have been vulnerable to attack if prisoners were held there other than temporarily. Stenton is of the opinion that the *ceorls* on an estate would have been responsible for prisoners. Unfortunately he does not reference this statement.

Were the 'original' Kingstons and the 'road/string' Kingstons kin?

In some essential respect they must have been. The 'original' Kingstons in the petty-kingdoms will have arisen from the need to manage the tribal lands and support the chief. We cannot be certain what its detailed function might have been, but in the light of subsequent estate development and circumstantial evidence, a collecting centre for renders must have been one of the functions. It will have been a compound of some sort, large enough to accommodate both produce and animal stock, and there must have been some built structures. No king, high or petty, would have wanted his hall to be too close to the noise and chaos of a collecting centre or a lock-up: but not too far away either.

Campbell is of the view that there would have been many more small kingdoms, with their *principes* and *subreguli*, than Bede records, and that all of these groups would have been led by similar potentates to those that Bede does records.[5] These petty kingdoms would have been a great deal more diverse than the expanded kingdoms we see when they come into view towards the end of the seventh century. The subsuming of these small territories into larger ones, the survival of some names, the loss of others, and the coining of new, reflecting changed circumstances, more than accounts for the loss of many of the Kingstons. With their built-in obsolescence, and their not being settlements as such, it is surprising that as many as 70 have endured. Superficially, a road/string Kingston would appear to have little in common with an 'original' Kingston, but behind their, no doubt dissimilar, day-to-day functions, they shared the same common purpose – the enforcement of royal power and control.

When were the Kingstons founded, what was the process, and by whose order?

As mentioned previously, whatever a *cyningestun* was it was known and in use by the beginning of the seventh century. Almost nothing is known of the earliest years of Anglo-Saxon settlement in relation to the polities of these early adventurers, and when the name *cyningestun* 'Kingston' comes into view, a hundred years or more will have passed since their arrival. One (vain) hope is that the

---

[4] Laws of Ine, *cap* 20.

[5] Campbell 1986: p. 91.

ground will offer up more Staffordshire hoards, Rædwalds, and Prittlewell princes. But even they, fabulous as they are, with their glorious grave goods, leave us with more questions than they answer.

Working with the evidence that we *do* have, what can be said is that the 'Kingston concept' must have been relevant and useful as its proliferation in Wessex and the Severn Valley would seem to suggest. It is not being suggested that this is where the 'Kingston concept' arose - that belongs to a time before written records began in this country, but it is where the name and concept seems to have come into their fullness. There must have been challenges, causes, threats, and opportunities that cried out for a response.

As noted throughout, the relative paucity of early/mid-Anglo-Saxon archaeological and documentary evidence restricts our understanding of these tantalisingly shadowy times. In recent years, Anglo-Saxon studies have experienced great advancements, with sophisticated electronic developments offering insights into the past, undreamed of heretofore. We know so much more than we ever thought we could, but much is still beyond our reach. The insights offered by the road/string distribution patterns are of particular significance, as they confirm what we had already deduced relating to the important political developments of the long eighth century: the militaristic expansion, the need for more sophisticated innovative reforms, and complex forms of socio-political organisation, to secure the realm. The king now had to establish, and maintain, his authority over the lesser kingdoms whose petty kings were once his enemies, but were now his clients. This would have been a monumental undertaking as warfare was part of the fabric of elite Anglo-Saxon society, a vital tool in the power politics of the day. The king had to appease his own retinue of aristocratic warriors and other nobles who were bound to him by his ability to be a munificent 'ring-giver'. A 'ring-stingy' king did not last long. The newly-enlarged kingdoms needed to be steadied if they were to survive and flourish. Innovative systems of governance were needed to secure the evolving new order. Land-holding procedures and regulation, obligations such as the *trinoda necessitas*; the *firma unius noctis*, the formalisation of trade, creation of law codes, and the general manipulation and regulation of judicial practice, were some of the innovative measures employed. As royal authority developed so the official function of kings would have changed, with radical state planning needed. Kingship which in origin was a personal role, the king was the leader of the kin and known to all, changed, to be replaced by an ever-increasing penetration of officialdom at a local level, with the various royal agents becoming increasingly visible as the king's enforcers. The adoption of Christianity, the development of the legal system, the introduction of increasingly institutionalised processes and procedures regarding the control of land, and the obligations that accompanied land holding, were developing, although some of these changes might not have been entirely home grown as there is evidence, admittedly slight, that some of these expanded kingdoms were influenced by Carolingian forms of governance.

Villæ regales and Kingstons

Through the exploration of the changes and mechanisms for social control adopted by the emerging super-kingdoms, it is now possible to propose a role the Kingstons might have had within that framework. The hypothesis that there could have been two separate origins for the 'original' and the road/string Kingstons has been tested thoroughly, and does not seem to have been the case. It seems clear that the road/string Kingstons developed from the earliest 'original' Kingstons. The idea that a Kingston was the centre of royal power is wrong. It was at the king's hall, the central place on a royal estate, that the king would have met with his council, the Witan, and from where decisions were agreed and the kingdom ruled.

Only five Kingstons and seven *villae regales* lie north of a line from Lancashire to the Wash, with the distributional bias towards areas broadly south of the Danelaw boundary being most the most pronounced. To some extent this is a reflection of the documentary source material, derived in the main from the *Anglo-Saxon Chronicle*, which is a Wessex history.

A statistical method, known as *Weighted Kernel Density Analysis*, reveals an illuminating distributional pattern regarding the Kingstons and the *villæ regales* in Greater Wessex and the kingdom of the *Hwicce*.

A Weighted Kernel Density Analysis is a statistical method for estimating the density of other points (in this case the Kingstons) around a feature (the *villae regales*), making it possible to define a smoothly-curved mathematical surface in which every position has a value. A Kernel Density estimation calculates the density of the *villæ regales*, the shading represents the calculated population field value for each cell. Dark shading shows a high density of *villæ regales*, whilst lighter shading represents a low density.[6] The resulting plot calculated for the *villæ regales* with the Kingstons superimposed, shows unambiguously the main areas of royal landed power. It is generally accepted that Wessex was formed from two districts: the 'core' lands comprised the shires of Hampshire, Wiltshire, and Berkshire, and the additional district formed of the western shires of Dorset, Somerset, and Devon, territories that were largely under British control until the early years of the seventh century. There is a marked difference between the two districts. Barbara Yorke has noted that both the Burhgal Hidage and the Domesday Book hidage assessments are more regular and substantial in the core lands of Wessex than in the western group. The distribution pattern is compelling and, given the early history of these territories as outlined in chapter four, it is hard to interpret the appearance of Kingstons in the documentary sources of the seventh to ninth centuries, and their manifestation in reality, in any way other than they represent a response related to the governance of people beyond the core lands which were

---

6   Silverman: 1986. p. 76, equation 45.

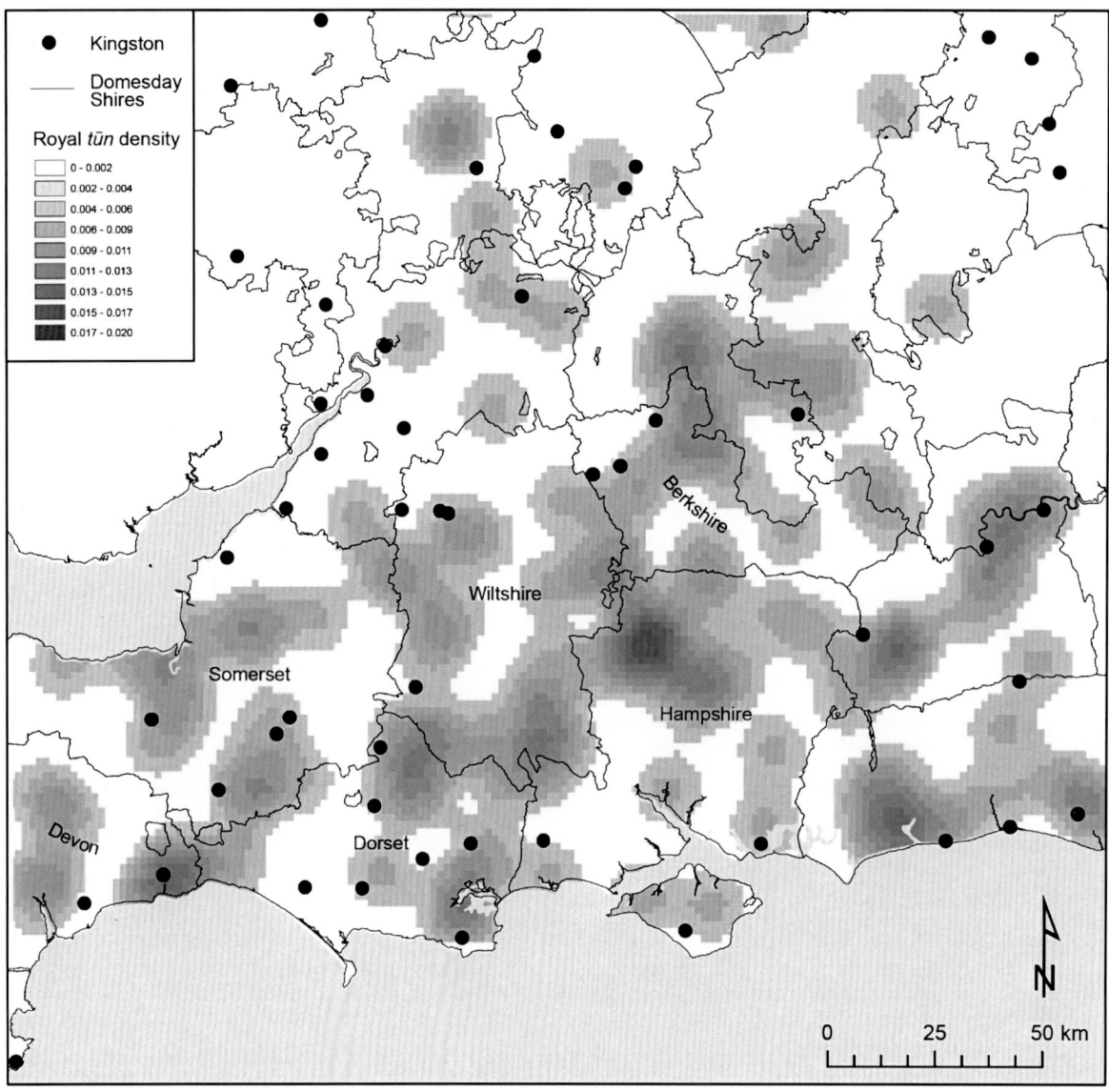

Figure 19: Kingstons and royal *tūn*s in Wessex as listed in Sawyer (1982), presented as a Weighted Kernel Density plot. Courtesy of Stuart Brookes, UCL *Landscapes of Governance Project*.

bereft of Kingstons, where they were clearly not needed. The Kingstons sited on the main routes through the dense forest of Selwood on the Wiltshire/Somerset border, the traditional division between east and west Wessex, have to be significant. Again, Ine is involved, enhancing and embedding his authority as he moves into Selwood. In 705 he divided the west Saxon diocese into two: one based on Winchester, the other on Sherborne, west of Selwood forest. His first bishop was his noble kinsman Aldhelm, who had strong connections with the royal court.

The extensive interdisciplinary research that has been undertaken with the *Landscapes of Governance* project has made it possible to set the Kingstons in, quite literally, a much wider landscape than would have been possible heretofore. By bringing together archaeology, place-names, and written sources in a national study of early medieval sites it has been possible to examine the social complexity and connectivity of Anglo-Saxon England.

Brookes has noted that the distribution patterns of the road/string Kingstons resemble, and in some cases might be supplementing, that of beacons which have been identified by the OE place-name elements *tot* 'a look-out', and *weard* 'watch, ward, protection'.

Brookes suggests that, if the beacons had a military function, and if the Kingstons could be shown to have been part of a beacon system, they might have been connected with the control and movement of troops. This proposal is worth consideration, particularly in Dorset, east Devon and the lower Severn valley, where the road/string pattern is pronounced. There is, however, no demonstrable connection, as the map shows clearly.

There is a hint of a possible military function with two of the Kingstons. Very few mustering sites are known from the records and one of these is the Iron Age hill fort of Badbury Rings, adjacent to which is Kingston (Lacy) DOR. Here,

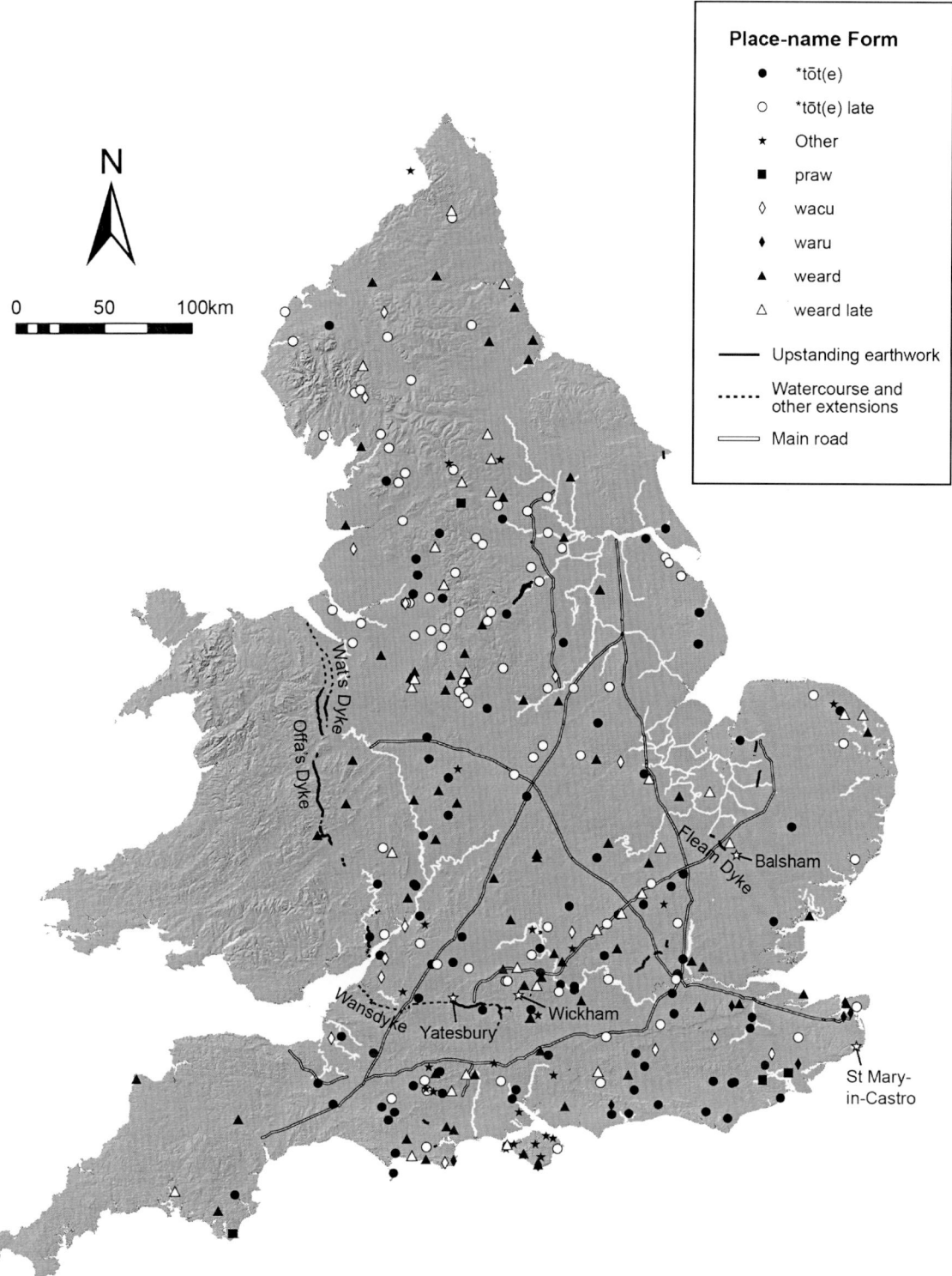

Figure 20: Map of medieval England showing look-out points derived from the written records (up to the Norman Conquest).

Edward the Elder mustered his men in order to repel his cousin Æthelwold, who, after the death King Alfred, was challenging Edward for the crown. In the event there was no fight. Æthelwold, who had been holed up at the convent at nearby Wimborne, fled under cover of night to join the Vikings. The second known mustering place is found in west Wiltshire at Egbert's Stone. This is where Alfred is believed to have mustered his men prior to the battle of

Edington, at which he defeated Guthrum, the Viking leader, in 878. The (claimed) original *Ecgbrihtesstan* stone, which (it is also claimed) once stood on nearby Court Hill, is now close by in the churchyard of Kingston (Deverill).

The Kingston phenomenon is best appreciated as a 'concept', whose reality 'on the ground' was a place called Kingston where 'Kingston things' happened, and where the king's authority ran in a specific, recognised way, and where supplementary laws, and more severe punishments, applied. Kingston was the generic technical term for these places, with the road/string Kingston name differing from the original Kingstons in one essential respect – they were also markers of hegemony.

When were the Kingstons founded?

The only known historical context that corresponds with the road/string systems is the long eighth century, the earlier years of which is when the expanding kingdoms, which later to became known popularly as the Heptarchy, began to develop. The 'core' was essentially Wessex, Mercia, Northumbria, East Anglia, Sussex, Kent, and Essex, with the numbers, and territorial extent, being fluid and unstable for at least two centuries, as small tribal territories were absorbed. This was a time when just one battle could change everything. Many territories would have collapsed without fighting, their petty-kings and nobles accepting the authority of their more powerful neighbours, and settling for a life as elite members of the kingdom they had been forced to join. It is likely, after their loyalty had been tested, they might have become agents of their new king in the governance of the enlarged kingdom. Smaller kingdoms would have been absorbed relatively easily, the larger less so. It would have taken generations to build and secure these new super-kingdoms.

In Summary

The small petty-kingdoms probably had a designated place, connected directly with the enforcement of royal authority, a 'compound', an 'enclosure', a '*tūn*' – the King's '*tūn*', sited somewhere within the tribal lands. There might have been an associated lock up. Whether the Kingston concept came over with the incomers, or emerged in the early years of settlement is not known. They might not have even been founded as such; they could have risen simply out of the day-to-day practicalities of managing the tribal lands. In contrast, the positioning of the road/string Kingstons cannot have been random. Beyond this there is little more to add. The stray examples of the name north and east of the Trent have their own, more individual, stories to tell. These have been explored within the text, and explanations suggested. They are Kingstons, and their stories, when they emerge more fully, will be Kingston stories: the evidence of this research points to Kingstons being, in one way or another, kin.

And finally, was there an architect?

The apparently geometric patterns of road/string Kingstons that have been identified in several places across much of the wider south-west landscape, suggest strongly a purposeful, royal, hand behind the patterns. If, as has been proposed, the most likely time, and circumstances, of the foundation of the road/string Kingstons, corresponds in some way to kingdom expansion, the strongest candidate has to be Ine of Wessex. There is no need to rehearse his

achievements again, other than to remind ourselves of the key advancements of his reign. The promulgation of the law codes; the creation and unification of the Wessex shires; the creation of the role of ealdorman; the end of multiple kingship; the establishment of a new diocese; the founding of 12 religious houses, and the creation of the *entrepôt* of *Hāmwīc*. We know for certain, that the place-name *cyningestune*, was a known term and a physical actuality eighty or so years before Ine's reign. It must, therefore, have been available for imitation and exploitation, but without written records we cannot know whether the term was used prior to the early years of the seventh century. It certainly could have been, and there were Wessex kings prior to Ine whose power, and length of reign, could have offered the opportunity for a system of control to be established; but this would seem to have been unlikely. Barbara Yorke notes that West Saxon kingship in the seventh century presents a confused picture, with multiple kingship seemingly the norm, and the evidence of the annals hinting at rivalry within the various branches of the royal house. She suggests that it is not until the reign of Ine, who was able to build on the successes of predecessors, and abolish the sub-kings, that there was stability in Wessex.[7]

Ine resigned the throne in 726 and travelled to Rome where he died. He was succeeded by Æthelheard, whose ancestry is not known but who it has been suggested was the brother of Ine's wife. Æthelbald of Mercia quickly imposed his authority over Wessex with Æthelheard ruling for the rest of his reign as a client king. It would seem to be unlikely that the road/string Kingston system was established in the reigns subsequent to Ine's although there is no reason to think that the system and the Kingston concept did not continue to be used in circumstances other than kingdom expansion.

It is hoped that this study of the origins, purpose, and development, of the place-name Kingston, offers a strong foundation on which further research can be built. As David Parsons has recently asserted, in his study of place-names referring to early English society – *churls, æthelings, kings*, and *reeves*, the key to understanding place-name evidence is context, and that the robustness of the context needs constantly to be assessed and reassessed.[8]

As the late James Campbell's words opened the first chapter of this study it seems fitting to close with them. Although Campbell was a passionate Anglo-Saxonist, he nevertheless, sounded a note of warning to all who would study the Anglo-Saxon period: 'If they wish for certainty in history, and like to feel the ground firmly under their feet, they would be best advised to study some other period'. This writer, hopefully not unwisely, chose to disregard this advice and set out to weave a narrative around the OE place-name Kingston. All the available source material, some of which is, admittedly, fragile and slight, has been

---

[7]   Yorke. B., in Lapidge. M., 1999: p. 470.
[8]   Parsons. D., 2013, pp, 54-6.

pressed into service, heeding Margaret Gelling's stricture that: 'evidence should not be sought to support a view that is already held, but the names should be allowed to speak for themselves'.[9] The Kingstons and their patterns have been allowed to emerge and speak for themselves, the consequence being that the ground on which they stand now is firmer than heretofore.

I leave the final judgement of this study to David Parsons who, in his paper (cited above) of place-names in early English society, affirms: 'It is in the pattern of names that we learn so much...', and when reflecting on the outcome of this [Jill Bourne's] research, it has crystallised my view that her conclusions are probable rather than possible.[10]

---

[9]   Gelling, 2002-03: 'English place-name studies', p. 16.
[10] Parsons 2013: p. 56.

PART II

The Data

The **Base Map** bound at the beginning of Part I shows the distribution in England of the place-name Kingston plotted against the historical county boundaries of 1850, and relevant long-distance Roman roads and some major ancient routeways. The lines of the roads are those described by I. Margary. A few additional roads, not identified by Margary, have been included. The source of these is largely from the records of English Heritage and a few from literature published subsequent to Margary. These roads and the relevant references are identified in the text, and on the Base Map (Fig. 1 p. 2).

The **Base Map** plots all 70 Kingstons with the additional identification of those recorded in DB or earlier.

The Material relating to the Kingstons is organised alphabetically by pre-1973 counties in the form of a gazetteer. Each entry is accompanied by a map which places each Kingston in its wider context, and in relation to any long distance Roman road or ancient routeway with which it appears to have been associated. The gazetteer entries and the maps are numbered as they appear on the Base Map, and the small maps in Part 1.

The Kingston data is listed alphabetically by pre-1974 county.

The names are listed within their county in order of their first appearance in the record.

AP. Ancient Parish, These are parishes known to have existed prior to 1597. The ecclesiastical status has been determined largely by reference to F.A. Youngs, 1979. *Guide to the Local Administrative Units of England*, vol. 1, Southern England; vol. 2, Northern England (Royal Historical Society, London). Some nineteenth-century county directories and Victoria County Histories also refer to the ecclesiastical status of a settlement.The form of the name is **emboldened** for its first entry in the record as are **all pre-DB and DB references**.

Domesday references are taken from the Phillimore Domesday volumes (see Bibliography).

(S 000): Refers to charter references from P.H. Sawyer, *A Revised Catalogue of Anglo-Saxon Charters*, 1968 and _www.esawyer.org.uk_.

(M 00): Refers to the number allocated to Roman roads by I. Margary.

Each individual map is numbered in the same order as the related material on the opposite page and as it appears on the **Base Map** (Fig. 1 p. 2).

Each entry follows this order:

1   The name, **emboldened**, in the form it appears in the one-inch Seventh Series OS map.
2   OS reference.
3   Hundred/Wapentake.
4   Ecclesiastical status and church dedication if known.
5   First recorded spelling and date: all pre DB forms are listed.
6   DB reference(s) for the Kingston or for the manor within which the Kingston lay.
7   DEPN E Ekwall, 4th edn, 1960: *The Concise Oxford Dictionary of English Place-Names*.
8   CDEPN: V. Watts ed., 2004. *The Cambridge Dictionary of English Place-Names*.
9   English Place-Name Society volume, e.g. PNGlo vol. 3, p. 133.
10 Site.
11 Additional notes.

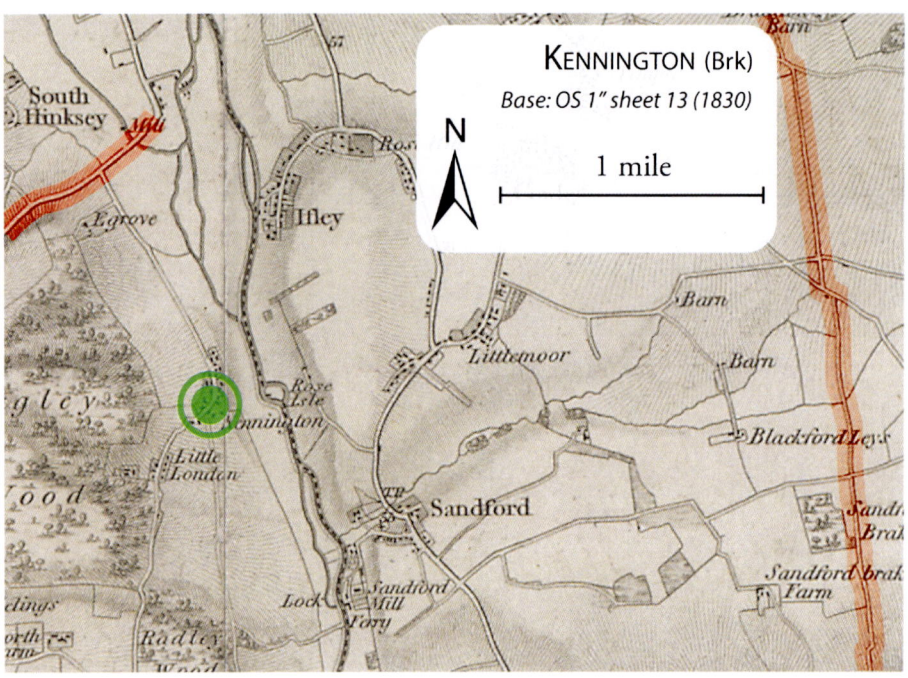

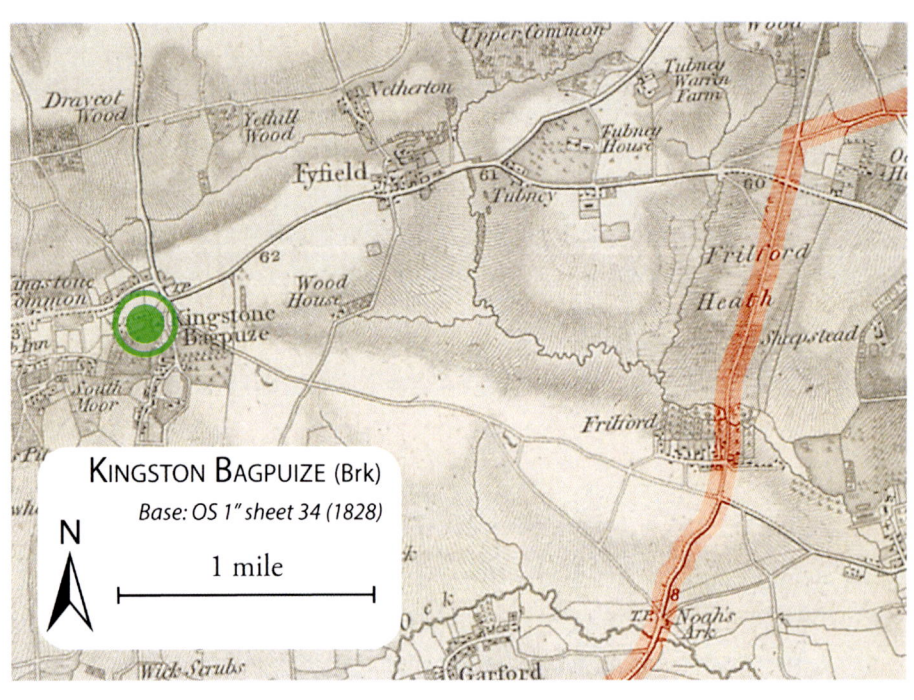

BERKSHIRE 1

1 **Kennington**

2 SP 522 025

3 Hormer Hundred

4 Originally a daughter of Sunningwell, now a separate parish

5 *Chenitun*, *Chenigtun* 821 Grant by Ceonwulf to Abingdon Abbey (S 183)

   Cenigtun 956 Grant by Eadwig to Brihthelm (S 614)

   æt Cenintune 956 Agreement between Brihthelm and Abingdon (S 1292)

6 *Chenitun, Genetune* DB

   DB Land of Abingdon Church TRW, 'Warin holds 4 hides of the same manor and (amongst others) the same land in *Chenitun*; Alwin one hide in *Genetun*. TRE Six Englishmen held them they could not withdraw from the church' (DBBrk 7,11)

7 DEPN p. 272

8 CDEPN p. 340

9 PNBrk vol. 2, p. 453

10 SITE Kennington lies two miles south of Oxford on the west bank of the River Thames, in the angle formed by the river and the Roman road from Wantage. This road crossed the river between New Hinksey and Iffley, continuing on into the north-east to Headington where it is joined at the Silchester to Towcester Roman road (M 160b/160c). The bounds of S 614 describe the modern parish of Kennington.

11 PNBrk interprets this name as *Cæna*'s (personal name) + *tūn*. Discussion with Dr David Parsons and Dr Paul Cavill suggests that, based on the thirteenth and fourteenth, century forms, an alternative interpretation of the first element of the name could be *Cyng* + *tun*. (See also Kennington KNT and Kennington SUR).

BERKSHIRE 2

1 **Kingston** (Bagpuize)

2 SU 407 981

3 Marcham Hundred

4 i **Cingestun** 970 in a charter of King Edgar, '...7 hides at *Cinges tun* ' Free of all but the three common dues (S 778)

   ii 956 for 975 x 978, a charter of King Edward of 13 hides *aet Cyngestun* (S 828)

   iii 965 for 975 x 978 (S 12) charter of King Edward, grant of 7 hides at *Cyngestune*' (S 829)

   iv 958, charter of King Eadwig, in the bounds of a grant of land at Longworth, '...*east onlong Temese þæt hit cymð to Cing hæma gemære*...' (S 654)

   v 958 for 959 charter of King Edgar contains a boundary reference *ondlang Temese to þa þorn stybbe æt Cingtuninga gemære* (S 673)

5 A chapelry of Longworth, now a parish, church dedicated to St James

6 *Chingestune* At DB there were two manors:

   i Land of Henry of Ferrers, held by Henry himself TRW, by Stankell TRE (DBBrk 21,14)

   ii TRW Land of William son of Ansculf; held TRE from King Edward by Thorkell who 'could go where he would' (DBBrk 22,12)

7 DEPN pp. 277–8

8 CDEPN p. 347

9 PNBrk vol. 2, pp. 412–13

10 SITE Kingston (Bagpuize) lies on an ancient long-distance route-way, which may have been Romanised. It broadly follows the line of the River Thames. This road runs north-eastwards to Bessels where it is joined by the present-day A338, which follows the line of a long-distance Roman road that ran north from the Roman small town of Wantage and on to Kennington, where it crossed the River Cherwell. The northern parish boundary follows the Thames.

11 It is not immediately obvious of which royal *vill* Kingston Bagpuize was a component part and the ecclesiastical connections do not help. The most likely candidate is Wantage. The identification of the 970 (S 778) charter of King Edgar granting to Brihtheah, his faithful deacon, seven hides at a place *appellatione dicitur Cinges tun* in Berkshire, is not entirely secure. Margaret Gelling is of the opinion that it is impossible to say to which of the Berkshire Kingstons this grant refers. It is possible that it may be one of the title deeds which Abingdon acquired when they purchased 20 hides at *Cingestune*, and could be referring to Kingston Lisle. See M. Gelling, 1979. *Early Charters of the Thames Valley*, no. 122, p. 58, pp. 345–7 (Leicester University Press).

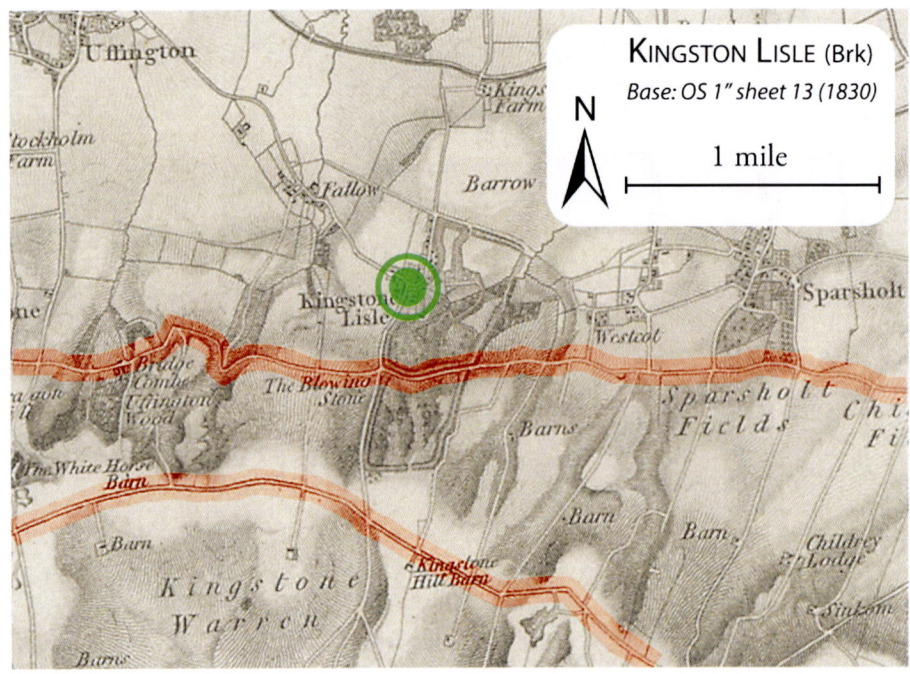

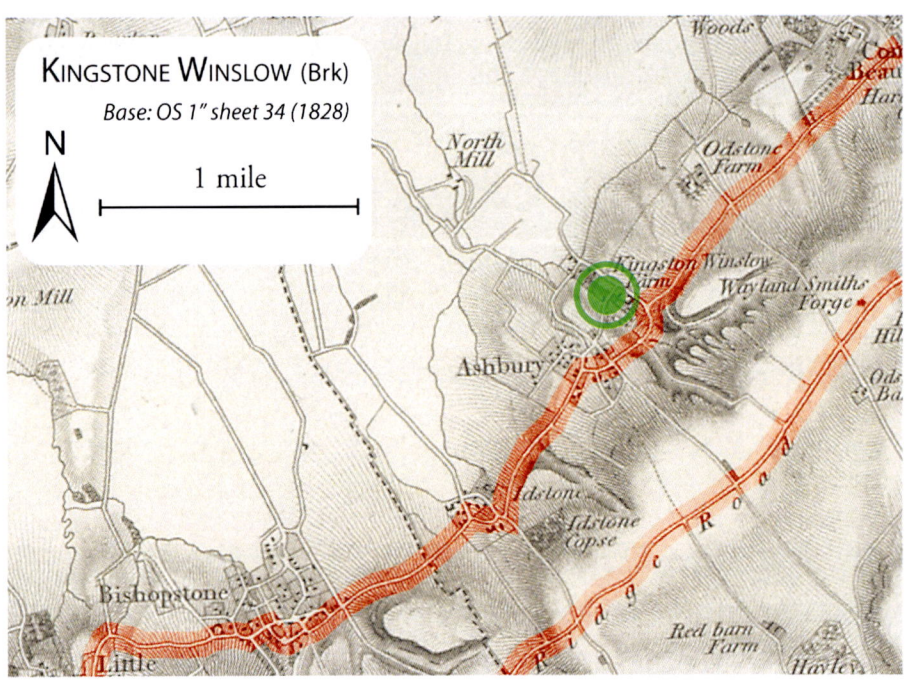

BERKSHIRE 3

1 **Kingston** (Lisle)
2 SU 326 876
3 Hillslow Hundred
4 Chapelry of Sparsholt; neighbouring Fawler is also a chapelry
5 *Kingeston* 1220
6 DB *Spersholt* (DBBrk 1,32) has been identified as Kingston (Lisle)
   At DB Sparsholt was held TRW by the king and TRE 'by three free men who held it as three manors' (DBBrk 1,10. 21,12. 35,5. 55,4.). It was assessed at 16 hides TRE but TRW nothing. These three manors appear to be represented by Fawler, Kingston, and Sparsholt. Only one was in royal demesne; this was almost certainly Kingston Lisle. Phillimore DB for Berkshire identifies entry 1,32 – *Spersolt*, as Kingston Lisle. See Gelling, 1979. *Early Charters of the Thames Valley*, pp. 345–7, (Leicester University Press).
7 DEPN pp. 277–8
8 CDEPN ~
9 PNBrk vol. 2, p. 372
10 SITE Sited on both the Icknield Way and the Ridge Way which cross the county broadly shadowing each other. The present-day north/south parish boundaries cross both of these roads, on which Kingston Winslow (below) also lies. Two miles to the west, just over the county boundary, the Ridgeway crosses the Roman road from Cirencester to Winchester.
11 The existence of Kingston prior to its first separate entry into the record in 1220 may be implied in the 963 land grant of King Edgar to Æthelsige, his *camerarius*, of 10 hides *æt Speresholte*, this is considered to represent Fawler in Kingston Lisle. (S 713) The bounds, which probably describe the western half of the present parish of Kingston Lisle refer to *'on þæs cinges scypena, of þan scypenum on þæt riscbed, of þan risc bedde on þæs cinges/þornas* the 'king's cow-shed', 'king's thorns'.
   It is unclear of which *villa regalis* Kingston Lisle once may have been a member as it shares boundaries with both Wantage and Lambourne, both of which were held TRW and TRE by the king. Wantage has perhaps the greater claim with Sparsholt, being both in Wantage Hundred at DB and sited on the Icknield Way at the point where it is crossed by another long-distance road. Originally all these lands may have been one large estate, which may broadly represent the land near Ashdown of 3,000 hides granted in 648 by Cenwealh of Wessex to his nephew Cuthred (*ASC* A 648).

BERKSHIRE 4

1 **Kingstone** (Winslow)
2 SU 263 857
3 Ashbury Hundred
4 Chapelry of Ashbury, church dedicated to St Mary
5 *Kyngeston Wendelsclev* 1252; there are early forms for Winslow, *Wend(e)l(es)cliva(m)*, c.1150, 1189, 1242–3
6 DB ~
   At DB Ashbury was held both TRW and TRE by Glastonbury Abbey. (DBBrk 8, 1)
7 DEPN p. 278
8 CDEPN ~
9 PNBrk vol. 2, pp. 345–6
10 SITE Kingstone Winslow lies on both the county boundary with Wiltshire and on the long-distance route-way known as the Icknield Way, which crosses the north of Berkshire, shadowing the Ridge Way for much of its length. The boundaries of the parish cross both of these roads.
   Two miles west of Kingstone Winslow, just across the county boundary with Wiltshire, is the long-distance Roman road between Cirencester and Winchester.
11 *Wendelsclev* was originally the name of a separate estate named from the escarpment. The wider area here is known as Ashdown.
   Lambourne, the south-eastern neighbour of Ashbury, might be the royal estate of which Kingston Winslow was a component part. At DB Lambourne was held both TRW and TRE by the king. (DBBr 1,29. 35, 3. 59,1.).

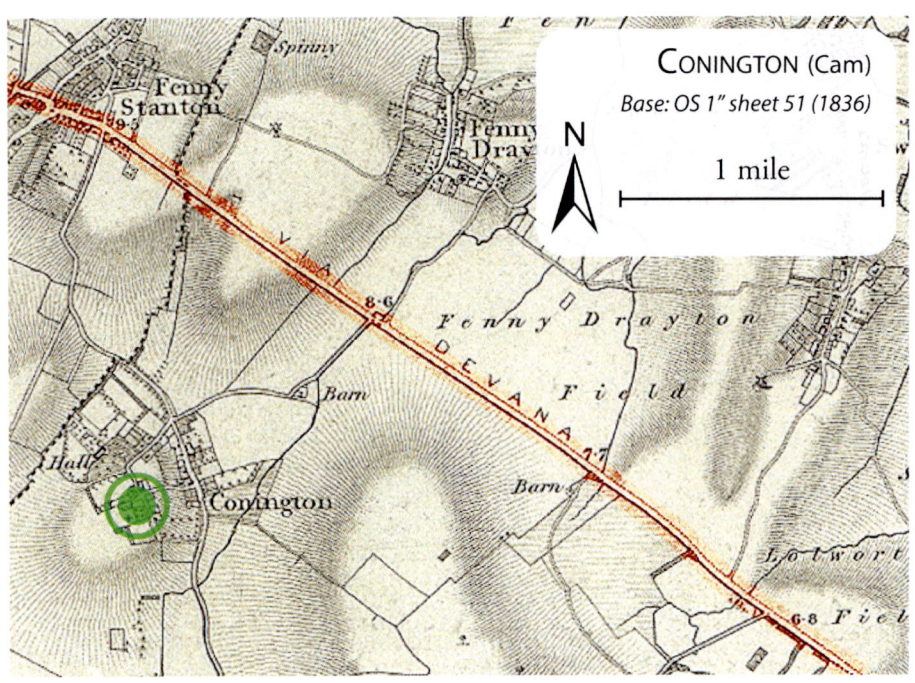

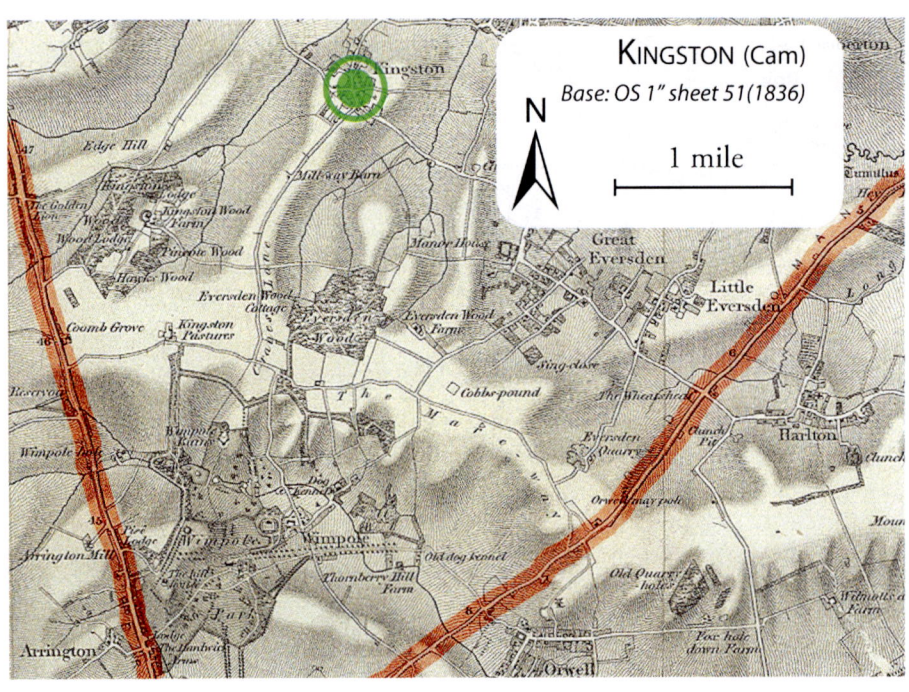

CAMBRIDGESHIRE 1

1 **Conington**
2 TL 320 661
3 Papworth Hundred
4 Ancient Parish, church, dedicated to St Mary; the manors of Seagraves and Smyths were once chapelries of Conington.
5 *aet Cunningtune* 975 x 1016, Will of Ælfhelm (S 1487)
6 DB: *Contone*, *Cunitone*, three manors:
   i   TRW Land of Robert Gernon, no TRE information given (DBCam 21,7)
   ii TRW Land of Gilbert of Ghent, no TRE information given (DBCam 23,3)
   iii TRW Land of Hardwyn of Scales, TRE '3 Freemen of King Edward's held this land' (DB Cam. 26,46)
7 DEPN p. 120
8 CDEPN p. 155
9 PNCam pp. 165–6
10 SITE Conington lies on the Roman road from Godmanchester to Cambridge (M 24). The north-east boundary of the parish follows the line of the road; the north-west parish boundary is the county boundary with Huntingdonshire.
11 ~

CAMBRIDGESHIRE 2

1 **Kingston**
2 TL 345 550
3 Longstow Hundred
4 Ancient Parish, church dedicated to All Saints and St Andrew
5 *Chingestone* DB
6 At DB there were six manors:
   i   Held by the King both TRW and TRE (DBCam 1,8)
   ii TRW Land of Earl Roger; TRE, Earl Waltheof (DBCam 13,12)
   iii TRW Land of Count Alan; TRE, Earl Algar's man held this land (DBCam 14,47)
   iv TRW Land of Eudo. TRE Earl Waltheof's man, held this land (DBCam 25,8)
   v TRW Land of Hardwyn of Scales, there are '2 men at arms; TRE Goding Thorbert, Edeva the Fair's man, held this land and could withdraw', also 'Wulfmer held this land and could grant' (DBCam 26,38–39)
   vi TRW Land of Picot of Cambridge; 'Ralph holds from Picot...'. 'TRE 14 Freeman held this land, 10 of them had 2 hides and 1½ virgates of the King's jurisdiction; they found 7 cartages and 3 escorts. 2 others, earl Agar's men had 1 virgate. 1 Archbishop Stigand's man held 3 virgates. One of them, the Abbot of Ely's man, had a virgate of the Abbot' jurisdiction. 2 others, Earl Algar's men, had 2 hides. They could all withdraw' (DBCam 32,21)
7 DEPN p. 277
8 CDEPN p. 347
9 PNCam p. 163
10 SITE Kingston lies in the angle between the Roman road which runs roughly south-west from Cambridge and Ermine Street, which is the south-west boundary of Kingston parish (M 23a; M 2b).
11 The DB reference 6 vi, which notes the duties of 10 freemen to find cartages and three escorts, is one of several DB Kingston entries where riding duties kind are listed.

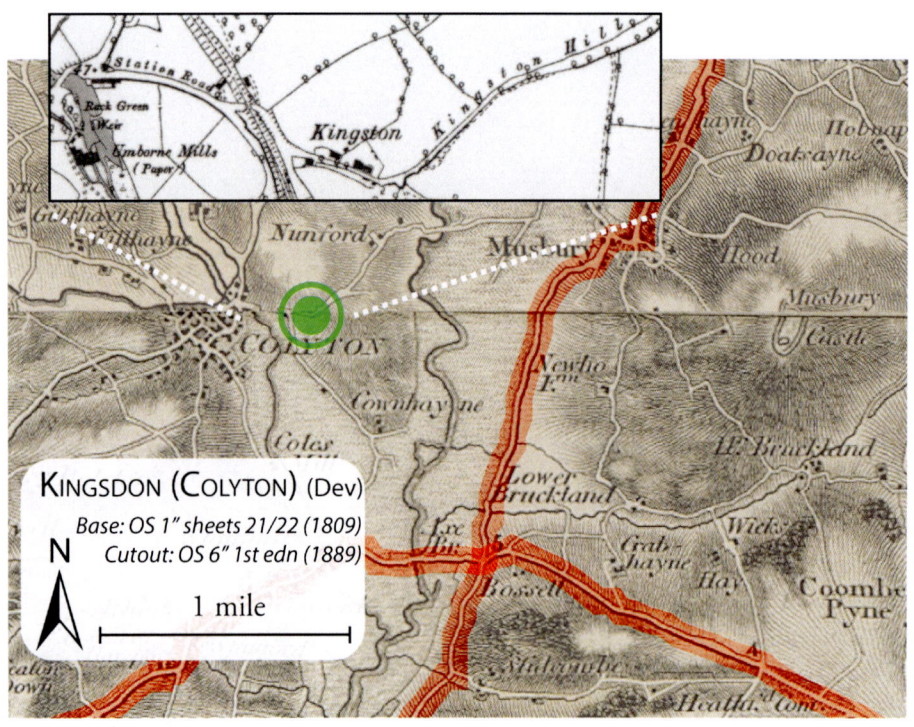

KINGSDON (COLYTON) (Dev)
Base: OS 1" sheets 21/22 (1809)
Cutout: OS 6" 1st edn (1889)

N

1 mile

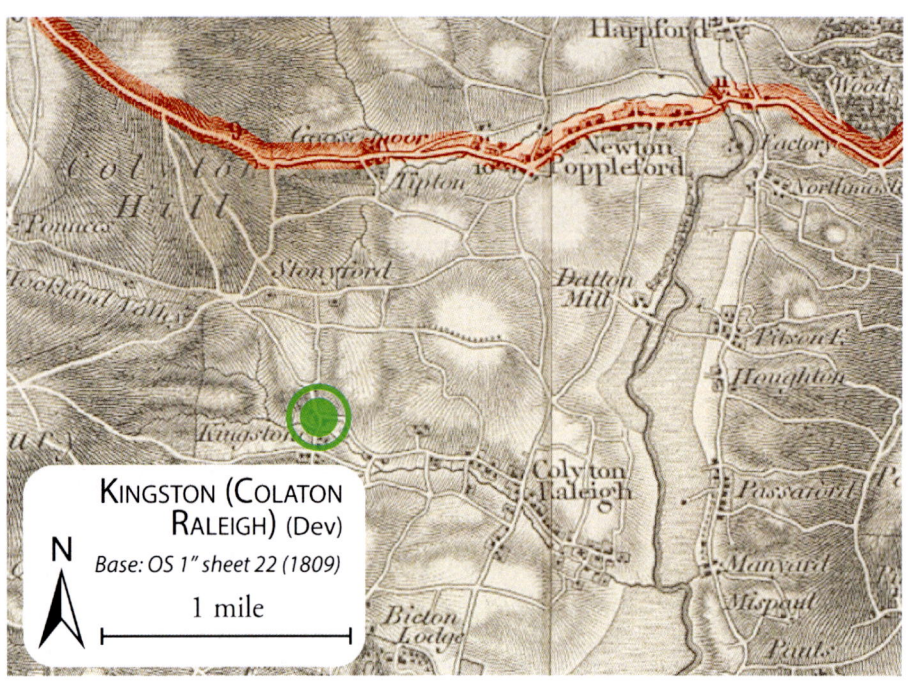

KINGSTON (COLATON RALEIGH) (Dev)
Base: OS 1" sheet 22 (1809)

N

1 mile

DEVON 1

1 **Kingsd(t)on** (Colyton)
2 ST 252 943
3 Colyton Hundred
4 Chapelry of Colyton, Parish of St Andrew
5 *Kyngesdon* 1539
   Kingston on second edition six-inch OS map
6 DB ~
   At DB *Culitone* was held TRW by the King; no TRE information is given (DBDev 1,13)
7 DEPN ~
8 CDEPN ~
9 PNDev vol. 2, pp. 623–4
10 SITE Kingston lies immediately to the east of Colyton, in the angle formed by the London to Exeter Roman road and the Lower Fosse Way.
11 Axminster is the nearest royal centre to which Kingsdon might have been attached. At DB TRW it was held by the King and was liable for the *firma unius noctis* (DBDev 1. 11; 19, 45)
12 A Saxon cross probably tenth century, found at SY 246 940 during reconstruction of the Norman tower, now incorporated into the reconstructed south transept.

DEVON 2

1 **Kingston** (Colaton Raleigh)
2 SY 065 877
3 East Budleigh Hundred
4 Chapelry of Colaton Raleigh, the church is dedicated to St John
5 *Kingeston* 1227
6 DB ~
   At DB Colaton was held TRW by Gytha, mother of Earl Harold, TRE it paid geld for 3 hides. The final entry notes 'to this manor has been added half a virgate of land which a thane held freely TRE' (DBDev 1,46).
7 DEPN ~
8 CDEPN ~
9 PNDev vol. 2, pp. 587–8
10 SITE Kingston lies in the parish of Colaton Raleigh adjacent to Newton Poppleford (also a chapelry of Colaton), which has been carved out of the larger land unit of Colaton Raleigh. The northern boundary of Newton Poppleford follows the line of the long-distance Roman road to Exeter, which crossed Dorset from Badbury Rings, and on which the Hampshire/Dorset 'string' Kingstons and Kingston (Colyton), ten miles to the east, are sited. The line of this road has been identified archaeologically one mile to the north-east of Colaton (M 49).
11 Cemetry 43AD-700 at SY 057 887

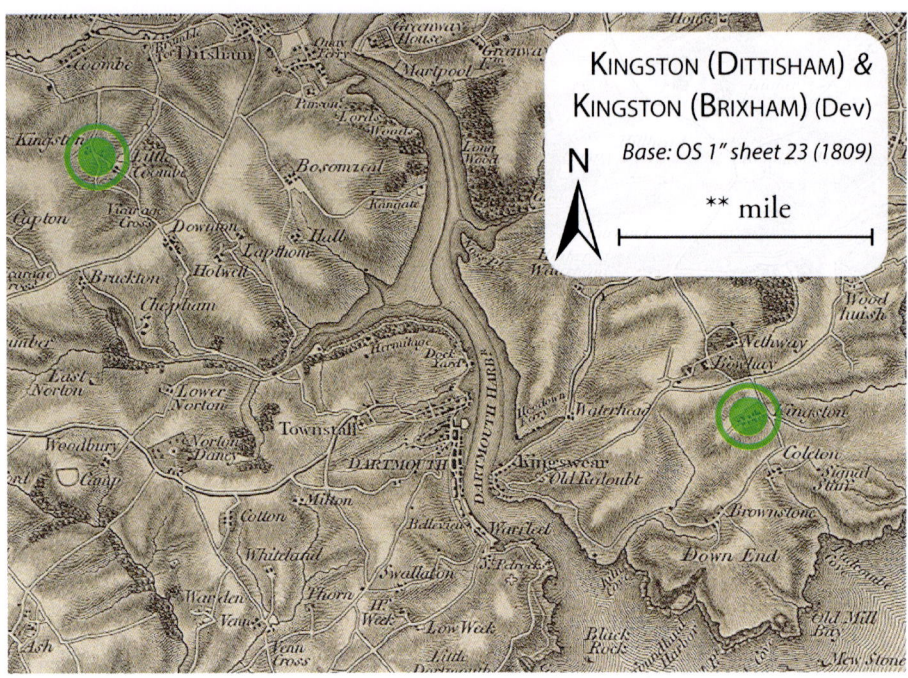

KINGSTON (DITTISHAM) &
KINGSTON (BRIXHAM) (Dev)

N

Base: OS 1" sheet 23 (1809)

** mile

DEVON 3

1 **Kingston** (Dittisham)
2 SX 846 540
3 Coleridge Hundred
4 Chapelry of Dittisham parish, church dedicated to St George
5 *Kyngestone* 1438
6 DB No
At DB Dittisham was held TRW by the Bishop of Exeter; no TRE holder is given (DBDev 2,23)
7 DEPN ~
8 CDEPN ~
9 PNDev vol. 1, pp. 322–3
10 SITE Kingston lies in the parish of Dittisham on the west bank of the River Dart. The parish boundaries go down to the banks of the river. Kingston lies just over one mile inland. On the opposite side of the river another Kingston lies, just inland from Kingswear in the parish of Brixham.
11 ~

DEVON 4

1 **Kingston** (Facy/Brixham)
2 SX 904 515
3 Haytor Hundred
4 Chapelry of Brixham, the church is dedicated to the Virgin Mary
5 *Kyngeston Facy juxta Dertemuth* 1292, *Kyningeston juxta Brikesham* 1302
6 DB ~
At DB Brixham was held TRW by Iudhael of Tones and TRE by Ulf (DBDev 17,29)
7 DEPN ~
8 CDEPN p. 347
9 PNDev vol. 2, p. 507
10 SITE Lies on the east bank of the River Dart one mile inland, north-east of Kingswear and opposite Dartmouth.
11 ~

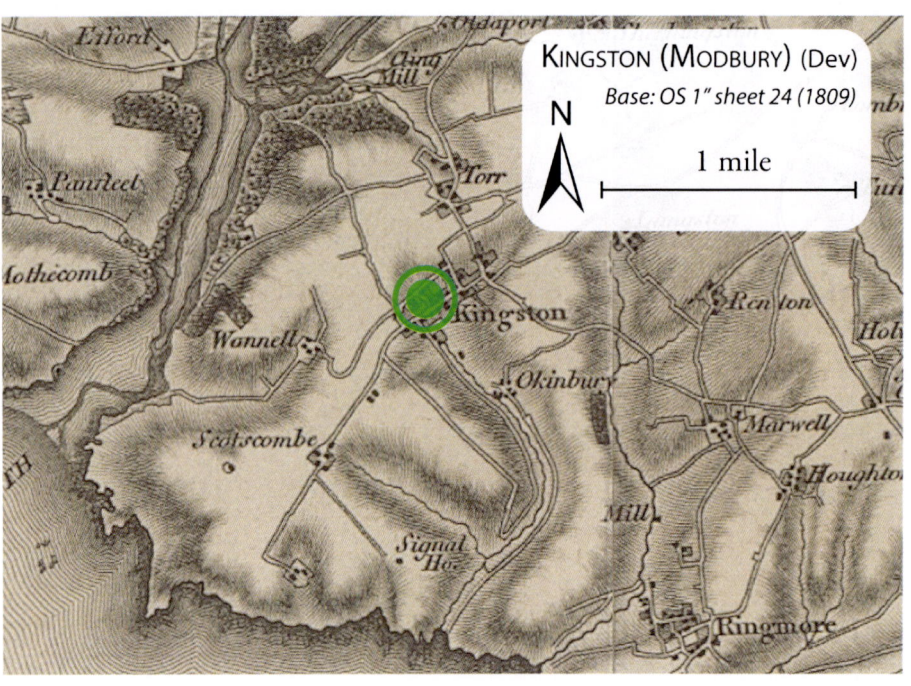

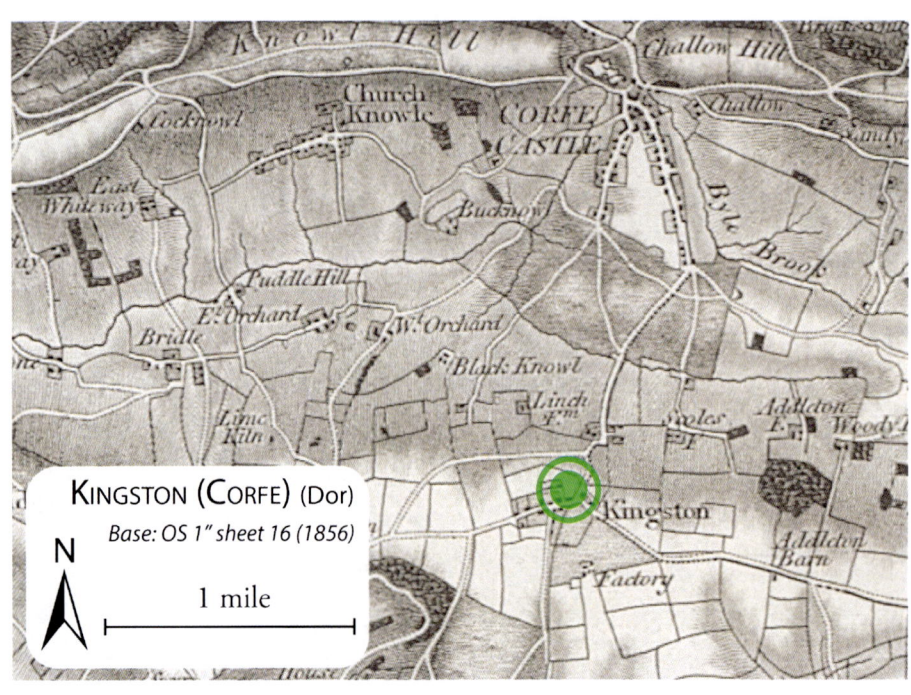

DEVON 5

1 **Kingston** (Modbury)

2 SX 635 478

3 Ermington Hundred

4 Chapelry of Ermington, the church is dedicated to St James the Less. The patronage of Ermington alternates between the Crown and the Rector. It is now an independent civil parish.

5 *Kingeston(e)* 1242–1394 with the variant *kyng*

6 DB ~
DB TRW Ermington is held by the king, TRE it was held by Asgar (DBDev 1,23; 15,67)

7 DEPN pp. 277–8

8 CDEPN p. 347

9 PNDev vol. 2, p. 279

10 SITE Lies on the south coast of Devon at the mouth of the River Erme, Three miles SSW of Modbury. The parish goes down to the sea where there is a Beacon Point.

11 ~

DORSET 1

1 Kingston (Corfe)

2 SY 956 797

3 Rowbarrow Hundred

4 Chapelry of Corfe Castle, independent civil parish since 1877

5 *Chingestone* DB

6 At DB, 'of the manor of ***Chingestone*** the king has I hide, on which he built Wareham Castle, for it he gave to St Mary's (Shaftesbury) the church of Gillingham with its dependencies' (DBDor 19, 10).

7 DEPN p. 277

8 CDEPN p. 347

9 PNDor vol. 1, p. 15

10 SITE Kingston lies in the centre of the Isle of Purbeck, two miles south of Corfe Castle, seven miles south-east of the Roman small town and Alfredian *burh* of Wareham, and six miles west of Swanage. Given the extensive Roman stone and shale quarries at Kimmeridge and the Isle of Purbeck, it is considered that the road which runs from Wareham to Swanage is probably following a Roman line. Kingston lies on this road.

11 The land at Kingston was granted to Shaftesbury Abbey by King Eadred in 948. It remained in the hands of the Abbey until the Dissolution. Wareham is the most likely Anglo-Saxon royal estatE of which Kingston might have been a component part.

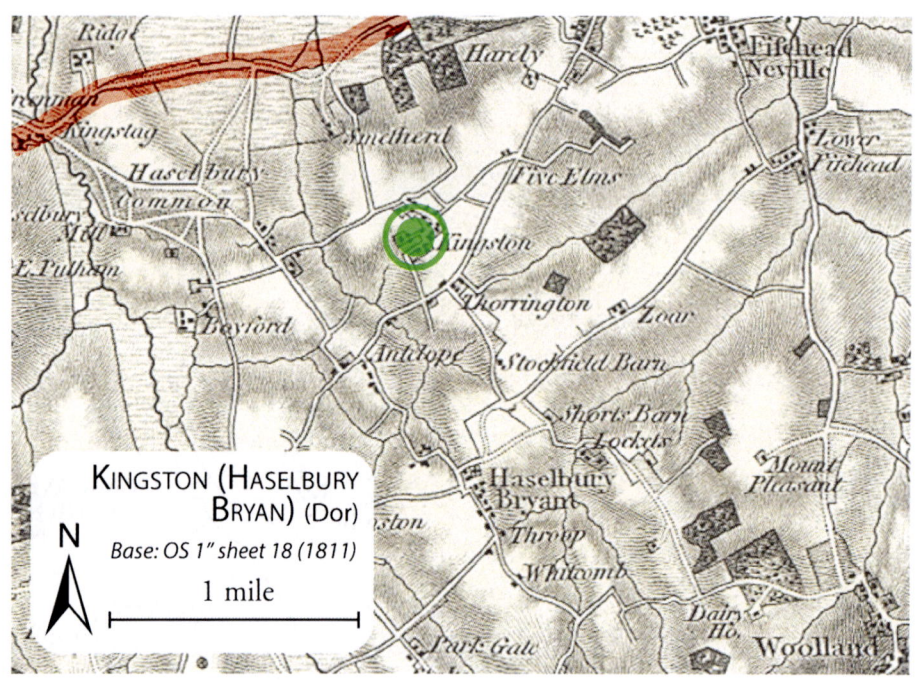

KINGSTON (HASELBURY BRYAN) (Dor)

Base: OS 1″ sheet 18 (1811)

N

1 mile

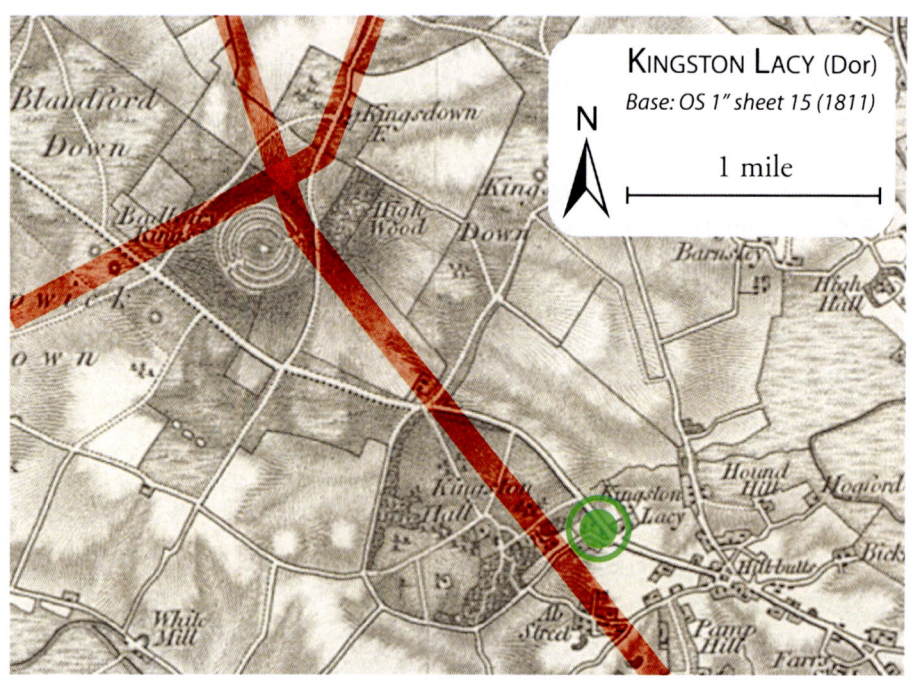

KINGSTON LACY (Dor)

Base: OS 1″ sheet 15 (1811)

N

1 mile

DORSET 2

1 **Kingston** (Hazelbury Bryan)
2 ST 750 098
3 Pimperne Hundred
4 Lies in the present-day parish of Hazelbury Bryan, church dedicated to St James. Both Kingston and Haselbury were originally chapelries of Sturminster Newton.
5 *Kingeston* 1580
6 DB ~ for both Kingston and Hazelbury.
   At DB (Sturminster) Newton was in the hands of St Mary's, Glastonbury. No TRE holder is given. (DBDor 28,2).
7 DEPN ~
8 CDEPN ~
9 PNDor vol. 2, p. 101
10 SITE Kingston lies in the centre of the county. Several roads cross here and an ancient trackway runs two miles south of Kingston, but no long-distance Roman roads have been identified here. The boundaries of Haselbury Bryan, Pulham, and Radlynch meet at King's Stag 'king's boundary stake' (ST 725 108). This is the *truncum qui stat in tribis divis*, 'the trunk which stands at three boundaries'. (PNDor vol. 3, p. 349). An ancient trackway runs east/west two miles to the south.
11 In 1361, Richard *di Hasilbere* held the manor of King John in chief.

DORSET 3

1 **Kingston** (Lacy)
2 SY 978 013
3 Hundred of Badbury
4 Chapely of Wimborne Minster
5 *Kingestune* c.1170
6 DB ~
   At DB Wimborne was held both TRW and TRE by the King. It did not pay tax TRE (DBDor 1.3, 21. (31. 14,1; 31,1).
7 DEPN pp. 277–8
8 CDEPN ~
9 PNDor vol. 2, p. 167
10 SITE The grounds of Kingston Lacy House are bounded on the east by the Roman road, which ran north out of Wimborne from the Roman fortress at Lake Farm, passing Badbury Rings towards Blandford Forum, and onwards to Bath and the early Roman harbour at Sea Mills on the River Avon (M 46). To the south, this road ran from Lake Farm to the sea at Hamworthy, where military stores have been found at the site of the Roman harbour (M 4d). Kingston Lacy is sited at the intersection of this road and the Roman road from London to Exeter. (M 4c/4e at this intersection. This is the site of the small Roman town of *Vindocladia*.

Kingston Lacy was probably a component part of the important royal estate that was centred on Wimborne, and which was founded at the latest by 718 (*ASC* C, D, 718) for Cuthburgh, sister of King Ine of Wessex, and her nuns. The *ASC* A 901 (899) records that after the death of King Alfred, Æthelwold, his nephew, opposed the succession of Edward the Elder by seizing Wimborne and Twinham. Edward mustered his men at Badbury, but there was no fight as Æthelwold and his men escaped, under the cover of darkness, to join the Vikings.

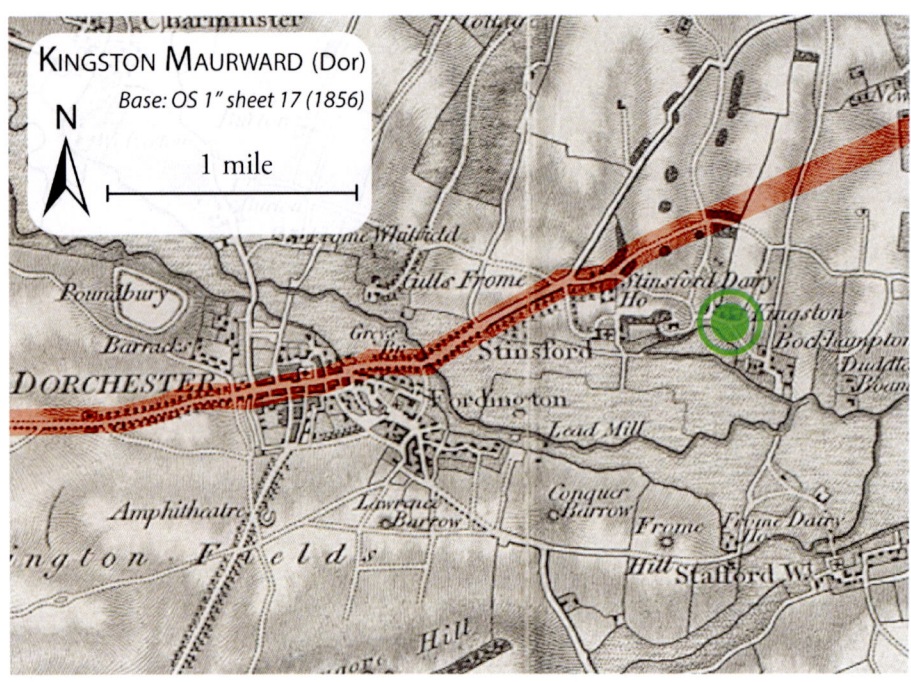

DORSET 4

1 Kin**gston** (Maurward) in the parish of Stinsford
2 SY 720 912
3 Puddletown Hundred
4 Now in the parish of Stinsford; church dedicated to St Michael.
5 *Kingeston* 1244
6 DB ~ Neither Stinsford nor Maurward are listed in DB.
7 DEPN ~
8 CDEPN ~
9 PNDor Part 1, p. 369
10 SITE Lies on the long-distance Roman road, one mile east of Dorchester, which crossed north-west/south-west across the county from Badbury Rings to Exeter, (M 4e).

   A (presumed) Roman milestone, without inscription, is still *in situ* on the south bank of the agger at the point where it joins the Wimborne to Dorchester Road. Margary vol.1, p.100

11 In 1894 part of Holy Trinity, Dorchester, beyond the limits of the borough on the north-east, together with a part of the parish of Fordington, were added to Stinsford parish, suggesting perhaps that Fordington may have been the mother church. At DB Fordington was held both TRW and TRE by the king (DBDor 1,4). It was liable for the *firma unius noctis*.

DORSET 5

1 **Kingston** (Russel)
2 SY 582 913
3 Uggescombe Hundred
4 Chapel of Long Bredy, the church is dedicated to St John the Baptist.

   Lewis notes that Kingston Russell was 'anciently in the parish of Whitchurch Canonicorum', ten miles to the west.
5 **Kingeston** 1212
6 DB ~

   At DB both Little and Long Bredy were held TRW by St Peter's of Cerne Abbey. (DBDor 11,10).

   At Long Bredy there was a Thane with one hide and one plough. No TRE information given (DBDor 11,12).

   At DB Whitchurch (Canonicorum) was held by the Abbey of St Wandrille, who also held the churches of Burton Bradstock, Bridport and Whitchurch.
7 DEPN p. 278
8 CDEPN ~
9 PNDor vol. 4 pp. 17–18
10 SITE The northern parish boundary of Kingston Russell follows the line of the Roman road from Dorchester to Exeter (M 4f).
11 The early tenth-century Burghal Hidage records a stronghold at *Brydie* which has been identified as Bredy, an immediate neighbour of Kingston Russel, which, once its military purpose was past, faded back into the landscape where it is now represented by an earthen rampart on a hill-top. Bridport, seven miles to the west, may have replaced Bredy as a burghal centre. Kingston Russell may have been connected with the *burh*, although its foundation could have been much earlier. Perhaps the initial decision to create a *burh* at Little Bredy was related to the (unrecorded) pre-existence of a Kingston here.

   There is a 1672 reference to 'land called Kingstone', and in 1678 to 'Kingstone Corner', in the neighbouring parish of Frampton. Dorset Record Office, Sheridan Collection (D 51).

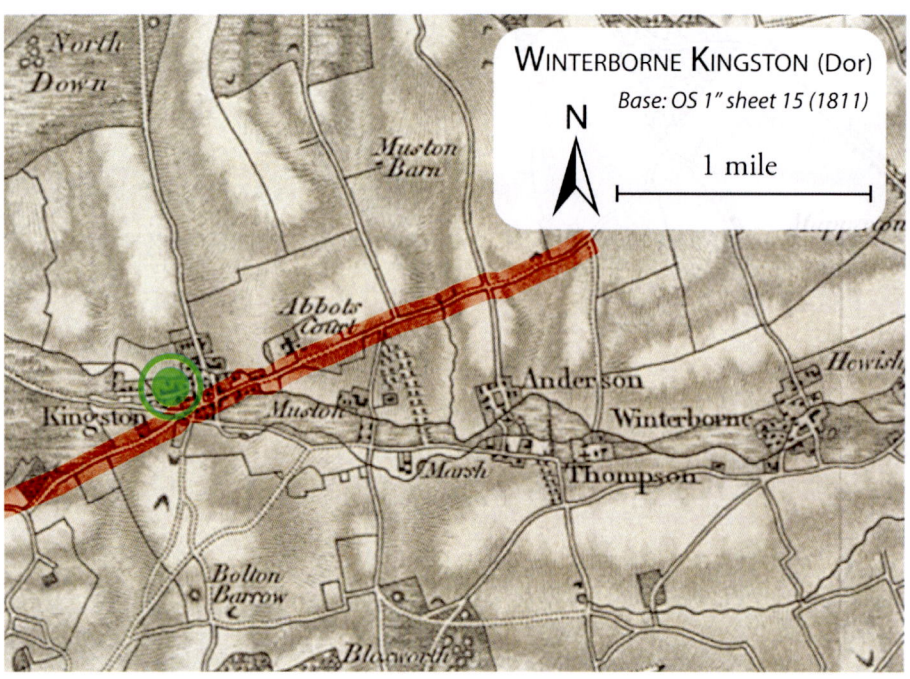

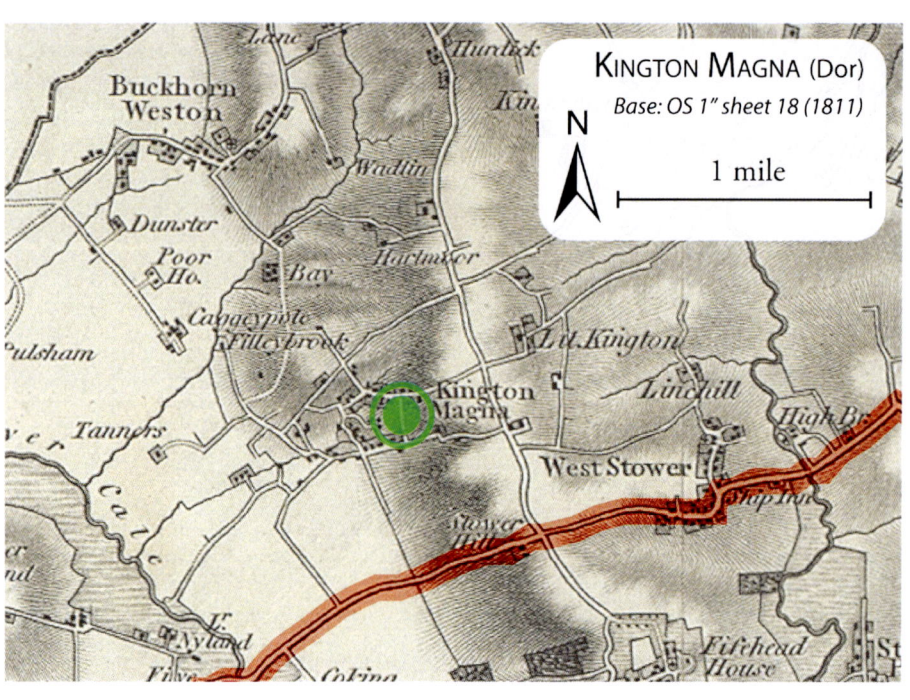

DORSET 6

1 **Kingston** (Winterborne)
2 SY 862 976
3 Bere Hundred
4 Chapelry of Bere Regis, church dedicated to St Nicholas. It is now a parish. No other chapelries of Bere have been identified.
5 *Kingeswinterburn* 1194
6 DB ~

At DB Bere Regis was held both TRE and TRW by the King, (DBDor 1,2. 24,1. 55,15).

Although Kingston is not listed independently at Domesday it has been suggested that the entry under the Land of the King's Thanes refers to Kingston (DBDor 56,6).

The manor of Bere and its dependencies were liable for the *firma unius noctis*.

7 DEPN ~
8 CDEPN ~
9 PNDor vol. 1, p. 283
10 SITE The line of the long distance Roman road which crossed the county from Badbury Rings to Dorchester runs through this parish; the church stands on this road (M 4e).
11 ~

DORSET 7

1 **Kington** Magna (also, Little Kington ST 775 233
2 ST 763 232
3 Redlande Hundred
4 AP, church dedicated to All Saints, originally part of the extensive parochia of Gillingham
5 *Chintone* DB. Little Kington is first recorded as *Parva Kynton* in 1239
6 At DB there were three manors:
  i TRW Land of Arnulf of Hesdin, TRE Edric held it (DBDor 32,1)
  ii TRW Land of Waleran, TRE Leofgeat held it. (DBDor 40,2)
  iii TRW Lands of the King's Thanes, Ketel holds *Chintone*; TRE Doda held it (DBDor 56,2
7 DEPN p. 279
8 CDEPN p. 349
9 PNDor vol. 3, p. 41, Parva Kynton PN Dor vol. 3, p. 71
10 SITE Kington Magna lies towards the north-west tip of Dorset on the boundary with Somerset. The southern parish boundary follows the long-distance ancient route-way, known in this part as Sherborne Causeway, which crosses the county from Old Sarum to Sherborne to Yeovil, crossing the Fosse Way at Coker.
11 Kington (Magna) shares a boundary with Gillingham which lies three miles to the north-east of Kington Magna. As Kington Magna was in origin a daughter of Gillingham, this was probably the royal *vill* of which it was a member.

At DB Gillingham was held both TRW and TRE by the King, and was liable for the *firma unius noctis*.

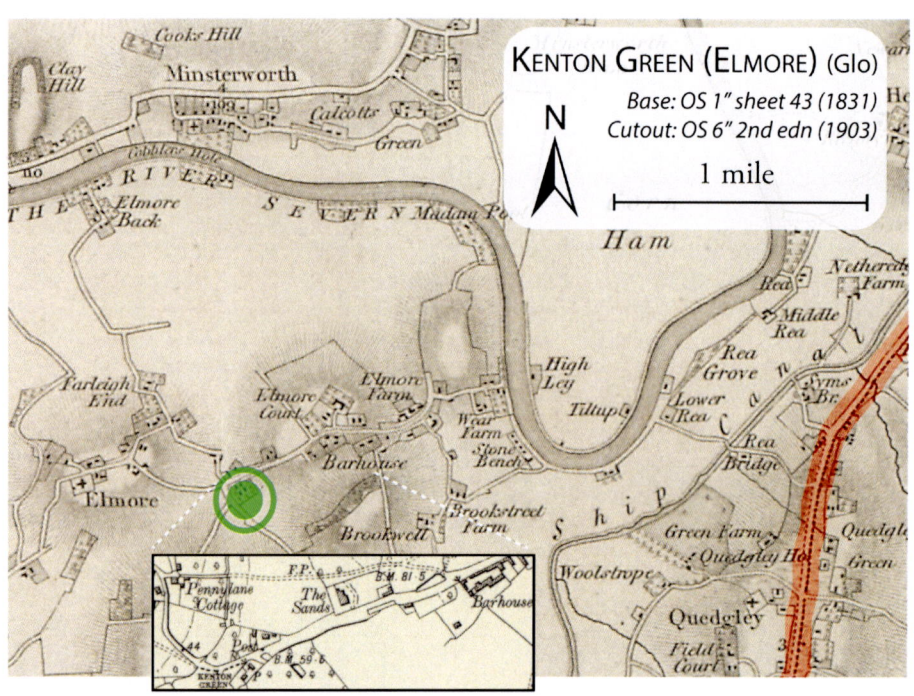

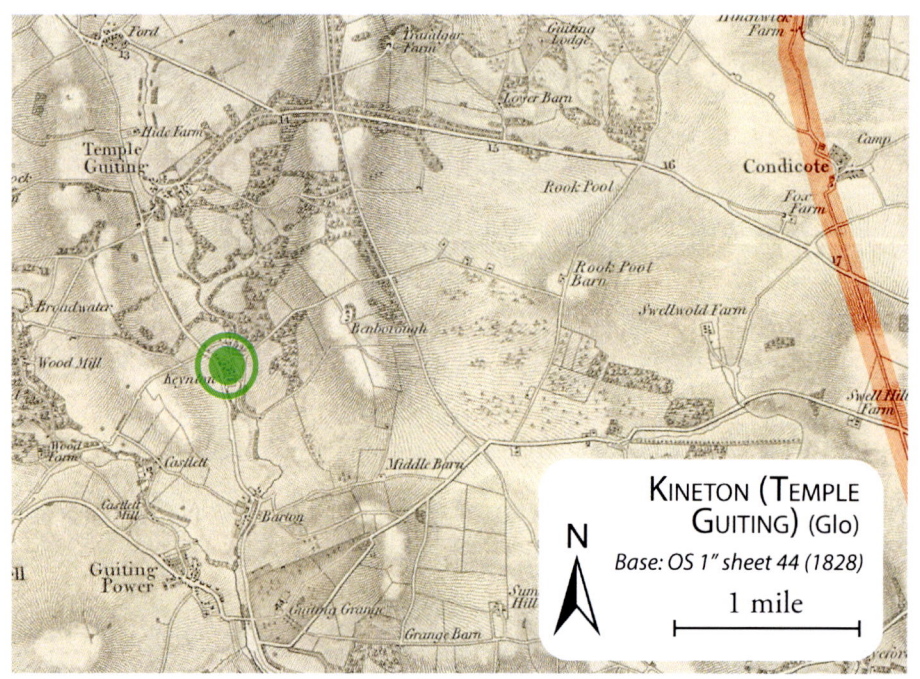

GLOUCESTERSHIRE 1

1 **Kenton Green** (Elmore)
2 SO 777 148
3 Dudstone and King's Barton, an area of royal demesne that surrounded Gloucester
4 Chapelry of Elmore, the church is dedicated to St John the Baptist
5 *Kyngtone* 1250–1457
6 DB ~

   At DB Elmore was listed under Land of the King's Thanes, 'Edward holds ½ a hide from the King (William) as a manor (DBGlo 78, 6 note)

7 DEPN ~
8 CDEP ~
9 PNGlo vol.2, p.162
10 SITE The present-day eastern boundary of the parish of Elmore lies just over a mile from the Roman road which ran from Gloucester to Sea Mills (M 541).

It is almost impossible to reconstruct this landscape as it would have been in Roman or early medieval times, as it has been altered radically by land reclamation, and the building of a canal and railway.

11 By 1095, Elmore was held by Walter of Gloucester, the castellan of Gloucester. It is listed as 'Land which John son of William Erins de la Strete de Kyngtone gave...' under the Lands and Tenements of the Berrow family in Elmore *c.* 1250–1457. Gloucestershire Archives D326

T 17/5. I am grateful to Simon Draper for drawing my attention to this reference.

GLOUCESTERSHIRE 2

1 **Kineton** (Temple Guiting)
2 SP 097 265
3 Holford Hundred
4 Chapelry of Temple Guiting, church dedicated to St Mary
5 *Kin-, Kynton(e), toniam, -tune,* 1185
6 DB ~

   At DB three manors are listed under Guiting.
   Temple Guiting:

   i   Land of Roger of Lacy TRW. TRE Brictric, a Thane of King Edward's held it. (DBGlo 39,6). TRW the 'lordship land' did not pay tax. Seven riding men are listed here.

   ii Land of Gerwy's Wife TRW. TRE 3 Thanes held it as three manors (DBGlo 76,1).

   Guiting is recorded in 814 in a charter of Ceonwulf, King of Mercia, issued from Tamworth to Deneberht, bishop of Worcester (S 171).

   Guiting Power:

   Land of William Goizenboded TRW. TRE King Edward held it and leased it to Alwin his sheriff so that he might have it for his lifetime.

7 DEPN p. 207
8 CDEPN p. 265
9 PNGlo vol. 2, p. 14
10 SITE Kineton lies in the present-day parish of Temple Guiting on the boundary between Guiting Power and Temple Guiting. The eastern boundary of the parish just skims the long-distance Roman road which ran from Bourton-on-the-Water to Alcester (M 18a). The western boundary of the parish follows the line of the Salt Way. This is the only Kingston that lies near a saltway.

The royal status of these manors is indisputable.

11 This is one of several Kingstons where special duties related to transport and communications are listed (DBGlo 39, 6).

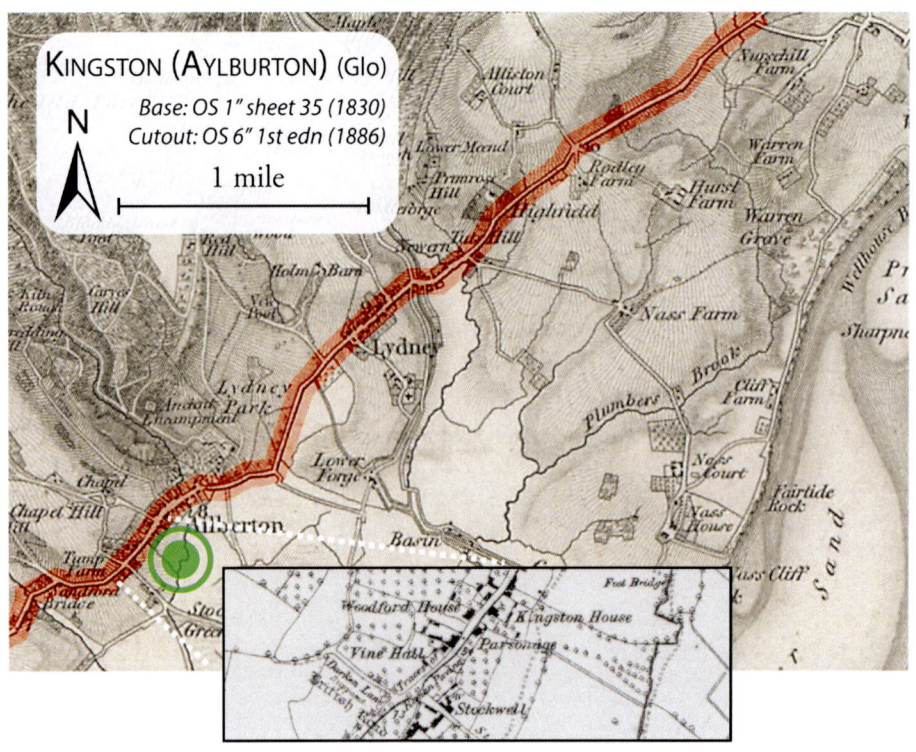

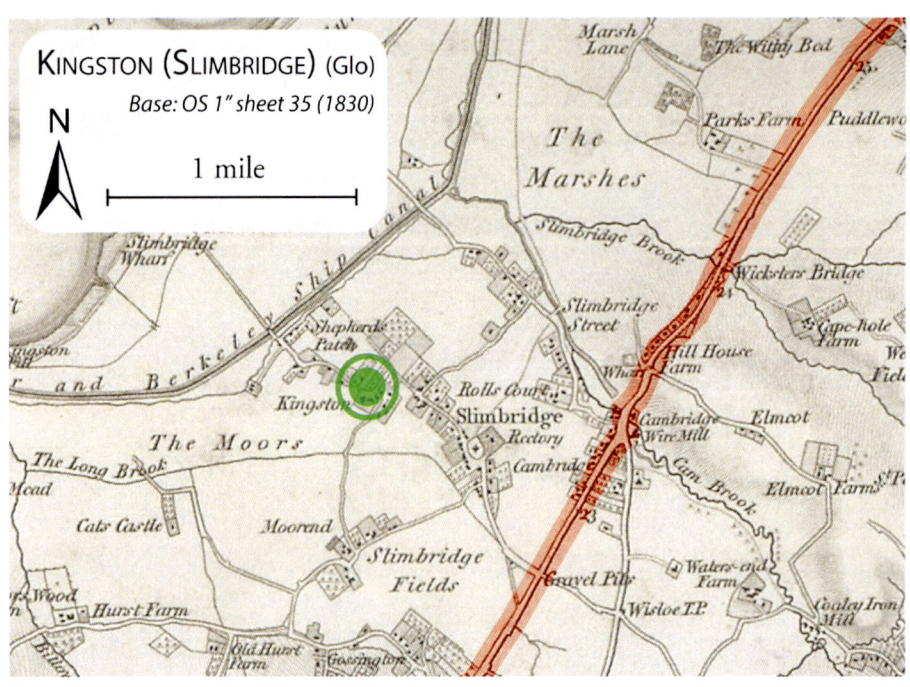

GLOUCESTERSHIRE 3

1 **Kingston** (Aylburton)
2 SO 618 019
3 Lydney Hundred
4 In the parish of Lydney
5 *Kinegerst'* 1221, ***Kingesterne*** 1221, ***Kyngeston*** 1385
6 DB ~
   At DB Kingston was probably subsumed under the entry for Lydney, its mother settlement.
   At DB Lydney was held TRW by the king and was the head of the Hundred. TRE it was held by Earl William who 'made a manor from 4 lands – the Bishop of Hereford, the monks of Pershore, and 2 thanes' (DBGlo 1.55; E5).
7 DEPN ~
8 CDEPN ~
9 PNGlo vol. 3, p. 255
10 SITE Kingston lies almost nine miles north-east of Kingston (Tidenham) on the Roman road from Chepstow to Gloucester and Weston under Penyard (HRE). At Lydney the road divides, the right fork going to Newnham which stands on the west bank of a large loop of the River Severn. Opposite Newnham is Arlington from where a Roman road ran south-east to Whitminster to join the Gloucester to Sea Mills road. There are several references to a ferry between Newnham and Arlington.

The first edition of the 1866 six-inch OS map shows a hamlet of a few houses along the line of the Roman road, which, along its length, is variously labelled, 'British Road' or 'Roman Road'. The line of this road has now been straightened and Kingston by-passed (M 60a).
11 It has been suggested that the name could be a compound of the OE *cyne* or *cyning* with *gærs-tūn* 'a pasture, enclosure' (PNGlo vol. 3, p. 255). Dr David Parsons disagrees with this interpretation.

GLOUCESTERSHIRE 4

1 **Kingston** (Slimbridge)
2 SO 733 038
3 Berkeley Hundred
4 A chapelry of Slimbridge, church dedicated to St John the Evangelist
5 First recorded as ***Ki-, Kyngeston(a)*** 1248
6 DB ~
   At DB Slimbridge was a manor of Berkeley. TRW it was held by the King; Roger had two hides of Berkeley here. TRE no information given (DBGlo 1,17).
7 DEPN ~
8 CDEPN ~
9 PNGlo vol. 2, p. 248
10 SITE Kingston is now represented by the name of a farm lying immediately west of Slimbridge Church and less than a mile from the River Severn. The eastern boundary of the parish of Slimbridge crosses the line of the Gloucester to Sea Mills Roman road (M 541).
11 ~

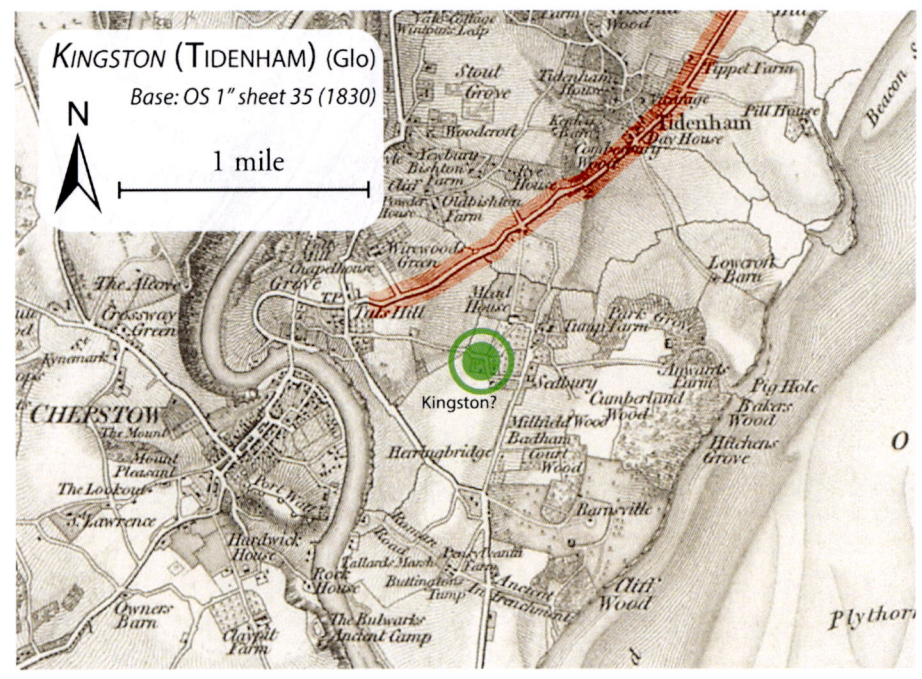

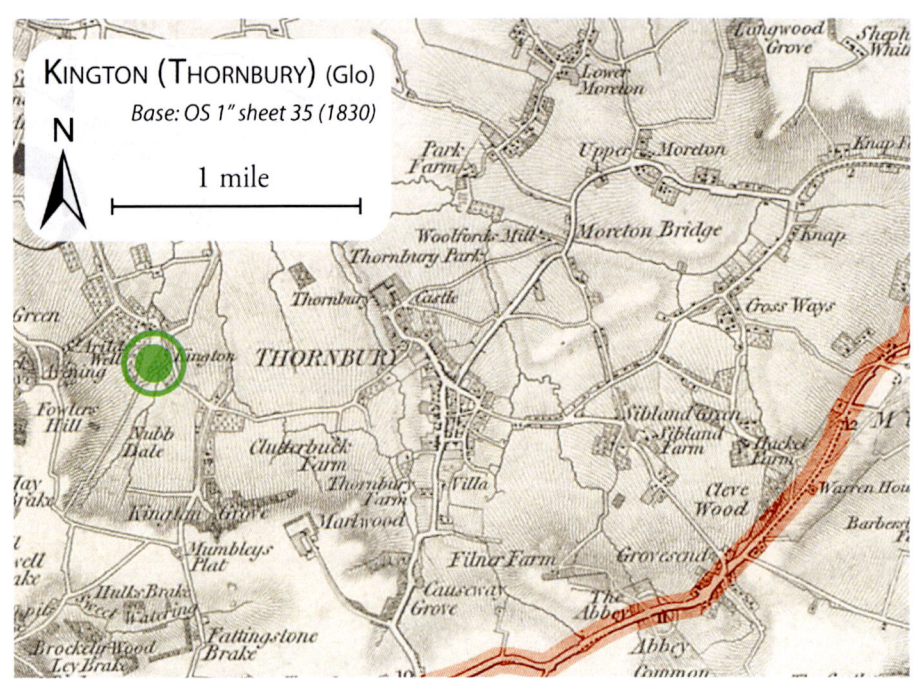

GLOUCESTERSHIRE 5

1 **Kingston** (Tidenham)

2 ST 55 93 (exact site unknown)

3 Tidenham Hundred

4 In the parish of Tidenham

5 *To cinges tun*, in the tenth-century bounds and customs of Tidenham (S 1555)

6 DB ~

At DB there were 3 manors at Tidenham:

i TRW Land of the King, 30 hides were held by the Abbot of Bath. TRE this manor was held by Archbishop Stigand. It did not pay taxes. (DBGlo1,56). This manor probably represents the 30 hides granted in the charter of King Eadwig.

ii TRW Land of William of Eu one and a half virgates. TRE Archbishop Stigand held it (DBGlo 31,6).

iii Land of Roger of Lacy half a hide. TRE Archbishop Stigand held it (DBGlo 39,11).

7 DEPN ~

8 CDEPN ~

9 PNGlo vol. 3, p. 266

10 SITE The exact position of *Cyningestune* is uncertain, but present-day Sedbury is considered to have been where Kingston lay. It lies between the east bank of the River Severn and the west bank of the River Wye, at the southern end of Offa's Dyke, two miles from Chepstow on the long-distance Roman road which ran south-west from Gloucester along the west bank of the River Severn (M 60a or 60aa).

Sedbury, the *sud burh*, may refer to the site of a Roman camp which overlooked the River Severn.

11 A survey of Tidenham made in the later tenth or earlier eleventh century extended the manor by 30 hides lying in six divisions: there were 12 hides at Stroat (the Roman road), five at Milton, six at Kingston, three at Bishton, and three at Lancaut. The remaining hide, described as lying 'outside the enclosed land' was apparently at Beachley.

C. Elrington *et al* 'Tidenham including Lancaut: Introduction', 1972. *A History of the County of Gloucester: Volume 10: Westbury and Whitstone Hundreds* pp. 50–62. URL: http://www.british-history.ac.uk/report.aspx?compid=15757

GLOUCESTERSHIRE 6

1 **Kington/Kyneton** (Thornbury)

2 ST 620 904

3 Langley Hundred (of which Thornbury is the head)

4 A tithing of the ancient parish of Thornbury, church dedicated to St Mary. Other tithings are Falfield, Morton, Oldbury, Rangeworthy.

5 First recorded as **Kin-**, **Kynton** 1248, **King-**, **Kyngton** 1322

6 At DB Thornbury was held TRW by the King. It had been a manor of Queen Matilda. TRE Thornbury was held by Brictric, son of Algar. 18 *radcenestre* are listed here. (DBGlo 1,47). This is the same Brictric who also held Temple Guiting TRE, a manor in which there is a Kingston and where seven riding men were listed at DB.

7 DEPN ~

8 CDEPN ~

9 PNGlo vol. 3, p. 15

10 SITE Thornbury lies nine miles south of Kingston (Slimbridge). The eastern boundary of the parish follows the line of the Roman road that ran from Gloucester to Sea Mills. (M 541)

Kington and Kyneton lie almost immediately next to each other, half a mile to the west of Thornbury church and castle. The first edition of the six-inch OS map shows Kington and Kyneton less than half a mile apart. They are represented today by Kyneton Quarry and Kington House respectively.

11 Underlying medieval Thornbury there is a settlement of Roman date. The earliest Anglo-Saxon settlement is close to the church and castle.

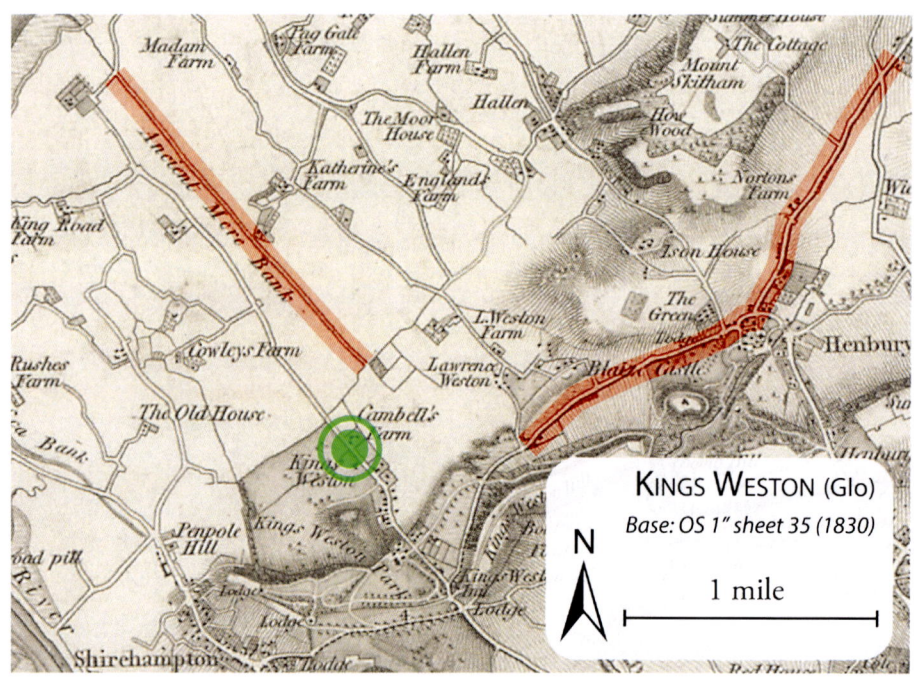

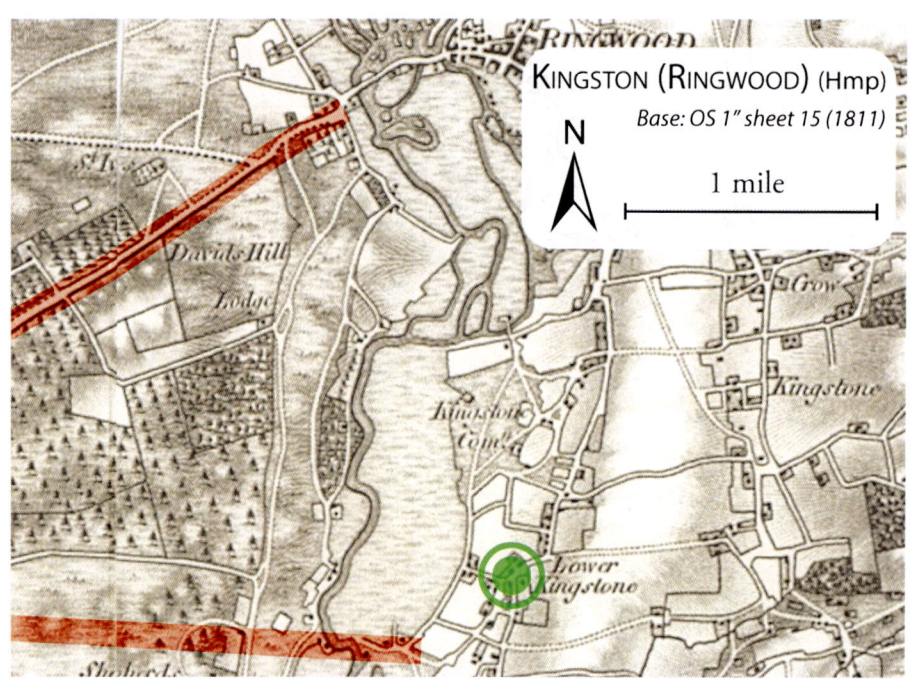

GLOUCESTERSHIRE 7

1 **Kingsweston**

2 ST 538 779

3 Henbury Hundred

4 Kings Weston is a chapelry of Henbury; the church is dedicated to St Mary. Other dependencies of Henbury are Lawrence Weston, Northwick, Redwick, Stowick, Charlton, Compton and Aust.

5 *Weston(e)* DB, *Ki-, Kynges- Weston*(e) 1248.

6 DB ~

At DB listed under Berkeley along with 19 other outliers.

Held both TRE and TRW by the king. Assessed in total at seven hides, one virgate (DBGlo 1,15)

7 DEPN ~

8 CDEPN ~

9 PNGlo vol. 3, p. 133

10 SITE Kingweston lies 10 miles south of Thornbury on the Roman road between Gloucester and the Roman port of *Abonæ* (Seamills) (M 541).The line of the road, which was aligned on the prehistoric earthwork at Henbury known as Blaise Castle, ran broadly parallel with the River Severn. This name is included in the corpus based on the place-name evidence and other factors. These are its location on a long-distance Roman road 10 miles south-west of Kington/Kyneton (Thornbury), and its proximity to a Roman port and small town. These suggest that it was part of the 'string' of Kingstons that lie roughly ten miles apart along this road. The remains of a Roman villa can still be seen at Kingsweston, where they have been consolidated.

On the first edition six-inch OS map, the road leaving Kingsweston is marked 'Roman Road'. It continues northward along the line of 'Cribb's Causeway' in the general direction of Gloucester.

It has been suggested that a Roman ferry may have run between Aust and Beachley, which lies just over a mile south of the suggested site of Kingston. Aust lies 8 miles north of Kingsweston; the most likely route between these two places would have been along the Gloucester road to just south of Alveston where it turned west towards the Severn.

11 Neighbouring Lawrence Weston was once one with Kings Weston, originally they were daughters of Henbury.

HAMPSHIRE 1

1 **Kingston** (Cross, Ringwood)

2 SU 149 020

3 Ringwood Hundred

4 Kingston is one of several tithings of the parish of Ringwood. The others are Burley, Bistern, Crow, Moortown and Poulner. The curacies of Bistern and Harbridge are annexed to the vicarage, but these may not be ancient connections. The church at Ringwood is dedicated to St Peter and St Paul; originally Ringwood was itself once part of the parish of Twynham/Christchurch.

5 *Kyngeston* 1280

6 DB ~

At DB Ringwood was held TRW by the king; TRE it was held by Earl Tosti and was the head of the hundred. It had been a substantial manor answering for 28 hides TRE, but at DB nothing is recorded; its change of fortunes may be connected with the establishment of the New Forest.

A significant entry listed under Ringwood is one 'riding man' with 'half a plough'. (DBHmp 1, 30) Ringwood is OE *rimuc* 'edge, border, boundary, ridge' + *wudu*. The wood on the boundary of Dorset.

7 DEPN ~

8 CDEPN p. 347

9 PNHmp ~

10 SITE Lies two miles south-west of Ringwood, on the River Avon, and two miles from the boundary with Dorset. A putative Roman road between the vexillation fortress at Lake Farm, Wimborne Dorset and west Hampshire has been confirmed recently by Arthur Clarke.The road left Kingston to the west, crossed the Avon at Watton's Ford (the lowest crossing point on the river) and carried on westward to the county boundary where it joined the Roman road between Winchester/ Dorchester. This lane is a public right of way. Arthur Clarke, Archaeology Officer of the Ordnance Survey, re-investigated the Roman road from Applemore Hill to Lepe, in the east of the county. He not only confirmed the line of the road, but was also able to trace it north-west to Shorn Hill where it joined the Roman road from Otterbourne to Stoney Cross, Picket Hill, Hightown, Watton's Ford on the River Avon and then to the vexillation fortress at Lake Farm, where it connected with the road Roman road which crossed Dorset to Dorchester and Exeter. Six Kingstons are sited on this road (Clarke 2003: pp. 35, 50).

11 Two charters relate to Ringwood:

955 Charter of Eadwig, bounds, '....to *rimuc wude...*' (S 582)

961 Charter King Edgar to Abingdon Abbey a grant of 22 hides at 'loco qui celebri *Rimecuda....*' (S 690)

At DB Twynham was held both TRW and TRE by the king: 'It was in King Edward's revenue'. At both Twynham and Ringwood there are references to 'riding men'. There were four 'riding men' with two and a half ploughs at Twynham and one riding man with half a plough at Ringwood. Outside the counties which border Wales there are only four DB references to riding men.

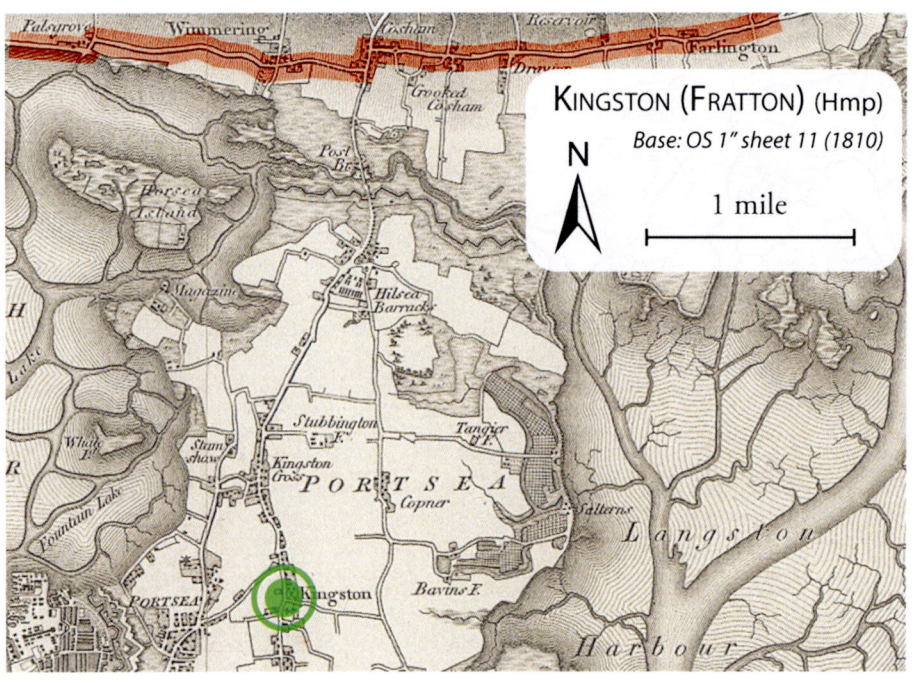

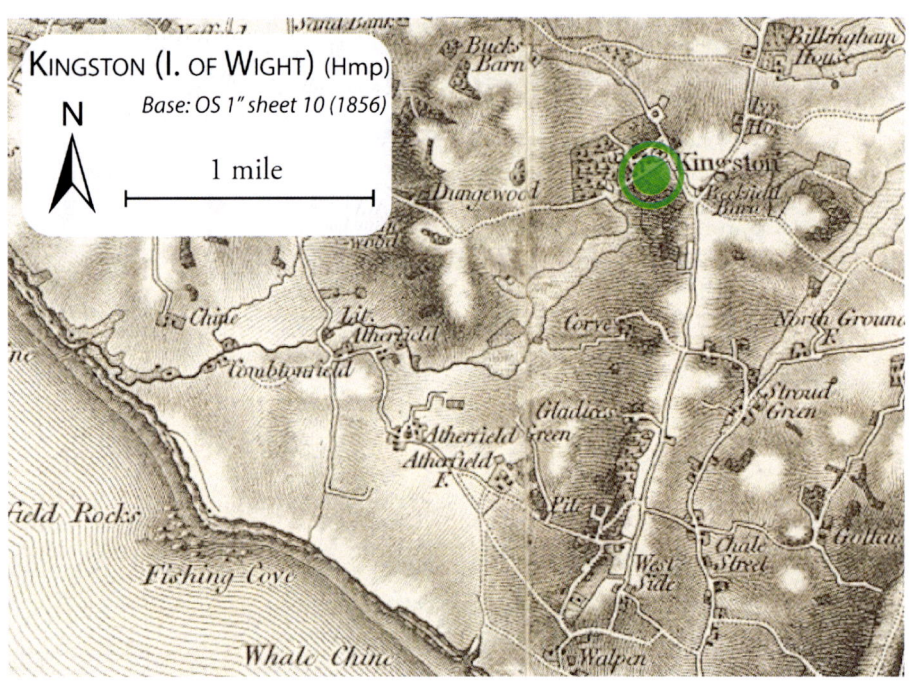

HAMPSHIRE 2

1 **Kingston** (Fratton/ Portsmouth)
2 SU 655 013
3 Portsdown Hundred
4 Chapelry of Fratton
5 *Kingeston* 1194
6 DB ~
   At DB Fratton is the land TRW of William of Warren, held by Osmelin. TRE Ketel held it from the king 'in freehold'. (DBHmp 34, 1).
7 DEPN p. 278
8 CDEPN ~
9 PNHmp ~
10 SITE Portsea is an island separated from the mainland by a small creek between Hilsea and Cosham. Portsmouth harbour lies on the west of the island, Langston harbour on the east. South is Spithead and the English Channel. The Roman road from Chichester to Bitterne ran along the north side of the creek, Portchester lies two miles to the west (M 421).
11 It has not been possible to establish the *villa regia* of which Kingston might have been a component part. Saxon Portsmouth has not yet been identified although its existence can be assumed. It appears in the *ASC* A text for the year 501 in the foundation myth, *her cuom Port on Bretene 7 his .ii. suna Bieda 7 Mægla mid .ii. scipum on þære stowe þe is gecueden Portesmuþa:* 'Here Port and his two sons Bieda and Mægla came with 2 ships to Britain at the place which is called Portsmouth'.

Portsmouth is not listed in DB.

It is possible that Kingston might have been part of the *villa regia* of Cosham which lies just across the creek. It was held at DB both TRW and TRE by the king, (DBHmp 1, 10. 23, 60. 68, 5.).

HAMPSHIRE 3

1 **Kingston** (Isle of Wight)
2 SZ 480 814
3 West Medina Liberty
4 Kingston is the smallest parish in the Isle of Wight
5 *Chingestune* DB
6 At DB held TRW by the King; TRE Wulfric held it jointly with the King. (DBHmp 1, 14).
7 DEPN p. 278
8 CDEPN p. 347
9 PNIOW ~
10 SITE Lies four miles south of Carisbrooke.
11 ~

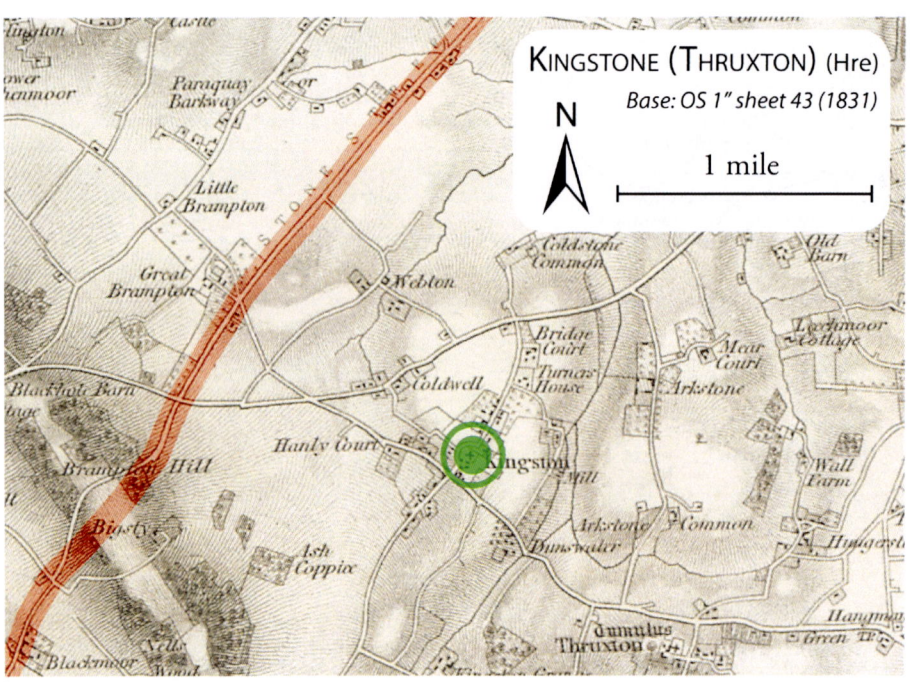

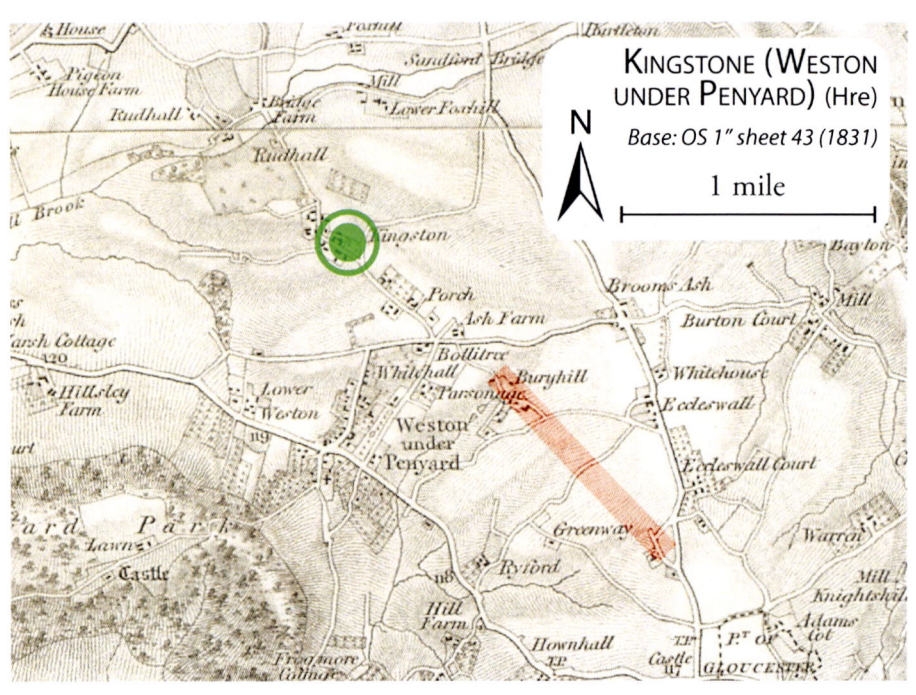

HEREFORDSHIRE 1

1 **Kingstone** (Thruxton)
2 SO 424 357
3 Stretford Hundred
4 Kingstone, which is now a parish, was a chapelry of Thruxton.
5 *Chingestone* DB
6 At DB TRW held by William, TRE held by King Edward along with the customary dues of one parcel of land in Cusop.

'A wood named Treville pays no customary dues except hunting rights. The villagers who lived there before 1066 carried the produce of the hunt to Hereford and did no other service'. (DBHre 1,3).

St Mary's of Cormeilles held the whole tithe of this manor.
7 DEPN p. 278
8 CDEPN p. 348
9 PNHre ~
10 SITE Lies six miles south-west of Hereford on the line of the long-distance Roman road, which ran from Abergavenny to Kenchester, beyond which it joined the Monmouth to Wroxter road. (M 630 and M 6c).
11 This part of Herefordshire lay within the small kingdom of *Ergyng* (later Archenfeld).

HEREFORDSHIRE 2

1 **Kingstone** (Weston under Penyard)
2 SO 631 246
3 Bromsash Hundred
4 AP, church dedicated to St Lawrence
5 *Chingestone* DB
6 At DB:

i TRW Land of the Church of Cormeilles held two hides here: 'They pay tax and do service in Gloucestershire, but the men who live there come to pleas in this Hundred to give and receive right'. No TRE information listed. (DBHre 3, 1).

ii Listed under Westbury is a reference to 8 hides in Kingstone (DBGlo 1, 11) This is Kingstone in Weston under Penyard: the confusion was brought about by the incorrect location of the documentation soon after Domesday Book was compiled.

At the time of DB the boundary between Herefordshire and Gloucestershire had not been finally established.
7 DEPN p. 278
8 CDEPN ~
9 PNHre ~
10 SITE Kingstone is sited where the Gloucester to Monmouth road crosses the road from South Wales via Chepstow and Lydney, where it forks and runs northwards to Weston under Penyard and on to Leominster. Weston under Penyard is the site of the small Roman town of *Ariconium*, the Roman administrative centre for the iron mines in the area, and itself a centre for iron-working for which there is considerable archaeological evidence reaching back into the Iron Age.
11 ~

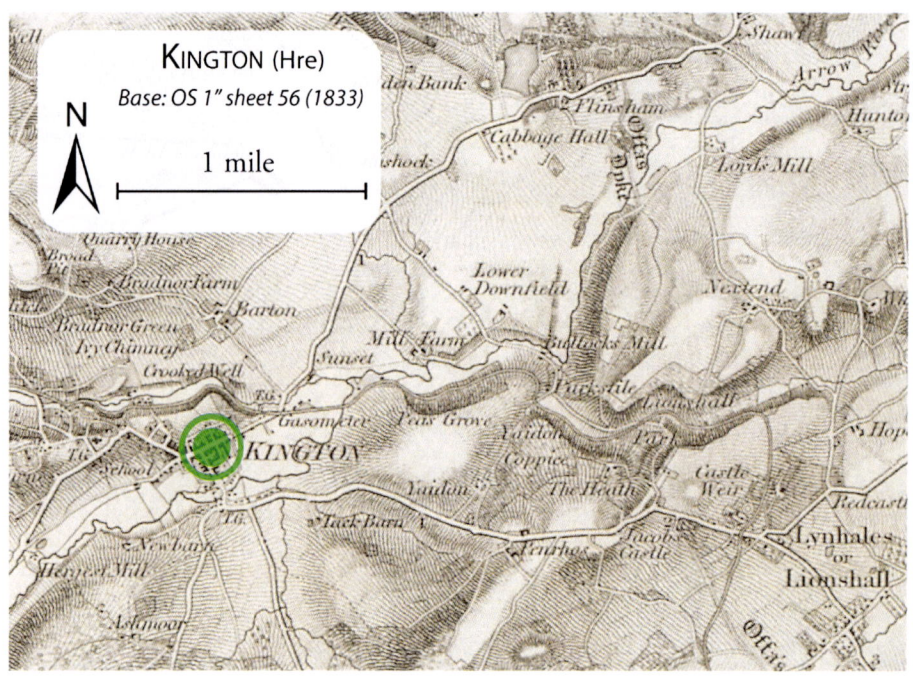

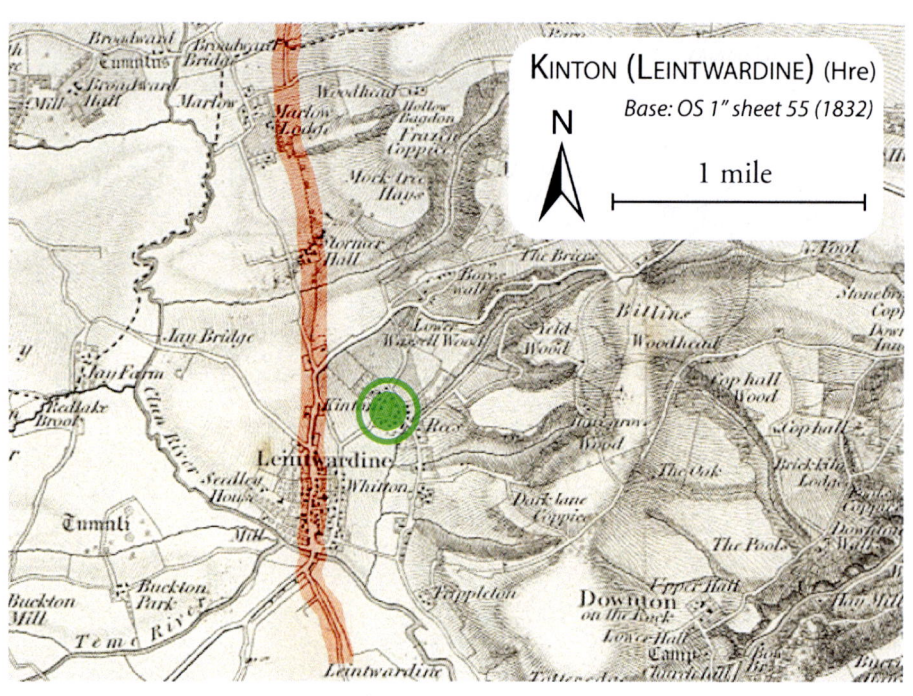

HEREFORDSHIRE 3
1 **Kington** (Welsh Border)
2 SO 291 568
3 Elsdon Hundred
4 AP, church dedicated to St Mary
5 *Chingtune* DB
6 At DB TRW Kington was held by the King and paid no
   dues due to the lands where being 'wasted'. TRE it was
   held by Earl Harold (DBHre 3, 69).
7 DEPN p. 278
8 CDEPN ~ pp. 348–9
9 PNHre ~
10 SITE Kington lies two miles from the Welsh border,
   looking westward along the valley of the River Arrow
   into Radnorshire, along which a major road runs. The
   parish boundary, to the north and east, follows the line
   of Offa's Dyke with Kingston lying on the west side of
   the dyke.
11 ~

HEREFORDSHIRE 4
1 **Kinton** (Leintwardine)
2 SO 405 747
3 Wigmore Hundred
4 In the parish of Leintwardine, church dedicated to St
   Mary Magdalene
5 *Kynton* 1249
6 DB ~
   Leintwardine entries are listed in the Shropshire folios
   (DBHre ES 1–2; 4)
   i   When the King left the City (Shrewsbury), the
       Sheriff sent him 24 horses from Leintwardine and
       the King took these as far as the first manor in
       Staffordshire (DBShr C10).
   ii TRW Holding of Picot under Earl Roger, three
       virgates of land in Leintwardine (DBShr 20, 20,
       20).
   iii TRW Land of Ralph of Mortimer. TRE held by
       King Edward. On this manor 2 'riders' are listed.
       (DBShr note 6, 11).
7 DEPN ~
8 CDEPN p. 278
9 PNHre p. 122
10 SITE Kinton is sited in the north-west of the county
   close to the Shropshire border. It lies on the line of
   the long-distance Roman road which ran north to
   south across the county from Wroxeter to Caerleon.
   Leintwardine, less than half a mile to the south, and lying
   on the same road, was the Roman fort and town known
   as *Bravinium/Branonium*. This has been identified as
   Branogenio in the Antonine Itinerary. *Branogenio*
   underlies the present village of Leintwardine. (M 6c).
11 References to various riding duties are found in several
   DB entries for Kingstons and/or the manors in which
   they lay.

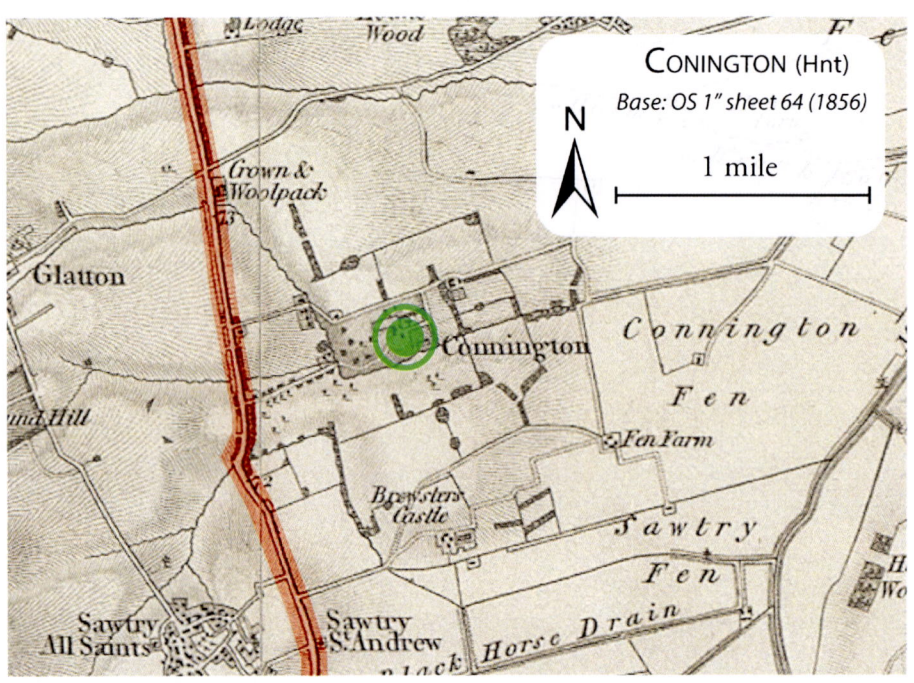

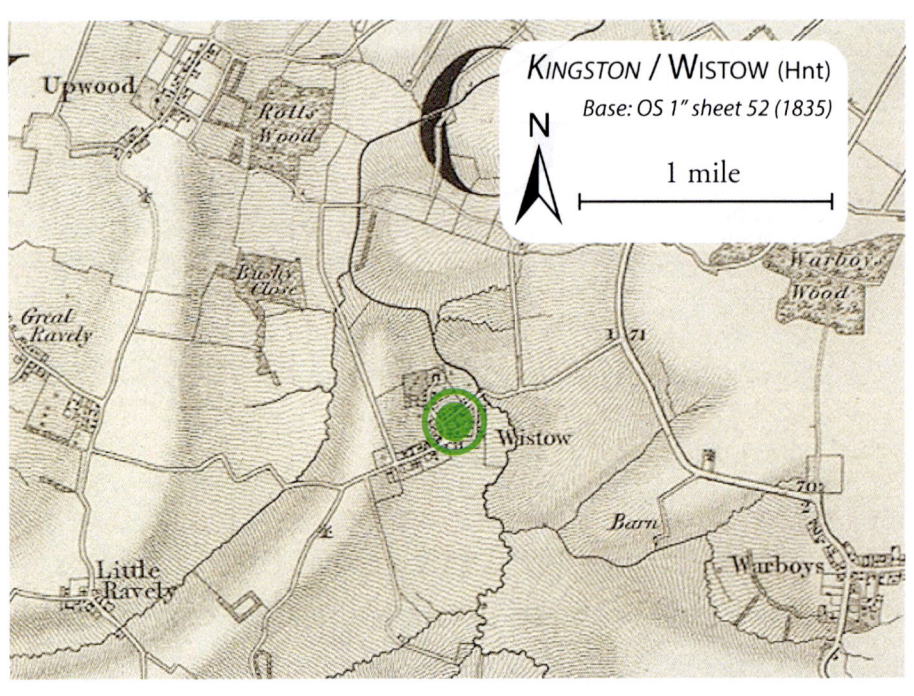

HUNTINGDONSHIRE 1

1 **Conington**
2 TL 180 859
3 AP, the church is dedicated to All Saints.
4 Norman Cross Hundred
5 First recorded in 957 in a grant of King Eadwig to Wulfstan, his faithful minister, at *Cunic tune* (S 649). Also recorded in 1017 x 1035 (S14) in the will of Mantat, the anchorite bequeathing land **at *Cunintun*** (S 1523).
6 DB *Coninctune*
 At DB held TRW by Countess Judith, 9 hides, there was a church and a priest. TRE held by Thorkell, six hides of this land belonged to the Church of St Mary of Thorney; Thorkell held these from the Abbot. (DBHnt 20,12.)
 The Men of the Hundred stated, 'that TRE the 6 hides in Conington formerly lay in the lands of the church of Thorney and they had been given to Thorkell on condition that after his death they should revert to the church with the other 3 hides of this village. (DBHnt note D 26).
7 DEPN p. 120
8 CDEPN p. 155
9 PNHnt p. 182
10 SITE Lies on the Roman Ermine Street, three miles south-east of Stilton (M 2b).
11 ~

HUNTINGDONSHIRE 2

1 *Kyngestone/*Wistow
2 TL 279 810
3 Hurstingstone Hundred
4 Lies in the parish of Wistow, dedicated to St John the Baptist
5 i 974 ***Kingeston** id est Wistowe cum Raue* and *Biri Berewycis*, charter of King Edgar (S 798). The charter is probably spurious, but it does not follow that the name is not genuine.
 ii 1062 ***Kingeston** cum Raffleya et Biri berewicis suis*, 1062, charter of King Edward a grant of land to Ramsey Abbey (S 1030). This charter has been dismissed by both Gelling and Wormald as bogus, but it is still evidence for the pre-Conquest existence of the name.
6 DB ~
 At DB TRW Wistow was held by the Abbey of St Benedict, Ramsey. No TRE information is given, but it will almost certainly have been a holding of the Abbey.
7 DEPN p. 526
8 CDEPN p. 689
9 PNHnt p. 228
10 SITE Lies three miles south of Ramsey almost on the fen edge; the whole area lies within the Bedford Middle Levels. There is no identifiable Roman/ancient through route-way here although, on the first edition six-inch OS map, one mile to the north of Wistow at Bury, a 'Roman camp' is noted. Ermine Street runs six miles to the east. The local road on which both Wistow and Ramsey lie appears to follow an ancient line. It was turnpiked in the eighteenth century. Today, *Kingestune* is represented by Kingston Way, a cul-de-sac west of the church.
11 Watts suggests that *wic-stow* in this context may have meant the site of the royal house (CDEPN p. 689).

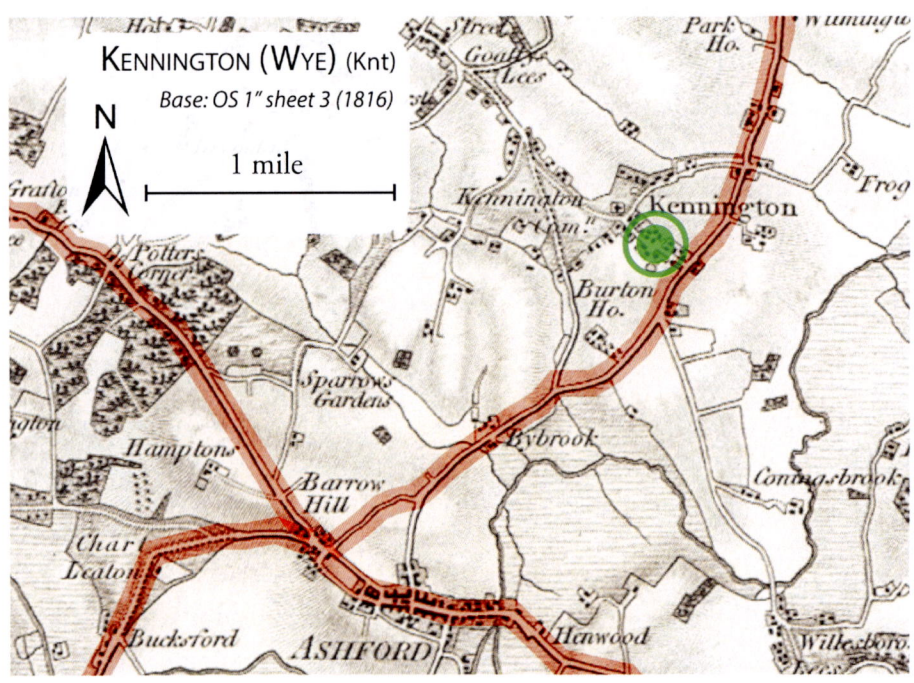

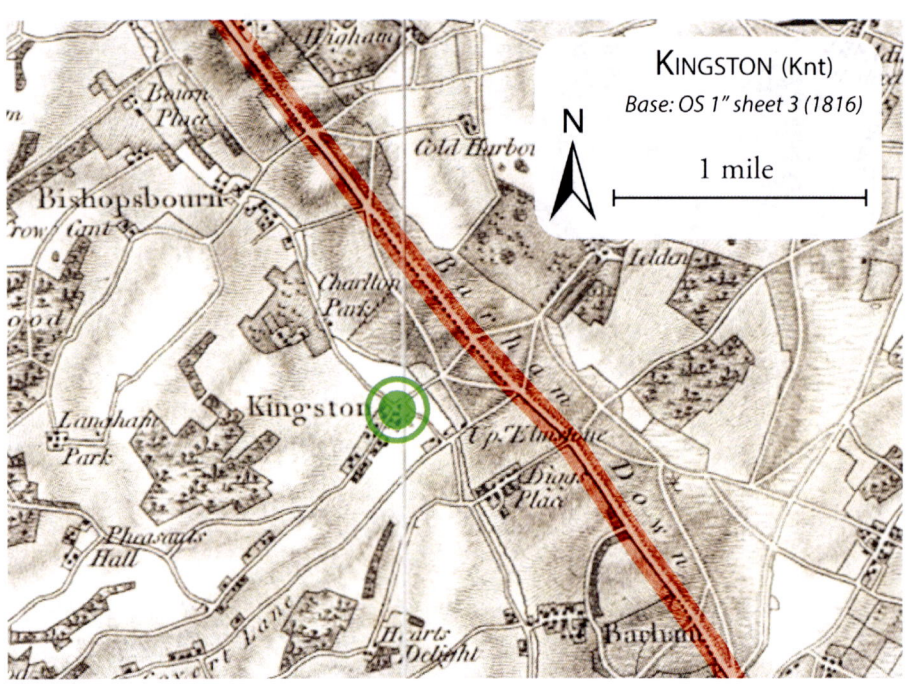

KENT 1

1 **Kennington** (Wye)
2 TR 022 452
3 Longbridge Hundred, Wye Lathe
4 AP, the church is dedicated to St Michael or St Mary.
5 *Chintune* 1072, Kyngtune eleventh century, *Chenetone* DB
6 At DB TRW Land of St Augustine's Church, the Abbot holds Kennington himself. TRE it answered for four sulungs and lay in Burmarsh: 'The villagers held it before 1066'. (DB Knt 7,28).
7 DEPN p. 272
8 CDEPN p. 340
9 PNKnt ~ ; Cullen, 1997: p. 119.
10 SITE Lies adjacent to Wye on the south-west, between Wye and Ashford on the Roman road from Canterbury to the Weald. (M 130) Wye lies on this Roman road and also on the ancient long–distance route-way, known for much of its length as the Pilgrim's Way'.
11 The first element is the OE *cyne*, Kentish *cene* varying with *cyning, cening*.

KENT 2

1 **Kingston**
2 TR 198 513
3 Kinghamford Hundred, St Augustine Lathe
4 AP, church dedicated to St Giles
5 *Kynigtune*, 1087 Domesday Monachorum
6 DB ~
7 DEPN p. 278
8 CDEPN p. 347
9 PNKnt p. 557
10 SITE Kingston lies ten miles south-west of Canterbury on the Roman road to Dove. (M 1a). The church is sited close to this road and the parish boundaries straddle it. Kingston may once have been a component member of the riverine estate of 'the Bourne people', based on and around the River Bourne. This estate has been reconstructed in Everitt 1986: pp. 79–81
11 Domesday Monachorum is a Domesday-related text which deals with estates of the archbishop of Canterbury, the monks of Christchurch Canterbury, the bishop of Rochester and some other landholders in Kent. In a list of the customs received by the archbishop at Easter *Kynigtune* paid *VII denarios*, *X denarios* was the highest assessment and *VII* the least.

An early medieval barrow cemetery on Kingston Downs was excavated 1767-70. There were over 300 burials, more than 180 with wooden coffins, most were marked by small mounds or barrows. All were buried with heads to the west. Numerous grave-goods including weapons, beads, Christian crosses, and glass vessels. The collection includes the famous 'Kingston Brooch' and the skeleton of a small woman who had been buried under a large mound.

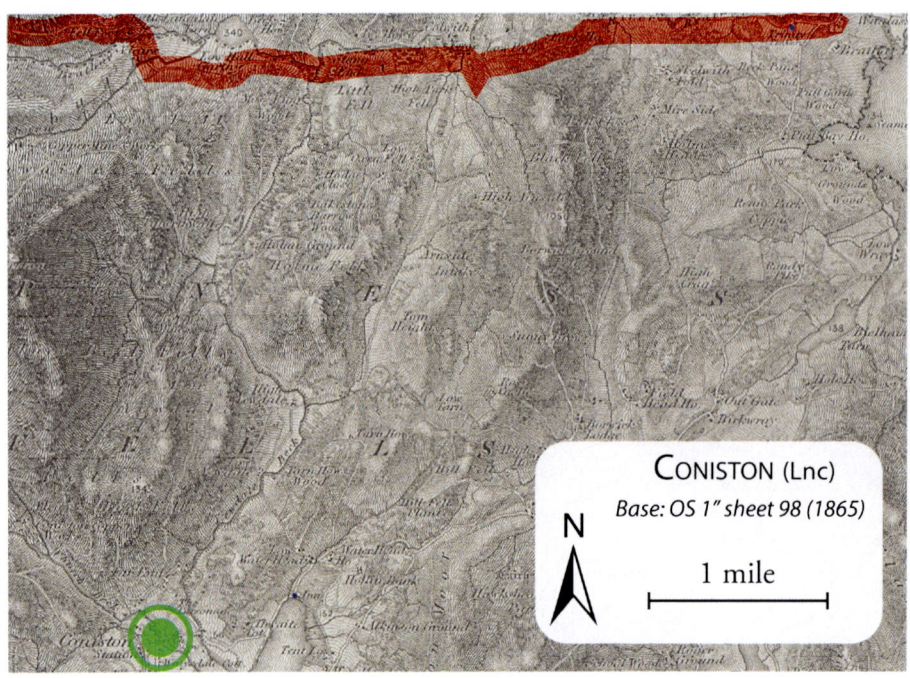

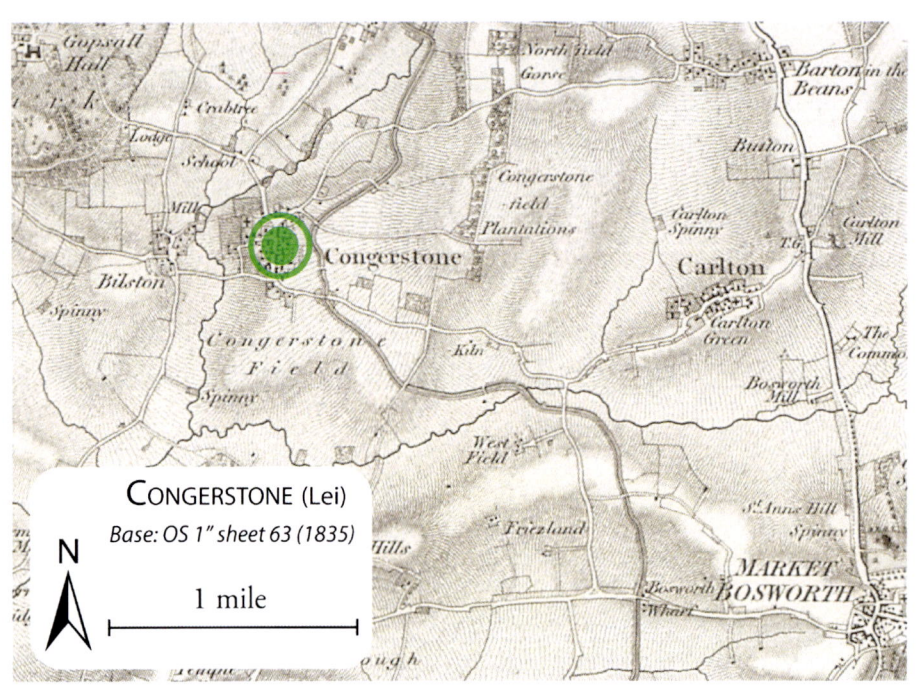

LANCASHIRE 1

1 **Coniston**
2 SD 302 976
3 Lonsdale Hundred
4 Chapelry of Ulverston, church dedicated to St Mary
5 *Coningeston* 1157–63
   The Scandinavianised first element may have replaced the OE *cyning*
6 DB ~
7 DEPN p. 121
8 CDEPN p. 155
9 PNLnc ~
   Whaley pp. 80–1
10 SITE Lies at the head of Coniston Water, which takes its present name from the settlement. In 1196 it was *Thurstainewater*. The road running north from here meets, three miles on, the long-distance Roman road (M 740) that came across from Kendal, through Ambleside (*Galava*) and on to Ravenglass. This is the same road on which Coniston Cold (WRY) is sited.
11 Ekwall speculated that this name may preserve the memory of a small Scandinavian mountain kingdom, although the Scandinavianisation of the OE *cyning* suggests that the name might indicate an earlier territory. E. Ekwall, *Place-Names of Lancashire*, p. 215.

LEICESTERSHIRE 1

1 **Congerstone**
2 SK 366 054
3 Sparkenhoe Hundred
4 Now a parish, originally a daughter of Market Bosworth.
5 *Cuningestone*, DB (Scandinavianisation of *Cyningestone* the OE *cyning* influenced by ODan *kunung*
6 At DB there were two manors at *Cuningestone*:
   i   Land of the Count of Meulan TRW the Count holds six carucates of land; TRE Saxi held all these lands and could go where he would. (DBLei 9,5)
   ii Land of Hugh de Grantmesnil TRW, two carucates held by Hugh from Hugh. No TRE information (DBLei 13,72)
7 DEPN p. 120
8 CDEPN p. 154
9 Cox, 1971. *The Place-Names of Leicestershire and Rutland*, unpublished Ph.D. thesis, University of Nottingham 1971. Sections of this thesis have been published by the English Place-Name Society: the volume covering this part of this county is yet to come.
10 SITE Congerstone lies three miles north-west of Market Bosworth and four miles from the Roman Watling Street, which is the county boundary with Warwickshire. (M 1g). Foss argues that Market Bosworth was the central place of a Mercian royal multiple estate of which Congerstone was a component part (Foss 1996: pp. 83–106). The southern boundary of the proposed Bosworth estate is defined by Watling Street, with the western boundary following the line of the Roman road, known locally as the Fenn Lanes, which ran south-westwards from Leicester to join Watling Street at Mancetter.
11 Cox suggests that this putative royal estate, petty-kingdom may have been the based on a small hundred which was later subsumed into the Danish wapentake of Guthlaxton.

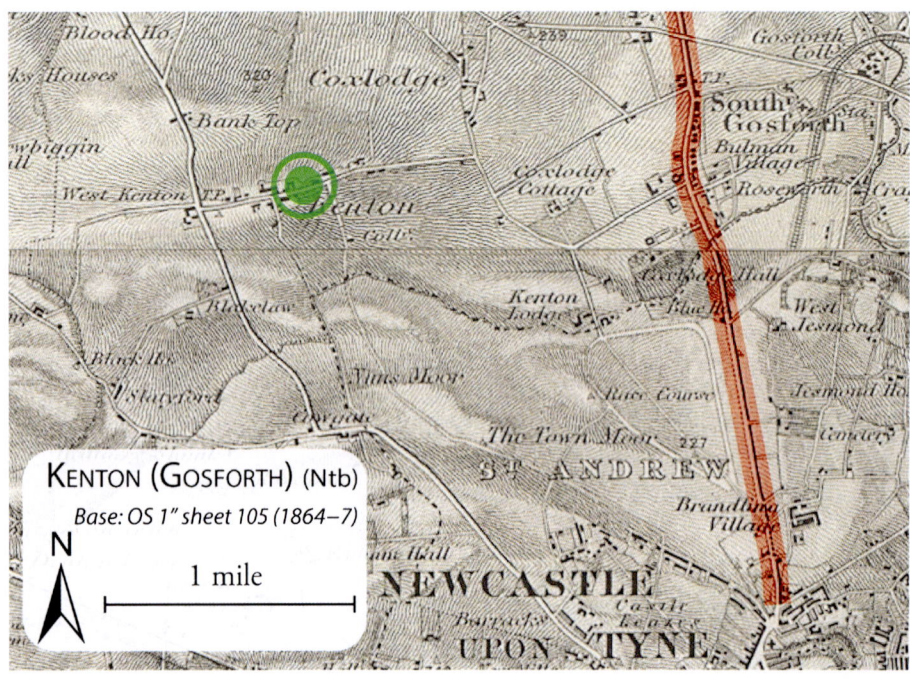

KENTON (GOSFORTH) (Ntb)
Base: OS 1" sheet 105 (1864–7)

N

1 mile

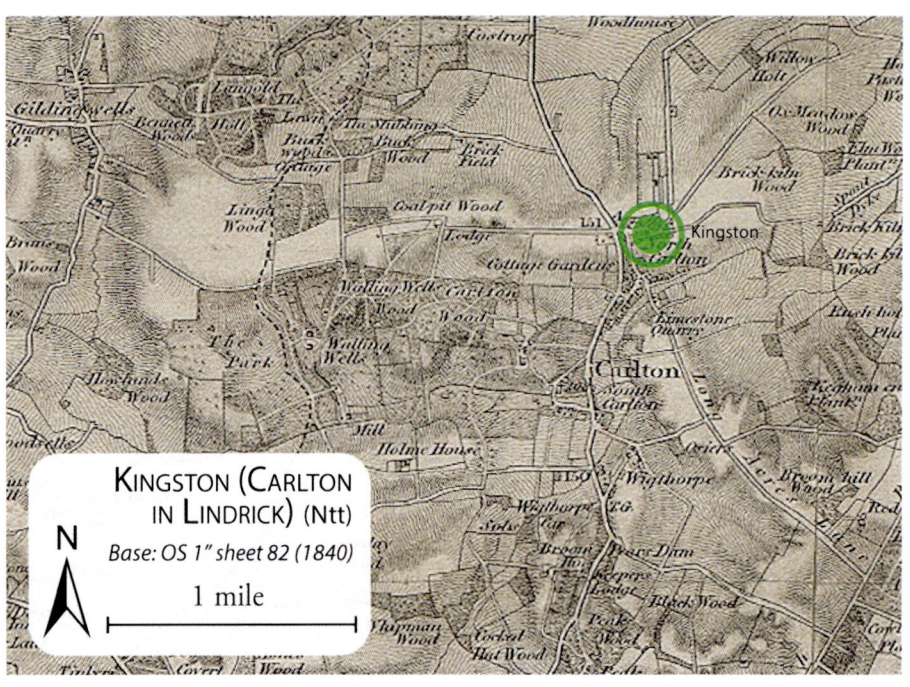

KINGSTON (CARLTON IN LINDRICK) (Ntt)
Base: OS 1" sheet 82 (1840)

N

1 mile

NORTHUMBERLAND 1

1 **Kenton** (Gosforth)

2 NZ 225 675

3 Tynedale Ward

4 Lies in the parish of Gosforth, the church is dedicated to St Nicholas; other chapelries are East and West Brunton, Coxlodge, Fawdon

5 *Kynton*, ***Quenton*** 1255

6 DB ~

   Gosforth DB ~

7 DEPN p. 272

8 CDEPN ~

9 PNNbDm pp. 125

10 SITE Kenton lies two miles north of Newcastle-upon-Tyne on the present-day A1. Although sections of this road further south follow a Roman line, (M 80b), the English Heritage map shows this road continuing on north of the river to join M 67 which is the Roman road from Corbridge northwards towards Berwick-on-Tweed. The line of this is marked clearly on the first edition six-inch OS map. Kenton might be associated with Walbottle which is thought to be the *Ad Muram*, *ASC* 653.

11 ~

NOTTINGHAMSHIRE 1

1 **Kingston** (Carlton in Lindrick)

2 SK 591 845

3 Bassetlaw Wapentake

4 Chapelry of Carlton

5 *Le Kynggeston* 1308 Imp, ***Kengeston*** in Carleton 1356

6 DB ~

   At DB Carlton was divided between King William and Roger de Busli. The king's part is probably represented by Kingston. No TRE information is given (DBNtt 1,24; 30,9; 50).

7 DEPN ~

8 CDEPN ~

9 PNNtt p. 72

10 SITE Kingston lies to the north of Carlton in Lindrick within which it is subsumed and now represented by a small housing estate. Carlton is sited on the present A60 road between Worksop, Tickhill and Blyth. No Roman road has been identified securely here, although two miles due north of Kingston at Oldcoates, and also on this road, a Roman villa site has been identified. Oldcoates lies on the E/W Roman road which ran from Ryknild Street to join the Roman road from Lincoln to Doncaster (M 28e). For much of the length of this road its line is almost impossible to identify, the reason for this being the destruction brought about by heavy industry. At Oldcoates, however, the *agger* can be seen in the fields for almost a mile along the north side of the present Firbeck to Oldcoates road. Margary vol. 2, 1957: p. 145.

11 ~

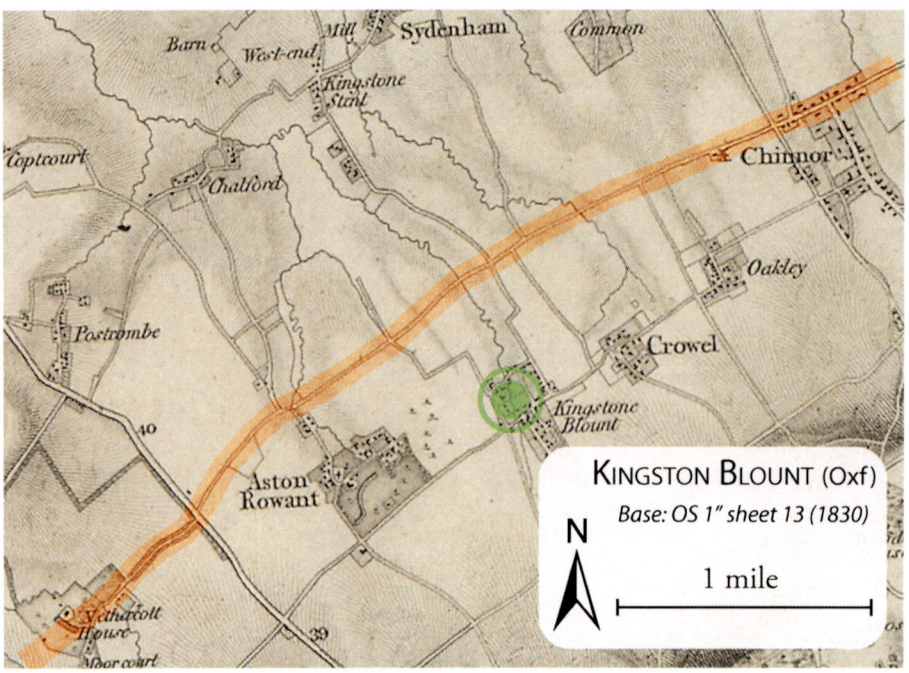

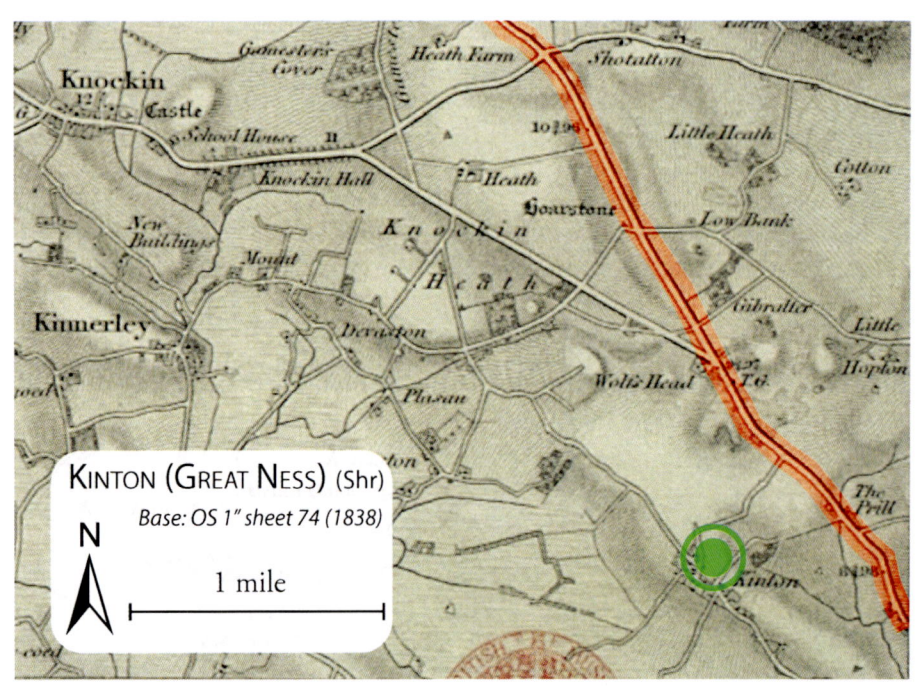

OXFORDSHIRE 1

1 **Kingston** (Blount)
2 SU 739 995
3 Lewknor Hundred
4 Chapelry of Aston Rowant, church dedicated to SS Peter and Paul
5 *Chingestone* DB
6 At DB there were two manors here:
   i   TRW Land of Miles Crispin; no TRE information (DBOxf 35,4)
   ii TRW Land of Miles Crispin; no TRE information (DBOxf 35,27)
7 DEPN pp. 277–8
8 CDEPN p. 347
9 PNOxf vol. 1, p. 103
10 SITE Lies on the central/eastern stretch of the Ickneild Way, two miles south-west of Chinnor and four miles north-east of Watlington.
11 Kingston Lisle and Kingstone Winslow BRK are sited on this same long-distance route-way.

Nearby is Grim's Ditch, a substantial linear earthwork constructed across the west end of the Chilterns, cutting off a loop of the Thames between Wallingford and Henley. It has not been possible to establish a wider context for this Kingston; neither is it clear of which royal estate it was attached.

Kingston (Stert), half a mile to the north, is part of the same land unit and most probably represents the second DB manor.

SHROPSHIRE 1

1 **Kinton** (Great Ness)
2 SJ 372 195
3 Great Hundred
4 Chapelry of Great Ness, church dedicated to St Andrew
5 First recorded in 1203–4 as *Kinetu', -ton*
6 DB ~
   At Ness at DB there were two manors:
   i   TRE it was held by Earl Roger himself with four berewicks. TRE it was held by Earl Morcar. This manor is represented by Great Ness (DBShr 4,1,17).
   ii TRW Land of Earl Roger held by Reginald the Sheriff. TRE It was held by Siward. This manor is represented by Little Ness. (DBShr 4,3,52).
7 DEPN ~
8 CDEPN ~
9 PNShr vol. 5, p. 99
10 SITE Kinton lies on the present-day A5 road midway between Shrewsbury and Whittington, approximately eight miles distance from each of them. White has noted that the vexillation fortress at Rhyn Park (SJ 30 37) would have needed connecting routes. He suggests a possible road that left M 64 at Washford where it crossed the Rea Brook (SJ 480 099), then headed north-west, meeting the line of the A5 at SJ 444 140, passing Kinton and the Roman sites at Nesscliffe (SJ 444 140)
11 It has not been possible to establish a context for this place.

KEINTON MANDEVILLE (Som)
Base: OS 1" sheet 18 (1811)

N

1 mile

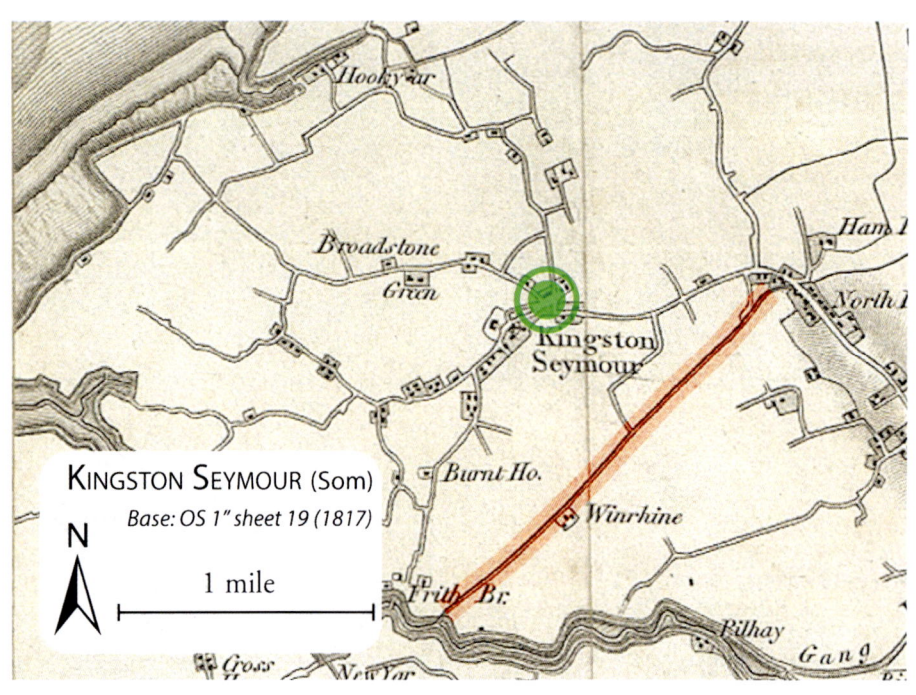

KINGSTON SEYMOUR (Som)
Base: OS 1" sheet 19 (1817)

N

1 mile

SOMERSET 1

1 **Keinton** (Mandeville)
2 ST 547 301
3 Catsash Hundred
4 It has a church, dedicated to St Mary Magdalene
5 *Chintune* DB
6 DB TRW Land of the Count of Mortain, Mauger holds Chintune. TRE twoThanes held it. (DBSom 19, 59)
  The DB entry for Barton St David, Keinton's neighbour on the north-west, records that TRE Keinton Mandeville lay in that manor (DBSom 21, 92).
7 DEPN p. 269
8 CDEPN p. 338
9 PNSom ~
10 SITE Keinton Mandeville is sited on the Fosse Way between Bath and Ilchester (M 5b). Three and a half miles and a half to the south-west is Somerton, the royal *vill*, of which Keinton may once have been a component part.
11 ~

SOMERSET 2

1 **Kingston (Seymour)**
2 ST 401 669
3 Winterstoke Hundred
4 Ancient parish church, dedicated to All Saints
5 *Chingestone* DB
6 At DB TRW two manors are listed here. Both are the Lands of the Bishop of Coutances and both manors were held from him by William de Moncells. One manor, the smaller, was held TRE by Eldred who paid tax for one hide. (DBSom 63). The other was held TRE by four thanes who, except for one hide, did not pay tax (DBSom 5, 63–4).
7 DEPN ~
8 CDEPN ~
9 PN Som ~
10 SITE Lies on the north-west coast of Somerset between Clevedon and Weston-super-Mare. It has been suggested that a Roman road ran down this coast from a point opposite the small Roman port of Seamills, which is adjacent to Kings Weston GLO and running on towards Taunton. The line of this road has been identified in the parish of Kingston Seymour, the north-east/south-west boundary of which follows the line of the road. This line can also be seen in Yatton, Nailsea and Wraxall. A Roman villa lay in the south of Kingston Seymour parish; another lies on the road between Nailsea and Wraxall.

11 Kingston Seymour may have been a component part of the royal estate of Congresbury which was given to Congar, a Welsh missionary, by King Ine of Wessex. A third-century Roman hoard has been found immediately to the north at Kenn Moor.

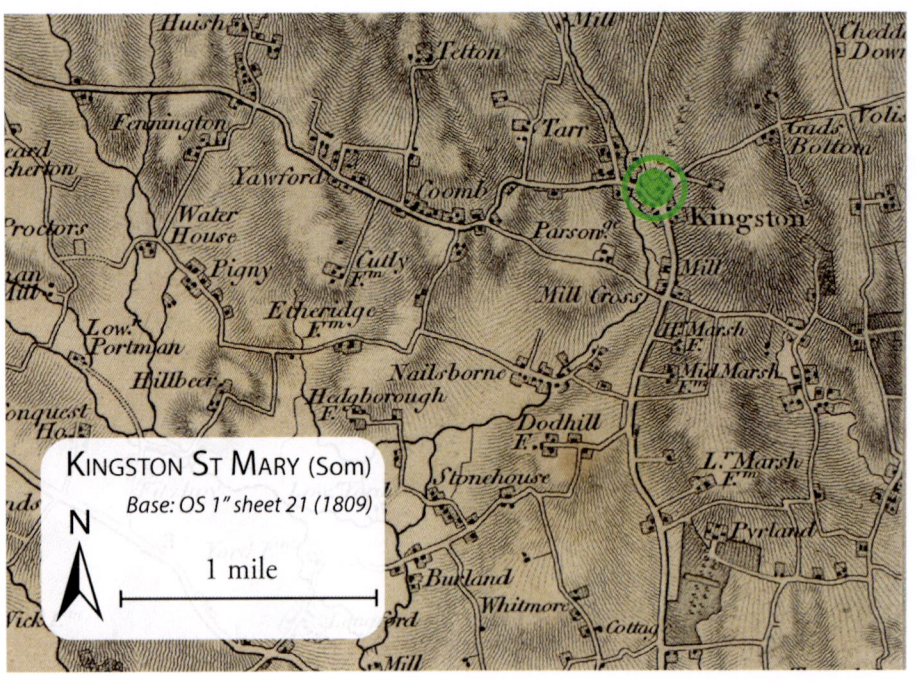

KINGSTON ST MARY (Som)
Base: OS 1" sheet 21 (1809)

N

1 mile

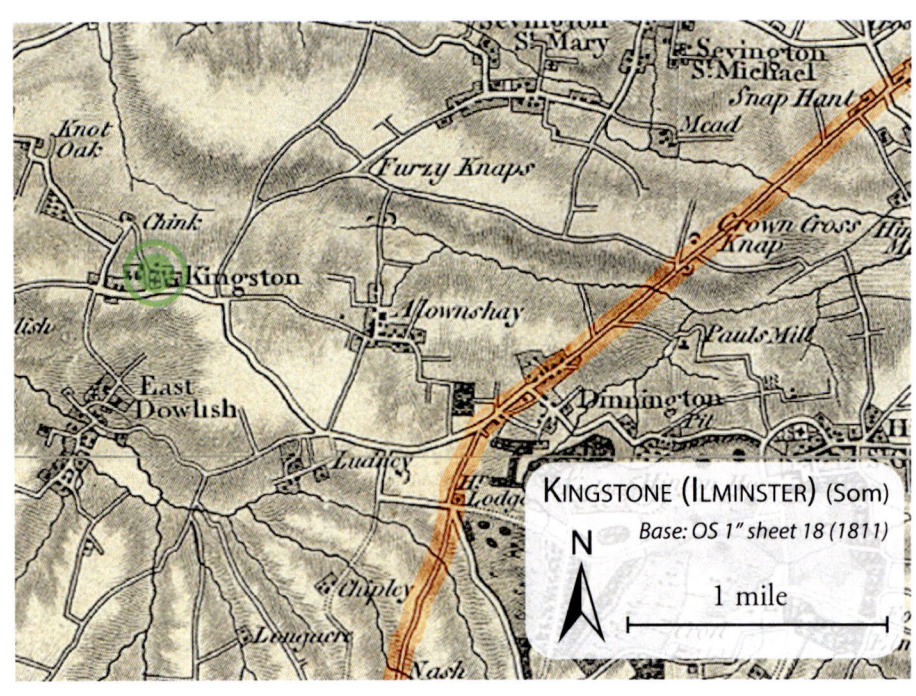

KINGSTONE (ILMINSTER) (Som)
Base: OS 1" sheet 18 (1811)

N

1 mile

SOMERSET 3

1 **Kingston** (St Mary, Taunton)
2 ST 223 297
3 Taunton and Taunton Dean
4 Ancient parish, church dedicated to St Mary. St Mary was added to the name in 1952. Cotherstone is a chapelry.
5 *Kyngestona* 1155–8
6 DB No

At DB Kingston was probably subsumed under the entry for Taunton, which was held TRW by the Bishop of Winchester and TRE by Archbishop Stigand (DBSom 2,1; 2–5; 8–9, 19, 40)

7 DEPN pp. 277–8
8 CDEPN p. 348
9 PNSom ~
10 SITE Kingston St Mary lies on the southern edge of the Quantocks, three miles north of Taunton. It has not been possible to establish the line of an ancient route-way here although there would have been one. A road runs north-westward from here towards Williton and the coast at Watchet. A minor Romano-British settlement is marked at Taunton on the OS map of Roman Britain.
11 There is considerable evidence for Taunton being an Anglo-Saxon centre of importance. During the final years of Ine's reign the record hints at internal unrest. A remarkable entry in the *ASC* A 722 notes that 'Queen Æthelburg (wife of Ine) threw down Taunton which Ine built earlier'. The significance of this is inscrutable but it does offer a *terminus post quem* for the foundation of Taunton. Taunton featured in seven royal charters, none of which were issued by Ine (S 254; S 311; S 443; S 521; S 806; S 818; S 825).

SOMERSET 4

1 **Kingstone** (Ilminster)
2 ST 379 136
3 Tintinhul
4 Ancient parish, church dedicated to All Saints. Allowenshay and Ludney are hamlets of this parish.
5 *Chingestone, Kingestona* DB, *Kingestan* 1194, 1212, *Kingeston* 1610
6 At DB there were two manors here:
   i TRW, Land of St Mary's of Glastonbury, which is also listed as being held from the King by the Count of Mortain. TRE these lands were thaneland in Glastonbury lands (DBSom. 8,39).
   ii TRW, Land of the Count of Mortain, TRE it was held by the church at Glastonbury (DBSom. 19,10).
7 DEPN p. 278
8 CDEPN p. 348
9 PNSom ~
10 SITE The parish boundary of Kingstone crosses the Fosse Way (M 5a). It lies in an apparently direct and significant relationship with the Anglo-Saxon royal *vill* of Ilminster.
11 The place-name evidence for the interpretation of this name is not without some ambiguity. A footnote to the entry in CDEPN (p. 348) notes: '*stane*, the identification of this form is not certain'. Margaret Gelling comes down on the side of 'stone'. On the place-name evidence alone, Margaret Gelling suggests that this is 'stone', but in this case it is possible to suggest that, by applying the 8–10 mile 'string' system that has been observed in the counties of Dorset, Gloucestershire and Sussex (and hinted at in other counties), this could be a Kingston.

Keinton Mandeville and Kingstone lie 19 miles apart on the Fosse Way, midway between them is Ilchester, an important Anglo-Saxon royal centre. (M 5a). No Kingston name is to be found here, although, one mile to the north-west, lying in the fork between the Fosse Way and the Roman road to Street, is Kingsdon. The elements *dūn* and *tūn* are often hard to disentangle in the early sources, but the name and its situation in an angle of tow Roman roads need to be noted.

Three charters granting land at Ilminster confirm its royal status:
i 693 ?692, Ine, a grant of 40 hides to Froda, Abbot of Muchelney (S 240)
ii 725, Ine, 20 hides to Froda Abbot of Muchelney, 20 hides at Ilminster. (S 249)
iii 995, King Athelred, confirmation of lands at Muchelney Abbey (S 884)

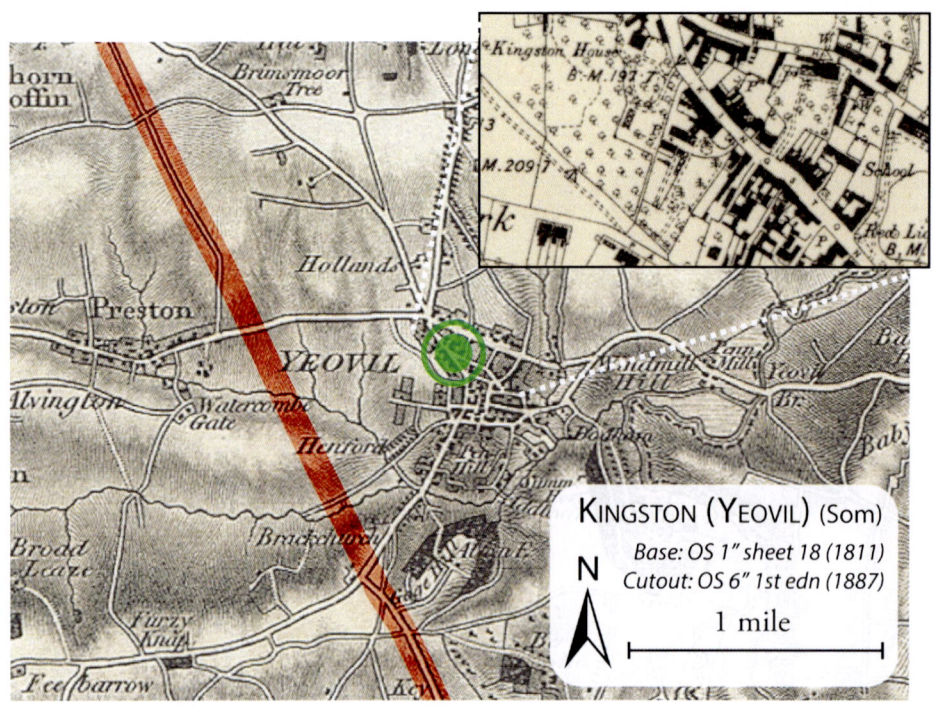

KINGSTON (YEOVIL) (Som)
Base: OS 1" sheet 18 (1811)
Cutout: OS 6" 1st edn (1887)

1 mile

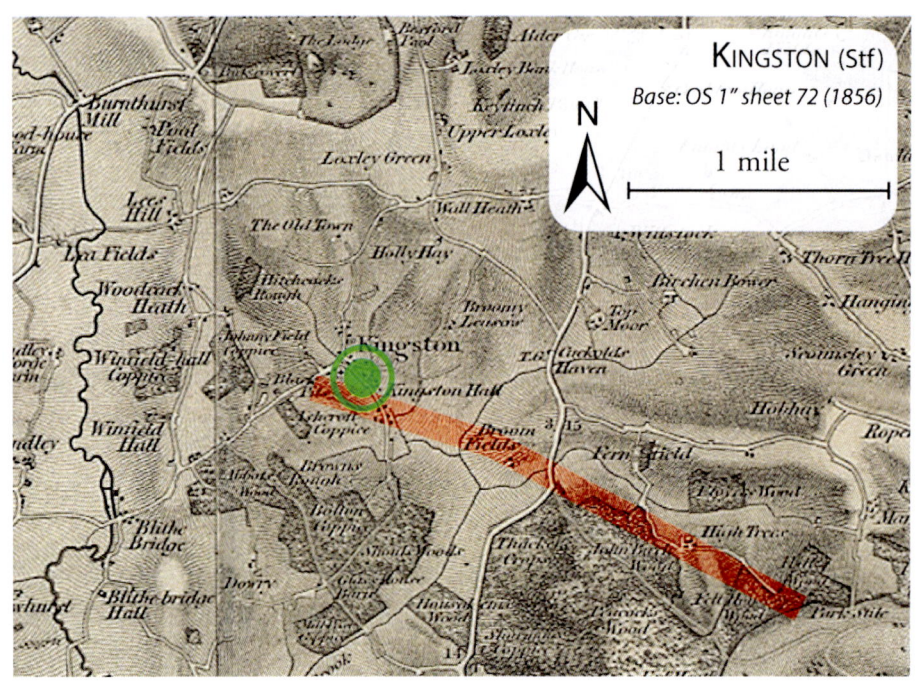

KINGSTON (Stf)
Base: OS 1" sheet 72 (1856)

1 mile

SOMERSET 6

1 Kingston (Yeovil)

2 ST 553 165

3 Hundred of Somerton

4 Chapelry of Yeovil

5. First recorded. There are no early forms for this name.

6 DB ~

At DB to manors were listed at Yeovil. One is held TRW by the Count of Mortain, with one hide. No TRE information is given.

The second was held by William of Eu TRW, no TRE information is given although it is specifically noted that 'in 1066 it paid tax for 6 hides but is not liable for the *firma unius noctis*. (DB SOM 19, 83-4; 6, 6).

7 DEPN ~

8 CDEPN ~

9 ~ not listed in the EPNS volume for Somerset

10 SITE Lies on the Roman road from Dorchester to Ilchester. It is hard to detect now but it is clearly visible on aerial maps. The name survives as a street name.

There was an early minster here; Kingston lies within its parish. See Blair 2005 p. 219; n. 326; n 446.

Yeovil was the site of a Roman small town, it lay on the area now known as Westland

Sherbourne Causeway enters Yeovil on the east side. The line is now almost impossible to trace through the suburban houses on the edge of the town, but it can be seen on the first edition of the six-inch OS map.

STAFFORDSHIRE 1

1 **Kingstone**

2 SK 060 295

3 Totmonslow Hundred

4 Chapelry of Gratwich

5 First recorded as *Kingeston* in 1166

6 DB ~

At DB Gratwich was held by Wulfheah from Robert of Stafford; TRE by Goding who was 'a free man' (DBStf 11,35).

7 DEPN ~

8 CDEPN ~

9 No PN volume. (See Horovitz 2005: p. 344)

10 SITE Lies three miles south-west of Uttoxeter on an old coaching road between Uttoxeter and Stafford, which crosses the River Blythe in this parish. No Roman road has been identified here or nearby, and the nearest known Roman settlement is the *vicus* of Rocester, seven miles to the north-east. Uttoxeter may have been the royal estate centre of which Kingston was a component part. It was held TRW by the king and TRE by Earl Agar.

11 ~

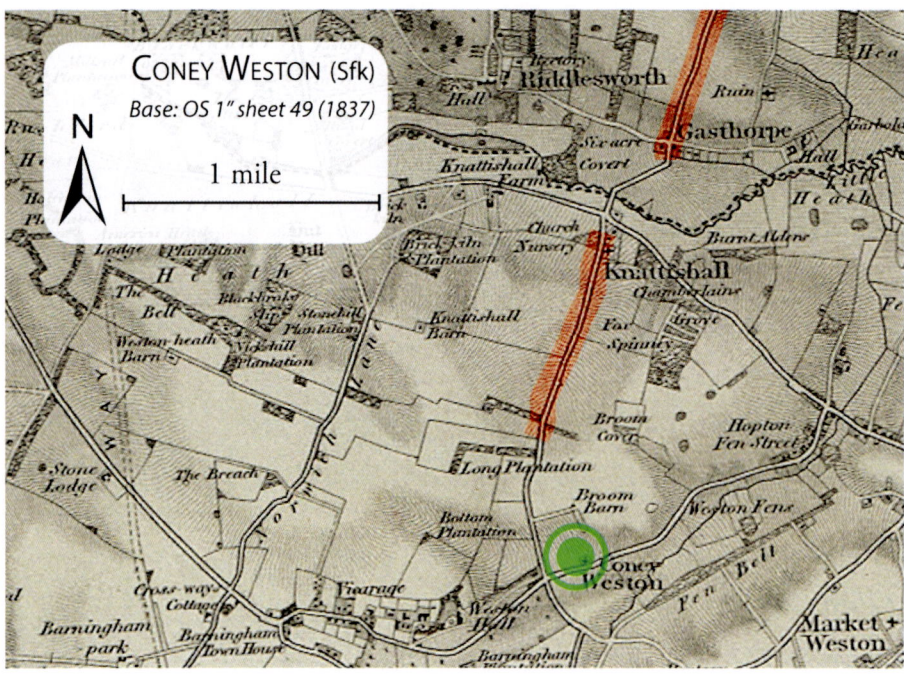

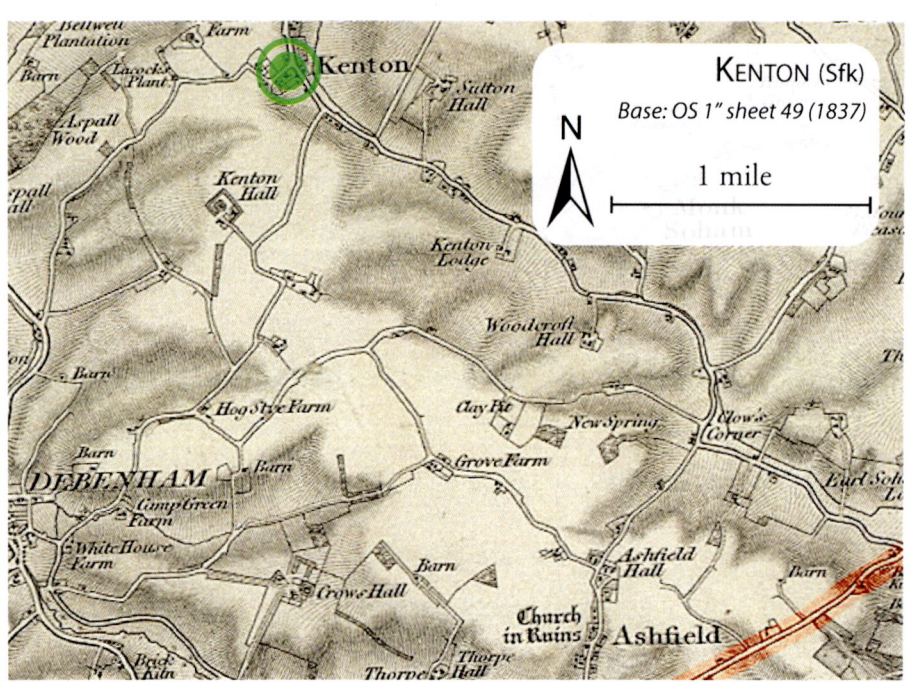

SUFFOLK 1
1 **Coney Weston**
2 TL 955 781
3 Blackbourn Hundred
4 AP, church dedicated to St Mary
5 *Cunegestone* 1051 x 1052 or 1053 x 1057, writ of King Edward declaring that the land at *Cunegestone* belongs to St Edmund's monastery (S 1080)
6 *Cunegestuna* DB
   i Land of St Edmunds both TRW and TRE (DBSfk 14,76)
   ii Under the entries for Hepworth, Hopton, and (Market) Weston is the note that 'service was due in Coney Weston' (DBSfk (14, 78; 14, 80; 84))
7 DEPN p. 120
8 CDEPN p. 667
9 PNSfk ~
10 SITE The line of the Roman road from London to Norwich crosses the parish of Coney Weston one mile south of the county boundary with Norfolk (M 331)
11 ~

SUFFOLK 2
1 **Kenton** SFK
2 TM 191 659
3 Loes Hundred
4 Chapelry of Soham
5 *Chene, Ketetuna* DB, *Keneton(a)* 1179 x 1286, *Kingeston* 1252
6 DB:
   i TRW manor held TRW by Malet's mother from Robert; TRE held by Edric (DBSfk 6,271)
   ii TRW manor held by Durand from Godric the Steward (DBSfk 14,119)
7 DEPN 272
8 CDEPN p. 341
9 PNSfk ~
10 SITE Kenton lies in central Suffolk adjacent to Debenham. It is sited two miles off the Roman road to Dunwich, which branched off the Roman Colchester to Norwich road at Baylham. (M 34b). This road crosses the neighbouring parishes of Earl and Monk Soham.
11 It has been suggested that the first element could be the personal names *Cēna* or *Cyna*. The 1252 form shows that this was a royal manor. (*CDEPN* p. 341). Having examined all the early forms, Dr David Parsons is of the opinion that the first element is *cyne*.

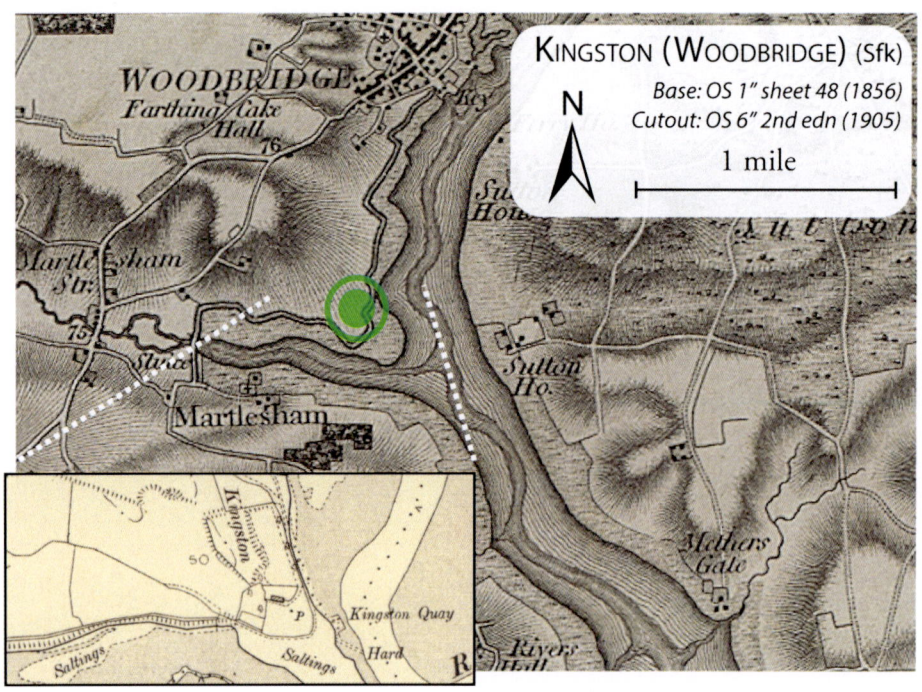

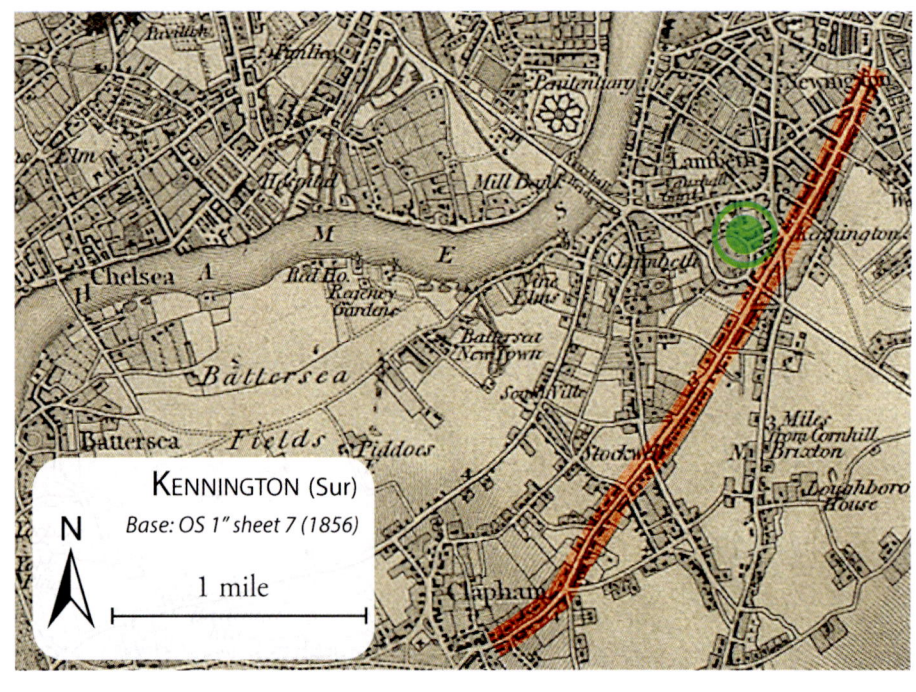

SUFFOLK 3

1 **Kingston** (Woodbridge)
2 TM 270 475
3 Loes or Carlford Hundred
4 Kingston lies in the parish of Woodbridge
5 *Kingestun*, 1042 x 1086, charter of King Edward granting land at Kingston to Ely Abbey (S 1051). Woodbridge (*Oddebruge* in the charter) is also included in the charter.
6 *Kyngestona* DB, no TRW; held TRE by St Etheldreda (DBSfk 21,53; 8,6 note)
7 DEPN p. 278
8 CDEPN ~
9 No PN volume
10 SITE Kingston lies in the parish of Woodbridge on the River Deben, directly across the river from the royal Anglo-Saxon burial ground at Sutton Hoo. It stands on a small promontory that juts out into the River Deben.
11 Rendlesham, lying six miles inland, is also sited on the River Deben. It has been identified as the place of the same name, described by Bede as 'the king's country seat' *HE* iii, 22. On-going archaeological research at the site confirms that this is an Anglo-Saxon site of the highest status.

SURREY 1

1 **Kennington** (Lambeth) SUR
2 TQ 312 778
3 Brixton
4 Chapelry of Lambeth
5 *Chenintune* DB
6 TRE and TRW Theodoric the goldsmith held *Chenintune* from the king. (DBSur 33,6)
7 DEPN ~
8 CDEPN ~
9 PNSur p. 23. This name is interpreted in PNSur as *Cena*'s (personal name) + *tūn*. Discussion with David Parsons and Paul Cavill suggests that, based on the thirteenth- and fourteenth century-century forms, an alternative interpretation of the first element of the name could be *Cyng* + *tūn*. The early forms are: *Keninton(e)* 1229, *Kyniton(e)* 1255, *Kenyngton* 1263, *Kenigton* 1316, *Kenintone* 1331.
10 Kennington is sited on the Roman road from London to Chichester that left London Bridge on the south side (M 15).
11 A royal palace lay in Kennington. It was here in 1041 that Harthacnut, king of England and Denmark, died, and where Harold Godwinson took the crown the day after the death of Edward the Confessor.

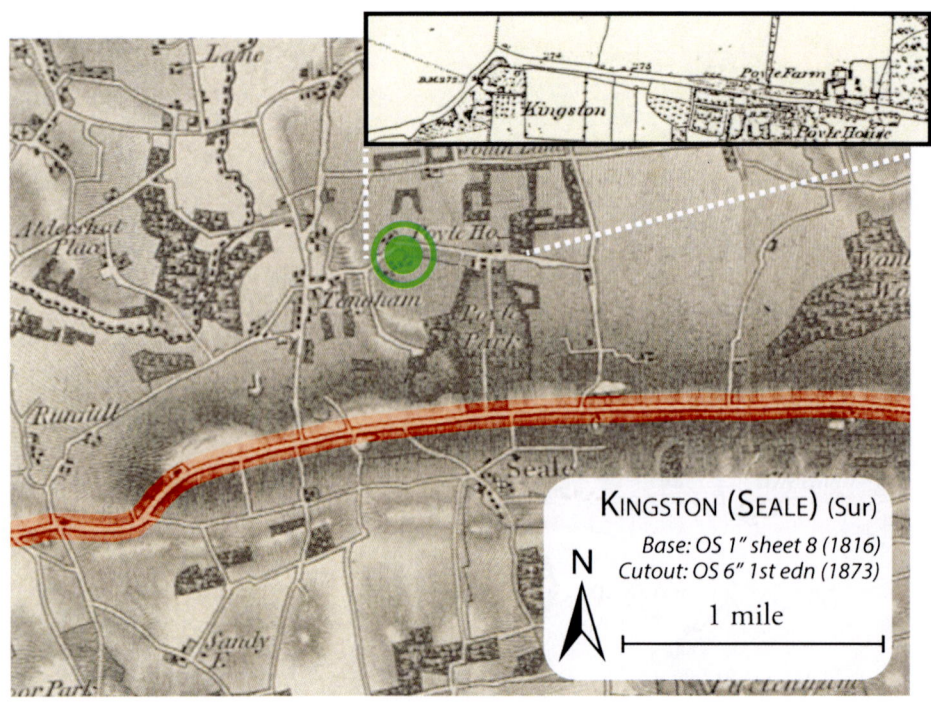

KINGSTON (SEALE) (Sur)
Base: OS 1" sheet 8 (1816)
Cutout: OS 6" 1st edn (1873)
N
1 mile

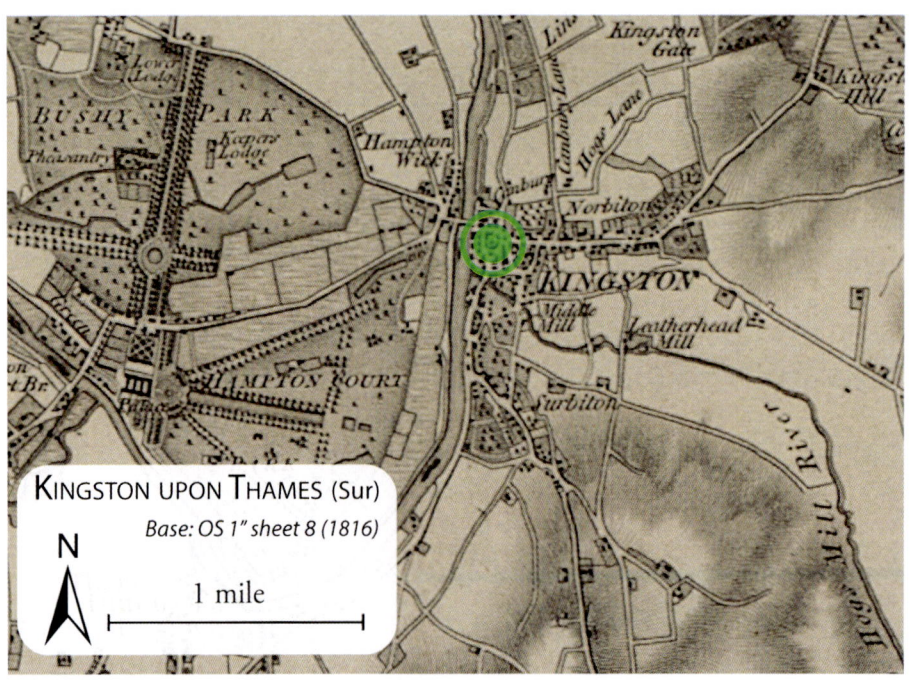

KINGSTON UPON THAMES (Sur)
Base: OS 1" sheet 8 (1816)
N
1 mile

SURREY 2

1 **Kingston** (Seale)
2 SU 891 491
3 Farnham Hundred
4 Chapelry of Farnham
5 *Kyngeston* 1288 Rental
6 DB ~
   Neither Kingston nor Seale are listed in DB. The first reference to Seale is *Sela* in a farm rental of 1210.
   At DB Farnham was held by the Bishop of Winchester. It features in seven charters (five royal) between 688 and 975 (Cædwalla, S 235, Edward, S 382, Edgar, S 818, Edgar, S 822, Edgar, S 823, S 1263, S 1274).
7 DEPN ~
8 CDEPN ~
9 PNSur pp. 181–2
10 SITE Kingston lies four miles east of Farnham, on the long-distance ancient route-way known at this point as the Pilgrim's Way and marked as such on the first edition of the six-inch OS map; its destination south-eastward is Canterbury.
11 PN Sur. suggests that the name is probably 'King's farm', but it may also be derived from the personal name of an early settler from Kingston.
   The name *Sele* is interesting. There are two possible meanings: OE *sele*, 'hall, building': or OE *sēale* 'at the willow'. If it was the former, the 'hall' might refer to building(s) that were still there or were known to have been there. The built structures must have been remarkable in some way for them to have given their name to a site. It is possible that the building referred to was the king's hall.

SURREY 3

1 **Kingston upon Thames**
2 TQ 179 693
3 Kingston Hundred
4 AP, church dedicated to All Saints
5 i *Cyninges tun* 838, *Cyninges tun* in regione Suðregiæ' (S 1438)
   ii *Cingestūn* 838, grant of Egbert king of Wessex issued from *Cingestun* in reggione
   Suðreie (S 281)
   iii *Cingestune*, *Cyngestune* ASC 924 (C, D)
   iv *Cyningestune*, *Cingestune* ASC 979 (C, E)
6 *Chingestune* DB, *Kyngeston super, juxta, Tamisian* 1321
   Land of the King, TRW and TRE (DBSur 1, 8; (2, 3. 5, 28, 8, 12. 22, 4)
7 DEPN p. 278
8 CDEPN p. 348
9 PNSur p. 59
10 SITE Lies on the south bank of the River Thames at the highest tidal point.
11 Chapter five offers a detailed discussion of Kingston upon Thames.

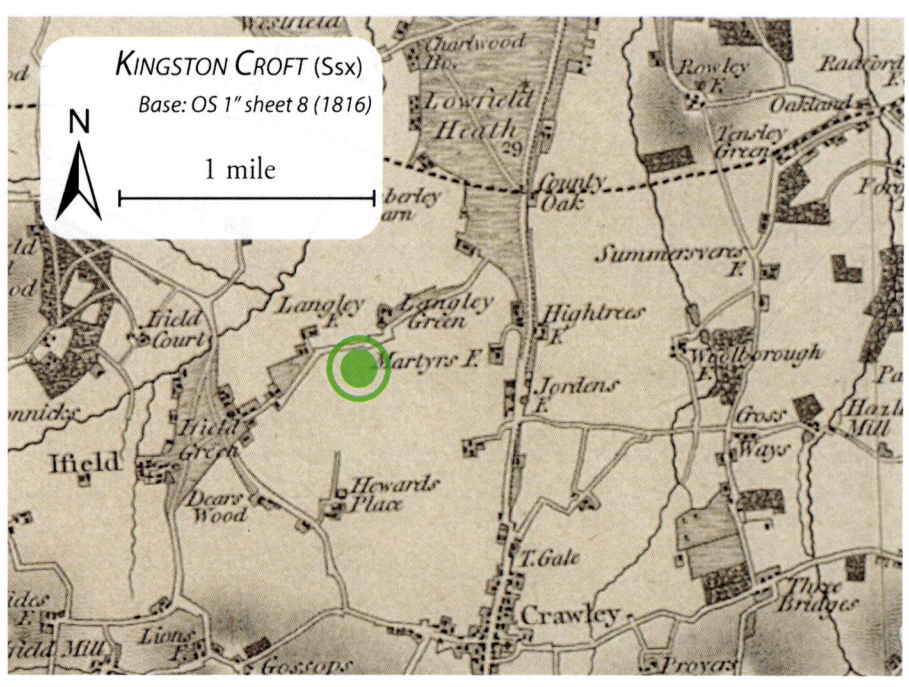

SUSSEX 1

1 **Kingston** (Bucy)
2 TQ 235 052
3 Hundred of Aldrington/Shermanbury, Fishergate/Bramber Rape
4 AP, church dedicated to St Julian
5 *Chingestone* DB
6 At DB there were two manors:
   i   Land of William of Braose, TRW 21 hides held by Ralph. TRE Azor held it from Harold (DBSsx 13,28).
   ii TRW '7 hides were held by William, son of Ranulf from William'. TRE Gunhild held it from Harold (DBSsx 13,29).

   A further eight and a half hides are listed under Hangleton, held TRW by William of Warenne, these hides 'lay in the lands of Kingston'. TRE they were held by Azor from King Edward. (DBSsx 12,23)
7 DEPN p. 278
8 CDEPN p. 348
9 PNSsx vol. 1 p. 245
10 SITE Kingston (Bucy) lies next to Shoreham, midway between Kingston (Lewes) (nine miles north-east) and Kingston (Ferring/*juxta* Arundel), nine miles west. A Roman road crossed the parish at the foot of the downs (M 153). The River Ardur forms the southern boundary. The coast of the parish has been subject to major changes in the course of the river, with the shingle bank changing over the centuries. A new coastal road was constructed n the eighteenth century, replacing an earlier road that had been washed away.
11 Kingston was the site of a large Roman villa. It is thought that there was a harbour and port here which has been swallowed up by the sea. It is possible that there may also have been an Anglo-Saxon harbour here. Kingston stands in a significant relationship to its neighbour Southwick which, although not listed in Domesday, is connected to Kingston with whose lands it intermingles on its western boundary.

SUSSEX 2

1 **Kingston** (Croft/Ifield)
2 TQ 263 383
3 Burbeach Hundred
4 In the parish of Ifield
5 *Kyngeston,* 1261
6 DB ~
   Ifield at DB was held TRW by William of Braose; TRE Alfwy held it from the King.
7 DEPN ~
8 CDEPN ~
9 PNSsx vol. 1, p. 209
10 SITE Kingston Croft lies on the boundary of East and West Sussex, and also on the boundary with Surrey. Although no long-distance Roman road is known here the road which forms the eastern boundary of the parish of Ifield follows a direct line to the south to Brighton. Paterson describes this road as starting from Westminster Bridge, then to Kennington, Clapham Common, Reigate, Crawley and on to *Brighthelmstone* (Brighton). (Paterson, Route 35). Kennington (Lambeth) SUR is sited at the start of this road on the south side of Westminster Bridge. Kennington also lies on the Roman road from London (Bridge) to Chichester.
11 ~

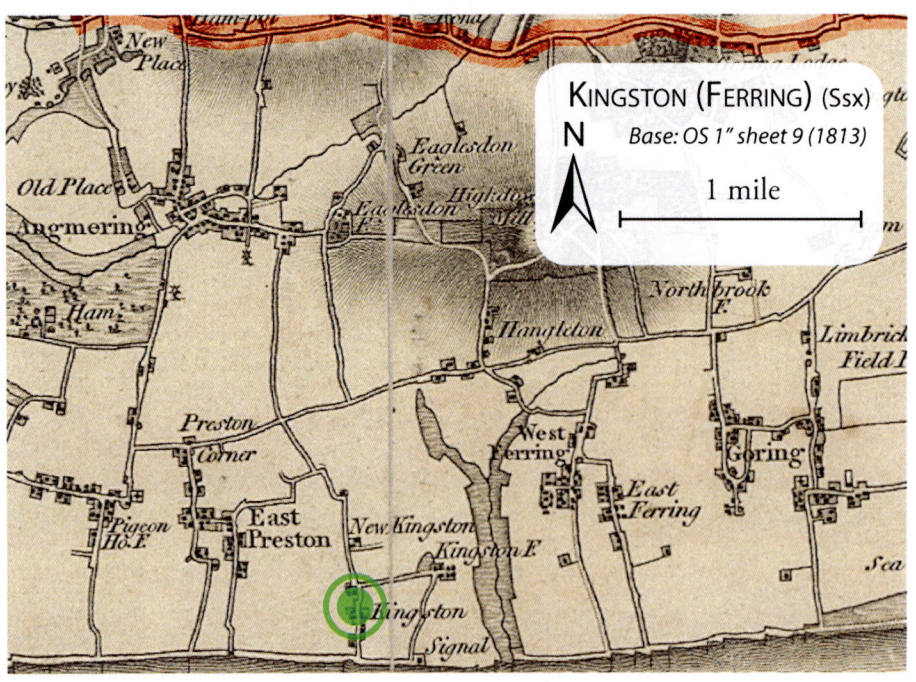

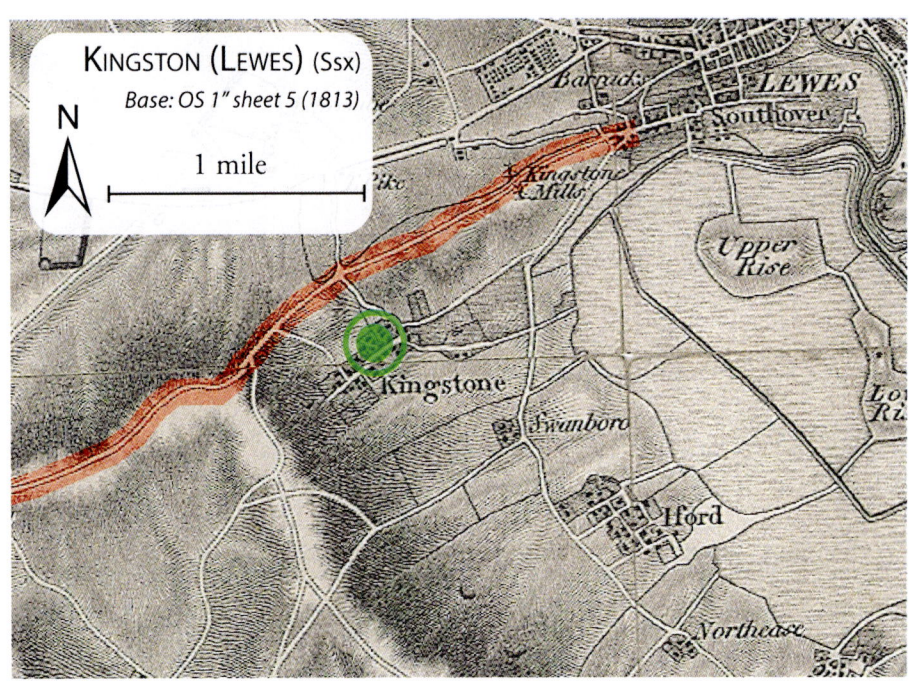

SUSSEX 3

1 **Kingston** (Ferring/Angmering)
2 TQ 086 020
3 Poling Hundred/Arundel Rape
4 There are sixteenth-century references to 'the Chappell of *Kyngston* which is now in the sea'. Report from Sussex Archaeological Collections XXII, MDCCCLX, p. 97.
5 *Kingeston* 1312, *Kingston juxta Arundell* 1316
6 DB ~
   Angmering was probably the *villa regia* to which Kingston stood in relationship.
   At DB Angmering there were two manors:
   i   TRW Land of Earl Roger, held by Warin from the Earl; TRE Earl Godwin held it. (DBSsx 11,65).
   ii   TRW Land of Earl Roger held by Geoffrey from the Earl; TRE three Freemen held it. (DBSsx 11,66).
   Angmering is listed in King Alfred's will; there is no evidence of a royal residence here.
7 DEPN ~
8 CDEPN ~
9 PN Ssx vol. 1, p. 168
10 SITE Immediately to the north of Kingston is Angmering, the site of a Roman villa. Two miles to the south-west in Rustington, the western neighbour of East Preston, is the site of another Roman villa; these villas lie on either side of the Roman road which crosses these parishes. A further five miles west at Arundel lies another villa (M 153).
11 The immediate neighbours of Kingston have royal connections.
   In 762 x 765 Ferring, to the west, featured in a charter of King Osmund who granted 12 hides at *Ferryng* for the construction of a minster (S 48).
   The DB West Preston entry is 'Nunminster', held TRW by Almenesches Abbey from Earl Roger and TRE by Esmelt, a priest, who held it from King Edward. (DBSsx. 11,63–64).
   Charter issued 711 or 791 by Eadwulf, *dux* of the South Saxons, with the consent of Offa, to Withun, bishop, for St Andrew's church, Ferring, woodland at *Cealtborgsteal* (S 1178) This may be the minster for which 12 hides at *Ferrying* were granted by King Osmund in 762 (S 48).

SUSSEX 4

1 **Kingston** (Lewes)
2 TQ 392 082
3 Malling Hundred
4 Parish, church dedicated is to St Pancras; Iford is part of this parish.
5 *Kyngestona*, 1087, William 2 x 1121, *Kyngeston juxta Lewes* 1340
6 DB ~
   Although not listed in DB, Kingston appears in the record just one year later. It must have been subsumed into the Lewis DB entry.
   At DB there were multiple TRW land holders at Lewis. TRE most of the Lewes lands were held by the King. (DBSsx 2,3 4; 3,2; 7,1; 12,1, 3; 4 (5–6; 8–9; 11; 14; 19; 26–28; 31–33; 37–44; 48; 50–51). Lewes was one of King Alfred's *burhs*.
7 DEPN p. 278
8 CDEPN p. 348
9 PNSsx vol. 2, pp. 310–11
10 SITE Kingston lies immediately to the south-west of Lewes. A Roman road, which has been identified archaeologically, crosses the parish in the general direction of Brighton.
11 A sixth/seventh-century Anglo-Saxon cemetery excavated here produced high-status grave goods.

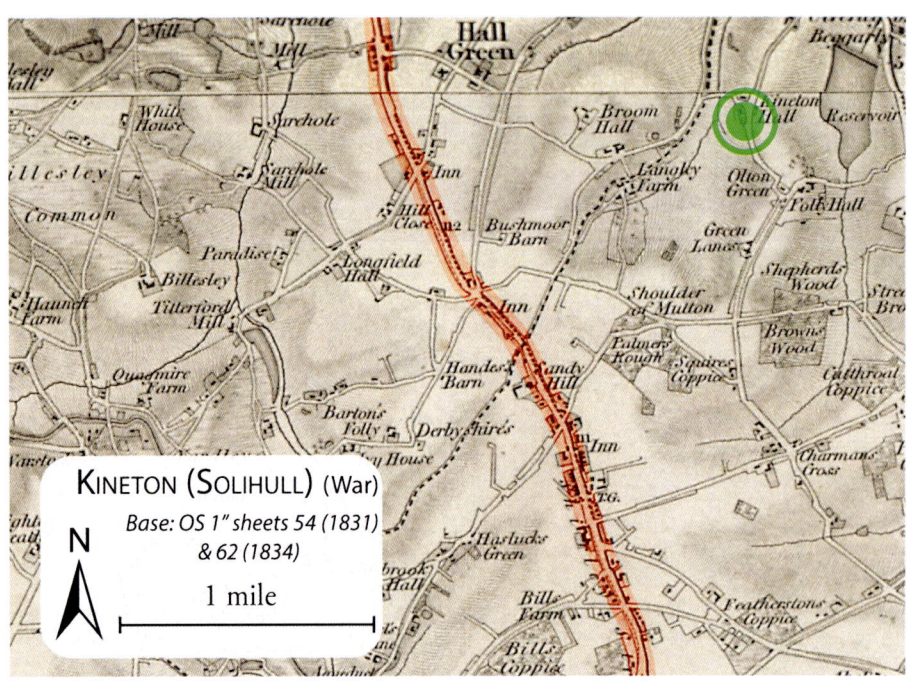

WARWICKSHIRE 1

1 **Kineton** WAR
2 SP 335 511
3 Fexhole Hundred
4 Chapelry of Wellesbourne. Now a civil parish, the church dedicated to St Peter is the same as that of the mother church.
5 *Cyngtun* 969 in a charter of King Edgar grant of 10 hides, '...*loco qui vulgari* **Cyngtun** *dicitur*....'
   The bounds of this charter refer to the royal *vill* of neighbouring Wellesbourne: '*Ðis synt ða lond gemæra into* **cyngtune** *of weles burnan...*'. (S 773)
6 *Quintone* DB
   At DB, Kineton is listed under the entry for Wellesbourne, both were held TRW and TRE by the king. 'This [Wellesbourne] is the manor and the outlier [Kineton] together.' The hidation is low, three hides, but the population is high, 93 villagers, 18 smallholders, five slaves. (DBWar 1, 2).
7 DEPN p. 277
8 CDEPN p. 346
9 PNWar p. 282
10 SITE The parish of Kineton lies five miles south of Kingston (Chesterton) on the Fosse Way, (M 5a). Combrook, its daughter settlement, lies between Kineton and the road. The *villa regalis* of Wellesbourne is sited two miles to the west across the Fosse Way. There does not seem to be any doubt that Kineton was a component part of the federative estate centred on Wellesbourne. The bisecting of the royal estate by the Fosse Way suggests that the land unit, at least at this part of the estate, could be pre-Roman in origin. A direct road connects the two settlements.
11 The 10 hides at *Cyngtun*, which had been granted out in 969 by King Edgar to Ælfwold by DB were back in the king's hands.
   A market charter was granted for Kineton in 1220 and at Wellesbourne (Hastings) in 1246.

WARWICKSHIRE 2

1 **Kineton Green** (Solihull)
2 SP 125 815
3 Coleshill Hundred
4 Lies in the parish of Solihull
5 *Cinctun*, *Cinctun*(*es broc*) 972, in a charter of King Edgar, (S 786)
6 *Cintone* DB
   TRW Land of William son of Corbucion, Aelmer holds two hides. TRE Thorkell held it freely. (DBWar 28,2).
7 DEPN ~
8 CDEPN ~
9 PNWar p. 70; also PNWor p. 330
10 SITE Lies in the forest of Arden on the Warwickshire/ Worcestershire border five miles south-east of Birmingham on the Roman road (present-day A34), known locally as Monkspath Street, which ran from the Roman garrison at Metchley, Edgbaston, in the direction of Stratford-upon-Avon.
   At DB Kineton (Green) was listed both in Warwickshire and Worcestershire.
11 Kineton Green is listed under the Worcestershire DB also.

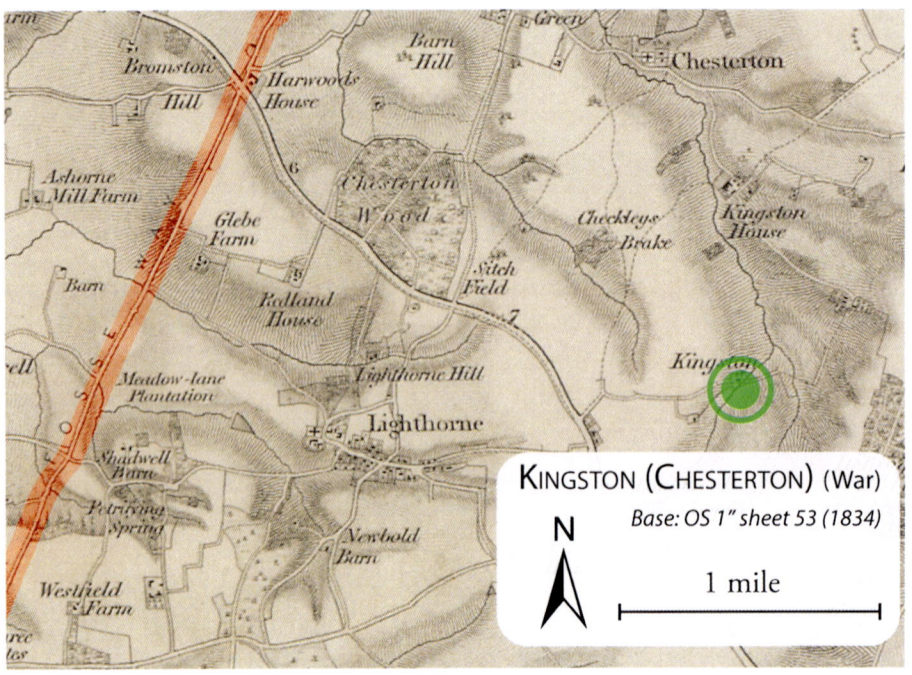

KINGSTON (CHESTERTON) (War)
Base: OS 1" sheet 53 (1834)
N
1 mile

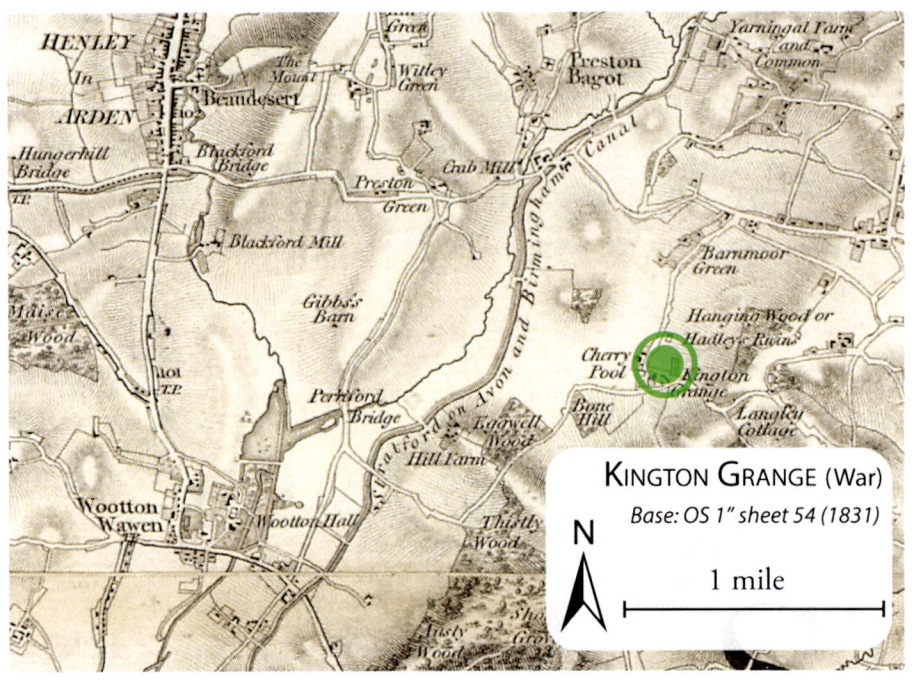

KINGTON GRANGE (War)
Base: OS 1" sheet 54 (1831)
N
1 mile

WARWICKSHIRE 3

1 **Kingston Farm** (Chesterton)
2 SP 352 583
3 Tremlow Hundred
4 Chapelry of Chesterton
5 *Kyngeston* 1262
6 DB ~
At DB Chesterton there were five manors:
i TRW Land of Coventry Church, one and a half hides plus one hide in pledge, no TRE information. (DBWar 6,17).
ii TRW Land of Thorkell of Warwick, Abbot of Abingdon holds one hide from him; TRE Alfwold held it. (DBWar 17,67).
iii TRW the Abbot holds one hide in pledge; TRE Alnoth, Brictwin, and Thori held freely. (DBWar 17,68).
iv TRW Land of Henry of Ferrers, Wazelin holds half a hide from him; no TRE information. (DBWar 19,5)
v TRW Land of Richard the Forester, Richard Hunter holds three hides from him; TRE four Thanes held it freely. (DBWar 44,8).
7 DEPN p. 101; pp. 277–8
8 CDEPN p. 131
9 PNWar p. 251
10 SITE Kingston lies on the Fosse Way, five miles north-east of Kineton; the parish boundaries of Chesterton cross the Fosse Way (M 5a). The earthworks of a Roman small town can be seen beside the line of the road in the north of the parish.
11 Kingston today is represented by a farm name.

WARWICKSHIRE 4

1 **Kington Grange** (Claverdon)
2 SP 180 642
3 Barlichway Hundred
4 Chapelry of Claverdon
5 *Cintone* DB
6 At DB *Cintone* was held TRW land of the Count of Meulan, one and a half hides. TRE Brictnoth held it; he was a free man (DBWar 16,19).
7 DEPN ~
8 CDEPN ~
9 PNWar p. 207
10 SITE Lies in the Forest of Arden, adjacent to Claverdon, which may have been the estate centre to which it was attached. The original central place of this estate has been shown by Steven Bassett to be Wootton Wawen. No Roman road has been identified here but Wootton Wawen lies close to an ancient route-way between south Birmingham and Stratford upon Avon. The first five miles of this road have been identified as Roman. Kington Grange lies too far away for the road to have been be its prime association.
11 Kingston lies in the small early Anglo-Saxon kingdom of the *Stoppingas.* This is explored fully in Chapter 4.

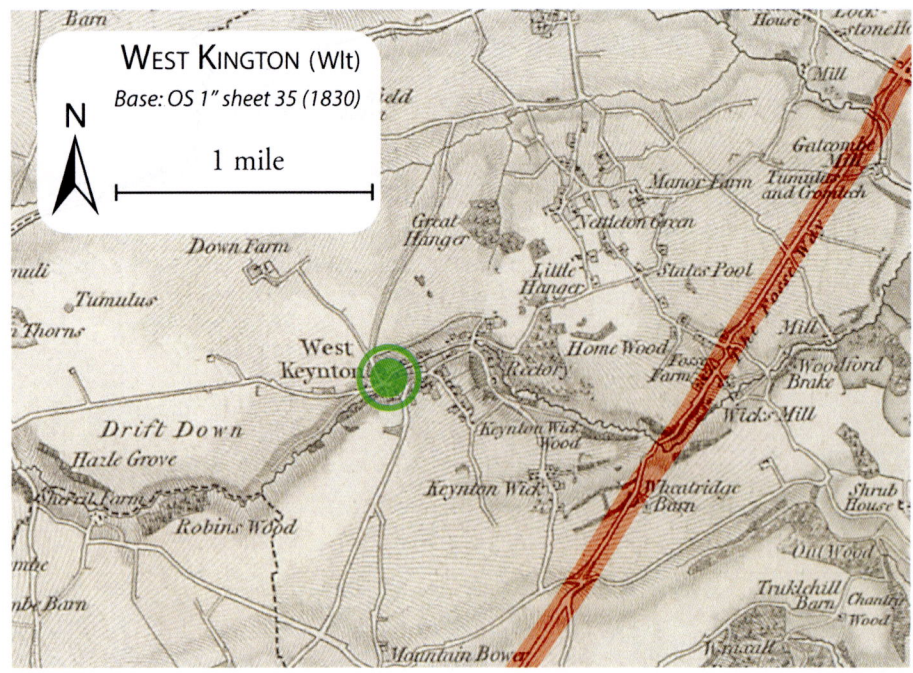

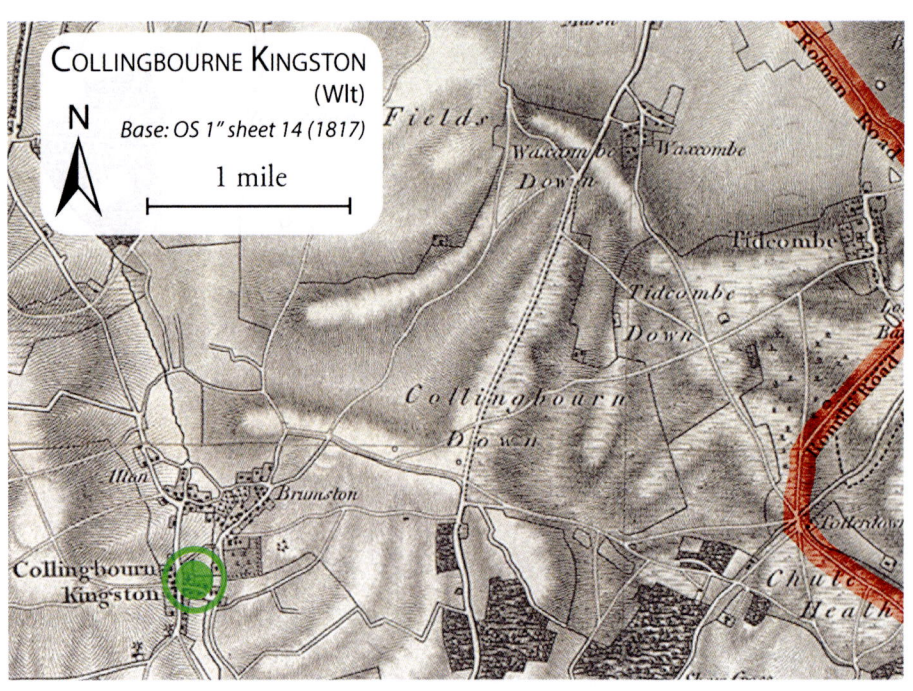

146

WILTSHIRE 1
1 **West Kington**
2 ST 813 776
3 Thorngrove Hundred
4 Lies in the parish of Nettleton, church dedicated to St Mary
5 *Westkinton*, 1195
6 DB ~
   At DB Nettleton was held TRW by the Church of Glastonbury. No TRE information (DBWlt 7, 9).
7 DEPN p. 278
8 CDEPN p. 349
9 PNWlt p. 80
10 SITE West Kington lies on the Fosse Way, six miles west of Chippenham and seven miles north of Bath (M 5c). Its immediate neighbour is Nettleton, the site of a Roman small town built on the site of a complex series of second- and third-century temples. After their abandonment at the end of the third century, the town became a centre for the production of pewter.
11 West Kington is one of seven Kingstons which are sited on or next to Roman small towns. The spelling of the name on the O.S. map is West Keynton.

WILTSHIRE 2
1 **Kingston** (Collingbourne)
2 SU 241 559
3 Kinwardstone Hundred
4 AP, church, dedicated to St Mary. Other tithings, Aughton, Cadly, Brunton, Southton.
5 *Colingeburne Kingeston* 1306
6 DB ~
   At DB there were two manors listed at *Coleburna* and *Colingeburne*
   i   Collingbourne (Ducis) was held TRW by the King and TRE by Earl Harold (DBWlt 1, 9).
   ii Collingbourne (Kingston) was held TRW Land of the Abbey of St Peter's Winchester. No TRE information is given but it was unlikely to have been any other holder other than the Abbey. (DBWlt 10,2).
7 DEPN ~
8 CDEPN pp. 150–1
9 PNWlt pp. 342–3
10 SITE The north-west tip of Collingbourne Kingston touches the boundary with north-eastern Hampshire and south-west Berkshire, where the three counties meet at Scot's Poor and Silver Down, the site of a cluster of Neolithic monuments. The long-distance Roman road which runs north-west/south-east between Cirencester and Winchester tips this north-eastern corner of the parish (M 44). Collingbourne was a riverine estate along the River Bourne, midway between Andover and Marlborough, eight miles south-west of Bedwyn.
11 Collingbourne was the subject of two royal charters:
   i   A Charter of King Edward issued from Southampton in 903 granting land at *Colengaburnan* for the founding of the New Minster at Winchester (S 370). Winchester still held this land at DB.
   ii A Charter of King Edward, issued from Wilton in 921 granting land at 'de villa de *Colingborne*', has been identified as the part of the estate of Colingbourne which later became known as Kingston (S 379).
   The name probably means the 'stream of the *Collingas*'. It is also possible that *Coll* was the original name of the stream.

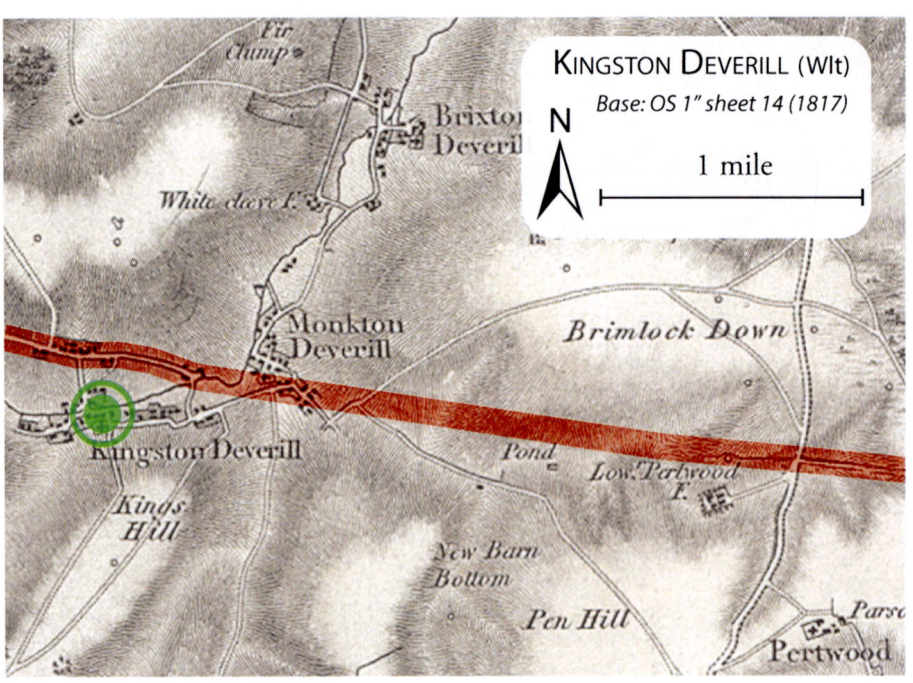

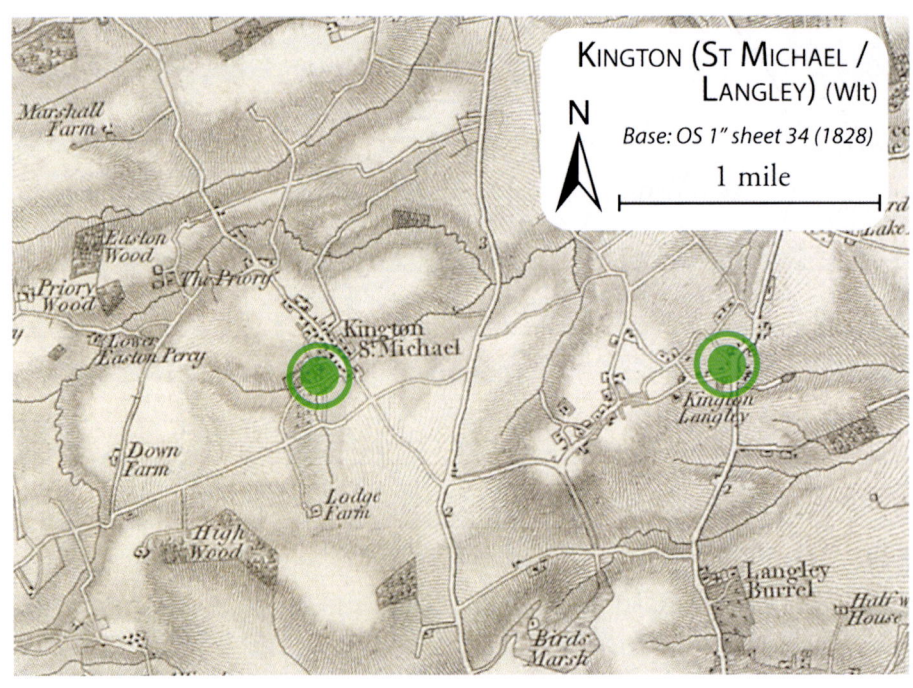

WILTSHIRE 3

1 **Kingston** (Deverill)
2 ST 845 370
3 Amesbury Hundred (part) Mere Hundred (part)
4 Daughter of Warminster
5 *Deverel Kyneston* 1249
6 DB ~

At DB there were four manors at Deverill:

i Deverill (Kingston) was held TRW by the Canons of Lisieux; TRE by (Queen) Edith. (DBWlt 19,1).

ii Deverill (Monkton) was held TRW by the church at Glastonbury. No TRE information. (DBWlt 7,3).

iii Deverill (Brixton) was held TRW by St Mary of Bec, Queen Matilda had held it and given its value to the church. TRE it was held by Brictric (DBWlt 17,1)

iv Deverill was held TRW by the church at Glastonbury, no TRE information is given although it is likely they also held this manor TRE.

7 DEPN p. 278
8 CDEPN p. 348
9 PNWlt p. 173
10 SITE Kingston (Deverill) lies in the south-western corner of the county, close to the Somerset border, at the junction of the Roman road which ran west from Old Sarum (M 45) and the Roman road which ran south to Fontmell Magna and Badbury Rings and north to Bath. (M 46). Kingston Lacy DOR is sited at Badbury Rings.

Kingston Deverill lies 11 miles north-east of Kington Magna DOR. They are connected by a through road via Gillingham.

11 The site of a Roman temple has been identified in the north-west corner of the parish.

WILTSHIRE 4

1 **Kington** (St Michael/Langley)
2 ST 903 773
3 Chippenham Hundred
4 Now a parish, previously a chapelry of Kingston (Langley) which was part of the extensive parochia of Chippenham.
5 i *Kingtone* 934, charter of King Æthelstan to Aethelhelm, minister (S 426).

  ii *Kyngtune* 987, charter of King Æthelred granting 40 hides at *Kyngtune* to Glastonbury Abbey. This charter refers to land in both Kington St Michael and Langley (S 866).

6 *Chintone* DB

At DB Kington St Michael was a small manor of one and a half hides, held TRW by Roger from Ralph Mortimer and TRE by Alwyn who held it from Glastonbury and 'could not be separated from it'. This is in contrast to Kington (Langley) which was a large manor assessed at 29 hides and also held both TRW and TRE by Glastonbury Abbey.

7 DEPN p. 278
8 CDEPN p. 349
9 PNWlt p. 100
10 SITE Kington (St Michael) lies two miles north of Chippenham. No long-distance ancient road has been identified here. The minor Roman town of *Verlucio* lay four miles to the south of Chippenham near Bell Farm (ST 972 673), on the Roman road that ran east-west between Silchester and Bath. *Verlucio* is known from its being mentioned in the Antonine Itinerary and from surface finds of Roman material. No above-ground structures survive and the extent of the town is not known.

11 Kington St Michael and its neighbour Kington Langley would once have been one unit, with Kington St Michael being the place of lower status as it became a dependency of Kington (Langley) after Langley became separate from Chippenham. The separation may date from the tenth century, when they were the subject of separate royal charters.

Whatever was the function of Kington St Michael (and possibly Langley) in relation to the royal *vill* of Chippenham, that function may have ceased by the tenth century for the king to have granted it away. This was the case at Kineton WAR, although Kineton had reverted to the king by DB.

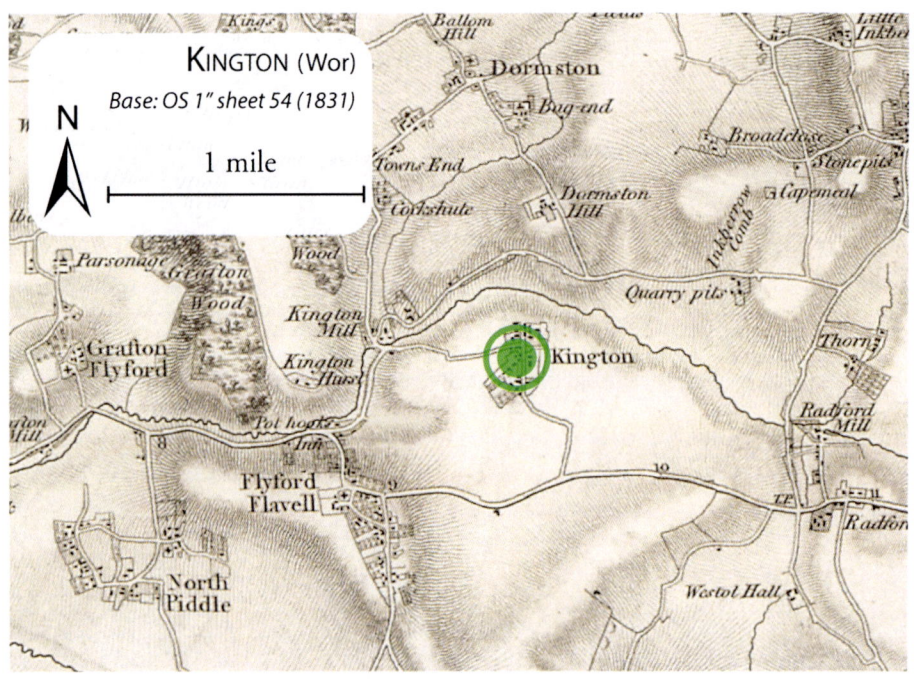

WORCESTERSHIRE 1

1 **Kington** WOR
2 SO 990 559
3 Doddingtree Hundred
4 AP, the church is dedicated to St James.
5 *Cyngtun* 930, Charter of King Æthelstan to Cynath abbot. (S 404)
6 *Chintune* DB, *c.* 1086 *Ki-Kyn(e)ton(e)*
   TRW Land of Roger of Lacy, Roger holds Kington (himself). TRE Alfwy, Elaf and Tori held it as three manors, these men 'could go where they would'. They had one hedged enclosure where wild animals were caught (DBWor 18, 4).
7 DEPN pp. 348-9
8 CDEPN p. 348
9 PNWor p. 330
10 SITE Lies nine miles east of Worcester and eight miles west of Alcester. There is no evidence of a Roman road here, although it has been suggested that the road from Worcester to Alcester, which crosses the southern part of the parish, may follow a Roman line.
11 The earlier name of this estate was *piduuella*, 930 (S 404), 1002 (S 901) from the Piddle Brook. In 930 it was granted by King Athelstan to abbot Cynath and in 1002 by King Æthelred to archbishop Ælfric. Watts suggests that this grant led to the descriptive term royal manor becoming current'. Watts 2000: p. 348.

Both of these charters relate to woodland at *Fleferth* (Flyford Flavell). This estate has been identified as the parish of Kingston, whose parish boundaries follow almost exactly those of the boundary clause.

YORKSHIRE EAST RIDING 1

1 **Kingston upon Hull**
2 TA 104 297
3 Harthill Wapentake, Hunsely Beacon
4 AP, church dedicated to the Holy Trinity
5 The town has been known at various times as *Wik(e)*, Hull and Kingston.
   i *Wyk* 1160 x 1180–1279
   ii '*portum, villa de Hul*' 1228
   iii *Kyngeston* - (*super, on, upon*) Hul(*l –e*) 1275–1548
6 DB ~
7 DEPN p. 278
8 CDEPN p. 348
9 PNYER & York pp. 209–10
10 SITE Kingston upon Hull stands on the River Hull on the north bank of the Humber estuary. The site, known as *Wyke* (an outlying corner of Myton), was a low-lying creek with no fresh water. *Wyke* means either the OE *wīc* 'a dairy farm, trading place' or ON *vik* 'a creek, an inlet'. Myton, now lost, is *myðe tūn,* the settlement at the confluence of the Hull and the Humber'. At DB *Mitun(e)* was an outlier of Ferriby, held by Ralph of Mortemer TRW and by Eadgifu (DBYOE14e 15).
11 In 1292, Edward I exchanged with the monks of Meaux lands he had in Wawne and Wilsby for *Wyke*, for the purpose of securing the port. This place was officially named *nomen dictæ villæ de Wyk mutavit et eandem villam Kingestonam super Hullo fecerat nominari'*.

The charter recording this exchange is preserved in the Guildhall of the city. There is no evidence for this site of a port before it was held by the king, although it is tempting to wonder whether the original name of *Wyke* hints at an earlier incarnation as a *wīc*, as in *Hamwīc*.

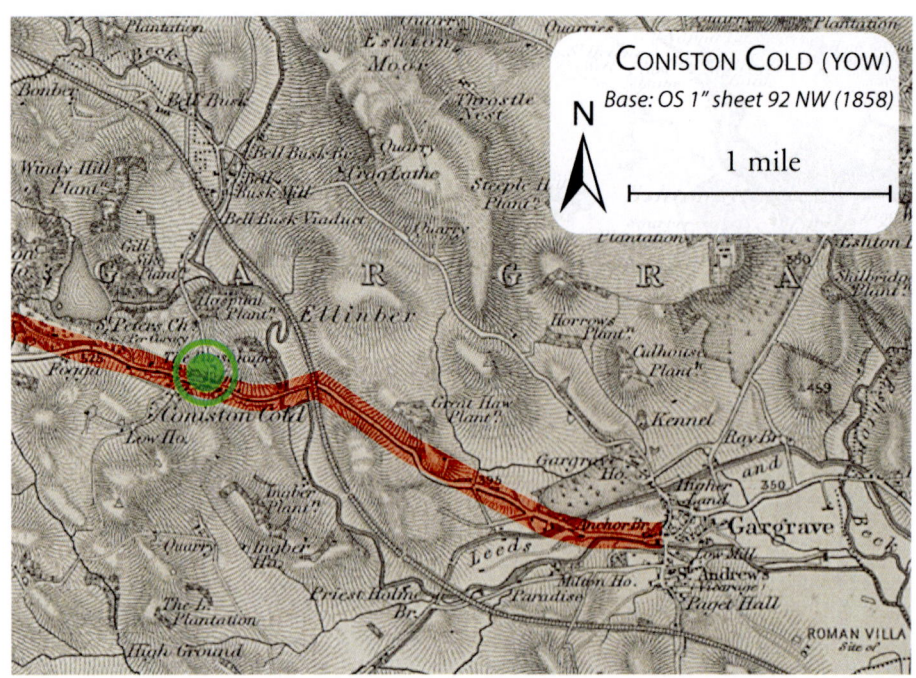

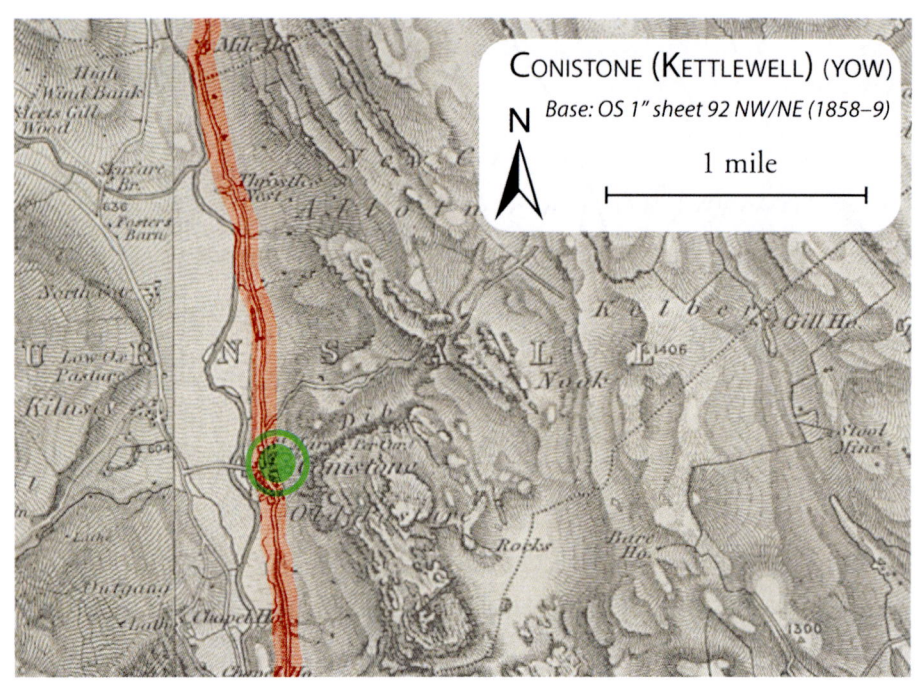

YORKSHIRE WEST RIDING 1

1 **Coniston** (Cold**)**

2 SD 902 552

3 Staincliffe Wapentake

4 Chapelry of Gargrave

5 *Co- Cuninges- Conegheston(e)* DB, *Cunyngeston in Craven* 1369

6 At DB there were four manors:

   i *Coneghestone*, three carucates (DBYOW 1W73)

   ii Land of William of Percy. In Swinden, Hellifield, Malham, *Cuningestune*, 13½ carucates taxable. 'These manors were (TRE) Bjornulf's; now William of Percy has them. Waste'. (DBYOW 13W44).

   iii In *Cuningestune* two carucates, William of Percy held it, but Roger of Poitou has it. (DBYOW 30W2).

   iv In *Coninestone* three carucates belongs to Bolton Abbey (DBWR SW, Cr 5)

7 DEPN p. 120

8 CDEPN p. 155

9 PNYOW vol. 6, p. 45

10 SITE Lies on the long-distance Roman road from Skipton to Kendal. (M 722 b), continuing on to Ambleside and Ravenglass. A Roman villa site has been excavated in neighbouring Gargrave, where a section of the Roman road has been exposed.

11 Both of these Yorkshire examples lie within the Anglo-Saxon (and possibly British) kingdom of Craven; the name was still in use as a district name at the time of DB.

YORKSHIRE WEST RIDING 2

1 **Conistone** (Kettlewell)

2 SD 981 675

3 Staincliffe Wapentake

4 Chapelry of Burnsall

5 *Cunestune* DB

6 DB Land of the King's Thanes. Arnketill held three carucates taxable, Ketil has it (DBYOW 29W 50M).

7 DEPN p. 120

8 CDEPN p. 155

9 PNYOW vol. 6, p. 85

10 SITE Conistone lies on the road from Kettlewell to Skipton, a long-distance ancient route-way which was used, and almost certainly improved, by the Romans. The OS Roman Britain map shows this road running south from Brough by Bainbridge (*Virosidum*) towards Kettlewell. The road follows the valley of the upper River Wharfe and, although no remains have yet been identified, Margary suggests the road continued on southward (M 730).

11. Both of these Yorkshire examples lie within the Anglo-Saxon (and possibly British) kingdom of Craven: the name was still in use as a district name at the time of DB.

Bibliography

Abels, R., 1988. *Lordship and Military Obligation in Anglo-Saxon England* (British Museum Publications, London).

Abrams, L., 1996. *Anglo-Saxon Glastonbury: Church and Endowment* (Boydell, Woodbridge).

Abrams, L. and Parsons, D., 2005. 'Place-names and the history of Scandinavian settlement in England', in Hines, J., Lane, A., and Redknapp, M., eds., *Land, Sea, and Home* (Society for Medieval Archaeology, Monograph Series, vol. 20 (Maney, Leeds and London).

Addison, W., 1980. *The Old Roads of England* (Batsford, London).

Anderton, M., 1999. *Anglo-Saxon Trading Centres: Beyond the Emporia* (Cruithne, Glasgow).

Andrews, P., 2004. 'Kingston – Saxon royal estate centre to post-medieval market town: the contribution of archaeology to understanding towns in Surrey', in *Aspects of Archaeology and History in Surrey: towards a research framework for the county* (Surrey County Council and Surrey Archaeological Society, Kingston upon Thames).

Andrews, P., *et al.*, 2003. *Charter Quay, the Spirit of Change: the Archaeology of Kingston's Riverside* (Wessex Archaeology, Salisbury).

Arnold, C., 1984. *Roman Britain to Saxon England* (Routledge, London).

Ashmore, O., 1969. *The Industrial Archaeology of Lancashire* (David and Charles, Newton Abbot).

Aston, M., 1984. 'The towns of Somerset', in Haslam, J., ed. *Anglo-Saxon Towns in Southern England* (Phillimore, Chichester), pp. 167–201.

Aston, M., 1986. 'Post-Roman central places in Somerset', in Grant, E., ed., *Central Places, Archaeology and History* (Department of Archaeology and Prehistory, University of Sheffield), Sheffield, pp. 49–77.

Aston, M. and Lewis, C., eds, 1994. *The Medieval Landscape of Wessex* (Oxbow, Oxford).

Attenborough, F. L., 1922. *The Laws of the Earliest Kings* (Cambridge University Press, Cambridge).

Aubrey, J., 1718–19. *Natural History and Antiquities of the County of Surrey*, vol. 1 (E. Curll, Fleet Street, London).

Bacon, G.W., 1891. *Through Airedale from Goole to Malham* (Walker and Laycock, Leeds).

Balkwill, C.J., 1993. 'Old English *wīc* and the origin of the hundred', *Landscape History*, 15, pp. 5–11.

Bassett, S., 1989. 'In search of the origins of Anglo-Saxon kingdoms', in Bassett, S., ed., *The Origins of Anglo Saxon Kingdoms* (Leicester University Press), Leicester).

Bassett, S., 1990. 'The Roman and medieval landscape of Wroxeter', in Barker, P.A., ed., *From Roman Viroconium to Medieval Wroxeter* (West Mercian Archaeological

Consultants, privately printed), pp. 10–12.

Bassett, S., 2000. 'How the west was won: the Anglo-Saxon takeover of the West Midlands', *Anglo-Saxon Studies in Archaeology and History*, 11, pp. 107–18.

Bassett, S., 2007. 'Boundaries of knowledge: mapping the land units of late Anglo-Saxon and Norman England', in Davies, W., Hassall, G.W., and Reynolds, A., eds, *People and Space in the Middle Ages, 300–1300* (Brepols, Belgium), pp. 115–42.

Behr, C., 2000. 'The origins of kingship in early medieval Kent', *Early Medieval Europe*, 9, pp. 25–52.

Biddle, M., 1976. 'Towns', in Wilson, D.M., ed., *The Archaeology of Anglo-Saxon England* (Cambridge University Press, Cambridge), pp. 99–150.

Bird, D., 2002. 'Roads and temples, Stane Street at Ewell', in *London Archaeologist*, 10, no. 2, pp. 41–5.

Bird, D., 2004. *Roman Surrey* (The History Press, Stroud).

Birkbeck, V., Smith, R.J. C., Andrews, P., and Stoodley, N., 2005. *The Origins of Mid-Saxon Southampton: Excavations at the Friends Provident St Mary's Stadium 1998–2000* (Wessex Archaeology, Salisbury).

Blair, J., 1988. 'Minster churches in the landscape', in Hooke, D., ed., *Anglo-Saxon Settlements* (Blackwell, Oxford), pp. 35–58.

Blair, J., 1989. 'Frithuwold's kingdom and the origins of Surrey', in Bassett, S., ed., *The Origins of Anglo-Saxon Kingdoms* (Leicester University Press, (Leicester), pp. 97–109.

Blair, J., 1991. *Early Medieval Surrey, Landholding, Church and Settlement before 1300* (Sutton, Stroud).

Blair, J., 1994. *Anglo-Saxon Oxfordshire* (Sutton, Stroud).

Blair, J., 1996. 'Palaces or minsters? Northampton and Cheddar reconsidered', *Anglo-Saxon England*, 25, pp. 97–121.

Blair, J. 1999. 'The Tribal Hidage', in Lapidge, M., *et al.*, *Blackwell Encyclopedia of Anglo-Saxon England* (Blackwell, Oxford).

Blair, J., 2005. *The Church in Anglo-Saxon Society* (Oxford University Press, Oxford). Bonney, D., 1979. 'Early Boundaries and Estates in Southern England', in Sawyer, P.H. ed., *English Medieval Settlement* (Edward Arnold, London), pp. 41–51.

Bradley, R., 1968. 'The South Oxfordshire Grim's ditch and its significance', *Oxoniensia*, 33, pp. 1–13.

Brandon, P., ed., 1978. *The South Saxons* (Phillimore, London and Chichester).

Briggs, K., 2009. 'The distribution of certain place-name types to Roman roads', *Nomina*, 32, pp. 43–57.

Brookes, S., 2007. *Economics and Social Change in Anglo-Saxon Kent AD 400–900 Landscapes, Communities and change* (BAR British Series 431, Oxford).

Brookes, S. and Harrington, S., 2010. *The Kingdom and People of Kent AD 400–1066* (The History Press, Stroud).

Brookes, S., date *Economics and Social Change in Anglo-Saxon Kent AD 400-900: Landscapes Communities and Change* BAR 441, Oxford.

Brooks, N., 1964. 'The unidentified forts of the Burghal Hidage', *Medieval Archaeology*, 8, pp. 74–89.

Brooks, N., 1971. 'The development of military obligations in eighth- and ninth-century England', in Clemoes, P. and Hughes, K., eds, *England Before the Conquest: Studies in Primary Sources presented to D. Whitelock* (Cambridge University Press), pp. 69–84.

Brooks, N., 1984. *The Early History of the Church of Canterbury* (Leicester University Press, Leicester).

Brooks, N., 1989a. 'The creation and early structure of the kingdom of Kent', in Bassett, S., ed., *The Origins of the Anglo Saxon Kingdoms* (Leicester University Press, Leicester), pp. 55–74.

Brooks, N., 1989b. 'The formation of the Mercian kingdom', in Bassett, S., ed., *The Origins of Anglo-Saxon Kingdoms* (Leicester University Press, Leicester), pp. 159–70.

Brooks, N., 1996. 'The administrative background to the Burghal Hidage', in Hill, D. and Rumble, A.R., eds, *The Defence of Wessex: The Burghal Hidage and Anglo-Saxon Fortifications* (Manchester University Press, Manchester), pp. 128–50.

Brooks, N., 2000. *Communities and Warfare 700–1400* (Hambledon Press, London).

Brooks, N., 2003. *Church, State and Access to Resources in Early Anglo-Saxon England*, 20th Brixworth Lecture, The Brixworth Lectures Second Series, no. 2 (The Friends of All Saints Church, Brixworth).

Brown, M. and Farr, C., eds, 2005. *Mercia, an Anglo-Saxon Kingdom in Europe*, Continuum Studies in Medieval History (Continuum International Publishing, London/New York).

Burnham, B. and Wacher, J., 1990. *The Small Towns of Roman Britain* (University of Califorrna Press, Berkeley).

Cadbury, G., 1920. 'The Roman roads of south Birmingham', *Trans. Birmingham and Warwickshire Archaeological Society*, 46, pp. 22–35.

Cam, H. M., 1963. *Liberties and Communities in Medieval England: Collected Studies in Local Administration and Topography*, 2nd edn (Cambridge University Press, Cambridge).

Cameron, K., 1959. *The Place-Names of Derbyshire*, 3 vols (English Place-Name Society, Nottingham).

Cameron, K., 1996. *English Place-Names*, revised edition (Batsford, London).

Campbell, A., ed., 1962. *The Chronicle of Æthelweard* (Nelson, London).

Campbell, J., 1979a. 'Bede's words for places', in *Essays in Anglo-Saxon History* (Hambledon Press, London), pp. 85–98.

Campbell, J., 1979b. 'Bede's *reges* and *principes*', in *Essays in Anglo-Saxon History* (Hambledon Press, London), pp. 99–119.

Campbell, J., ed. 1982. 'The lost centuries: 400–600', in Campbell, J., ed., *The Anglo- xxxxx*

Campbell, J., 1986. 'Early Anglo-Saxon society according to the written sources', in *Essays in Anglo-Saxon History* (Hambledon, London), pp. 131–8.

Campbell, J., 2003. *The Anglo-Saxon State* (Hambledon, London).

Carroll, J., and Parsons, D.N., 2007. *Anglo-Saxon Mint-Names 1. Axbridge-Hythe* (English Place-Name Society, Nottingham).

Carroll, J., and Parsons, D. N., eds, 2013. Perceptions of Place (English Place-Name Society, Nottingham).

Chadwick, H.M., 1963. *Studies on Anglo-Saxon Institutions* (Cambridge University Press, Cambridge).

Chaney, W.A., 1970. *The Cult of Kingship in Anglo-Saxon England* (Manchester University Press, Manchester).

Charles-Edwards, T., 1989. 'Early medieval kingships in the British Isles', in Bassett, S., ed., *The Origins of Anglo Saxon Kingdoms* (Leicester University Press, Leicester).

Clarke, A., 2003. 'A Roman road on the eastern fringe of the New Forest from Shorn Hill to Lepe', *Proceedings of the Hampshire Field Club and Archaeological Society*, 58, pp. 33–58.

Cleere, H. and Crossley, D., 1985. *The Iron Industry of the Weald* (Leicester University Press, Leicester).

Coates, R., 1984. 'Coldharbour for the last time?', *Nomina*, 8, pp. 73–8.

Coates, R., 1993. *Hampshire Place-Names* (Batsford, London).

Cochrane, C., 1969. *The Lost Roads of Wessex*, 2nd edn (David and Charles, Newton Abbot).

Cohen, N., 2003. 'Boundaries and settlements: the role of the River Thames', in Griffiths,

D., Reynolds, A., Semple, S., eds, *Boundaries in Early Medieval Britain: Anglo-Saxon Studies in Archaeology and History*, 12, pp. 9–20.

Cole, A., 1985. 'Topography, hydrology and place-names in the chalklands of southern England: *Funta, Aewiell* and *Aewielm*', *Nomina*, 9, pp. 3–19.

Cole, A., 1991. '*Burna* and *Brōc*: problems involved in retrieving the OE usage of these place-name elements', *Journal of the English Place Name Society*, 23, pp. 26–48.

Cole, A., 1994. 'The Anglo-Saxon Traveller', *Nomina*, 17, pp. 7–18.

Cole, A., 2011. 'The Place-Name Evidence for a Routeway Network in Early Medieval England', 2 vols, unpublished DPhil thesis, University of Oxford.

Colgrave, B. and Mynors, R.A.B., eds, *Bede's Ecclesiastical History of the English People* (Clarendon, Oxford).

Cooper, A., 2002. 'The Rise and Fall of the Anglo-Saxon Law of the Highway', in *The Haskins Society Journal*, 12, pp. 39–69.

Corcos, N.J., 1983. 'Early Estates on the Poldens and the origin of the settlement at Shapwick', *Proceedings of Somerset Archaeological and Natural History Society*, 127, pp. 47–54.

Costen, M., 2011. *Anglo-Saxon Somerset* (Oxbow, Oxford).

Cotton, J., Crocker, G. Graham, A., eds, 2004. *Aspects of Archaeology and History in Surrey* (English Heritage, London).

Courtney, P., 1981. 'The early Anglo-Saxon fenland: a reconsideration', *Anglo-Saxon Studies in Archaeology and History*, 2, pp. 91–103.

Cousins, N., *Cumbria Amenity Trust Mining History Society*, at www.catmhs.org.uk.

Cox, B., 1971. 'The Place-Names of Leicestershire and Rutland', unpublished Ph.D. thesis, University of Nottingham.

Cox, B., 1972–73. 'The significance of the distribution of the English place-names in *hām* in the Midlands and East Anglia', *Journal of the English Place-Name Society*, 5, pp. 15–73.

Cox, B., 1975–76. 'Place-names of the earliest English records', in *Journal of the English Place-Name Society*, 8, pp. 12–66.

Cubitt, C., 1995. *Anglo-Saxon Church Councils c.650–c.850* (Leicester University Press, London).

Cullen, P., 1997. *The Place-Names of the lathes of St Augustine and Shipway Kent*, unpublished Ph.D. thesis, University of Sussex.

Cullen, P., Jones, R. and Parsons, D., 2011. *Thorps in a Changing Landscape* (University of Hertfordshire Press, Hatfield).

Cunliffe, B., 1993. *Wessex to A.D. 1000* (Longman, London and New York).

Darby, H.C. and Campbell, E.M.J., 1962. *The Domesday Geography of South-East England* (Cambridge University Press, Cambridge).

Darby, H.C. and Terrett, I.B., 1954. *The Domesday Geography of Midland England* (Cambridge University Press, Cambridge).

Dark, K.R., 1994. *Civitas to Kingdom: British Political Continuity 300–800* (Leicester University Press imprint, Bloomsbury, London).

Dark, K.R., 2000. *Britain and the end of the Roman Empire* (Tempus, Stroud).

Davies, W., 1982. *Wales in the Early Middle Ages* (Leicester University Press, Leicester).

Davies, W. & Vierk, H., 1974. *The Contexts of the Tribal Hidage: Social Aggregates and Settlement Patterns,* (Frühmittelalterliche Studien).

De la Bedoyere, G., 1991. *Roman Towns in Britain* (Batsford, London).

Dodgson, J. McN., 1970–97. *The Place-Names of Cheshire,* 7 vols (English Place-Name Society, Nottingham).

Dornier, A. ed., 1977. *Mercian Studies* (Leicester University Press, Leicester).

Draper, S., 2004. Roman Estates to English Parishes, in Collins, R. and Gerrard, J., *Debating Late Antiquity, Britain AD 300–700'* (BAR British Series number 36, Oxford).

Draper, S., 2006. *Landscape, Settlement and Early Society in Roman and Early Medieval Wiltshire* (BAR British Series 149, Oxford)

Draper, S., 2009. '*Burh* place-names in Anglo-Saxon England', *Journal of the English Place-Name Society*, 41, pp. 103–17.

Dumville, D., 1977. 'Kingship, Genealogies and Regnal Lists', in Sawyer, P. and Wood, I.N. eds, *Early Medieval Kingship* (School of History, University of Leeds) pp. 72–104.

Dumville, D. 1985. 'The West Saxon genealogical regnal list and the chronology of early Wessex', *Peritia*, 4, pp. 21–66.

Dumville, D., 1989. 'The Tribal Hidage: an introduction to its texts and their history', in

Bassett, S., ed., *The Origins of Anglo-Saxon Kingdoms* (Leicester University Press, Leicester).

Dumville, D., and Lapidge, M., ed., 1985. *The Annals of St Neots with Vita Prima Sancti Neoti* (Boydell, Woodbridge).

Dumville, D., 1986. 'The West Saxon genealogical regnal list: manuscripts and texts', *Anglia*, 104, pp. 1–32.

Dymond, D., and Martin E., eds, 1999. *An Historical Atlas of Suffolk* (Suffolk County Council Planning Department, Bury St Edmunds).

Edwards, H., 1988. *The Charters of the Early West Saxon Kingdom*. (BAR series needed Oxford).

Eilersgaad Christensen, L; Lemm, T; Pederson, A; eds., 2016. *Hysebyer - status quo, open questions and perspectives*. Papers from a workshop at the National Museum, 2014, PNM, Copenhagen)

Ekwall, E., 1922. *The Place Names of Lancashire* (Manchester University Press, Manchester).

Ekwall, E., 1980. *The Concise Oxford English Dictionary of English Place-Names*, 4th edn (Oxford University Press, Oxford).

Elrington, C.R., Herbert, N.M., Pugh, R.B., Morgan, K., eds, 1972. *A History of the County of Gloucester: Volume 10: Westbury and Whitstone Hundreds* (Victoria County History).

Evans, S.S., 1997. *Lords of Battle* (Boydell, Woodbridge).

Everitt, A., 1986. *Continuity and Colonisation; The Evolution of Kentish Settlement* (Leicester University Press, Leicester).

Everitt, A., 1997. 'River and Wold: reflections on the historical origin of regions and

pays', *Jnl Historical Geography*, 3(i), pp. 1–19.

Faith, R., 1999. *English Peasantry and the Growth of Lordship* (Leicester University Press, London).

Faulkner, N., 2004. 'The case for the Dark Ages' Collins, R. and Gerrard, J. *Debating Late Antiquity in Britain AD 300–700*, (BAR British Series 365, Oxford)

Finberg, H., 1961. *The Early Charters of the West Midlands* (Leicester University Press, Leicester).

Finberg, H., 1964. *The Early Charters of Wessex* (Leicester University Press, Leicester).

Finberg, H., 1972. *The Agrarian History of England and Wales AD 43–1042*, vol. 1, part (ii), pp. 482–99 (Cambridge University Press, Cambridge).

Finberg, H., 1973. *Lucerna: Studies of Some Problems in the Early History of England* (Macmillan, London).

Finberg, H., 1975. *The Gloucestershire Landscape* (Hodder and Stoughton, London).

Finch-Smith, R., 1987. *Roadside Settlements in Lowland Roman Britain* (BAR British Series 157, Oxford).

Foot, S., 2009. *Monastic Life in Anglo-Saxon England, c.600–900* (Cambridge University Press).

Foss, P., 1988. 'Market Bosworth and its region – clues to its early status and connections', in Bourne, J., ed., *Anglo-Saxon Landscapes in the East Midlands* (Leicestershire Museums Service, Leicester), pp. 83–106.

Freeman, J., 2008. 'The name of the *Magonsæte*', in Padel, O.J., and Parsons, D.N., eds, *A Commodity of Good Names* (Shaun Tyas, Donington), pp. 101–16.

Freeman, S., Hiller, J., Petts, D., 2002. *Gathering the People, Settling the Land, the Archaeology of a Middle Thames Landscape: Anglo-Saxon to Post-Medieval*, Thames Valley Landscapes Monograph (Oxford Archaeology, Oxford).

Gelling, M., 1954. *The Place-Names of Oxfordshire* (English Place-Name Society, Cambridge).

Gelling, M., 1968. 'The Charter Bounds of *Æscesbyrig* and Ashbury', *Berkshire Archaeological Journal*, 63, pp. 5–13.

Gelling, M., 1971. *The Place-Names of Oxfordshire*, 2 vols (English Place-Name Society, Cambridge).

Gelling, M., 1973. *The Place-Names of Berkshire*, Part 1 (English Place-Name Society, Nottingham).

Gelling, M., 1974. *The Place-Names of Berkshire*, Part 2 (English Place-Name Society, Nottingham).

Gelling, M., 1976. *The Place-Names of Berkshire*, Part 3 (English Place-Name Society, Nottingham).

Gelling, M., 1977. 'English place-names derived from the compound *wīchām*', in Cameron, K., ed., *Place-Name Evidence for the Anglo-Saxon Invasions and Scandinavian Settlements* (English Place-Name Society, Nottingham). pp. 8–26.

Gelling, M., 1979. *The Early Charters of the Thames Valley* (Leicester University Press, Leicester).

Gelling, M., 1990. *The Place Names of Shropshire*, Part 1 (English Place-Name Society, Nottingham).

Gelling, M., 1992. *The West Midlands in the Early Middle Ages* (Leicester University Press).

Gelling, M., 1997. *Signposts to the Past*, 3rd edn (Phillimore, Chichester).

Gelling, M., 2001. *The Place Names of Shropshire*, Part 3 (English Place-Name Society, Nottingham).

Gelling, M., 2004. *The Place Names of Shropshire*, Part 4 (English Place-Name Society, Nottingham).

Gelling, M., 2006. *The Place Names of Shropshire*, Part 5 (English Place-Name Society, Nottingham).

Gelling, M., and Cole, A., 2000. *The Landscape of Place-Names* (Shaun Tyas, Stamford).

Gelling, M., 2006. 'English Place-Name studies: some reflections', *JEPNS 35* (English Place-Name Society, Nottingham) pp. 5-16.

Gelling, M., with Foxall, H., 1995. *The Place Names of Shropshire, Part Two: The Hundreds of Ford and Condover* (English Place-Name Society, Nottingham).

Good, R., 1940. *The Old Roads of Dorset* (H.G. Commin, Bournemouth).

Gover, J.E.B., Mawer, A. and Stenton, F.M., 1927. *The Place-Names of Worcestershire* (English Place-Name Society, Cambridge).

Gover, J.E.B., Mawer, A. and Stenton, F.M., 1929. *The Place-Names of Sussex,* Part 1 (English Place-Name Society, Cambridge).

Gover, J.E.B., Mawer, A. and Stenton, F.M., 1930. *The Place-Names of Sussex,* Part 2 (English Place-Name Society, Cambridge).

Gover, J.E.B., Mawer, A. and Stenton, F.M., 1931. *The Place-Names of Devon,* Part 1 (English Place-Name Society, Cambridge).

Gover, J. E. B., Mawer, A., and Stenton, F. M., 1932. *The Place-Names of Devon,* Part 2 (English Place-Name Society, Cambridge).

Gover, J.E.B., Mawer, A.,and Stenton, F.M., 1934. *The Place-Names of Surrey* (English Place-Name Society, Cambridge).

Gover, J.E.B., Mawer, A, and Stenton, F.M., 1936. *The Place-Names of Warwickshire* (English Place-Name Society, Cambridge).

Gover, J.E.B., Mawer, A, and Stenton, F.M., 1939. *The Place-Names of Wiltshire* (English Place-Name Society, Cambridge).

Gover, J.E.B., Mawer, A. and Stenton, F.M., 1940. *The Place-Names of Nottinghamshire* (English Place-Name Society, Cambridge). 216

Green, D., 1998. *Language and History in the Early Germanic World* (Cambridge University Press, Cambridge).

Hadley, D., 2007. *The Vikings in England: Settlement, Society and Culture,* Manchester Medieval Studies (Manchester University Press, Manchester).

Hall, T., 2000. *Minster Churches in the Dorset Landscape* (BAR British Series 304, (Oxford).

Hamerow, H., 1991. 'Settlement mobility and the "Middle Saxon Shift"', *Anglo-Saxon England*, 20, pp. 1–17.

Hart, C., 1971. 'The Tribal Hidage', *Transactions of the Royal Historical* Society, 5th series, 21, pp. 133–57.

Hart, C., 1977. 'The Kingdom of Mercia', in Dornier, A., *Mercian Studies* (Leicester University Press, Leicester), pp. 53–61.

Harvey, S., 1967. 'Royal revenue and Domesday terminology', *Economic History Review*, second series, vol. 20, pp. 221-8.

Hase, P., 1994. 'The Church in the Wessex Heartlands', in Aston, M. and Lewis, C., *The Medieval Landscape of Wessex*, Monograph 44 (Oxbow, Oxford).

Haslam, J., ed., 1984. *Anglo-Saxon Towns in Southern England* (Phillimore, Chichester).

Hawkins, D., 1996. 'Roman Kingston-upon-Thames: a landscape of rural settlements', *London Archaeologist*, vol. 8, no. 2, pp. 46–50.

Hawkins, D., 1998. 'Anglo-Saxon Kingston: a shifting pattern of settlement', *London Archaeologist*, vol. 8, no. 10, pp. 271–8.

Hawkins, D., 2007. 'A product of its environment: revisiting Roman Kingston', in *London Archaeologist*, vol. 11, no. 8, pp. 199–203.

Heighway, C., 1984. 'Saxon Gloucester' in Haslam, J., ed., *Anglo-Saxon Towns in Southern England* (Phillimore, Chichester).

Heighway, C., 1987. *Anglo-Saxon Gloucestershire* (Alan Sutton & Gloucestershire County Library, Gloucester).

Higham, N., 1993. *The Kingdom of Northumbria AD 350–1100* (Sutton, Stroud).

Higham, N., 1994. *The English Conquest: Gildas and Britain in the Fifth Century* (Manchester University Press, Manchester).

Higham, N., 1995. *An English Empire: Bede and the Early Anglo-Saxon Kings* (Manchester University Press, Manchester).

Higham, N., 1997. *The Convert Kings: Power and Religious Affiliation in Early Anglo-Saxon England* (Manchester University Press, Manchester).

Higham, N., and Hills, D., eds, 2001. *Edward the Elder 889–924* (Routledge, London).

Higham, N., ed. 2007. *Britons in Anglo-Saxon England* (Boydell, Woodbridge).

Higham, R., 2008. *Making Anglo-Saxon Devon* (The Mint Press, Exeter).

Hill, D., 1981. *An Atlas of Anglo-Saxon England* (Blackwell, London).

Hill, David and Rumble, A., eds, 1996. *The Defence of Wessex: the Burghal Hidage and Anglo-Saxon Fortifications* (Manchester University Press, Manchester).

Hines, J., 2004. '*Sūðræ-gē* – the foundations of Surrey', in Cotton, J., Crocker, G. and

Graham, A., eds. *Aspects of Archaeology and History in Surrey* (English Heritage, London).

Hodges, R., 1989a. *Dark Age Economics: The Origin of Towns and Trade AD 600–1000* (Duckworth, London).

Hodges, R., 1989a. *The Anglo-Saxon Achievement* (Duckworth, London).

Holland, E., 1986. *Coniston Copper: a History* (Cicerone, Milnthorpe, Cumbria).

Hooke, D., 1981. 'The Droitwich salt industry', *Anglo-Saxon Studies in Archaeology and History*, 2, pp. 123–69.

Hooke, D., 1985. *The Anglo-Saxon Landscape: The Kingdom of the Hwicce* (Manchester University Press, Manchester).

Hooke, D., 1986. 'Territorial organisation in the Anglo-Saxon West Midlands: central places, central areas', in Grant E., ed., *Central Places and Archaeology and History* (Department of Archaeology and Prehistory, University of Sheffield), pp. 79–93.

Hooke, D., 1987. 'Anglo-Saxon estates in the Vale of the White Horse', *Oxoniensia,* 52, pp. 129–43.

Hooke, D., 1990. *Worcestershire Anglo-Saxon Charter Bounds* (Boydell, Woodbridge).

Hooke, D., 1992. 'Early units of government in Herefordshire and Shropshire', *Anglo-Saxon Studies in Archaeology and History*, 5, pp. 47-64.

Hope-Taylor, B., 1977. *Yeavering* (HMSO, London).

Horovitz, D., 2005. *The Place-Names of Staffordshire* (self-published, Brewood).

Hough, C., 1997. 'The place-name Kingston and the laws of Æthelberht', *Studia Neophilologica*, 69, pp. 55–7.

Hunter Blair, P., 2003. *An Introduction to Anglo-Saxon England*, 3rd edn (Cambridge University Press, Cambridge).

Jackman, W., 1966. *The Development of Transportation in Modern England*, with introduction by W.H. Challoner (Frank Cass, London).

John, E., 1996. *Reassessing Anglo-Saxon England* (Manchester University Press, Manchester).

Jones, B. and Mattingley, D., 1990. *An Atlas of Roman Britain* (Blackwell, Oxford).

Jones, G., 1979.'Multiple estates and early settlement', in Sawyer, P., *English Medieval Settlement* (Edward Arnold, London).

Kain, R., and Oliver, R., 2001. *Historic Parishes of England & Wales: an Electronic Map of Boundaries before 1850* (Colchester History Data Service).

Keen, L., 1984. 'The towns of Dorset', in Haslam, J., ed., *Anglo-Saxon Towns in Southern England* (Phillimore, Chichester), pp. 203–47.

Kelly, 1885. *Directory of Shropshire* (Strand, London).

Kelly, 1896. *Directory of Warwickshire* (Strand, London).

Kelly, 1899. *Directory of Hull and its Neighbourhood* (Strand, London).

Keynes, S., 1995. 'England 700–900', in McKitterick, R., ed., *The New Cambridge Medieval History II, c.700–900* (Cambridge University Press, Cambridge), pp. 18–42.

Keynes, S., 2001. 'Mercia and Wessex in the ninth century', in Brown, M. and Farr, C., *Mercia, an Anglo-Saxon Kingdom in Europe*, Continuum Studies in Medieval History (Continuum International Publishing, London/New York).

Keynes, S. and Lapidge, M., trans. and eds, 1983. *Alfred the Great: Asser's Life of King Alfred and Other Contemporary Sources* (Pengin Books, London).

Kirby, D., 1991. *The Earliest English Kings* (Unwin Hyman, London).

Lafflin, S., 2001. 'Roman roads and ford place-names in Shropshire', *Shropshire History and Archaeology*, 76, pp. 1–11.

Lapidge, M., ed., Collected edition, 1958–93 vol. 2. *Bede and his World: the Jarrow Lectures, 1958–93* (Variorum, Rugby).

Lapidge, M., Blair, J., Keynes, S. and Scragg, D., eds, 1999. *Encyclopedia of Anglo-Saxon England* (Blackwell, Oxford).

Lavelle, R., 2007. *Royal Estates in Anglo-Saxon Wessex: land, politics and family strategies* (BAR British Series 439, Oxford).

Lavelle, R., 2010, *Alfred and His Wars,* (Boydell Press, Woodbridge).

Lawson, T. and Killingray D., eds, 2004. *An Historical Atlas of Kent* (Phillimore, Chichester).

Laycock, S., 2004. *Warlords: the Struggle for Power in Post-Roman Britain* (The History Press, Stroud).

Leather, P., 1994. *West Midlands Archaeology*, 37, p. 9.

Leech, R., 1975. *Small Medieval Towns in Avon: archaeology and planning* (Committee for Rescue Archaeology in Avon, Gloucestershire and Somerset, Bristol).

Leighton, A,, 1972. *Transport and Communications in Early Medieval Europe 500–1100 AD* (David and Charles, Newton Abbot).

Leslie, K. and Short B., eds, 2010. *An Historical Atlas of Sussex* (Phillimore, Chichester).

Letters, S., *Online Gazeteer of Markets and Fairs in England and Wales to 1516*, at www.history.ac.uk

Lewis, G., 1907. *The Stannaries: A Study of the English Tin Miner*, Harvard Economic Studies 3.

Lewis, S., 1833. *Topographical Dictionary of England*, 4 vols (Samuel Lewis & Co., London).

Liebermann, F., 1903–16. *Die Gesetze der Angelsachsen*, 3 vols (Niemeyer, Halle).

Loveluck, C., ed., 2007. *Rural Settlement, Lifestyles and Social change in the later first millennium AD. Anglo-*

Saxon Flixborough in its wider context. Excavations at Flixborough, vol. 4 (Oxbow, Oxford).

Loyn, H. 1984. *The Governance of Anglo-Saxon England* (Edward Arnold, London).

Lunn, N., Crosland, B., Spence, B., Clay, G., 2008. *The Romans came this way: the story of the discovery and excavation of a Roman Military Way across the Yorkshire Pennines* (Huddersfield and District Archaeological Society, Huddersfield).

Margary., 1955. *Roman Roads in Britain*, vol. 1 (Phoenix House, London).

Margary, I., 1957. *Roman Roads in Britain*, vol. 2 (Phoenix House, London).

Margham, J., 1992. 'Carisbrooke: a study in settlement morphology', *Southern History*, vol. 14, pp. 1–28.

Margham, J., 2000. 'St Mary's, Brading: Wilfrid's Church', *Proceedings of the Isle of Wight Natural History and Archaelogical Society*, 16, pp. 117–35.

Margham, J., 2003. 'Charters, landscapes and hides on the Isle of Wight', *Landscape History*, 25:1, pp. 17-43

Mattingley, H. and Handford, S. trans. 1970. *Tacitus: The Agricola and the Germania* (Penguin, London).

Mawer, A., 1920. *Place Names of Northumberland and Durham* (Cambridge University Press, Cambridge).

Mawer, A., 1922. *Place-Names and History* (University of Liverpool, Liverpool).

Mawer, A. and Stenton, F.M 1926. *The Place-Names of Bedfordshire and Huntingdonshire* (English Place-Name Society, Cambridge).

Mawer, A. and Stenton, F., and Houghton, F., 1927. *The Place-Names of Worcestershire* (English Place-Name Society, Cambridge).

Meaney, L., 1981. *Anglo-Saxon Amulets and Curing Stones* (BAR British series 96, Oxford).

Meeson, R. and Rahtz, P., 1992. *Anglo-Saxon Watermill at Tamworth*, Research Report 83 (Council for British Archaeology, London).

Mills, D., 1977. *The Place-Names of Dorset*, Part 1 (English Place-Name Society, Nottingham).

Mills, D., 1980. *The Place-Names of Dorset*, Part 2 (English Place-Name Society, Nottingham).

Mills. D., 1989. *The Place-Names of Dorset*, Part 3 (English Place-Name Society, Nottingham).

Mills, D., 1990. *Dorset Place-Names: their origins and meanings* (Ensign Publications, Southampton).

Mills, D., 2010. *The Place-Names of Dorset*, Part 4 (English Place-Name Society, Nottingham).

Moore, J., 1987. 'The Gloucestershire section of Domesday: geographical problems of the text, Part 1', *Transactions of the Bristol Archaeological Society*, 105, 109–32.

Morris, J., gen. ed., *Domesday Book*, 35 vols (Phillimore, Chichester).

Morton, A., ed., 1992. *Excavations at Hamwic Vol i, : Excavations 1946–83, excluding Six Dials and Melbourne Street*, CBA Research Report 84 (Council for British Archaeology, London).

Newton, S., 1993. *The Origins of Beowulf and the pre-Viking Kingdom of East Anglia* (Brewer, Cambridge).

Oliver, J., 1936. *Ancient Roads of England* (Cassell, London).

Ordnance Survey Map of Roman Britain, 5th edn, 2001.

Osborne, B.J., 2010. *Epsom and Ewell Wells: the Historic Spa, Salts and Springs of Epsom and Ewell*, (SPAS Research Fellowship, www.EpsomWells.com)

Padel, O., 1985. *Cornish Place-Name Elements*, vol. 16. (English Place-Name Society, Nottingham).

Pantos, A., 2004. 'The location and form of Anglo-Saxon assembly places: some Moot Points', in Pantos, A. and Semple, S., eds, *Assembly Places and Practices in Medieval Europe* (Four Courts Press, Dublin, Portland, Oregon), pp. 155–80.

Parsons, D.N., 2013. 'Churls and *aethelings*, kings and reeves: some reflections on place-names and Early English Society', in Carroll, J. and Parsons, D.N., eds, *Perceptions of Place: twenty-first century interpretations of English Place-Names Studies* (English Place-Name Society, Nottingham), pp.45-72.

Paterson, D., 1799. *A New and Accurate Description of all the Direct and Principal Cross Roads in Great-Britain* (London).

Pelteret, D., 1999. 'Anglo Saxon Roads', in Lapidge, M. et al,. eds, *Blackwell Encyclopaedia of Anglo-Saxon England*, p. 395.

Phythian-Adams, C., 1977. 'Rutland reconsidered', in Dornier, A., ed., *Mercian Studies* (Leicester University Press), pp. 63–84.

Pickles, T., 2009. '*Biscopes-tūn, muneca-tūn* and *prēosta-tūn*: dating, significance and distribution', in Quinton, E., ed., *The Church in English Place-Names*, English Place-Name Society Extra Series, 4 (English Place-Name Society, Nottingham), pp. 39–108.

Probert, D., 2008. 'Towards a reassessment of Kingston place-names', *Journal of the English Place-Name Society*, 40, pp. 7–22.

Putnam, W., 1984. *Roman Dorset* (Dovecote Press, Wimborne).

Rackham, O., 1986. *The History of the Countryside* (Dent, London).

Rahtz, P., 1977. 'The archaeology of West Mercian towns', in Dornier, A., *Mercian*

Studies (Leicester University Press, Leicester), pp. 107–29.

Rahtz, P., 1979. *The Saxon and Medieval Palaces at Cheddar* (BAR British Series 65, Oxford).

Raistrick, A., 1948. *Grassington and Upper Wharfedale* (Dalesman, Lancaster).

Reaney, P., 1935. *The Place-Names of Essex,* vol. 12 (English Place-Name Society, Cambridge).

Reaney, P., 1943. *The Place-names of Cambridgeshire and the Isle of Ely* (English Place-Name Society, Cambridge).

Rigold, S., 1975. 'The Sutton Hoo coins in the light of the contemporary background of coinage in England', in Bruce-Mitford, R., *The Sutton Hoo Ship Burial I* (British Museum Publications), pp. 653–77.

Riley, H., 2006. *The Historic Landscape of the Quantock Hills* (English Heritage, Swindon).

Rivet, A., and Smith, C., 1979. *The Place-Names of Roman Britain* (Batsford, London).

Roffe, D., 1990-1. 'Place-naming in Domesday Book: settlements, estates and communities. *Nomina*, 14, pp. 47–60.

Rowley, R., 1969. 'Metchley Roman Fort, Birmingham', *West Midlands Archaeology*, 12, p. 24.

Ruskin Museum, Coniston Coppermine LNC, at wwwruskinmuseum.com

Sawyer, P., 1968. *Anglo-Saxon Charters: an annotated list and bibliography*. Royal Historical Society. Updated online at, http://www.esawyer.org.uk.

Sawyer, P., ed., 1976. *Medieval Settlement: continuity and change* (Edward Arnold, London).

Sawyer, P.. 1978. *From Roman Britain to Norman England* (Methuen, London).

Sawyer, P., 1983. 'The Royal *Tun* in pre-conquest England', in Wormald, P., Bulloch,

D., and Collins, R., eds, *Ideal and Reality in Frankish and Anglo-Saxon Society: studies presented to J. M. Wallace-Hadrill* (Blackwell, Oxford), pp. 273–99.

Scragg, D., 2008. 'The Late Old English 'King'', in Padel, O.. and Parsons, D.N., eds., *A Commodity of Good Names* (Shaun Tyas, Donnington), pp. 117–22.

Scull, C. 1999., 'Social archaeology and Anglo-Saxon kingdom origins', *The making of Kingdoms: Anglo Saxon studies in Archaeology and History*, 6, pp. 65–82.

Silverman, B.. 1986, *Density Estimation for Statistics and Data Analysis* (Chapman and Hall, New York).

Sims-Williams, P., 1983. 'The Settlement of England in Bede and the Chronicle', *Anglo-Saxon England*, 12, pp. 1–41.

Sims-Williams, P., 1990. *Religion and Literature in Western England, 600–800*, Cambridge Studies in Anglo-Saxon England, 3 (Cambridge University Press, Cambridge).

Smith, A. H., 1956. *English Place-Name Elements*, 2 vols (Cambridge University Press, Cambridge).

Smith, A., 1961a. *Place-Names of the West Riding of Yorkshire*, Part 1 (English Place-Name Society, Cambridge).

Smith, A.H., 1961b. *Place-Names of the West Riding of Yorkshire*, Part 2 (English Place-Name Society, Cambridge).

Smith, A.H., 1961c. *Place-Names of the West Riding of Yorkshire*, Part 3 (English Place-Name Society, Cambridge).

Smith, A H., 1961d. *Place-Names of the West Riding of Yorkshire*, Part 4 (English Place-Name Society, Cambridge).

Smith, A H., 1961e. *Place-Names of the West Riding of Yorkshire*, Part 5 (English Place-Name Society, Cambridge).

Smith, A H., 1961f. *Place-Names of the West Riding of Yorkshire*, Part 6 (English Place-Name Society, Cambridge).

Smith, A H., 1961g. *Place-Names of the West Riding of Yorkshire*, Part 7 (English Place-Name Society, Cambridge).

Smith, A H., 1962. *Place-Names of the West Riding of Yorkshire*, Part 8 (English Place-Name Society, Cambridge).

Smith, A H., 1963. *Place-Names of the West Riding of Yorkshire*, Part 8 (English Place-Name Society, Cambridge).

Smith, A.H., 1964a. The *Place-Names of Gloucestershire*, Part 1 (English Place-Name Society, Cambridge).

Smith, A.H., 1964b. The *Place-Names of Gloucestershire*, Part 2 (English Place-Name Society, Cambridge).

Smith, A.H., 1964c. The *Place-Names of Gloucestershire*, Part 3 (English Place-Name Society, Cambridge).

Smith, A.H., 1965. The *Place-Names of Gloucestershire*, Part 4 (English Place-Name Society, Cambridge).

Snyder, C., 1998. *An Age of Tyrants* (Sutton, Stroud).

Speed, G., 2014. *Towns in the Dark? Urban Transformations from Late Roman Britain to Anglo-Saxon England* (Archaeopress, Oxford).

Stafford P., 1980. 'The "Farm of One Night" and the organisation of King Edward's estates in Domesday', *Economic History Review*, 33, pp. 491–502.

Stafford, P., 1985. *The East Midlands in the Early Middle Ages* (Leicester University Press, Leicester).

Stenton, F. M., 1934. 'Pre-Conquest Herefordshire', *Royal Commission on Historical Monuments: Herefordshire*, vol. iii, pp. lv–lxi.

Stenton, F.,1936. 'The road system of medieval England', *Economic History Review*, 7, 1936, pp. 1–22.

Stenton, F., 1970 [1918]. 'The supremacy of the Mercian kings', in *Preparatory to Anglo-Saxon England* (Oxford University Press, Oxford).

Stenton, F., 1971. *Anglo-Saxon England*, 3rd edn (Oxford University Press, Oxford).

Stubbs, W., ed., 1876. *Radulfi de Diceto Decani Lundoniensis Opera Historica*, vol. i, Rolls Series.

Swanton, M., trans., 1996. *Anglo-Saxon Chronicle* (Dent, London).

Taylor, C., 1957. 'The origin of the Mercian Shires', in Finberg, H., ed., *Gloucestershire Studies* (Leicester University Press), pp. 17–51.

Taylor, C., 1979. *Roads and Tracks of Britain* (Dent, London).

Taylor, J., 2007. *An Atlas of Roman Rural Settlement in England*, CBA Research Report 151 Council for British Archaeology, (York).

Timperley, H., and Brill, E., 2005. *Ancient Trackways of Wessex* (The History Press, Stroud).

Thacker, A., 2000. 'Two frontier states – Northumbria and Wessex 650–750', in

Maddicott, J. and Palliser, D. eds.. *The Medieval State: Essays presented to James Campbell* (Hambledon Press, London).

Trevarthen, M., ed., 2008. *Suburban Life in Roman Durnovaria* (Wessex Archaeology, Salisbury).

Ulmschneider, K., 1999. 'Archaeology, history, and the Isle of Wight in the Middle Saxon period', *Medieval Archaeology*, 43, pp. 19–44.

Ulmschneider, K., 2003. 'Markets around the Solent: unravelling a "Productive" site on the Isle of Wight', in Pestell, T. and & Ulmschneider, K., eds, *Markets in Early Medieval Europe: Trading and 'Productive' Sites, 650-850* (Windgather Press/Oxbow, Oxford), pp. 73–83.

Walker, B., 1936. 'The Rycknield Street in the neighbourhood of Birmingham', *Transactions Birmingham and Warwickshire Archaeological Soc.*, 60, pp. 42, 55.

Walker, H., 1956. 'Bede and the Giwissæ: the political evolution of the heptarchy and its nomenclature', *Cambridge Historical Journal*, xii, pp. 174–86.

Walker, I., 2000. *Mercia and the Making of England* (Sutton, Stroud).

Wallace-Hadrill, J., 1971. *Early Germanic Kingship in England and on the Continent* (Oxford University Press, Oxford).

Wallenberg, J., 1934. *Place-Names of Kent* (Lundequistska Bokhandein, Uppsala).

Walters, B., 1992. *The Archaeology and Ancient History of Ancient Dean and the Wye Valley* (Thornhill Press, Cheltenham).

Warner, P., 1996. *The Origins of Suffolk* (Manchester University Press, Manchester).

Watts, V., 2004. *Cambridge Dictionary of English Place-Names* (Cambridge University Press, Cambridge).

Whaley, D., 2006. *A Dictionary of Lake District Place-Names* (English Place-Name Society, Nottingham).

White, R. and Barker, P., 1998. *Wroxeter: Life and Death of a Roman City* (Tempus, Stroud).

White, R., 2007. *Britannia Prima: Britain's Last Roman Province* (Tempus, Stroud).

White, W., 1850. *Directory of Devonshire* (London).

White, W., 1851. *Historical Gazetteer and Directory of Staffordshire* (London).

White, W., 1859. *History, Gazetteer, and Directory of the Isle of Wight* (London).

Whitwell, B., 1991. 'Flixborough', *Current Archaeology*, 126, pp. 224–7.

Williams, A., Smyth, A. P., and Kirby, D. P., eds., 1991. *A Biographical Dictionary of Dark Age Britain, England, Scotland and Wales c.500–c.1050* (Seaby, London).

Williamson, T., 2008. *Sutton Hoo and its Landscape: the Context of Monuments* (Windgatherer Press/Oxbow, Oxford).

Wiltshire County Council Archaeology Service, Libraries and Heritage, 2004. *The Archaeology of Wiltshire's Towns: an Extensive Urban Survey.*

Witney, K., 1982. *The Kingdom of Kent* (Phillimore, Chichester).

Wood, P., 1990. 'On the little British Kingdom of Craven', *Northern History*, 32, pp. 1–20.

Wormald, P., 1999. *The Making of English Law: King Alfred to the Twelfth Century: Legislation and its Limits* (Oxford University Press, Oxford).

Yorke, B., 1981. 'The vocabulary of Anglo-Saxon overlordship', *Anglo-Saxon Studies in Archaeology and History*, 2, pp. 171–200.

Yorke, B.,1983. 'Joint Kingship in Kent c.560–785', *Archaeologia Cantiana*, 99, pp. 1–19.

Yorke, B., 1989. 'The Jutes of Hampshire and Wight and the origins of Wessex', in Bassett, S., ed., *The Origins of the Anglo-Saxon Kingdoms* (Leicester University Press, Leicester), pp. 84–96.

Yorke, B., 1990. *The Kings and Kingdoms of Early Anglo-Saxon England* (Seaby, London).

Yorke, B., 1995. *Wessex in the Early Middle Ages* (Leicester University Press, London).

Yorke, B., 1999. 'The origins of Anglo-Saxon kingdoms: the contribution of written sources', *Anglo-Saxon Studies in Archaeology and History*, 10, pp. 25–9.

Yorke, B., 2003. *Nunneries and the Anglo-Saxon Royal Houses* (Continuum, London/New York).

Yorke. B., 2006. *The Conversion of Britain: Religion, Politics and Society in Britain c. 600-800* (Pearson Longman, Harlow).

Yorke, B., 2009. '*Bretwaldas* and the origins of overlordship in Anglo-Saxon England', in Baxter, S., Karkov, C., Nelson, J., and Pelteret, D., eds, *Early Medieval Studies in Honour of Patrick Wormald* (Ashgate, Aldershot), pp. 81–96.

Youngs Jnr., F., 1979. *Guide to the Administrative Units of England,* vol. I *Southern England,* vol. II *Northern England* (Royal Historical Society, London).

Index

References in **bold** denote maps and those in *italic* refer to tables.

Æthelbald 4, 10, 27
Æthelberht of Kent, King 8
Alfred, King 8, 25, 26
Anglo-Saxon Chronicle 7, 11, 22, 24
Anglo-Saxon period
    continental homelands and early Anglo-Saxon kingship
        11–12
    earliest petty kingdoms 12–13
    kingship, early kingdoms and royal power 10–11
    regnal practices 14
    Tribal Hidage 13–14, **13**

Bassett, Stephen 9–10, 13, 14, 30, 38
Bede 7, 11, 12, 14, 27, 41
Bede's Words for Places (Campbell) 7
Berkshire 28–9
    Domesday Book, royal connections, charters and
        ecclesiarical status 29–30
Blair, John 9, 13
Briggs, Keith 9
Brooks, N. 13, 23

Cambridgeshire 40–1
Cameron, Kenneth 8, 11
Campbell, James 7, 10, 11, 12
Cenred of Wessex, King 14
Chadwick, H. M. 14
churches, mother-church parishes 9, 10
Clarke, Arthur 21
Claverdon (Warwickshire) 10
    St Peter's Church 9, 10
Cole, Anne 5, 9, 21
Collingbourne (Wiltshire) 26
Coney Weston (Suffolk) 41
Congerstone (Leicestershire) 39–40
Conington (Cambridgeshire) 41
Conington (Huntingdonshire) 41
Coniston (Cold, Yorkshire) 43
Coniston (Lancashire) 42–3
Conistone (Kettlewell, Yorkshire) 43
Costen, Michael 5
Cullen, P. 3
cyng 3
cyning/cyning(e)s+tun 3, 7, 8–9, 10, 12

Devon 20–1, 23, 28
Domesday Book (DB) 4, 5
    Berkshire 29–30
    Cambridgeshire 40–1
    Dorset 22–3

first recordings of Kingstons *16–17*
Gloucestershire 35–6
Hampshire 24–5
Herefordshire 36, 37
Huntingdonshire 41
Kent 33
Leicestershire 39–40
Nottinghamshire 40
Oxfordshire 30
Somerset 27–8
Suffolk 41–2
Surrey 30–1
Sussex 32–3
Warwickshire 38–9
Wiltshire 26
Worcestershire 39
Yorkshire 43
Dorset 19–22, *21*
    Domesday Book, royal connections and ecclesiarical
        status 22–3
Dumville, David 11
-dun names 21

Ecclesiatical History of the English People (Bede) 11
Edwin, King 14
Ekwall, E. 42–3
English Place-Name Society 3

Gelling, Margaret 8, 19, 21, 27–8
Germania (Tacitus) 11–12
Gildas 11
Gloucestershire 33–5
    Domesday Book, royal connections and ecclesiarical
        status 35–6
Green, D. 12
Gumley (Leicestershire) 4

Hampshire 21
    Domesday Book, royal connections and ecclesiastical
        status of 24–5
Harthacnut, King 31
Herefordshire 36, 37
Heritage England 4
Higham, N. 13
Holland, Eric 42
Hough, Carol 4, 8
Huntingdonshire 41
Hurstingas 13–14
Hurstingstone (Huntingdonshire) 14

Ine of Wessex, King 12, 14, 22, 28

Isle of Purbeck 21–2

Jones, R. 3
Jones, Richard 7

Keinton (Mandeville, Somerset) 26, 27
Kennington (Berkshire) 29–30
Kennington (Lambeth) 31
Kennington (Wye, Kent) 33
Kent 14, 33
Kenton (Gosforth, Northumberland) 43
Kenton (Suffolk) 42
Kineton Green (Elmore, Gloucestershire) 34, 35
Kineton Green (Solihull, Warwickshire) 38
Kineton (Temple Guiting, Gloucestershire) 36
Kineton (Warwickshire) 26, 38–9
Kingsdon (Somerset) 26–7
kingshaeme 4
kingship 10–11, 14
kingslea 4
Kingston (Aylburton, Gloucestershire) 35–6
Kingston (Bagpuize, Berkshire) 28–9
Kingston (Blount, Oxfordshire) 30
Kingston (Bucy, Sussex) 32–3
Kingston (Cambridgeshire) 40–1
Kingston (Carlton in Lindrick, Nottinghamshire) 40
Kingston (Colaton Raleigh, Devon) 20
Kingston (Collingbourne, Wiltshire) 25, 26
Kingston (Corfe, Dorset) 21–2
Kingston (Croft/Ifield, Sussex) 31, 32
Kingston (Deverill, Wiltshire) 25, 26
Kingston (Dittisham, Devon) 28
Kingston (Facy/Brixham, Devon) 28
Kingston Farm (Chesterton, Warwickshire) 38
Kingston (Ferring/Angmering, Sussex) 32
Kingston (Fratton/Portsmouth, Hampshire) 24–5
Kingston (Haselbury Bryan, Dorset) 21, 22
Kingston (Isle of Wight) 24
Kingston (Kent) 33
Kingston (Lacy Dorset) 5, 19, 22
Kingston (Lewes, Sussex) 31–2, 33
Kingston (Lisle, Berkshire) 29, 30
Kingston (Maurward/Stinsford, Dorset) 19, 20, 23
Kingston (Modbury, Devon) 28
Kingston (Ringwood, Hampshire) 21
Kingston (Russell, Dorset) 20, 23
Kingston (Seale, Surrey) 31
Kingston (Seymour, Somerset) 27, 28
Kingston (Slimbridge, Gloucestershire) 34, 35
Kingston (St Mary, Taunton, Somerset) 27, 28
Kingston (Tidenham, Gloucestershire) 35
Kingston upon Hull 43
Kingston upon Thames (Surrey) 6, 9, 30
Kingston (Winterborne, Dorset) 19, 22–3
Kingston (Woodbridge, Suffolk) 41
Kingstone (Ilminster, Somerset) 27–8
Kingstone (Staffordshire) 37
Kingstone (Thruxton, Herefordshire) 37
Kingstone (Weston under Penyard, Herefordshire) 37
Kingstone (Winslow, Berkshire)

Kingstons 8
    alphabetical list of, by pre-1974 counties *15–16*
    association with Roman roads/ancient trackways 3–5,
        9, 10, *18–19*, 19–21, 25
    distribution of *cyninges + tun/kyne* by pre-1974 county
        Group 1a counties which comprised the core of
            ancient Wessex before 726 *17*, 19–28, **20**
        Group 1b counties which had close associations
            with ancient Wessex before 726 *17*, 28–31, **29**
        Group 1c Kingstons in counties over which Wessex
            had established lordship before 726 *17*, 31–3, **31**
        Group 2 Kingstons in the lower Severn Valley and
            West Midlands *17*, 33–9, **34**
        Group 3 Kingstons between Watling Street and the
            Mersey/Humber line *18*, 39–42, **40**
        Group 4 Kingstons in counties north of the Mersey/
            Humber line *18*, 42–3, **42**
    first recordings in Domesday Book (DB) *16–17*
    geographical groups 15
    listed by date of first documentary reference *16*
    mapping the Kingstons 5–6
    place-name of 7–14
        distribution map of the place-name **2**
        example of *cyning(es)+tun* 3
        example of *villa regalis* 3
        lateness of the name 8–9
        origin and survival of the name 7–8
        origin of the name 3
        previous work on 8–9
        statistical analysis 9–10
        status of names 4
    royal connections 8, 9–10
        Berkshire 29–30
        Cambridgeshire 40–1
        Dorset 22–3
        Gloucestershire 35–6
        Hampshire 24–5
        Herefordshire 36, 37
        Huntingdonshire 41
        Kent 33
        Leicestershire 39–40
        Nottinghamshire 40
        Oxfordshire 30
        Somerset 27–8
        Suffolk 41–2
        Surrey 30–1
        Sussex 32–3
        Warwickshire 38–9
        Wiltshire 26
        Worcestershire 39
        Yorkshire 43
    sited in relation to a river or the coast *19*
    sited on old-established long-distance roads *19*
Kingstonsweston (Gloucestershire) 34–5
Kington Grange (Claverdon, Warwickshire) 10, 38
Kington/Kyneton (Thornbury, Gloucestershire) 34, 35
Kington Magna (Dorset) 21, 22
Kington (St Michael, Wiltshire) 25, 26
Kington (Warwickshire) 9, 10
Kington (Welsh Border) 36–7

Kington (Worcestershire) 10, 39
Kinton (Great Ness, Shropshire) 37
Kinton (Leintwardine, Herefordshire) 36
Kinton (Shropshire) 4–5
Kolmogorov-Smirnov test 9
konungr 3
kuning 12
kunung 3
Kyngestone/Wistow (Huntingdonshire) 41

Lancashire 42–3
laws 8
Leicestershire 39–40
London to Exeter roman road 19–21

maps 3–4
Margary, Ivan 4, 5, 20, 21
Mercia 9
milestones 5, 20

Nether Stowey (Somerset) 5
Northumberland 43
Nottinghamshire 40

Offa of Mercia, King 4, 9
The Origins of the Anglo-Saxon Kingdoms (Bassett) 10
Ornance Survey 3–4
Over Stowey (Somerset) 5
Oxfordshire 30

Parsons, D. 3
Pelteret, David 6
Penda of Mercia 10, 12
piudans 12
principes 12
Probert, Duncan 8–9
proviniœ 11, 14
Putnam, W. 22

reges 12
regiones 11, 14
rex 12
Roman roads
    identification of 4–5
    Kingston associations with 3–5, 9, 10, *18–19*, 19–21

Sawyer, Peter 6, 9
Scragg, D. 3
Sedbury (Gloucestershire) 35
Sense of Space in Anglo-Saxon England 7
Sherborne Causeway 21
Shropshire 37
Signposts to the Past 8
Slaithwaite (Yorkshire) 5
Somerset 26–7
    Domesday Book, royal connections and ecclesiarical
        status 27–8
Somerton (Somerset) 27
Stafford, Pauline 14
Staffordshire 37

Stenton, F. M. 10
Stoppingas 10, 13, 26, 30, 38
Suffolk 41–2
Surrey 30–1
Sussex 31–3

Tacitus 11–12
Taunton (Somerset) 28
Taylor, Christopher 5, 19
terminology 11
    king, terms for 12
Thorps in a Changing Landscape (Cullen) 3
Topographical History of England (Lewis) 23
Tribal Hidage 13–14, **13**
truhtin 12
-tun names 7, 21

Ulmscheider, Katharina 24

Victoria County Histories 3
villa regia/villa regalis 3, 6, 7, 8, 9, 22, 26, 27, 30

Warwickshire 37–9
Watts, V. 39, 41
Welsh border counties 36
Wessex 4, 6, 14, *17*
West Kington (Wiltshire) 25, 26
White, Philip 4–5
White, Roger 37
Wiltshire 25
    Domesday Book, royal connections and ecclesiarical
        status 26
Wootton Wawen (Warwickshire) 9
Worcestershire 39

Yorke, Barbara 13, 14
Yorkshire 43

Zanella, Giacomo 9